*Women Peasant Poets in Eighteenth-Century
England, Scotland, and Germany*

*Studies in German Literature, Linguistics, and Culture*

Edited by James Hardin
*(South Carolina)*

# Women Peasant Poets in Eighteenth-Century England, Scotland, and Germany

*Milkmaids on Parnassus*

Susanne Kord

CAMDEN HOUSE

Copyright © 2003 Susanne Kord

*All Rights Reserved.* Except as permitted under current legislation,
no part of this work may be photocopied, stored in a retrieval system,
published, performed in public, adapted, broadcast, transmitted,
recorded, or reproduced in any form or by any means,
without the prior permission of the copyright owner.

First published 2003
by Camden House

Camden House is an imprint of Boydell & Brewer Inc.
PO Box 41026, Rochester, NY 14604–4126 USA
and of Boydell & Brewer Limited
PO Box 9, Woodbridge, Suffolk IP12 3DF, UK

ISBN: 1–57113–268–6

**Library of Congress Cataloging-in-Publication Data**

Kord, Susanne.
    Women peasant poets in eighteenth-century England, Scotland, and Germany : milkmaids on Parnassus / Susanne Kord.
    p. cm. — (Studies in German literature, linguistics, and culture)
Includes bibliographical references and index.
ISBN 1–57113–268–6 (hardcover : alk. paper)
    1. European poetry — 18th century — History and criticism. 2. European poetry — Women authors — History and criticism. 3. Peasants as authors — Europe. I. Title. II. Series.

PN1241 .K67 2003
821'.5099287—dc21

2002015252

A catalogue record for this title is available from the British Library.

This publication is printed on acid-free paper.
Printed in the United States of America.

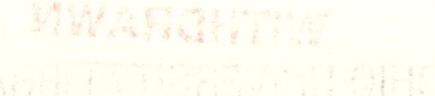

*To my friend and mentor,
Susanne Zantop (1945–2001)*

*We go to Nature for comfort in trouble, and sympathy in joy, only in books. Admiration of those beauties of the inanimate world, which modern poetry so largely and so eloquently describes, is not, even in the best of us, one of the original instincts of our nature. As children, we none of us possess it. No uninstructed man or woman possesses it. Those whose lives are most exclusively passed amid the ever-changing wonders of sea and land are also those who are most universally insensible to every aspect of Nature not directly associated with the human interest of their calling. Our capacity of appreciating the beauties of the earth we live on is, in truth, one of the civilised accomplishments which we all learn as an Art...*
— Wilkie Collins, *The Woman in White* (1859–60)


*What you call rags I call romance. What seems poverty to you is picturesqueness to me.*
— Oscar Wilde, "The Model Millionaire" (1887–91)


*[...] if Alexander and Caesar had been born in a cottage, they would have died in obscurity.*
— Ann Cromartie Yearsley, *The Rural Lyre* (1796)

# Contents

| | |
|---|---|
| List of Illustrations | ix |
| Acknowledgments | xix |
| Introduction: Aesthetic Evasions and Social Consequences | 1 |
| **1: Back to Nature: Bourgeois Aesthetic Theory and Lower-Class Poetic Practice** | 19 |
|    Visionaries: The Artist As Servant, God, or Vegetable | 19 |
|    Window Shoppers: The Servant As Artist | 39 |
| **2: The Wild and the Civilized: Poet Making** | 48 |
|    The Wages of Suffering and the Wages of Sin: Class Issues and Literary Patronage | 48 |
|    "Menial Maids, with No Release from Toil": Some Paradigms | 54 |
|    "The Poet's Silence is the Triumph of Taste": The Case of Anna Louisa Karsch | 70 |
|    "Drive Your Cows from the Foot of Parnassus": The Case of Ann Yearsley | 93 |
| **3: The Life As the Work: Counterfeit Confessions, Bogus Biographies, Literary Lives** | 105 |
|    Arcadian Shepherdesses and Toiling Peasants: On Poetry and Poverty | 108 |
|    The German Sappho: Controversies Surrounding a Legend | 118 |
|    A Man or a Mother? Anna Louisa Karsch Forgets Her Gender | 123 |
|    Beauty and the Beasts: Fairy Tale Imagery | 133 |
|    Unhappy Endings: Biographical Punishment | 153 |

4: A Literature of Labor: Poetic Images of Country Life  160
   Physical Labor and Poetic "Idleness"  160
   Rural Realities I: Pastoral Landscapes and Village Scenes  161
   Rural Realities II: The Rustic at Work  176
   Pastorals and Power: Social and Aesthetic Considerations  192

5: Inspired by Nature, Inspired by Love:
Two Poets on Poetic Inspiration  194
   The Rural Muse: On Nature Inspiration
     and Book Learning  195
   Under Love's Spell: Authors and Readers  208

6: Of Patrons and Critics:
Reading the Bourgeois Reader  216
   Reading the Reader: Of Critics and Posterity  216
   Castle-Building: Of Patrons and Their Empty Promises  231

Conclusion: On the Gender and Class of Art  240

Appendix: Short Biographies of Women Peasant Poets  259

Works Cited  273

Index  315

# Illustrations

1. Karoline Leonhardt Lyser (1811–99), "Anna Louisa Karsch, geb. Dürrbach." Ink and water color painting. Courtesy of the Städelsches Kunstinstitut und Städtische Galerie Frankfurt.   136

2. "Encounter with the herder boy." Etching by W. Arndt, ca. 1790. From: Gisela Brinker-Gabler, *Deutsche Literatur von Frauen*, vol. 1 (1988).   137

3. Anna Louisa Karsch. Etching by Georg Friedrich Schmidt, 1764. Frontispiece to Anna Louisa Karsch's *Auserlesene Gedichte* (1764).   143

4. "Meierei auf dem Hammer bei Schwiebus." Drawing by Daniel Nikolaus Chodowiecki. Courtesy of Archiv für Kunst und Geschichte, Bildarchiv Preussischer Kulturbesitz, Berlin.   143

5. Anna Louisa Karsch at her desk. Drawing by Ernst Wilhelm Hempel. Courtesy of Societätsverlag Frankfurt.   144

6. Anna Louisa Karsch. Oil painting by Karl Christian Kehrer, 1791. Notation on the back: "Painted for Gleim, more on account of her virtue than of her genius." Courtesy of the Gleim-Haus, Halberstadt.   144

7. Anna Louisa Karsch. Etching by Johann Heinrich Lips. In: Johann Kaspar Lavater, *Physiognomische Fragmente*, 1777.   144

8. Ann Cromartie Yearsley, 1787, from a reprint of 1814. Engraving by [Wilson?] Lowry (1762–1824). Courtesy of the British Library.    149

9. "British Liberty." Etching by William Cromartie Yearsley, 1796. Frontispiece to Ann Cromartie Yearsley, *The Rural Lyre*. Courtesy of the British Library.    151

# Acknowledgments

IF WRITING WERE, as so many aesthetic treatises have claimed, inspired by Nature, authors would be entirely self-sufficient. To perceive writing, including one's own, within a context is to acknowledge a debt. My work on this book over the years has benefited from an excellent support system composed of friends, colleagues and institutions. I would here like to express my gratitude to some of them:

John Landau, my best friend and first reader, for being there from beginning to end;

Jim Hardin, my editor, for his faith in this project, his hawk eyes for everything from typos to methodological glitches, and for challenging me on every single thing that wasn't quite right;

Sarah Colvin, University of Edinburgh, for her hard work in procuring for me a Visiting Fellowship in German at the University of Edinburgh, for her supportive yet critical reading of chapter 2 and for the truly inspiring brainstorming sessions over peppermint tea;

David Hill, University of Birmingham, for providing me with an edition of the letters of Anna Louisa Karsch and other important literature, and for his expert reading of the manuscript and helpful suggestions;

Susan Cocalis, University of Massachusetts, Amherst, for her ability to read the manuscript simultaneously with a scholar's critical detachment and with a reader's anticipation and amusement;

Howard Gaskill, University of Edinburgh, for his generosity in sharing his ideas and sources;

My research assistants: Aida Premilovac, Ivan Parkinson, and Elisabeth Frech, Georgetown University, for their dependability, enthusiasm and resourcefulness;

Carol Tully, University of Wales Bangor, for providing me with the poems of Margaret Crawford, a later Scottish "peasant poet";

Margaret Ives, University of Lancaster, for granting me a sneak preview of her then unpublished work on Anna Louisa Karsch and sending me copies of her conference talks on Karsch;

Mark Taplin, Scottish Parliament, for sharing his insights on the status of Scots as a language;

Robert Crawford, University of St. Andrews, John Frow, University of Edinburgh, and Heidi Byrnes, Georgetown University, for pointing me to some important literature;

Ruth Dawson, University of Hawaii, for bringing the author Sophie Ludwig to my attention;

Justine Jordan from *The Guardian*, for kindly searching the newspaper archives for information about the Edinburgh novelist Kate Atkinson;

Kate Atkinson, for her gracious willingness to make a brief appearance in the conclusion;

Peter Pfeiffer, Georgetown University, for his unwavering support of my research;

The Graduate School of Georgetown University, for their repeated and generous support of my research and writing of this book in the form of summer grants and travel money;

The British Academy, who funded part of the archival research for this book in the form of a grant in the Spring of 1999;

The School of Languages and Cultures, German Section, and the Institute for Advanced Studies in the Humanities, both at the University of Edinburgh, for supporting the research and writing of this book by granting me Visiting Fellowships in the Spring of 1999 and Fall of 2000;

The German Department, Georgetown University, for its support of this project through Research Assistants;

The many librarians and archivists at various libraries in the US, UK, and Germany who have helped me track down authors, sources, and information: the National Library of Scotland and the Scottish Poetry Library (both in Edinburgh), the Staatsbibliothek in Berlin, the Bodleian Library in Oxford, the British Library, the Library of Congress, and the libraries at the universities of Edinburgh, St. Andrews, Glasgow, Berlin (both Humboldt and Freie Universität), and Georgetown University in Washington, DC;

The audiences at the following universities and conferences where I lectured on materials on which this study is based: the Institute for Advanced Studies in the Humanities, Edinburgh; the German Section, School of European Languages and Cultures, University of Edinburgh; the Day School on Eighteenth and Nineteenth-Century Women Writers, University of Glasgow; the Modern Language Association conventions in Chicago (1999) and New Orleans (2001); the University of Alberta, Edmonton; The Faculty, The Queen's College, University of Oxford; Myths and Mythmaking: International Women in German Studies Conference, University of Edinburgh; Image Into Identity Conference, University of Hull; and the German Department at the University of Sheffield.

None of these lectures ended up in this book, but the responses, criticisms, and questions of colleagues and students who heard me speak on related issues have nonetheless shaped this project in fundamental ways.

\* \* \*

This book is dedicated to the memory of Professor Susanne Zantop of Dartmouth College. As my friend and mentor, Susanne has centrally influenced my writing, from my first project — my dissertation, which she read chapter by chapter although she wasn't on my committee — to this one. This book, more than any other I have written, is indebted to her: her expertise in Comparative Literature, her pioneering role in unearthing early women writers, her concerns with the rediscovery and re-evaluation of lesser-known but no less interesting literary traditions, her interest in the social history of literature, her fearlessness and sense of joyous exploration in venturing into a new field are the models this project has sought to emulate. To both her and her husband Half, who died with her in January 2001, I owe a debt of gratitude for their unvarying friendship and their company and conversation whenever time and distance allowed. I will remember each of these occasions with fondness and gratitude, and I consider myself blessed to have known them both.

# Introduction: Aesthetic Evasions and Social Consequences

LITERARY HISTORY, as it has been written for eighteenth-century Britain and Germany, has traditionally assumed three things: first, that most, if not all, "great" writers of the age were male and middle class; second, that this was directly related to the bourgeoisie's rise to power and cultural preeminence following the emancipation of the middle-class artist from seventeenth-century aristocratic patronage; and finally, that the two aspects that make the new bourgeois art "Art"[1] and that have, in fact, from the eighteenth century on defined *all* Art as such, are its independence from social, political, and biographical context and its resulting ability to embody universally *human* values, transcending all specificities of gender and class. If this study concentrates on women writers of the lower orders — authors who were neither male nor middle-class —, if it moreover professes itself indebted to both Marxist and feminist criticism, it places itself outside of these parameters. In contrast to books on Goethe or Coleridge, whose relevance is assumed, such a study is forced to explain *why* it makes its subject literature that is so manifestly not "Art" by the bourgeois definition, why it should matter that this literature was produced by lower-class women rather than proper writers, and why a study that will automatically be assumed to be

---

[1] Throughout the book, I use lower-case "art" neutrally to refer to any art form (writing, painting, music, sculpture, etc.), with my concentration in this book on the art of writing, and capitalized "Art" to refer to the *sanctification* of art throughout its reception since the eighteenth century as transcendentally human, moral, or humane. The same will apply to all derivatives of the term, such as artistic, art form, or artist. Two exceptions will be the eighteenth-century usage of the term "art" or its derivatives in other meanings (e.g., "artless" to mean innocent, "art" as indicating artificiality, or "arts" as indicating skills) and usage of the term in quotations from other authors. In the first instance, all occurrences of "art" are rendered in lower case; in the second, the original author's spelling is retained.

A problem with the distinction between "art" and "Art" occurs in passages where I have translated German quotations using the term "Kunst" into English. In all such cases, I have tried to avoid preempting the reader's interpretation of the passage by translating "Kunst" neutrally as "art," even in cases where I believe the author's usage of "Kunst" to be closer to my usage of "Art."

social and political in outlook should be able to lay claim to a readership primarily interested in the aesthetic.

This book is the first comparative investigation of the literature of lower-class women poets in eighteenth-century England, Scotland, and Germany. It links this literary tradition with one of the major eighteenth-century aesthetic trends in all three countries: the Natural Genius craze, which culminated in highland primitivism in Britain and in the Sturm und Drang in Germany. One of the main considerations that have influenced this study is the idea that aesthetic theory and poetic practice were *mutually* influential, that not only poetic practice was judged within the parameters of contemporary aesthetics, but also that this aesthetic was re-evaluated in direct response to some of this literature. Thus, a link can be drawn between the reception of female lower-class poets and the establishment of aesthetics that ultimately conceptualized all forms of Art, including writing, as predominantly male-produced and as chiefly originating in the middle classes.

This book introduces the reader to some of this fascinating literature, a task that has already been begun by pioneering scholars like Donna Landry, Moira Ferguson, Mary Waldron, and Richard Greene. However, in contrast to these previous studies, which have concentrated on the lives and works of women peasant poets, my project is as concerned with the bourgeois response and the consequences for the development of middle-class aesthetics as it is with these women authors themselves. This book explores four related areas: It traces the now-common establishment of writing, understood as Art, as a predominantly male and middle-class tradition back to the reception of eighteenth-century lower-class poets and the aesthetic debate this phenomenon sparked. It thus establishes that this identification of Art with masculinity and the middle classes was not exclusively, as is commonly held, developed in dissociation from aristocratic culture, but also and more significantly in dissociation from lower-class art forms. It then links this phenomenon with the reception of middle-class women's writings by examining the role that works by women of their own class played in the theorizing of eighteenth-century bourgeois men. And finally, it examines how peasant poets responded to their becoming instruments in the service of middle-class aesthetics, how they viewed the bourgeois project of Art and authorship, and how they sought to participate in this project.

For reasons that will be explained later,[2] not the least of which is the much higher lower-class literacy rate in England and Scotland compared

---

[2] See chapter 1.

with Germany, poetry by women peasants is a tradition much better established in Britain than it was in Germany.[3] We know of at least thirteen published lower-class women poets in eighteenth-century England: the Norwich cordwainer's daughter Elizabeth Bentley (1767–1839); the domestic servants Jane Cave (ca. 1754–1813), Elizabeth Hands (Bourton, no dates available), Susannah Harrison (no dates available), Jane Holt (Oxford, no dates available), and Molly Leapor (Northamptonshire, 1722–46); the Suffolk cottager Ann Candler (1740–1814); the Hampshire washerwoman Mary Collier (1689/90–after 1762); possibly Mary Masters (occupation unknown, 1694?–1771 or 1706?–59?); the Somerset linen merchant's daughter Mary Scott (ca. 1752–90); the farmers Jane West (Leicestershire, no dates available) and Mary Whateley Darwall (Worcestershire, 1738–1825); and — most famously — the Bristol milkmaid Ann Cromartie Yearsley (1752–1806).[4] In Scotland, at least five peasant women published or publicly performed their work: Jeanie Glover from Kilmarnock (1758–1801), "a — and a thief" according to Robert Burns;[5] the Ayrshire milkmaid Janet Little (1759–1813); the Aberdeen carpenter's wife Christian Milne (1773–after 1816); Jean Murray from Muir near Mauchline (late eighteenth century); and the Muirkirk cottager Isobel (Tibbie) Pagan (1741–1821).[6] In Ireland, three lower-class poets have been documented: the Dublin wool clothier's wife Mary Barber (1690?–

---

[3] This is a point already made by Klaus, who claims that there was no such tradition in Germany (*Literature of Labour*, 1).

Throughout the book, citations refer to author and page numbers only (for full bibliographical information, see Works Cited at the end of the volume), or author, abbreviated title and page numbers in cases where more than one work by the same author appears in the list of Works Cited.

[4] Brief biographies and bibliographical references to the poets' publications and relevant secondary sources appear in the Appendix for all poets whose poetry is interpreted in this volume. Information on these poets can be found in the following sources: Landry, *Muses* (on Mary Collier, Molly Leapor, Ann Yearsley, Elizabeth Hands, Elizabeth Bentley, and Janet Little); Ferguson, *Eighteenth-Century Women Poets* (on Mary Collier, Mary Scott, Ann Yearsley, and Janet Little); Klaus, "Stephen Duck und Mary Collier"; Landry, "The Resignation" (on Collier); Ferguson, "The Cause of My Sex" (on Scott); Rizzo, "Christopher Smart" and "Molly Leapor" (on Leapor); Messenger on Whateley Darwall; and Ferguson, "Unpublished Poems," Waldron's works, Demers, Tompkins, Zionkowski, and the anonymously published "An Historical Milkwoman" on Yearsley. Carter's dissertation also includes one chapter on Yearsley. There is no sustained analytical literature to date on Susannah Harrison, Jane Cave, Jane Holt, Ann Candler, Mary Masters, or Jane West.

[5] Burns's remark is quoted in Paterson, 34.

[6] For information on Janet Little, cf. the sources cited in footnote 2 as well as Bold and Hilton Brown. Little, Glover, and Pagan make a brief appearance in Paterson; Milne is treated briefly in Spence. I have been unable to find any sources on Murray.

1757), Constantia Grierson (1704–33), and the domestic servant and cottager Ellen Taylor (late eighteenth century).⁷ Whereas there seems to have been something of a tradition of lower-class women's writing in the British Isles, the only lower-class women writers to have come out of Germany, to my knowledge, were the celebrated and comparatively well researched case of the Silesian cowherd Anna Louisa Karsch (1722–91)⁸ and the forester's wife Sophie Ludwig (1764–1815).⁹ We do know that

---

⁷ Cf. Tucker's introduction, Isdell-Carpenter, and chapter 5 in Fagan's study on Barber; Elias, Lilley, and the brief introductory passages in Colman/Thornton I, 241 on Grierson. I have been unable to locate sources on Taylor.

⁸ In including Karsch in this volume, I am disagreeing with some scholars who consider Karsch a bourgeois author based on her thirty-year career in Berlin. In my view, this interpretation erases the fine, but nonetheless crucial, line between *bürgerlich* and *verbürgerlicht*. That Karsch's lower-class origins were a matter of self-stylization and self-representation in her writing does not mean they were not also rooted in biographical fact. Karsch spent most of her childhood years doing manual labor rather than being groomed for marriage; she ended up marrying two men from the peasant and artisan class; and the few years she spent with her uncle learning to read and write hardly equal a bourgeois education, even for girls of the time. Conversely, Karsch's schooling — a rudimentary literary education provided by a male relative — seems quite typical for lower-class women writers. Many of her writings, written both before and after her transplantation to Berlin, were influenced by and depict thematically her rural background and early poverty. To consider her a bourgeois author seems to me to disregard available biographical data, as well as her career as a poet, before her transplantation to Berlin in 1761.

To date, short and mostly biographical works on Karsch considerably outnumber studies of her writing; the most important analytical sources on her are the works by Ute Pott, Uta Schaffers, and the collection of essays edited by Bennholdt-Thomsen and Runge.

All translations from German sources, primary or secondary, are mine unless otherwise indicated. In my translations, especially of Karsch's poetry, I have attempted to retain the metric and rhyme scheme Karsch employed and have tried to approximate her punctuation wherever possible: Karsch's usage of meter and rhyme becomes relevant to a reading of the poet as either within or independent of existing literary traditions, and her almost complete lack of punctuation in her letters is one of the most distinctive features of that correspondence. No attempt was made to approximate Karsch's usage of dialect or her erratic orthography in the translations. Due to my misgivings as to the justifiability of aesthetic judgments, particularly of noncanonized literature (see later in text), I have also made no attempt to avoid those of Karsch's poems that traditional readers would undoubtedly declare inferior in "quality" or to clean up Karsch's occasionally clumsy phraseology in translation. On the contrary, I hope to have approximated that clumsiness as well as the tremendous expressiveness of other poems.

⁹ I thank Ruth Dawson for bringing Sophie Ludwig to my attention. Brief biographical and bibliographical entries on the author can be found in Friedrichs, 191; Schindel, I, 359–66 and III, 213; Groß, 69–70; Goedeke, V, 542; Touaillon, 302–4; Frels, 190; Kosch, II (1953), 1586; Krüger, 275; Rassmann, *Deutscher Dichternekrolog* I, 122, and *Literarisches Handwörterbuch*, 296; Brümmer, *Lexikon*, 312–13, and *Deutsches Dichter-Lexikon*, I, 540–41. Sophie Ludwig was primarily a prose author, but published some poems in the 1797 edition of the *Göttinger Musenalmanach*.

some lower-class peasant women wrote but were never published or discovered: Robert Burns complimented an unnamed farmer's wife in Tiviotdale on her poetry,[10] and Anna Louisa Karsch discovered a field hand named Maria Catharina Dippen (ca. 1737–62) with poetic talent she deemed equal to her own.[11] All of these women, particularly those who were published, wrote within a tradition largely established and dominated by the male poets of their class — most famously, the thresher Stephen Duck (1705–56) in England and the "heaven-taught ploughman" Robert Burns (1759–96) in Scotland.[12] In Germany, as well, a few male poets from the lower classes have been documented, including the hatmaker and poet Städele in Memmingen, the impoverished village teacher Johann Heinrich Thomsen,[13] and the late eighteenth- and early nineteenth-century broommaker Gottlieb Hiller.[14]

With the exception of Burns, studies of peasant poets are in short supply;[15] studies of peasant women writers are, unsurprisingly, even more scarce. The only two extensive studies on this subject to date, Donna Landry's *The Muses of Resistance* (1990) and Moira Ferguson's *Eighteenth-Century Women Poets* (1995), both indispensable to further research in the area, are introductory studies that limit themselves largely to the English context (both include a chapter on the Scottish poet Janet Little). Other introductory studies concentrate on single writers and their works (Mary Waldron's works on Ann Yearsley, Ann Messenger's studies of Mary Whateley Darwall, Richard Greene's book on Molly Leapor, Uta Schaffers's monograph on Anna Louisa Karsch, Ute Pott's analysis of the correspondence between Karsch and her patron Johann Wilhelm Ludwig Gleim, and the conference proceedings volume on Karsch edited by Anke Bennholdt-Thomsen and Anita Runge). Re-

---

[10] Burns's letter is in the National Library of Scotland, MS. Acc. 7748, catalogued as "Answer to a Tiviotdale Farmer's Wife's Epistle." It is addressed to "Guidwife"; the relevant passage in the rhymed letter reads as follows: "For you wha, bred to barn an' byre, / Sae sweetly tune the Scottish lyre, / Thanks to ye for your lines!"

[11] Cf. Karsch's letters to Sulzer, June 10, 1762, in *"Bruder in Apoll"* I, 426–30, where she also cites some of Dippen's poetry.

[12] The appellation for Burns is Henry Mackenzie's in the *Lounger* of December 1786; cf. Bold, 21.

[13] Both are briefly mentioned in the correspondence between G. A. Bürger and Boie, cf. the letters in Strodtmann, I, 37, 46, 362, and II, 158–60 and 166.

[14] On his autobiography and reception, cf. Stüssel, 226–33.

[15] The most comprehensive studies of this phenomenon include Klaus's *Literature of Labour* and Ashraf's study, both of which include one chapter on eighteenth-century poets, as well as the works by Carter, Henry Shanks, Unwin, Southey, the *Sketches of Obscure Poets*, and Paterson.

editions of the poets' works, aside from occasional appearances of poems in modern anthologies,[16] exist only for three poets: Mary Barber (1992), Ann Cromartie Yearsley (1994 and 1996), and Anna Louisa Karsch (1966, 1981, 1987, 1996); Karsch's letters are now available in a reliable form (ed. Nörtemann and Pott, 1996[17]), as well as in various other earlier editions (ed. Hausmann, 1933, and Beuys, 1981).

My treatment — particularly of the best researched authors, Anna Louisa Karsch, Ann Cromartie Yearsley, and Molly Leapor — is indebted to these pioneering studies; however, my goals, and therefore the book's organization, are not that of an introductory study in which every poet is granted more or less equal space and treatment. Some writers, usually those on whom there is the most material available, reappear throughout the book; others are accorded only brief mention. All of them, however, have influenced my thinking and my conclusions. Rather than reintroducing those who have already been competently analyzed (Karsch, Yearsley, or Molly Leapor) or introducing women like Christian Milne or Mary Masters who have, so far, attracted little or no scholarly attention, I discuss their work within the context and from the perspective established by major aesthetic and social shifts occurring in the eighteenth century. Whether an author is accorded extensive treatment in this study is thus dependent on her works' pertinence to the contexts in which I discuss it, rather than the degree to which the author is known or has been previously researched. Assessments of the author's "importance" or the "quality" of her writing, however defined, have also played no part in my decision to discuss or ignore an author. For reasons I will explain later, I find assessments of literary "quality" highly problematic; they would be particularly misplaced in a study like this one, in which one of my aims is to question the processes by which such judgments are made.

The aesthetic context that furnished the frame for the publication of lower-class poets of either gender is the tradition epitomized by the writings of Edward Young in England, James Macpherson in Scotland, and Johann Gottfried Herder and the Sturm und Drang authors in Germany. Their conviction that true artistic inspiration stemmed from Nature rather than erudition, their identification of "nature" with the rustic

---

[16] For the reader's convenience, I provide references for reprints of poems discussed in this book, even in cases in which I cite from the original edition.

[17] Nörtemann's and Pott's edition of the correspondence between Karsch and Gleim is not only considerably more comprehensive than all previous editions of Karsch's letters, but also the only one that neither corrects nor modernizes Karsch's erratic orthography and that has chosen to publish her letters complete, unabridged, and without interpretive or biographical editorial comments interspersed throughout the correspondence.

(*Volk*) and "natural" Man with precivilized or unlettered Man, their juxtaposition of the "original" author with the imitator whose claim to poesy rests on his familiarity with literary traditions furnished an indispensable context for the marketing and publication of peasant poets.

Although the aesthetic constitutes one of the primary topics of this book, it is also crucial to consider aspects pertaining to class and gender, given that this body of literature was produced by one social group (peasant women) but fashioned into an aesthetic *tradition* by another (bourgeois men). This context alone brings up a question that will remain central throughout this book — namely, the question of what the existence of these poets meant to bourgeois men and how it impacted their ideas about literary Art. Reading the literature of peasant women in the context of the aesthetic theorizing of bourgeois men means questioning some of our most dearly held assumptions about eighteenth-century culture, one of them being that the eighteenth-century bourgeoisie, following its emancipation from aristocratic patronage, established itself as the ruling cultural class in dissociation from aristocratic predilections and values.

It is my contention that bourgeois claims to intellectual and artistic distinction, as they were formulated during the eighteenth century in Britain as well as in Germany, rested not only on a rejection of aristocratic values, but even more centrally on the bourgeoisie's dissociation from lower-class culture on the one hand and from bourgeois women writers on the other. This point has acute consequences for the common conception of bourgeois Art as transcendent, all-encompassing, or representing transcendentally human values: art that becomes Art through a process of limitation and exclusion based on gender and class can be seen as no more than class- and gender-specific. Nineteenth- and twentieth-century interpretations of eighteenth-century bourgeois Art as transcendentally human(e) have only been able to uphold this fiction by a process in which the aesthetic, defined by the terms established within that same process, is privileged over the social and in which social and political considerations came to be defined as anathema to art.

If the eighteenth-century nature craze had a discernible impact on how work by lower-class authors was read, a reverse influence might be postulated as well. One could speculate that the failure of eighteenth-century nature aesthetics in nineteenth- and twentieth-century assessment was due, in no small measure, to its damning association with lower-class art forms. In the nineteenth and twentieth centuries, the concept of art as erudite, as produced by an educated masculine elite, re-established itself with a vengeance.[18] The highest respect accorded in literary histories has been lavished on those movements that most closely correspond to these definitions — for example, the Enlightenment or Classicism. Literary movements that proposed definitions of Art deviating from the erudite model have been nearly universally presented as short-lived fads. Germany's Sturm und Drang, for example, is widely represented as a movement launched by a group of overenthusiastic and inexperienced juveniles, bursting with a revolutionary fervor they could not express politically and therefore rather ineffectively channeled into literary theory and practice. In traditional literary histories, these authors without exception either die off within a few years or "grow up" to produce "true" — that is, erudite — Art forms (such as German Classicism).[19] Small wonder, then, that the nineteenth- and twentieth-century verdict was that the movement ran its course within less than a decade. The extent to which erudition and membership in the bourgeoisie, the so-called *Bildungsbürgertum,* have become prerequisites for the production of Art can be assessed by the extent to which eighteenth-century defenders of alternative models (for example, nature aesthetics) are discredited or belittled in nineteenth- and twentieth-century literary criticism.

If the dissociation of Art from erudition has had such acute consequences for the canonization of perfectly respectable (that is, masculine

[18] Cf., e.g., Kontje, 9.

[19] On the early death or insanity of many writers of the movement, cf. Schneider, 35; Garland, 127–9 and 152–3; Kistler, 31–8; Kaiser, 192–3; Luserke, *Sturm und Drang,* 9–10. On the transition from the juvenile predilections of the Sturm und Drang to the maturity of Classicism, cf., paradigmatically, Fritz Martini on Goethe in "Von der Aufklärung zum Sturm und Drang," 461–2: "Duke Karl August's invitation to Weimar brought him the liberating call to a greater, less restricted life, to a multitude of new tasks and duties, which meant, for Goethe, the metamorphosis into the actively forming, self-educating maturity of manhood, from the Sturm und Drang to Classicism" ("Herzog Karl Augusts Einladung nach Weimar brachte dann den befreienden Ruf in ein größeres, weiteres Leben, in eine Fülle neuer Aufgaben und Pflichten, die für Goethe die Metamorphose zur tätig-geformten, sich selbst erziehenden Reife des Mannesalters, vom Sturm und Drang zur Klassik bedeuteten"). Occasionally, Herder is cast in a comparable role: "The ecstatic youth Herder has matured into the level-headed man who decisively turns his back on the genius-enthusiasm of his youth. . . . The 'demonic wildness' of the Storm-and-Stress Herder settles into the 'divine mildness' of the apostle of humanity" (Herman Wolf, "Die Genielehre des jungen Herder," 214: "Der ekstatische Jüngling Herder ist zum besonnenen Mann gereift, der sich entschieden von dem Genieenthusiasmus seiner Jugend abwendet. . . . Das 'Dämonisch-Wilde' des Stürmers und Drängers Herder klärt sich ab zum 'Göttlich-Milden' des Humanitätsapostels").

Most recently, Kagel has attributed the predominantly negative reception of Lenz's work until the mid-twentieth century to a near-universal scholarly "fixation" on the concept of Classical Art (1; cf. also the literature cited therein). Within the context of that obsession, Lenz is discounted as a writer precisely because he did *not* funnel the rebelliousness of the Sturm und Drang into Classical "maturity" (Kagel, 2).

and bourgeois) authors, the nineteenth- and twentieth-century reception of less respectable (female and lower-class) authors is, unsurprisingly, even more devastating. Their fame is viewed as fleeting and undeserved, based on "poems effortlessly cobbled together, improvised rhymes for every occasion."[20] Their work, thus defined by the moment and tied to specific occasions, is deemed ineligible for the posthumous fame to which the true Artist aspires: "It is certainly unlikely that her poems will ever be republished, and indeed the reading public has no need of them."[21] Where the traditional metaphor of childbirth for Artistic creativity is applied to these authors, what ensues is not a birth but a miscarriage: "In her painful births she could not impart life, and nothing remains of her poetry in the sense in which alone poetry can be said to live."[22] The utter unthinkability of the idea that such a poet could command any kind of posthumous esteem is, at times, reinforced by the use of witty epitaphs, such as the one published on the milkmaid Ann Yearsley: "Anne [*sic*] Yearsley tasted the Castalian stream, / And skimmed its surface as she skimmed her cream; / But struck at last by fate's unerring blow, / All that remains of Anne is — 'Milk below!'"[23] Robert Burns, possibly the only lower-class poet except for John Clare to have garnered any respect in posthumous criticism, is accused of inspiring other peasant poets — by example rather than by active support — who would have been "better discouraged."[24] Even in latter-day twentieth-century criticism, peasant poets are routinely presented as "craftily transform[ing their] ignorance into a virtue"[25] by jumping on the bandwagon of the nature craze, thus calculatedly insinuating themselves into an Artistic scene to which they have nothing to offer. Their work is characterized not only as substandard, as offering "nothing at all tempting,"[26] but also as disingenuous: utterly conventional verse produced in hopes of social

---

[20] Beuys on Anna Louisa Karsch, 7: "Das, worauf ihr frischer Ruhm sich gründet, ist das leicht hingeworfene Gedicht, der Reim aus dem Stegreif zu jedem Anlaß." On Karsch's reception as a mediocre occasional poet, cf. also Pott, "Berlin — Halberstadt — Berlin," 94.

[21] Tompkins, 96, on Ann Yearsley, whose poems were republished in 1994 and 1996.

[22] Tompkins, 102, on Ann Yearsley.

[23] The epitaph is cited in "An Historical Milkwoman," 398 (this citation), and Tompkins, 101.

[24] Hilton Brown on the "miscellaneous characters" attempting to write verse; his list includes Sillar, Simpson, Campbell, Fisher, and Walker the Tailor (15).

[25] Carter, 234, on Robert Burns; Janet Todd has made similar statements on the opportunistic self-representation of lower-class authors (*Sensibility*, 58).

[26] Paterson on Isobel Pagan, 118.

ascent.[27] In contemporary and later reviews, peasant poets are often held to *both* definitions of Art, forced to represent nature inspiration on the one hand and upbraided for their failure to follow the rules of erudite writing on the other.[28]

The quotability of blatantly biased reviews aside, there is good reason to look at this reception history closely. Contemporary reviews as well as nineteenth- and much twentieth-century criticism of lower-class women's works did more than merely disparage their writing: they established, and in my opinion consciously, a discourse that defined and still defines these works as *fundamentally* incompatible with true Art. Condemning reviews of individual poets often led straight into general remarks on the humiliating incompetence of these poets as a group. "There are those," the latter-day critic intoned, "whom even Pegasus cannot lift above the ground, and it is a waste of time for Pegasus to try."[29] Faced with the *principal* opposition between peasant poetry and Art, as Henry Shanks affirmed it in his 1881 study *The Peasant Poets of Scotland* when he assertively juxtaposed "*peasant* and *artisan*" and "*great* poets,"[30] the question becomes what the common factor is that would automatically and in every case except that of Robert Burns disqualify the works of peasant authors from consideration as Art. Part of the answer to this central question can be provided by an examination of how literature by bourgeois authors, in contrast with works by lower-class writers, has traditionally been read: as disconnected from Life in the case of bourgeois authors; as biographically descriptive and unproblematically transferable material in the case of peasant authors. During a century in which Art increasingly defined itself through its *dissociation* from Life, the works of peasant poets are marketed as representative for and expressive of their biographies.[31] What Achim von Arnim once stated about

---

[27] Janet Todd, *Sensibility*, 87–88. Cf. also Waldron's remarks on Yearsley's reception in the nineteenth century in *Lactilla*, 278, and Klaus, *Literature of Labour*, 19–20, on the regrettable conformity of the writing of peasant poets.

[28] Cf., e.g., Uta Schaffers's analysis of the reception of Anna Louisa Karsch, 109–11, 169–72, and 183–84. An excellent example supporting Schaffers's claim can be found in Muncker's assessment of Karsch's poetic activity, in which he upbraids the "child of nature" for her inability to conform to erudite rules (300–301). Cf. also Rizzo's remarks on Molly Leapor's and other English lower-class poets' attempts to conform to bourgeois aesthetic mandates, "Molly Leapor," 329–33.

[29] Hilton Brown on Janet Little, 20.

[30] Shanks, 113, the emphases are original.

[31] It is important to distinguish here between the self-representation of the artist (e.g., Goethe frequently emphasized the biographical origins of his writing) and the critical

Anna Louisa Karsch applies to other lower-class authors as well: the poet's work is only interesting to the reader to the extent that it describes the peasant's life.[32] In the absence of the traditional erudite context, the life of the "natural genius" furnishes the only context available or necessary for the interpretation of the work.[33] But this emphasis on the author rather than the work directly contradicts the emerging definition of Art as a work independent from its author. "Those who view the work of Art should never encounter in it the Artist, so that the work is the sole recipient of all attention. That is why it is said that the greatest art is to conceal Art."[34] This is precisely what the work of peasant poets does not do and indeed cannot do: if the greatest achievement of bourgeois Art is to conceal, the peasant's poetry is charged to reveal, to grant the bourgeois observer insight into the terra incognita of spontaneous nature inspiration on the one hand and a life dominated by labor and poverty on the other. In an aesthetic context that demands the complete dissociation of Art and Life, the peasant's work disqualifies itself by its direct applicability to the poet's biography.

The common juxtaposition of Life and Art has not only had consequences for the writing *by* women peasant poets, but also for writing *about* them. Biographical approaches to literary interpretation have long been considered outdated and unsophisticated; similarly, autobiographical works have had difficulty establishing themselves as respectable art forms. Yet much of the writing of peasant poets was necessarily and unabashedly autobiographical: Karsch, for example, often made no distinction between the author of the poem and the poetic speaker; Molly Leapor's "Mira" is an easily recognizable poetic stand-in for the author herself, as is Ann Yearsley's "Lactilla," a name she used both as her pen name and to describe an autobiographical persona in her poems. Works where this is obviously the case must be read as reflecting or alluding to events in the author's life, regardless of modern judgments of the sophistication or lack thereof of such a methodology, and it must be possible to consider the life in a reading of the work without deleting the multifaceted nature of the

requirement (throughout the eighteenth century and thereafter) that Art *transcend* Life, as described by Christa Bürger in her *Leben Schreiben*.

[32] Arnim on Karsch, 55–56. Arnim's essay was reprinted as "Ein Nachruf" in Gerhard Wolf, 260–63. The identical claim (that Karsch's poems are only relevant as descriptions of her life) is made in the review of Karsch's work in the *Journal Encyclopédique*, 78.

[33] Cf. Stüssel's analysis, 115–20, particularly 115.

[34] Sulzer, "Allgemeine Theorie der schönen Künste," quoted in Stüssel, 101: "Diejenigen, welche das Werk betrachten, müssen nirgends den Künstler erblicken, damit die Aufmerksamkeit allein auf das Werk gerichtet werde. Darum sagt man, es sey die größte Kunst, die Kunst zu verbergen." Cf. also Stüssel's discussion of this concept, 100–101.

work by reducing it to an expression of the life. What I find problematic, and have sought to avoid in my interpretations, is not a biographical reading per se but the unilateral designation of an author's complete work as autobiographical based on a few clearly autobiographical poems, the equation of "autobiographical" with "nonliterary,"[35] and the equation of "autobiographical" with "historical." As is discussed more extensively in chapter 3, autobiographical self-representation on the part of peasant poets was subject to as many pressures and prevarications as was their representation through their patrons or critics.

In my discussion of these authors' poems, I have sought to accord them the dignity of a literary reading that they have, so far, received only in rare cases. A "literary" reading means considering even blatantly autobiographical works as literature in the sense of presupposing a poetic license that transcends the purely autobiographical or historical. It does *not* mean an aesthetic judgment of these works, which would merely reiterate the very power relations that this project seeks to confront. My readings, in every case, distinguish between clearly autobiographical work and other poems, assume a distinction between poetic speaker and author in all works that are not ostentatiously autobiographical, and consider even works clearly intended to be autobiographical as literary documents as well as documents of self-representation that may contain significant deviations from the author's actual life.

To discuss the work of peasant poets in a context that does not automatically juxtapose it to Art means to rethink the terms of the debate from the outset. Reading their work from a nonpejorative viewpoint is impossible from a perspective that defines Art "by its capacity to evoke this special response: initially the perception of beauty; then the pure contemplation of the object, for its own sake and without other ('external') considerations."[36] Williams has shown to what extent the modern definition of art involves a dissociation not only from biography but also from all other contexts: "Art and thinking about art have to separate themselves, by ever more absolute abstraction, from the social processes within which they are

---

[35] For a more concrete problematization of this issue, cf. my concluding remarks to chapter 3.

[36] Williams, *Marxism*, 150. Cf. also Jameson's "assertion of a political unconscious" in interpretation (402) and Barrell's *Poetry, Language and Politics*. Particularly in his introduction, Barrell critically sums up the aesthetic mandate that the "process of judging truth and value is a process to be conducted with reference only to the text itself . . .," i. e. the idea that a text is best judged aesthetically through "the refusal of the historically-specific nature of the writing of literary texts . . . [which] is also a refusal of the political" (3–4).

still contained. Aesthetic theory is the main instrument of this evasion."[37] It is this principle that is responsible for the rather simplistic division of all literature into "good" literature (literature that can be assessed exclusively by aesthetic criteria, most or all of which happens to have been produced by middle-class men) and mediocre/trivial literature (that is, women's literature or lower-class art forms which can justifiably be discussed only by recourse to social or historical "interest"[38]). To simply apply aesthetic criteria to the work of lower-class authors, as both Waldron and Greene have attempted to do,[39] is no solution: at best, such a move would result in the inclusion of the few authors who have managed to conform to the bourgeois definition of Art in the exclusive club of noteworthy literati. At worst, it perpetuates the traditional definition of Art as the standard by which the works of peasants and women should be measured even today, thus implicitly sanctioning the processes by which bourgeois and masculine specificity misrepresents itself as all-encompassingly human. It neither answers the question of the *principal* ineligibility of lower-class authors and women for consideration as true Artists nor does it re-examine the criteria, aesthetic or social, by which male bourgeois art establishes itself as Art. My project, rather than attempting to assign an "aesthetic quality" to the writing of lower-class women, seeks to use their literature and their reception by male bourgeois readers to question how judgments of "quality" are made in the first place. This book, in other words, is as centrally concerned with the bourgeois response as it is with the work of peasant authors: of the six principal chapters, chapters 1 through 3 concentrate on the bourgeois conceptualization of writing as an Art form as it manifested

---

[37] Williams, *Marxism*, 154.

[38] Cf., paradigmatically, Southey, one of the rare anthologists of women's writing, whose excuse for doing so was to represent as accurately as possible the common taste of the era, a goal that he saw as better served by collecting the work of indifferent poets than that of good ones who wrote for posterity rather than pandering to contemporary tastes. The example is cited in Eger, 213–14.

[39] Waldron sees no alternative to either making aesthetic judgments or tacitly accepting the writer's exclusion from dominant literary discourse as justified; asserting that social and political reasons are not sufficient to justify the rediscovery of lower-class women authors, her study strives to establish Yearsley as "a writer of talent and originality" (*Lactilla*, 79–80; the quotation, 80). Greene, in his study of Molly Leapor, likewise states that a re-examination of the canon can only be effected based on "aesthetic value" (205), indicating that it would be sufficient to include those poets who had managed to conform to bourgeois criteria as having produced work of "sustained quality" (206) without actually re-examining these criteria. The sole effect the "inclusion" of a lower-class writer can have under these circumstances is that of reaffirming the canon: "to raise the status of a poet like Mary Leapor has the interesting and desirable effect of revealing something new about established figures, and may even raise the value of those who have been most valued" (Greene, 208).

itself in relation to peasant poetry and chapters 4 through 6 examine the work of peasant poets in relation or direct response to bourgeois aesthetics or critique. I have thus tried to take Williams's advice to examine literature not exclusively from the aspect of its reception, as the aesthetic response does, but also from that of its production. "Literature" is viewed, in accordance with Peter Bürger, not as a timeless phenomenon endowed with unchanging values, but as an institution that defines and redefines itself through aesthetic codices which simultaneously become the basis for the exclusion of undesirable art forms. From this perspective, the existence of peasant poets, women writers, and other unauthorized authors cannot be seen as indicating the collapse of "the patrician walls of art,"[40] but provides, on the contrary, the foil against which definitions of Art are established. Within the institution of Literature, aesthetic debates such as the ones that took place in eighteenth-century Britain and Germany, can be seen as struggles for the formulation of new norms. It is particularly important to view these processes, as Bürger has done, not as aesthetic debates comfortably divorced from "external" considerations but, conversely and pointedly, as expressions of *social* conflict.[41] What is needed for a fair assessment of the literature of peasants, women, or other authors who have been principally excluded from consideration as Artists by the bourgeois definition, is neither an assessment of their literature *within* the bourgeois aesthetic framework (as of "aesthetic value," however defined) or *outside* of this framework (as merely of historical or social interest), but a demolition of the framework itself. To this worthy goal, my book hopes to make a small contribution.

The deconstruction of the bourgeois conceptualization of Art could unquestionably be attempted with reference to other historical epochs and other national contexts. Presupposing an interest in the literary activity of lower-class and women authors, however, there are some good reasons for focusing on the eighteenth century on the one hand and Britain and Germany on the other. The eighteenth century, supposedly so central for the establishment of bourgeois art because of the bourgeoisie's emancipation from seventeenth-century aristocratic patronage, was also the first in which the bourgeoisie defined itself as clearly distinct from "the people."[42] Ideas about authorship as well as ideas about femininity underwent a significant change during that century;[43] particularly relevant for this con-

[40] Cf. Harris's introduction to Duncombe's *Feminiad*, viii.

[41] Peter Bürger, *Funktionswandel*, 13.

[42] Cf. Balet, 31–32; on the establishment of the bourgeoisie as a literary class, cf. Luserke, *Bändigung*, 147–49.

[43] Cf. Gray and Schabert/Schaff, 10–11, as well as Fulford's study of masculinity.

text is the development of ideas on patronage and original creativity versus imitation in Art, which are also commonly identified as originating during the eighteenth century.[44] The concentration on English, Scottish, and German authors seems warranted in view of the tremendous influence that English and Scottish aesthetics exercised on German theorists of literature.[45] If there is hardly, as Schmidt has phrased it, a single thought on poetic genius in eighteenth-century Germany that was not imported either from France or England,[46] one might identify, as German aesthetic theorists usually did, the erudite principle (the German Enlightenment) as derivative of the French[47] and the counterculture of nature inspiration as indebted to the English and Scottish tradition(s).[48] Some of the most

[44] Cf. Wunberg, 88–91; Huyssen, 71; Schmidt, I, 2; and McKeon, *Origins* 119–20, on the belief in the autonomy of the aesthetic from the eighteenth century on.

[45] Cf. Garland, 10–17; Huyssen, 70; Luserke, *Sturm und Drang*, 83–85 (on Herder's reception of Ossian); Schneider, 31 and 74–77. Herder famously defended his near-exclusive concentration on English aesthetics and literature by claiming a principal kinship between the two nations: he supported his findings of the many similarities between English and German folk and fairy tales by avowing that originally the Anglo-Saxons had been Germans. Cf. the introductory passage in his "Von Ähnlichkeit der mittlern englischen und deutschen Dichtkunst" (486).

[46] Schmidt, I, xii and 114.

[47] Particularly with respect to lyric genres, however, one could also argue a close affinity between German and French nature aesthetics; cf., e.g., Gay's dissertation on "Rousseau and the Lyric Natural."

[48] I find it necessary to distinguish between the English and Scottish traditions, although Scotland lost its political independence in the Act of Union with England in 1707 and did not regain it until 1999. Throughout the eighteenth century, Scotland would have been considered within the same national context as England, with the result that the significant differences in the cultural (especially literary and philosophical) scene were frequently erased by "subsuming" Scottish writings into English cultural discourse. (Even today, university curricula in both England and Scotland commonly teach Scottish authors such as Robert Louis Stevenson and even Walter Scott as "English" writers or as part of courses on English literature.) Eighteenth-century German writers (or, for that matter, Swiss writers) describing the influence of English or Scottish writings on German thought often fail to distinguish between the two. Where necessary and appropriate, I will refer to Scottish works and authors explicitly as Scottish or Scots, in an attempt to counteract the cultural "union" that many other writers have assumed as a given.

Of course, a similar principle can be applied to the German states of the eighteenth century: the context in which Anna Louisa Karsch lived and wrote, for example, was influenced both by French enlightened interests in Prussia and the reputation of the Prussian king Frederick II, throughout "Germany," as a patron of the arts. Referring to "Germany" at a time of particularism is, in itself, problematic. In discussing Karsch as a "German" (rather than a Prussian) writer, I do not intend to generalize the Prussian context to apply to all of Germany but to indicate that both her origins and early works (she was not originally from Prussia) and the aesthetic context in which she wrote, which was defined by treatises by authors from numerous German states and generally perceived as a "national" issue by later writers like Schiller, tran-

significant works on eighteenth-century genius aesthetics have centered on England and Germany and justified the concentration on these countries and the exclusion of, for example, the French context, with the intimate interrelationship between English/Scottish and German aesthetic thought during the eighteenth century.[49] My book, in seeking to debunk some fundamental assumptions about Art as they were developed in eighteenth-century aesthetics and perpetuated in nineteenth- and twentieth-century criticism, uses these assumptions as a necessary point of departure.

Some terms are used in this book differently from the way they appear in traditional literary criticism and also in earlier works on lower-class authors. Because this book is largely concerned with the *establishment* of terms describing the aesthetic, it concentrates on texts written before these terms solidified into discourse. Thus, some of the most central terms of the debate, including nature, genius, bourgeoisie, and art, are used in the literature in variant ways. I try to problematize the usage of terms in chapters which deal extensively with one term or another (for example, "nature," "genius," and *Volk* in chapter 1). In particular, class labels have turned out to be a complex issue; my designation of the two classes with which this book is most concerned, the "middle class" or "bourgeoisie" and the "lower class," expresses a compromise between traditional usage and applicability to this context. I use "the middle classes" (rather than "the middle class") to express an awareness of the amorphous nature of the class in the eighteenth century, particularly in Germany. "Bourgeoisie" and "bourgeois" are understood less as a denominator of social rank or economic class than as a designation for a *cultural* group, as defined in the work of Jürgen Kocka and others.[50] The term that has caused me the most headaches is simultaneously the most central for this study — namely, how to refer to the authors treated in it. "Proletarian poets" seems to imply an urban context and a class consciousness in the political sense that did not develop on a broad scale until the nineteenth century. "Working-class authors" seems inaccurate in its implication that members of the upper classes did not work. Klaus's term, "plebeian poets,"[51] is technically the most encompassing because it can be applied to rural as well as domestic workers. Nonetheless, I have

---

scended the Prussian setting. In this book, I will distinguish between German and Swiss writers and contexts and specify according to German states wherever this is relevant to the argument.

[49] For example, Engell's *The Creative Imagination* (cf. ix-x for a justification of his concentration on these two countries and the exclusion of the French context).

[50] Cf. Kocka, especially his essay "Bürgertum und Bürgerlichkeit"; and Bausinger. On issues of status and class, especially the middle class, see McKeon, *Origins,* 162–69.

[51] In *Literature of Labour;* cf. his explanation for choosing that particular designation, 2.

declined to use it: as one of the terms expressly developed by the upper classes to describe the lower orders in nonpejorative terms, "plebeian," at least to my ears, expresses the same genteel condescension as that which found its most apt manifestation in the patronage system. "Natural poets," finally, seems to authenticate an ideology that I find highly problematic and that this study challenges. I have finally settled, with some misgivings, on two terms which are used more or less interchangeably: "lower-class authors" and "peasant poets." "Lower-class authors" is used quite consciously in the way in which the term was originally designed, as an indication of the poets' class status vis-à-vis the bourgeoisie — a useful reminder, since their position *relative* to each other is one of the central aspects determining aesthetic theory and poetic response and therefore one of the main subjects of this book. "Peasant poets" is admittedly an inaccurate term because "peasant," in its dictionary definition, defines an occupation and implies a geographical setting, thus excluding domestic servants, artisans, and urban dwellers. I find it nonetheless useful — and use it to apply to all authors discussed here, regardless of whether or not they were technically "peasants" — because it best captures the sense of bourgeois superiority and contempt with which "peasants" are often discussed in bourgeois writings. In a book that primarily concerns itself with attitudes — that of the bourgeoisie toward lower-class authorship and that of the peasant poets toward bourgeois aesthetics and patronage — the angry, ill-mannered, and ungrateful "peasant" of bourgeois writings should perhaps be granted a more central and unapologetic role, if only evocatively, than is usually the case.

Because patronage is a central theme in this book, I have only included poets who published at least one volume of poetry with the help of a patron. The German novelist and essayist Sophie Ludwig is excluded for that reason.[52] Although not all of the poets treated in this volume were rural workers, all of them were "peasants" as far as their reception

---

[52] Sophie Ludwig's social background and literary career offer some interesting similarities to that of the other poets considered here: of rural origins, she married a forester and spent her married life as the head of a rural household. She established a relationship with many male bourgeois writers, including Weiße, Nicolai, Seume, and Rochlitz, that can be considered at least in terms of literary mentorship, if not patronage (Schindel, I, 364). I have chosen not to include her in this study for two reasons: her economic status seems closer to the lower-middle or artisan class than to the servant class which forms the background of the writers discussed here (according to Schindel, she employed a servant to help her run her household; I, 364). Second, Sophie Ludwig, a prolific prose author, published only single poems in the *Göttinger Musenalmanach*. To my knowledge, she did not publish a volume of poems, with or without the help of a patron.

in bourgeois writings is concerned. Not all of them worked on the land, but all of them worked physically and relied on this labor for their subsistence. Two of these poets would have continued to work physically for a living had it not been for their discovery and subsequent transplantation into the bourgeois literary scene (Anna Louisa Karsch and Ann Cromartie Yearsley); all other poets discussed here did. Class distinctions as defined by the division between those who need to labor physically for their subsistence and those who do not are the most crucial to my argument. For that reason, I chose to exclude some rural and poor poets who did not perform physical labor outside of the bourgeois confines of the home (such as Mary Scott) as well as well-to-do farmers (such as Jane West) or the daughters of "gentleman" farmers (such as Mary Whateley Darwall, who also did not work outside of the home). It is particularly in a discussion of *laboring* poets that both bourgeois and lower-class attitudes toward lower-class poetic activity come to the fore. Poetry was seen by many laboring poets as the antithesis and alternative to physical labor, by others as a ticket out of poverty, whereas the bourgeois reader took the fact that the author was a physical laborer as a guarantee that the poet would return, postpublication, to physical labor. Although there was also an aesthetic debate going on in peasant poetry as well as in bourgeois theoretical works and reviews, poetry can in neither case be read as assuming a purely aesthetic function; in both cases, social considerations outweigh aesthetic ones. I am most concerned with the relationship between the aesthetic and the social, between physical and intellectual, so-called creative labor, and these relationships can best be traced in the writings and bourgeois response to writings by authors who did both kinds of work.

# 1: Back to Nature: Bourgeois Aesthetic Theory and Lower-Class Poetic Practice

## Visionaries: The Artist As Servant, God, or Vegetable

THE DEVELOPMENT OF bourgeois aesthetic thought in England, Scotland, and Germany was intricately linked with the social ascendancy of the middle classes in these countries. The eighteenth century is commonly acknowledged as the first century marked by the bourgeois author's emancipation from aristocratic patronage; linked with that notion are two assumptions that are central to modern understanding of eighteenth-century aesthetic thought. First, the theory that bourgeois literature, newly liberated from its seventeenth-century mercenary and submissive context, was now free to aspire to the sublime and the eternal[1] — the hallmarks of all eighteenth-century art forms that were, and are, acknowledged to be Art. Second is the idea that bourgeois poetologies emphasizing the "natural" and seeking their inspiration in the "folk" were developed in express opposition to the aristocracy,[2] an opposition that is, in various contexts,

---

[1] Cf., for example, Schmidt, who expressly connects the new "extraordinary status of poesy" (I, 1: "außerordentlichen Rang der Dichtkunst") with the end of aristocratic patronage (I, 1–3). Similarly, Huyssen draws a direct link between aesthetic ideas of originality in writing and the changes in the literary market, citing Hans Jürgen Haferkorn's formula of the genius and originality aesthetic as originating in the sociological shift from rank-dependent to rank-independent authorship ("literatursoziologischen Übergang vom ständischen zum freien Schriftsteller," 71). Wunberg asserts that *inventio* and its attendant ideas *genius* and *ingenium* appeared in the eighteenth century for the first time, thereby supplanting *imitatio*, the poetological principle of earlier ages (89). McCann states the firm establishment of the profoundly redemptive function of culture as a mainstay in aesthetic theory in Britain and on the continent by the mid-eighteenth century (4). Engell goes so far as to define the very idea of *imagination*, as understood today, as an eighteenth-century invention: he traces the term "creative imagination" back to no earlier than 1730 and states that this idea reached "a level of completeness before 1800" (vii-viii).

[2] For example, Balet, who views the entire bourgeois self-definition as an opposition to the aristocracy (cf. his chapters III, IVB, and V); Kaiser, 53; and Gerth, 57. McCann draws the same conclusion for the English context when he defines the cultural revolution in Britain as "most emphatically. . . a middle class revolution directed against the vestiges of aristocratic and courtly culture" (3). On the rise of the middle class, its relationship to the aristocracy and the rise of the English novel, cf. the work of Ian Watt and Michael

interpreted to have been social and political as well as cultural.[3] German aesthetics, in the second half of the century, clearly took its cue from the English context;[4] conversely, some German poetological thought found

---

McKeon's response in "Generic Transformation." Ian Watt, whose history of the English novel professes a considerable awareness of class issues, views "the supersession of patronage by the booksellers, and the consequent independence of [middle-class novelists] from the literary past" as "reflections of a larger and even more important feature . . . — the great power and self-confidence of the middle class as a whole" (*Rise*, 59). Whereas most scholars posit an oppositional middle-class attitude toward the aristocracy, McKeon interprets this relationship as both identificatory and antagonistic, referring to the bourgeois desire to simultaneously imitate and supplant the aristocracy as the defining impulses of middle-class consciousness (*Origins*, 174).

[3] Political significance is most often claimed for the German Sturm und Drang movement, which can be viewed as the culmination of the German interest in the "natural" and the "folk"; even there, however, it is a contested area in scholarship. There is a plethora of sources claiming the political relevance of the movement: for example, Gerth, who asserts the movement's political significance as a vehicle for bourgeois emancipation and explains the uniqueness of the Sturm und Drang to Germany with the fact that the bourgeoisie in England and France enjoyed greater participation in political processes (57; cf. also Duncan, 9, who claims the existence of parallel movements in both Britain and the Netherlands). Although such psychological connections are difficult to substantiate, it is important to note that all evidence for the political involvement or interest of Sturm und Drang authors is based on *literary* sources, primarily the occasional criticisms hurled at the aristocracy in dramas and the frequent treatment of the infanticide theme. Recent literature has painstakingly documented that the recurrence of this theme had nothing to do with a political interest in either the status of women or that of the lower classes (cf. Madland, "Infanticide as Fiction" and "Marianne Ehrmann's Infanticide Fiction"; Kord, "Women as Children, Women as Childkillers"; Goetzinger; and Mabee).

There is also a sizable body of scholarship contesting the political dimension of the Sturm und Drang. Huyssen speaks of a "democratic genius-utopia" of the movement ("demokratische Genie-Utopie der Stürmer und Dränger," 59), but views the fact that the rebellious heroes of Sturm und Drang drama are usually set far in the past — whereas contemporary dramas of the movement do not depict such characters, but limit themselves to the portrayal of oppression and suffering (59, 78) — as an implicit admission of the impossibility of "Selbsthelfertum" in "real life" (59, 79). Manfred Wacker reads the absence of political writings in the movement in much the same way (13); Bruce Duncan has pointed out that the members of the Sturm und Drang generation generally showed little interest in major political events of their day, including the first partition of Poland (1772) or the Bavarian War of Succession (1778–79; cf. Duncan, 30). Garland rather contemptuously posits the revolutionary rhetoric of the movement against its political inefficacy: "Genius, as they conceived it, was a pistol pointed at the head of authority. When it fired it went off with a formidable detonation, and proved only to be loaded with powder" (140).

[4] The influence of English and Scottish poetology and literature on German nature aesthetics has often been noted by the following reviewers: Kistler, 12–14; Garland, 10–17; Engell, 87; Martini, *Literarische Form*, 14; Schneider, 24, 74–76; Pascal, 56; Stellmacher, 115–16, 129–32; Wolf, "Genielehre," 189; Kaiser, 186–93; Balet, 472–76; Abrams, 201–4; Hauser, *Social History*, II, 611; and Huyssen, 70. For examples of influ-

its way back across the channel.⁵ For this reason, it is generally assumed that these two central ideas — the sublime as a new, distinct quality of postpatronage poesy and culture as a means of distinguishing the middle classes from the aristocracy — determined, to a great degree, developments in bourgeois aesthetics on both sides of the channel.

This assessment is problematic because it obscures substantial differences in the social and political status of the middle classes in England, Scotland, and Germany⁶ and draws a line between the seventeenth century as the age of patronage and the eighteenth century as the age of liberated bourgeois literary production, which does not correspond to known history of either patronage or poetology. Because a broadened literary marketplace, defined by new publication venues, publishing houses, lending libraries, circulation of weekly magazines, and a tremendous increase in the number of both writers and readers, did emerge in the eighteenth century,⁷ aristocratic patronage of bourgeois writers changed form; however, it did not disappear.⁸ Aristocratic patronage and the new bourgeois literary life were

---

ential English poetological texts in Germany, cf. Engell, 80, 109, 114, and 123, and Schmidt, I, 150–52.

⁵ Cf. Luserke, who traces the influence of the German Sturm und Drang on English Romanticism through Matthew Lewis's reception of the Sturm und Drang *(Sturm und Drang,* 40), and Abrams, 200–202 and 218–25, who describes Young's influence in England as initially minimal and in Germany as decisive. Not until Coleridge reimported Young back to England, via his reception of the Sturm und Drang interpretation of Young, did Young gain any influence on English aesthetics. Osborn briefly describes the same complex process: " . . . Edward Young was formulating his *Conjectures on Original Composition,* completed for publication in 1759. When this concept became implanted in Germany it flowered into the literary period sometimes called the 'Geniebewegung,' though nowadays 'Sturm und Drang' has become the preferred label. Soon the German attitude was exported back to England and resulted in the common acceptance of the definition of the genius as an original creative mind" (144).

⁶ In England, the bourgeoisie had a long history of limited participation in political life under the auspices of a constitutional monarchy; in Scotland, the bourgeoisie had been recently disenfranchised by the parliamentary Act of Union with England in 1707; in Germany, particularism and absolutism effectively prevented the bourgeoisie's participation in the political process. Despite these differences in political and social status of the respective middle classes, scholars frequently insist on a congruity, or at least comparability, of the poetologies developed within these classes (cf., e.g., Gerth, 55–56).

⁷ Cf. Huyssen, 71, Kiesel/Münch, and Watt, *Rise,* 35–49.

⁸ Hauser states (for the English context), "After the middle of the century, patronage comes to an absolute end, and round about the year 1780 no writer any longer counts on private support" (*Social History,* II, 547); similarly, Gerth writes (for the German context), "In the eighteenth century, bourgeois art supplants aristocratic-courtly artforms" (55–56: "Im 18. Jahrhundert löst die bürgerliche Kunst die aristokratisch-höfische ab"), by which he means not so much art produced *by* the aristocracy as art produced *on behalf of* the aristocracy, under its protection and reflecting its worldview.

not only, by some, experienced as diametrically opposed, but also, by others, as complementary: until at least the 1760s, the job description of the professor of rhetoric at Königsberg included the requirement to function occasionally as court poet if called upon by the university — supposedly one of the reasons for Immanuel Kant's refusal to accept the position in 1764.[9] Kant's discomfort notwithstanding, it would be dubious to conclude that bourgeois writers throughout the eighteenth century defined their literary existence in opposition to the aristocracy.[10] For the German context, Frevert argues that it was the aristocracy that shaped the bourgeoisie as an educated class: the expansion of the absolutist state in Germany gave rise to a need for an army of civil servants that could not be provided by the nobility, and these civil servants — university-educated lawyers, judges, priests, professors, teachers, and doctors — formed the core of the "new bourgeoisie."[11] Most male bourgeois writers in the eighteenth century belonged to these professions. In Germany, a glance at the biographies of some of these writers shows a lifelong and ardent struggle with the concept and reality of aristocratic patronage, rather than a clear-cut emancipation that would have freed these writers to produce independently. More often, it was aristocratic patronage, rather than independence from it, that enabled literary careers: if not free from aristocratic influence, at least the writer was free from the need to earn a living by other means. Gotthold Ephraim Lessing repeatedly tried to obtain a post that would have given him the financial security to write, but concluded his career as librarian to the Duke of Wolfenbüttel; Johann Wolfgang Goethe spent most of his writing life in the service of the Duke of Weimar; the significance of Friedrich Schiller's "blocked passage to Weimar" lies in his ardent — and for a long time unsuccessful — attempts to secure just such security and support for his writing;[12] and Jakob Michael Reinhold Lenz's short-lived writing career can clearly be linked to the fact that he was a relatively independent author, largely owing to the fact that his attempts to follow in Goethe's footsteps — which led him to court — were clumsy, sporadic, and unequivocally rejected.[13] Christian August Vulpius,

---

[9] Cf. Hausmann, 79.

[10] Cf. Dan Wilson's essay "The Young Goethe's Political Fantasies," in which he counters the consistent attempts of Goethe scholarship to portray the young Goethe as a political revolutionary, a claim frequently made with respect to other authors of the Sturm und Drang as well.

[11] Cf. Frevert, *Women*, 32.

[12] Cf. Hammer; the quotation is taken from her title.

[13] Although there are many interpretations of Lenz's interlude in Weimar, it is clear that he was temporarily employed at court as Karl August's *Vorleser* and literary *Gesellschafter*; after the breach with Goethe, the Duke withdrew his support and banned Lenz from the

whose father had spent a decade making increasingly desperate and ultimately unsuccessful attempts at obtaining a position as a copyist at the court of Weimar, dedicated his verse drama *Oberon und Titania* (1783) to Duke Karl August, probably in the hopes of obtaining the Duke's patronage.[14] Johann Gottfried Herder and Christoph Martin Wieland tutored the children of princes; Friedrich Gottlob Klopstock, Johann Heinrich Voß, and Jean Paul Richter were all granted pensions by aristocratic patrons; the aging Johann Georg Hamann was supported by the Princess Gallitzin in Münster. Aristocratic support of these authors — or the lack thereof — does indeed differ from seventeenth-century patronage in that none of these authors were court poets, and the purpose of their employ on the part of the aristocrat was not to enable them to produce literature, but to support the absolutist state as members of the newly created class of civil servants: for example, Lessing was appointed Duke Karl August's librarian; Goethe was the Duke's Privy Councilor and right-hand man; and Lenz was briefly employed as the Duke's literary chamberlain. But this arrangement, for those bourgeois authors who were successful in obtaining it, undoubtedly enabled their literary careers by providing them with financial security, relieving them of the necessity to make a living by hawking their literary wares on the newly established "free" literary market. The long list of eighteenth-century German bourgeois authors who were ennobled during their lifetimes — among them Albrecht von Haller, Goethe, Schiller, Friedrich Maximilian Klinger, Herder, Theodor Gottlieb von Hippel, August von Kotzebue, Friedrich von Matthisson, Friedrich Wilhelm von Schelling, and Friedrich and August Wilhelm Schlegel — is strangely inconsistent with the idea that their literary production defined itself in opposition to the aristocracy, an idea that seems to owe its longevity to a critical tradition of over-reading plot strands in some of these authors' works.

If the connection between the death of patronage and the birth of the bourgeois aesthetic of originality and genius is not as uncomplicated as scholars have made it out to be, neither can aesthetic treatises produced by eighteenth-century bourgeois authors be read in as straightforward a manner as has often been done. Complicating the interpretation of these treatises is the fact that the most central terms of the debate, such as "originality," "nature," "genius," "bourgeois" (*Bürger*), and *Volk*, often remain undefined, which makes it a dubious undertaking to equate the meaning of these

---

city. Lenz's period of literary success at the court of Weimar is often linked with his brief interlude as *Vorleser* and literary companion to the Duke; conversely, Lenz's problems in Weimar are frequently seen as caused by his failure to secure a permanent function at court (e.g., Winter, 88). For a recent assessment of Lenz's time in Weimar, cf. Kaufman.

[14] Cf. Damm, 102; on Vulpius Sr.'s applications to the court, cf. 22–28.

terms in one author's vocabulary with that in another's. If poetic "genius" is inspired by "nature," this latter term can oscillate, depending on the author's predilections, among the poet's "inner" poetic nature, a precivilized state, the absence of poetic rules, and actual (contemporary) rural landscape;[15] "genius" can mean anything from a privileged and divinely inspired creative mind, symbolized by God or Prometheus,[16] which distinguishes itself through extreme rarity, to a guiding spirit common to all men.[17]

[15] Runge defines the term as describing an "inward state" and sees no evidence of a return to nature in the sense of abandonment of civilization (ix-x). Conversely, both Ossian's Scottish highlands and Haller's alpine landscape are frequently cited as defining influences on the Sturm und Drang concept of nature (Kistler, 14, and Schneider, 24); Kaiser reads works by Brockes and Haller as expressions of a "human relationship with nature," clearly intending nature in the physical sense (95); Goethe's dictum of "Mother Nature as the only true Artist" (quoted in Runge, 4) and La Riviere's idea that poetry flourishes best in "simple and natural surroundings" (quoted in Runge, 130) seem to point to the same interpretation. On the definition of "nature" as a prehistoric state, cf. Kistler, 11, and Hauser, *Social History*, II, 559; Bürger uses the term *Naturkatechismus* of poesy, as opposed to corrupted "Kunst," indicating a disregard for poetic rules ("Herzensausguß," 333). Williams, in his discussion of the English context, uses the term interchangeably to mean a principle of order, a principle of creation (an aspect that was emphasized during the industrial revolution), and as indicating physical nature in the sense of unblemished landscape (*Country*, 127–28). Dedner has pointed to the contradictory interpretations of *Volk* and "nature" in contemporary writings and adds another term, *Landmann*, which, used in poetry, can indicate anything from a wealthy landowning farmer to a day laborer ("Schäferleben," 47).

[16] The understanding of the poet as divine, which was first used by Shaftesbury, is a popular image in early aesthetics and becomes firmly established as a discourse in the Sturm und Drang. Bürger returns to the divinity image frequently throughout his writing — for example, in his image of Nature "blowing living breath into the nose of the work" ("Vorrede," 359: "keinem darstellenden Werke, welchem die Natur lebendigen Odem in die Nase geblasen hat") or in the following rhapsodic outburst describing poetry: "Living breath, gusting over the hearts and senses of all humankind! Breath of God which wakes the dead, gives sight to the blind, hearing to the deaf, movement to the lame and health to the leper! And all this for the good and gain of humankind in this vale of tears!" ("Herzensausguß," 336: "Lebendiger Odem, der über aller Menschen Herzen und Sinnen hinweht! Odem Gottes, der vom Schlaf und Tod aufweckt; die Blinden sehend, die Tauben hörend, die Lahmen gehend und die Aussätzigen rein macht! Und das alles zum Heil und Frommen des Menschengeschlechts in diesem Jammertale!").

[17] On the exclusivity theory, cf. Herder, "Grundsätze," 425; Huyssen, 73; Schmidt, I, 100 (on Hamann); Wacker, 9; Wolf, "Genielehre," 195–201; Stüssel, 55, 119; Wolf, *Versuch*, 148 (on Sulzer); and Abrams, 188 (on Spenser). On the definition of the genius as an inner guide, cf. Wolf, "Genielehre," 191–93 (on Herder). On the commonality theory, cf. Müller, "Einleitung," I, lxvi; Carter, 10; and Wolf, "Genielehre," 214: "Genius to him [Herder, S. K.] is not an exceptional apparition of divine provenance, not a 'chosen' gifted personality, but a universal aspect of humanity" ("Das Genie ist in ihm keine Ausnahmeerscheinung höherer Ordnung, keine 'auserwählte' begnadete Persönlichkeit, sondern es ist eine allgemein-menschliche Eigenschaft"). In Herder's ideas of the "genius" as an inner "Dämon" (Wolf, "Genielehre," 191–93), the distinction between metaphysics and aesthetics blurs to a considerable degree.

"Originality," the most important prerequisite for genius, can mean refusal to adhere to Aristotelian rules, imitation of Nature, imitation of Homer, imitation of the Creator, imitation of folklore, or total and divinely inspired independence from all previous models — even, in this context, an ignorance of previous literary models, which would, by default, ensure the desired originality of expression.[18] The *Volk*, in the German debate, variably includes or excludes the *Pöbel*, the poorest and least educated segment of society;[19] in the English context, a similar debate takes place with regard to sensibility and the educability of the masses.[20] And, although few of these

---

[18] Cf. Young's comparison of the original genius (defined as an imitator of Nature) with merely "imitative" writers (defined as an imitator of other authors; see also Duncan, 18–20; Abrams, 199; Schmidt, I, 156; Schneider, 19–20) vis-à-vis the idea, in part based on his *Conjectures*, that genius "creates Nature from within" (Mattenklott, 45), "intuit[s] the immutable rules of art inherent in Nature" (Carter, v-vi), and refers back to earlier literary models only by way of differentiation (Stüssel, 115). The notion of the poet as an imitator of God the Creator ("Prometheus under Jove") is originally Shaftesbury's (Wolf, *Versuch*, 20–21) and later taken up in Sturm und Drang aesthetics. Meier's question of whether imitation of nature ("die Nachahmung der Natur") or imitation of nature's *methods* ("ahme der Natur nach") should be considered the guiding principle of poesy (Vollhardt, 31) already transcends Young's original definition. Herder's writings demonstrate that one author's ideas on the subject could change considerably over time: his early rejection of any models, particularly Greek and Latin, on behalf of the titanic original genius (Wolf, "Genielehre," 196) could be seen as compatible with his later suggestion to aspiring geniuses of "studying" genius in ancient folk songs (Schneider, 69, 74), along with a rejection of the classical (French) norm in favor of these primitive cultures (in his *Journal meiner Reise*, Kontje, 18), but clearly stands in stark contrast to his even later recommendation to use "the ancients" as models (Schneider, 90).

[19] Gottfried August Bürger, one of the most ardent proponents of *Volkspoesie* in Germany, distinguished strictly between the *Volk* and the *Pöbel* and understood *Volk* as restricted to the "educated folk" (Luserke, *Sturm und Drang*, 85). Herder saw the *Pöbel* as incapable of poetic sentiment and contrasted the poetic folk with the screaming rabble: "By 'people' I do not mean the rabble on the streets who never sings and composes but shrieks and defiles" ("Volk heißt nicht, der Pöbel auf den Gassen, der singt und dichtet niemals, sondern schreyt und verstümmelt"; quoted in Luserke, *Sturm und Drang*, 86, and Huyssen, 34–35). Lavater saw the *Volk* as incapable of reading his *Physiognomische Fragmente* (Wacker, 11) as Meier held it incapable of understanding poetry (Krauss, 73). Johann Gottlob Benjamin Pfeil's treatise *Vom bürgerlichen Trauerspiele* (1755) excluded the rabble not only from poetic production but also from poetic representation: because that class of people was, he argues, too stupid for great virtues and too cowardly for great vices, they could not credibly appear as characters on stage (Luserke, *Bändigung*, 147–48). Lenz is the only German writer in aesthetics who spoke of the "whole people" (*ganzes Volck*) and expressly refused to exclude the *Pöbel* from his audience (ibid.; see David Hill, 32–33, on Bürger's concept of the term). Martini concludes from this that for writers like Herder and Goethe, the term *Volk* merely referred to a historical category, a poetic tradition rather than a present-day social community (*Literarische Form*, 20–21).

[20] For example, Hannah More's poem "Sensibility," in which she advocated the view that sensibility could only be experienced by a refined mind, although she saw sensibility as an

bourgeois authors ever use the words "bourgeois" or *bürgerlich* in their treatises — the fact that these authors rarely mention the terms adds to their literature's ambiguity — there is an implied struggle discernible in many writers' works between the inherent contradictions contained in the term *Bürger*.[21] Burghard Dedner has pointed out that *Bürger* can indicate the *Stadtbürger* (city dweller) as well as the *Staatsbürger* (citizen of a state), the bourgeois as well as the *citoyen*. In Dedner's analysis, the *Bürger* vacillates between adaptation and rejection of aristocratic norms; he views the supremacy of the state as support for his existence as *citoyen* and simultaneously as a threat to his existence as a bourgeois.[22]

In the following paragraphs, I concentrate on the terms that are most central to the debate as it relates to lower-class authors — namely, "nature" and the "original genius" in connection with ideas of the *Volk* and its derivatives (primitives, barbarous people, simple folk, rustics). These terms were originally defined in a now-standardized canon of aesthetic writings,[23] which have, for the most part, been reviewed chronologically and descriptively, showing links and influences, rather than inconsistencies.[24] In many of these assessments, a connection is made between the frequent postulation

---

entirely nonrational quality: "Let not the vulgar read this pensive strain, / Their jests the tender anguish wou'd prophane" (More, *Poems,* 166–87, the citation 174; cf. also Whitney, 100–104, and Janet Todd, *Sensibility,* 13). A similar phenomenon is Lavater's distinction between the "sublime melancholy" of the genius as opposed to the "lethargic melancholy" of the common man; cf. Mattenklott, 43–44. Whitney states, not without a sense of irony, that primitivism in educational theory in England was directed exclusively at the bourgeoisie (122–24). On theories of the educability of the masses in England, cf. Osborn, 123.

[21] Cf. Kaiser, 41–42.

[22] Cf. Dedner, *Topos,* 162. For a discussion of *Bürger* as a term, cf. also Marion Gray, 36–39, and 123–40.

[23] The texts that are most frequently reviewed in scholarship include Addison's article "On Imagination" in *The Spectator* (1711); Shaftesbury's *Soliloquy or Advice to an Author* (1711); Baumgarten's *Aesthetica* (1750–58) and Meier's popularization of his work in *Anfangsgründe aller schönen Wissenschaften* (First Principles of Aesthetics, 1748–50); Lowth's *Lectures on the Sacred Poetry of the Hebrews* (1753); Hamann's *Sokratische Denkwürdigkeiten* (Socratic Memorabilia, 1759); Young's *Conjectures on Original Composition* (1759); Gerstenberg's *Schleswigsche Literaturbriefe* (Literary Letters from Schleswig, 1766–70); Duff's *Essay on Original Genius* (1767); Sulzer's *Theorie der schönen Künste* (General Theory of the Fine Arts, 1771–74); Gerard's *Essay on Genius* (1774); Lavater's *Physiognomische Fragmente* (Physiognomic Fragments, 1775–78); Herder's treatises *Ueber die Neuere deutsche Litteratur* (On Recent German Literature, 1766–67), *Auszug aus einem Briefwechsel über Oßian und die Lieder alter Völker* (Excerpts from a Correspondence on Ossian and the Songs of Ancient Peoples, 1771), and *Von deutscher Art und Kunst* (On German Mentality and Art, 1773); and Bürger's *Aus Daniel Wunderlichs Buch* (From the Book of Daniel Wunderlich, 1776).

[24] Cf. Schmidt, Schneider, Engell, Abrams, and Wolf, *Versuch.*

of the "natural" poetic genius in contemporary aesthetics and the careers of peasant poets,[25] and it is this relationship that I revisit. In linking English, Scottish, and German poetologies, as many writers have done before me, I do not intend to either compare or equate them, nor do I necessarily treat them chronologically or look for cross-fertilizations of aesthetic thought, a path already well trodden by scholars. Instead, I point to functional correlations in some of these texts with an eye to whether the aesthetic inherent in them can indeed be employed as theoretical grounding for the careers of the "uneducated poets" with whom this book is concerned.

The most important question is therefore to what extent ideas of "genius," as presented in these various aesthetic treatises, are identified with primitive societies (either ancient or, more interesting for this context, contemporary, in the form of savage tribes or rural communities). The definition of nature (as an inward poetic state, a precivilized state, as being absent or ignorant of poetic rules, or as rural landscape) is an integral part of this concept. The link between the primitive and the genius seems much more important with regard to eighteenth-century peasant poets than, for example, the question of whether genius is, by authors of aesthetics, held to be universally applicable ("democratic," as one scholar has said[26]) or exclusionary — that is, applicable only to a chosen few. For despite all avowals that the genius spurns formal education (a facet of genius theory that would seem, once again, to open the door to uneducated authors), no clear-cut conclusions on lower-class authors can be drawn either from the exclusion or the inclusion theories, as they are presented in the various aesthetic works examined here. Kerstin Stüssel has described the new genius aesthetic, assuming the exclusion theory, as a means of specifically excluding lower-class authors: in her model, the belief in the innate genius of rare individuals functions as a measure of buttressing class distinctions against the aspirations of lower-class writers and thus neatly replaces erudition, which formerly served as the basis for accepted literary activity and which

---

[25] For example, Janet Todd, who claims that "rustics" were perceived, by the authors of contemporary aesthetic treatises, to be "naturally poetic. . . . Consequently, poetry in its purity should spring from the most primitive and untrained rustics, who would be spontaneously sensitive in apprehension of nature and tenderly sentimental in response to people" (*Sensibility*, 57). Stüssel, Carter, Abrams, and Waldron all make a similar connection when they examine contemporary lower-class authors against the background of contemporary aesthetics of primitivism (Stüssel, 217–35; Carter, 6–22; Abrams, 83; Waldron, *Lactilla*, 9–10). Nonetheless, as I explain later, there is not a single aesthetic treatise that expressly makes the connection that these modern critics see, namely, the seemingly direct line between an aesthetic of the primitive and the potential existence of a real-life primitive (rustic) poet.

[26] Cf. Müller, I, lxvii.

was inaccessible to the lower orders.[27] However, the inclusion theory (the idea that genius is inherent in all men[28]) also does not extend the potential base of authors to the lower orders: although it transcends class lines in theory, the few authors who claim the universal existence of genius, such as Herder in his later works, have no comments on the *manifestation* of such genius in individual cases. Presumably, such manifestations would be recognized and interpreted by the bourgeoisie, who had, by virtue of their theoretical writings on genius, taken care to establish themselves as experts on the theme, thus assuming a gatekeeping function. More revealing than the discussion on the universality or uniqueness of genius are the following two aspects of aesthetic writings: one, of all authors of aesthetics, only Lenz was willing to stretch class lines enough to include the "rabble" in his definition of the *Volk*, and, two, that few authors of aesthetics could envision members of the lower classes as characters in the new literature. Given the presumed strong sense of identification of both producers and recipients of literature with literary characters, *particularly* along class lines,[29] that fact is significant: a bourgeois aesthetic incapable of imagining members of the lower orders as either literary characters or readers would presumably be even less likely to view them as authors.

If one reads these texts with an eye to the question as to what extent the existence of contemporary "natural geniuses" is already either prefigured or preempted in this aesthetic — or, whether there is indeed a correlation between the bourgeois aesthetic thought and peasant poetic practice, as many scholarly readers of these treatises have proposed — one finds that few authors ever refer to their contemporary literary scene except ad negativum. Poetic genius is frequently seen as an occurrence so ancient and remote that it is virtually not recoverable in the modern age. In his *Essay on Original Genius* (1767), William Duff asserts of poetry that it is "an unquestionable truth . . . that this divine art . . . should attain its utmost perfection in the infancy of society, when mankind are only emerging from a state of ignorance and barbarity." He concludes that original poetic genius "will seldom appear in a very high degree in cultivated life"; the only modern authors he acknowledges to be geniuses are Shakespeare and Milton.[30] Robert Lowth makes the same

---

[27] Cf. Stüssel, 119.

[28] "Men," in this instance and in the following, is not used to denote "humans" but to indicate males: the possibility of genius inherent in *women* was not even remotely considered by any of these authors (cf. the conclusion).

[29] On this identification pertaining to the new bourgeoisie, cf. Luserke, *Bändigung*, 149, and Kaiser, 52.

[30] Duff, 261, 286–87.

claim in his *Lectures on the Sacred Poetry of the Hebrews* (1753) when he describes Hebrew poetry, which he labels sublime and which he extols as superior to anything Greek culture ever produced, as written by an ancient race of husbandmen and shepherds.[31] John Brown, in his *Dissertation on the Rise, Union, and Power, the Progressions, Separations, and Corruptions, of Poetry and Music* (1763) claims that a true unity of the arts existed only in primitive (by which he means precivilized) societies; once such societies were exposed to education and civilization, "a *Separation* of the several Parts . . . would naturally arise."[32] Alexander Gerard, in *An Essay on Genius* (1774), exalts Homer as the quintessential original genius who "lived in times of ignorance, when poetry remained almost in its first rudeness."[33] Herder similarly praises Ossian's poetry as an example of the wild songs of an ancient and primitive race[34] and calls for a recovery and collection of ancient German folklore.[35]

Of all authors who situate original genius, apparently irrecoverably, in ancient history, Herder is one of the few who makes reference to his own era when he declares the best orators of his age to be "unspoiled children, women, people of good natural sense, formed more by an active life than a life of speculation."[36] But instead of taking the mental leap for which he seems to be preparing — that of declaring contemporary children, women, and people working with their hands instead of their heads to be the most expressive in *writing* as well as oral expression — he interprets the contemporary rural population as a mere repository to be mined for that ancient treasure of folklore and song which could, in his view (and later in Bürger's and Goethe's), rejuvenate bourgeois literature.[37] *Volksdichtung*, like the *Volk* itself, functions collectively in his writing: there is no admis-

---

[31] Lowth, 71, 73–80.

[32] John Brown, 40 (the emphasis is original).

[33] Gerard, 11.

[34] Herder, "Auszug," 234–37, 262.

[35] Herder, "Von Ähnlichkeit," 491, 494–95.

[36] Herder, "Auszug," 256: "unverdorbne Kinder, Frauenzimmer, Leute von gutem Naturverstande, mehr durch Tätigkeit als Spekulation gebildet, die sind, wenn das, was ich anführete, Beredsamkeit ist, alsdenn die einzigen und besten Redner unsrer Zeit."

[37] The fact that the intended beneficiary of his interest is not the *Volk* but the bourgeoisie is expressed in a passage in "Auszug" that mirrors the previously described sentiment almost exactly — namely, in Herder's elaborate daydream to "become, for a time, an ancient Caledonian" and sail, uprooted from civilization, the rough seas, past the coast where Fingal's deeds were done and Ossian's songs were sung ("zu den Schotten! Zu Macpherson! Da will ich die Gesänge eines lebenden Volkes hören, . . . eine Zeitlang ein alter Kaledonier werden — "; "jetzt von fern die Küsten vorbei, da Fingals Taten geschahen und Ossians Lieder Wehmut sangen. . . . "; 240 and 242, respectively).

sion that this poetry was *authored* by anyone (it "originated in the folk, living and toiling among them") and a flat denial that it could ever be classed with written literature ("Naturally, it wasn't meant for paper and is barely legible on it"[38]). That there could be individual authors "living and toiling" among this *Volk* of Herder's own time clearly becomes unthinkable in this context, since *Volk*, like its poetry, is thought of only as an amorphous mythical entity that cannot be divided into its individual components. This *Volk*, in Herder's treatises, may "sing" — and Herder *does* imply originality and creativity in his description[39] — but it does not "author." It is not presented as the potential source of a new, more "natural" literature, but as the educator of a corrupt civilization. Herder proposes, with an unmistakable sense of superiority, "With gentle forbearance one transports oneself back into the olden days, lowers oneself to the mind of the people, one lies down, listens, smiling perhaps, sharing in the people's pleasures, or reflects and learns":[40] the purpose is to lower oneself to the "people," not to raise the people up to one's own level of literary achievement, corrupt as it may be. Just as Herder presents his *Volk* not as the producer, but merely as the repository and recipient of literature ("How the people stood and hearkened!"[41] he exclaims during one of the more visionary passages of his treatise), Bürger, one of his disciples when it came to folklore, recommends study of the "people" for the renewal of the bourgeois literary enterprise: "Let the poet get to know the people as a whole, let him explore their fantasies and feelings, in order to fill the former with appropriate images and express the latter in the appropriate mood. To then wave the magic wand of the natural epic poem!"[42] As in

[38] Herder, "Von Ähnlichkeit," 493: "im Volk entsprungen, unter ihnen lebend und würkend"; "Freilich nicht fürs Papier gemacht und auf ihm kaum lesbar."

[39] "Old national songs that were and still are sung by the people which enable the listener to learn something of the people's mentality, language and feelings" (Herder, "Von Ähnlichkeit," 493: "alte Nationalstücke, die das Volk singt und sang, woraus man also die Denkart des Volks, ihre Sprache und Empfindung kennenlernet"): if these pieces can indeed function as illustrative of folk mentality and language, then they must be both indigenous and particular to the *Volk*.

[40] Herder, "Von Ähnlichkeit," 493: "Mit milder Schonung setzt man sich also in die alten Zeiten zurück, in die Denkart des Volkes hinab, liegt, hört, lächelt etwa, erfreuet sich mit oder überschlägt und lernet."

[41] Herder, "Von Ähnlichkeit," 493: "Wie das Volk dastand und horchte!"

[42] Bürger, "Herzensausguß," 333: "Man lerne das Volk im ganzen kennen, man erkundige seine Phantasie und Fühlbarkeit, um jene mit gehörigen Bildern zu füllen und für diese das rechte Kaliber zu treffen. Alsdann den Zauberstab des natürlichen Epos gezückt!" In a certain sense, Bürger follows Herder's recommendation to lower himself to the "people" when he claims to be one of them in his modest reading habits: "I rarely read such scribblings [critical reviews, S. K.] and much prefer to hear what people say here and there, rather

Herder's treatises, folk songs function as a gold mine of instruction for bourgeois literati[43] whose rejuvenated "natural" poetry would in turn benefit readers from the *Volk:* Herder claims that "that venerable portion of our public called the people," to whom bourgeois literature is dedicated, would, in its current corrupted form, not understand a single word of it;[44] Bürger, playing on more traditional views of the "people" as concerned only with their next meal, calls for poetry that is "digestible and nutritious for the entire people."[45]

Where the "folk" is discussed in aesthetics, it functions either as the *ancient producer* or as *contemporary preserver and potential recipient* of idealized poetic production. Surprisingly, or so it may seem, given the interests and predilections of these works, the contemporary natural poet from the *Volk,* endowed with the same primitiveness and lack of erudition that are eulogized at such length in the ancient bards, is nowhere prefigured in these writings. We must therefore look for him (or her) in the genius theories of the age.

In these theories, there are a number of aspects that could feasibly serve as a theoretical support structure for a contemporary peasant genius, among them the definition, in many treatises, of genius as imagina-

---

than reading what one of those stay-at-home bookworms has written" ("ich lese solches Geschreibsel blutwenig und höre überhaupt lieber, was man hier und da sagt, als ich lese, was ein Stubenschwitzer schreibt"; "Vorrede," 360). In one sentence, Bürger succeeds in alluding to two principal contrasts between "the people" and the educated bourgeoisie and in allying his own inclinations with the former: orality/literacy (hören/lesen) and outside/inside (suggested in the "Stubenschwitzer" versus the implied image Bürger manages to evoke of himself going "out" among the people to "hear" what they have to say).

[43] Bürger, "Herzensausguß," 337.

[44] "As if the great and venerable portion of our public called the people, for whom these songs are after all produced, could feel a single one of the beautiful rules according to which they have been constructed" (Herder, "Auszug," 271: "Eben als wenn der große ehrwürdige Teil des Publikums, der Volk heißt und für den doch die Gesänge kastigiert werden, eine von den schönen Regeln fühle, nach denen man sie kastigiert!") Bürger, in his "Vorrede," proudly states the popularity of his own poetry among readers from the *Volk* (360).

[45] "We are Germans! Germans who should not write Greek, not Latin, not any hackneyed poems in the German tongue, but German poems in the German tongue, digestible and nutritious for the entire people" (Bürger, "Herzensausguß," 336: "Deutsche sind wir! Deutsche, die nicht griechische, nicht römische, nicht Allerweltsgedichte in deutscher Zunge, sondern in deutscher Zunge deutsche Gedichte, verdaulich und nährend fürs ganze Volk, machen sollen"). Bürger's exclamation adds yet another facet to an already complex term, namely that of *Volk* as describing members of a national community, which also figures prominently in Herder's writings. Cf. especially David Hill for meanings of the term in Bürger's work, as well as in that of some of his contemporaries, and Koepke for definitions of *Volk* in writings by Herder.

tion and invention;[46] the frequent opposition of genius with book learning, rule-based poesy, or imitation of any kind;[47] the idea that poetry originates in nature (understood as an organizing principle) and is inspired by nature (understood as rural landscape);[48] the frequent identification of genius with passion and enthusiasm rather than reason or judgment;[49] the description of the writing process of the genius as a kind of automatic writing, produced spontaneously, unconsciously, rapidly, and in the raptures of poetic inspiration and "divine fury," without pre-

---

[46] Gerard, 17, 36–37; Duff, 6–9, 35, 37–38, 89, 99, 125–26, 147, 188; Sulzer, *General Theory*, 34; Wolf, "Genielehre," 195–96; and Engell, 47.

[47] Gerard, 17; Duff, 262, 273–74, 281, 295; Herder, "Auszug," 237–38, 255–56, 269–71, and "Von Ähnlichkeit," 490–92; Bürger, "Herzensausguß," 333 (cf. also his *Briefe*; Strodtmann, I, 240); Sulzer, *General Theory*, 33; Stüssel, 113–17, 204–5; Runge, 50, 58; Schmidt, I, 99–116 (on Hamann); and Schneider, 58–59 (on Hamann). Rowe argues as early as 1709 that knowledge of the "ancients" would have restrained Shakespeare's creative spirit (I, iii-iv). Duff proposes that the inability of artists to profit from earlier examples of the art is particular to poetry alone: whereas painters, architects, and musicians profit from the work of previous artists (262–63), an "effect of learning is, to *encumber* and *overload* the mind of an original Poetic Genius" (281), and all "acquaintance with *Literary* and *Critical Knowledge* . . . must be equally unfavourable to the exertion of original Poetic Genius" (295, emphases original).

[48] Gerard, 104–5, 128–29, 356, 388–89; Lowth, 71–74; Duff, 271; Herder, "Auszug," 267, and "Grundsätze," 425 (in which he defines genius as "an exaggeration of Nature"); and Sulzer, *General Theory*, 34.

Duff describes the state of poetic inspiration as follows: "Happily exempted from that tormenting ambition, and those vexatious desires, which trouble the current of modern life, he wanders with a serene, contented heart, through walks and groves consecrated to the Muses; or, indulging a sublime, pensive, and sweetly-soothing melancholy, strays with a slow and solemn step, through the unfrequented desert, along the naked beach, or the bleak and barren heath. In such a situation, every theme is a source of inspiration" (271–72). It is one of the many passages in these treatises where "nature" as an inner poetic state becomes indistinguishable from nature as physical reality and outward inspiration.

[49] For example, Gerard, 66–69, 356, 388; Duff, 8–9, 97, 162, 168–71; and Martini, *Literarische Form*, 3 (on Hamann). In contrast to other critics like Sulzer, Mendelssohn, and Duff, all of whom viewed judgment as a natural restraint on the imagination, Gerard pronounces judgment as fatal to poetic inspiration: "In genius of the arts, an uncommon strength of judgment is so far from being necessary, that a degree of imagination which would have produced genius, if it had been joined to an ordinary judgment, may be rendered abortive, and unable to display itself, by being united to a very nice judgment. . . . It is almost better to give fancy an uncontrouled range, than to break its vigour by the continual restraint of an overscrupulous judgment. . . . In the arts, then, an uncommon acuteness of judgment is so far from constituting genius, that it will absolutely destroy genius" (388–90). Herder takes the concept to its logical conclusion when he claims a close relationship between genius and insanity: "Most inmates in lunatic asylums are geniuses, but they are in the minority: most of their brothers still run around free" ("Die meisten, die in den Tollhäusern liegen, sind Genies; nur sind sie die wenigsten: die meisten ihrer Brüder laufen frei umher"; *Grundsätze*, 425).

meditation or intent;[50] the description of the genius's themes as partly autobiographical;[51] and the idea of genius as called to its vocation and irrepressibly drawn toward its goal.[52] Any or all of these theoretical postulates could be applied to the lives of peasant poets in the early to mid-eighteenth century: they originated in the country (in "nature"); they were or presented themselves as largely or utterly uneducated and therefore thrown completely on their imagination and their passions; and they overcame severe hardship to achieve literary fame, thus demonstrating the "irrepressibility" with which they were drawn toward their calling. All of them laid claim to unerudite poetic production, and examples for swift, spontaneous, and near-automatic writing could certainly be found among them, the most famous case being that of Anna Louisa Karsch.

Most prominent among these points seems to be the interpretation of poetic practice as unconscious rather than premeditated, a process that is graphically described in aesthetics through the use of nature metaphors. In fact, the location of the *furor poeticus* either in a rural setting or its circumscription with rustic metaphors — taken from both plant and animal life — can be considered *the* most frequently recurring facet in bourgeois aesthetic treatises. Young claims an affinity between original genius and plant life: "An original may be said to be of a vegetable nature; it rises spontaneously, from the vital root of Genius, it grows, it is not made."[53] Young's sentiment is echoed in many aesthetic treatises,

---

[50] Abrams, 198, 209–16; Sulzer, *General Theory*, 32; Stüssel, 99–102, Huyssen, 63–64. The term "divine fury" is Duff's (171). Such spontaneity, according to Janet Todd, is the principal reason why "the most primitive and untrained rustics" were singled out for poetic genius (*Sensibility*, 57).

[51] Gerard describes the poetic theme as "sentiments suggested by a man's own situation, [which] mix with all the exertions of his genius, on whatever subjects it be employed" (191). Cf. also Stüssel's theory of the new link between autobiography and poetology in the absence of the erudite context (113–17).

[52] Duff views the vocation to poetry as an early childhood experience: "Imagination, which in every man displays itself before any of the other faculties, will be discernible in him in a state of childhood, and will strongly prompt him to Poetry" (37). Similarly, Sulzer states, "One can recognize such originality in persons by the irresistible drive they have for their art, by the way they overcome all obstacles that lie in the way of their work" (*General Theory*, 34); in "Entwickelung des Begriffs vom Genie," he sees genius as both independent of outside support ("Ohne alle Aufmunterung") and capable of overcoming all hindrances (311). Johann Joseph Spazier defines the overcoming of all obstacles as one of the signs of genius (1797, cited in Stüssel, 204).

[53] Quoted in Wolf, *Versuch*, 34, and Schmidt, I, 132; cf. Schmidt, I, 133, for further examples. On the immense popularity of nature and rustic metaphors in describing the creative process, cf. Engell, 3–4. At times, this discourse has reverberated in the works of modern scholars, as in Kaiser's paraphrase of Herder's theories: "Like a plant, the great poet takes

most notably in Sulzer's and Herder's. In Sulzer's near-identical wording, the genius's thoughts "grow . . . much as . . . plants germinate unnoticed and all at once burst into full bloom";[54] elsewhere, in a comparable depiction of the creative process as unconscious and unintentional, he likens the poet's "soul" to an "imperceptibly flowing brook."[55] In Herder's aesthetics, the plant figures as the prototype for the development of an Art form in the soil of its own time and place.[56] Lowth's entire treatise is built on such metaphoric usage of fauna and flora. According to Alexander Gerard, the process of collecting materials for a new work unfolds for the genius as follows:

> When a vegetable draws in moisture from the earth, nature, by the same action by which it draws it in, and at the same time, converts it to the nourishment of the plant: it at once circulates through its vessels, and is assimilated to its several parts. In like manner, genius arranges its ideas by the same operation, and almost at the same time, that it collects them.[57]

Animals, too, are treated metaphorically in aesthetic treatises — for example, in Sulzer's attribution of "genius" to animals[58] or in Meier's recommendation to the poet to get in touch with the "animalistic" part of his soul.[59] Such metaphors, which Abrams has analyzed for the English

---

root in the historical ground of his people" ("Wie eine Pflanze wurzelt der große Dichter im geschichtlichen Boden seines Volkes," 187).

[54] Sulzer, *General Theory*, 63.

[55] "The soul, by surrendering to a gentle distraction, produces without force or effort a series of pleasing thoughts. Like a brook whose waters flow imperceptibly, it does not sense its own activity, it forgets itself in the process" ("Von der Kraft," 124: "[D]ie Seele, indem sie sich einer sanften Zerstreuung überläßt, [bringt] ohne Zwang und ohne Anstrengung eine Reihe ergötzender Ideen hervor. . . . Gleich einem Bache, dessen Wasser unmerklich dahinfließt, fühlet sie ihre eigne Geschäfftigkeit nicht; sie vergißt sich selbst darüber. . . .").

[56] Abrams, 205.

[57] Gerard, 63–64.

[58] Quoted in Wolf, *Versuch*, 148.

[59] "You improve the spiritual part of your soul, utterly neglecting the lower sensual and animalistic parts" (quoted in Balet, 314: "Ihr verbessert den geistigen Theil eurer Seele und versäumt den unteren sinnlichen und thierischen ganz und gar"). Where animals occur in other treatises, they are at times — in contrast to plant imagery — used negatively. Cf., for example, Bürger's satirization of the "divine language" advocated in traditional poetry versus the simple language he advocates: "This divine language, in which many of our infants of the muses wish to babble, is often nothing better than the coarse bellowing of oxen and roaring of lions, whinnying of horses, howling of wolves, barking of dogs and cackling of geese" ("Diese Göttersprache, die viele unserer Musensäuglinge lallen wollen, ist oft nichts anderes als rauhes Löwen- und Stiergebrüll, Roßwiehern, Wolfsgeheul, Hundegebell und Gänsegeschnatter"; "Herzensausguß," 333).

context, served "to identify the element of nature in the natural genius with those instinctive activities of animals" and thus stood as "examples of unlearned behaviour *par excellence*."[60] Hazlitt, another genius theorist who drew an analogy between the creative process and a growing plant, states:

> The definition of genius is that it acts unconsciously, and those who have produced immortal works have done so without knowing how or why . . . Corregio, Michael Angelo, Rembrandt, did what they did without premeditation or effort — their works came from their minds as a natural birth — if you had asked them why they adopted this style or that, they would have answered, *because they could not help it*. . . .[61]

The metaphorical *Stadtflucht* that is going on in these works thus seems to serve a twofold purpose: to define the creative process as unconscious (and therefore as neither imitable nor attainable by training) and to emphasize the aspect of poetic *vocation* in the presentation of the poet as helpless in the firm grip of the muse, as *unable to help it*, as Hazlitt asserts. In later reviews, the same metaphorical discourse is used to dismantle the unconditional supremacy of the genius — as in an anonymous reviewer's claims that Karsch's writing was a wildly flowering tree in urgent need of pruning[62] — but, in aesthetics, plant metaphors demonstrate the effortlessness of poetic production, much as harvests occur in traditional pastoral poetry without labor or effort.[63] Noticeable, too, is the *indiscernibility* of the creative process that endows it with additional mystery and defies analysis in the treatise: if Sulzer's brook flows "imperceptibly," the poetic genius is not a plant one could watch grow.

Although references to primitive societies in aesthetic treatises invariably place the idealized poet in a precivilized age, thus overtly ignoring the poetic potential of contemporary rustics, the dominant portrayal of the poetic genius seems at least to allow for comparisons between the hypothetical genius advocated in aesthetics and real-life poets from the

---

[60] Abrams, 197 (emphasis original); for many examples from both plant and animal life in both English and German treatises, cf. 197–99, 202–5, and 213–20. Williams reads the frequent employment of negative rustic metaphors, the "creation of a desert landscape" in poetry, as a sublimation of the increased commercial use of the land (*Country*, 78–79).

[61] Hazlitt, "Is Genius Conscious of Its Powers?," quoted in Abrams, 215 (emphasis original). (One wonders whether a female aesthetician could have chosen the metaphor of a "natural birth" for a process she describes as taking place "without premeditation or effort.")

[62] Cited in Mödersheim, "Fruchtbarste Bäume," 33: "Auch die fruchtbarsten Bäume wollen beschnitten sein."

[63] For a more extensive discussion, cf. chapter 4.

"people." However, this fact should not tempt us to infer a prefiguration of contemporary peasant poets in bourgeois aesthetics, as scholars have at times done; the complete absence of contemporary examples of peasant poets in all treatises — where the paradigmatic genius is, invariably, exemplified in either Shakespeare or Milton — would make it difficult to uphold such a claim. The process that links contemporary peasant poets with bourgeois aesthetics was not prefigurative, but retrospective: comparisons between the ideal and reality were made frequently in reviews of peasant poets, comparisons that indirectly *refer back* to the best-known aesthetic treatises of the age. In such reviews, the unconsciousness of poetic production in aesthetic treatises is turned critically into the poet's lack of knowledge and awareness, his helplessness in the grip of the muse metamorphoses into his inability to take control of his writing, the idea of the unintentionality of poetic production is transformed into the mandate that the poet refrain from authorial ambition or intent to publish, and the imperceptibility of the plantlike poetic process reappears in the verdict that plants should not be uprooted from their rural environment, cannot be successfully transplanted into the literary scene, and that, consequently, the poet would have done better to *remain* imperceptible: in other words, obscure.

To women peasant poets, an added obstacle presents itself in contemporary aesthetics — namely, the near-universal identification of genius with masculinity. Young's definition of the superior genius as "masculine"[64] and Herder's interpretation of Ossian's language as "manly"[65] are just two examples; the fervent "masculinity" of the Sturm und Drang — which expresses itself, in scholarly interpretations, in the complete absence of women from the movement — is legendary.[66] The same rural imagery that had served to illustrate the creative process of the primitive genius was employed in late-eighteenth-century aesthetics as evidence that women were incapable of artistic creativity. In Schiller's analysis, Art is a harvest that men produce and women merely enjoy —

---

[64] Quoted in Schmidt, I, 156; Messer-Davidow has stated that Young's definition of the genius as a rebel against the ancient fathers is not a role that women could have assumed (51).

[65] "Leaps and bounds are particular to this original, not debilitated, free and manly language" ("Würfe und Sprünge . . . sind der ursprünglichen, unentnervten, freien und männlichen Sprache besonders eigen"; "Auszug," 270). On Herder's praise of "manly" language, cf. Lugowski, "Der junge Herder," 226–28.

[66] Cf., among others, Duncan, 28; Stephan, 46–50; Roebling, 63; Kistler, 14, 23; and my article "Discursive Dissociations."

in other words, women of any class are relegated, similar to the folk of earlier writings, to the exclusive status of recipients of Art:

> As, therefore, nature has not only dispensed but cut off the other sex from this task, man must give a double attention to it.... Consequently he will try to transfer all that he can from the field of abstraction, where he is master, to that of imagination, of feeling, where woman is at once a model and a judge. The mind of woman being a ground that does not admit of durable cultivation, he will try to make his own ground yield as many flowers and as much fruit as possible, so as to renew as often as possible the quickly fading produce on the other ground, and to keep up a sort of artificial harvest where natural harvests could not ripen. Taste ... nourishes and adorns the mind of woman with the productions of that of man, and allows the fair sex to feel without being previously fatigued by thought, and to enjoy pleasures without having bought them with labours.[67]

No aesthetic treatise written by a male bourgeois author has ever envisioned genius as feminine, and it would be easy enough to demonstrate that this implicit — or, in Schiller's case, explicit — prohibition left traces in the works of women peasant poets: although many of these women identified their poetic production as works of genius or personified genius in their works (at times with direct autobiographical references), this personification is, as in the aesthetics of male bourgeois authors, invariably male.[68] In an aesthetic context that ignored the potential of lower-class poets and tabooed the literary activity of women of any class,

---

[67] Schiller, "Necessary Limitations," 237. ("Das Geschäft also, welches die Natur dem andern Geschlecht nicht bloß nachließ, sondern verbot, muß der Mann doppelt auf sich nehmen.... Er wird also soviel, als er nur immer kann, aus dem Reich der Abstraktion, wo er regiert, in das Reich der Einbildungskraft und Empfindung hinüberzuziehen suchen, wo das Weib zugleich Muster und Richterin ist. Er wird, da er in dem weiblichen Geiste keine dauerhaften Pflanzungen anlegen kann, so viele Blüten und Früchte, als immer möglich ist, auf seinem eigenen Feld zu erzielen suchen, um den schnell verwelkenden Vorrat auf dem andern desto öfter erneuern und da, wo keine natürliche Ernte reift, eine künstliche unterhalten zu können. Der Geschmack ... nährt und schmückt den weiblichen Geist mit den Produkten des männlichen und läßt das reizende Geschlecht empfinden, wo es nicht gedacht, und genießen, wo es nicht gearbeitet hat"; "Über die notwendigen Grenzen beim Gebrauch schöner Formen," 683–84). Significant differences between Schiller's view of Art and earlier aesthetics that extol the natural genius include his identification of Art with intellectuality rather than feeling (which becomes a new trend in late-eighteenth- and early-nineteenth-century Germany) and his depiction of Art as *work* — both aspects that exclude women from all Artistic activity. For a brief discussion of eighteenth-century attitudes toward women and work, cf. the conclusion.

[68] For a more extensive discussion, cf. chapters 3, 4, and 5; for a discussion of bourgeois women authors in the context of the presumed masculinity of authorship, cf. the conclusion.

women peasant poets were subject to a double prohibition. But, as with Anna Louisa Karsch and others, aesthetic prohibition did not automatically ostracize the actual poet; rather, the confrontation between the aesthetic mandate and the existence of the actual poet resulted, in many cases, in a post facto — and highly instructive — attempt to reassess the aesthetic situation in light of this poet's existence, which represented the personification of the "natural genius" of earlier aesthetic treatises.

One might suspect a relationship, more likely analogous than causal, between the short duration of the nature craze in aesthetics and the brevity of most peasant poets' careers. The nature craze in aesthetics did not stand undisputed in either country: like the peasant poets who could have served as the best exemplification of the natural genius in aesthetic theory, that concept, along with the bourgeois interest in folk poesy, soon became an object of ridicule. Possibly the most famous example was Nicolai's satire "Eyn feyner kleyner Almanach vol schönerr echterr liblicherr Volckslieder, lustigerr Reyen unddt kleglicher Mordgeschichte" (A Lytle and Fyne Allmanac ful off beiautifulle, orriginalle, and lovlie folcke songes, cherfulle dannces, and sorowfulle murderr misterryes, 1777–78), whose very title reduces the aesthetic notion that the natural genius had no need of formal literary training to a mockery of the genius's copious spelling mistakes.[69]

In aesthetics, the concept of the natural and uneducated poetic genius was contested in treatises that claimed reason, erudition, and training to be the guiding principles of poesy (mentioned in Sulzer, later in Mendelssohn and others),[70] and ultimately supplanted by classical aesthetics in Germany and mainstream Romanticism in England. In many cases — for example, in Mendelssohn's *Rezensionsartikel* (Review Articles) — what ultimately turns into an aesthetic treatise begins as a review of an actual peasant poet — in this case, Anna Louisa Karsch. Such a point of departure naturally necessitates, implicitly or explicitly, a re-examination of earlier treatises celebrating the unlettered, natural poet *in light of that particular poet's work*, and ultimately leads — *in critical dissociation from*

---

[69] Cf. Dedner, "Schäferleben," 63–65; Nicolai's erratic spelling, intended to be both flawed and archaic, is an obvious spoof not only on the genius's lack of formal education but also on the presumed ancientness of folk literature. For a list of contemporary satires on the "natural genius" in Germany, cf. Schmidt, I, 148.

[70] Cf. Sulzer, "Entwickelung," 320, in which he considers exposure to literature and literary training indispensable to the development of true poetic genius, and Mendelssohn, who views "nature, without the direction of art, a very poor guide" (" . . . so ist die Natur ohne den Leitfaden der Kunst eine sehr misliche Führerin," 587). In England, Sharpe was one of the main opponents of nature aesthetics; in his *Dissertation on Genius* (1755), he attempted to show that genius was not a gift from Nature but the result of acquisition and study (cf. Osborn, 144).

*that particular poet's work* — to the development of an aesthetic alternative that pronounces erudition and poetic training, inaccessible to that poet and all others like her, as indispensable for the exercise of Art.

## Window Shoppers: The Servant As Artist

Even in the days when literary training was still viewed as a hindrance, rather than a prerequisite, for natural poetic genius, literacy was a precondition for writing of any kind, and the extent of lower-class literacy therefore becomes a subject of some interest in this context. Exact figures are difficult to come by for the lower orders (and impossible to come by for lower-class women), but most scholars who have studied the history of literacy estimate that England and Scotland were well ahead of continental Europe in this respect. In part, this is based on indirect evidence, such as the frequent reports of foreign visitors' (which included many Germans) astonishment at the high rate of literacy among the lower classes in Britain.[71] In England, the literacy rate of society overall has been estimated at 45 percent in 1714 and 60 percent in the mid-eighteenth century; for women, that rate is approximately 25 percent in 1714 and 40 percent in 1750, with the highest incidence of illiteracy occurring in the lower classes (especially among laborers and maidservants).[72] Stone records a sharp rise in literacy in England around 1780; his estimate of a 64 percent literacy rate in the late 1700s seems to match Thomas's estimate, but is unfortunately based exclusively on a group of men that includes only a small number of lower-class members.[73] His comparative estimate by class shows the literacy rate of laboring classes of the West Midlands in England to be approximately 35 to 48 percent (depending on geographic area) at the end of the eighteenth century;[74] Klaus estimates the literacy rate among working people in eighteenth-century England to have been as high as 40 percent.[75] Literacy estimates for Scotland are considerably higher: in comparison with England and France, the literacy rate of men is estimated as 47 percent in France, 65

---

[71] Cf. Stone, "Literacy," 85–86; Klaus, *Literature*, 2; Neuburg, 94.

[72] Thomas, 102.

[73] Stone, "Literacy," 95 and 103, respectively.

[74] Stone, "Literacy," 109–10.

[75] Klaus, *Literature*, 10, 179 n. 25. Overall, these figures correspond to the ones published by Neuburg (170–73), who defines "literacy" as the ability to *read*. The only dissenting voice on the subject of the extraordinarily high literacy among the lower classes in England is Patton's, who offers the unsubstantiated claim that as a rule, the poorer classes in eighteenth-century England were illiterate (26).

percent in England and Wales, and 88 percent in Scotland in 1800, with a postulated literacy rate for Scotland of about 75 percent in 1750.[76] Scotland, in the wake of the parliamentary reform acts of 1646 and 1696, enjoyed the best educational system in Europe, in part due to a broad (and compulsory) elementary-school system, which provided great social mobility and gave the lower orders broader access to education than they would have enjoyed in other national contexts.[77] In addition, schools dedicated to the education of the poor were instituted in every parish.[78] Shortly after the turn of the nineteenth century, a contemporary observer noted, "In the very humblest condition of the Scottish peasants, every one can read, and most persons are more or less skilled in writing and arithmetic."[79] Johnson described England in 1781 as "a nation of readers," and the "cries of alarm from their betters at this debauching of the minds of ploughboys and servants" testifies to the fact that reading had indeed spread to the lower classes.[80] Conversely, historians of German literacy have surmised that rural children in Germany, despite compulsory elementary education in some states, were usually not educated at all, but integrated into the workforce as early as possible to replace paid day laborers.[81] Beyond the general assumption that the literacy rate was higher in Scotland than in England and lowest in Germany, these figures are of limited use in a book on lower-class women writers because

---

[76] Stone, "Literacy," 120–21 and 127, respectively.

[77] Stone, "Literacy," 135–36. At Cambridge University, none of the students enrolled between 1752 and 1849 were working-class children; at the University of Glasgow, that figure is estimated to have been one third for the same time period (Stone, "Literacy," 136).

[78] This law was instituted by parliamentary decree in 1646, repealed by Charles II in 1660, and reenacted after the Revolution by the Scottish parliament (cf. Currie, I, 4).

[79] Currie, I, 3.

[80] Christopher Hill, 230; but see also Watt, *Rise,* 37–49, who claims that "there is much evidence to suggest that in the country many small farmers, their families, and the majority of labourers, were quite illiterate" (37).

[81] Cf. Wittmann; Frevert, *Women,* 24; Schlumbohm, 77–78, 91–92; Jacobeit/Nowak, 33–35; and Becker-Cantarino, "Belloisens Lebenslauf," 17, n. 8 (on compulsory elementary education in Prussia since 1713, reinforced by additional decrees in 1717 and 1763). The report of the "travelling village preacher" who praised the high degree of literacy among the rural population around Magdeburg in 1800 refers clearly and exclusively to wealthy landowning farmers and not to rural laborers or the poor (quoted at length and analyzed in Jacobeit/Nowak, 31–32). For women specifically, Becker-Cantarino surmises, without documentation, that lower-class women in Germany around 1800 were largely illiterate in the sense of being unable to write ("Leben als Text," 131).

literacy studies either examine the "general" population (usually with little attention to the lower classes) or describe male literacy only.[82]

A more general trait that makes the use of literacy studies highly problematic is the underlying definition of what constitutes literacy: most studies, which are based on marriage and church records, assume a person's literacy is defined by his or her ability to write, more specifically, the ability to sign his or her name. But, as Thomas has pointed out, a mark instead of a signature does not necessarily indicate illiteracy since many literate people used marks to indicate their occupations.[83] The greater problem with defining literacy as the ability to write is the fact that the ability to read was much more widespread in the eighteenth century: schools for the poor charged more for teaching children to write than they charged to teach them to read;[84] some schools refused on principle to teach writing to lower-class children. In *An Essay towards the Encouragement of Charity Schools* (1728), Isaac Watts states, "I will by no means contend for writing as a matter of equal necessity or advantage with that of reading.... I would not therefore by any means have it made a necessary part of a Charity-School, that the children should be taught to write."[85] James Nelson, in *An Essay on the Government of Children* (1756), advocated restricting the education of girls of the peasant class to reading and needlework and placed great emphasis on the exclusion of writing.[86] At the turn of the century, Hannah More still had to placate opposition to her school by reassuring her critics that "I allow of no writing."[87] In the 1740s, an examination of a group of 74 Scotswomen found all of them able to read and only eight able to write.[88] Because even fluent readers at times signed their names with a mark, Thomas's conclusion is that most literacy studies, which are based on

---

[82] Studies on women's education usually also pay little or no attention to women of the lower classes. For an overview of (mostly bourgeois) women's education in Germany and England, see the "window" chapters in Sotiropoulos (35–52 and 217–26, for Germany, and 152–66, for England).

[83] Thomas, 102.

[84] Cf. Neuburg, 55 and 93–96, on the curriculum of charity schools and Currie, I, 5–6, on the costs of schooling in various disciplines. To learn Latin, for example, at a county parish school was approximately twice as expensive (10–12 shillings per year) than to learn English, writing, and accounting (5 shillings per year; Currie, I, 6). On charges for reading versus other instruction in Scottish schools, cf. Gibson/Smout, 352.

[85] Quoted in Bridget Hill, *Eighteenth-Century Women*, 66.

[86] Quoted in Neuburg, 8.

[87] Cited in Stone, "Literacy," 89.

[88] Thomas, 103.

samples of signatures and which equate the abilities to read and write, greatly underestimate the number of fluent readers.[89]

Hannah More's assurances to her critics that she would never teach writing to a lower-class learner points to another aspect that seems relevant, namely, the *purpose* behind the middle-class education of the poor. Although it would be tempting to view increased literacy of the lower orders exclusively as a means for popular emancipation, it clearly also functioned as a means of upper-class hegemony by consolidating the authority of the educated classes over their inferiors.[90] Claude Levi-Strauss has suggested that "the primary function of writing . . . is to facilitate the enslavement of other human beings. . . . The struggle against illiteracy is indistinguishable, at times, from the increased power exerted over the individual citizen by the central authority."[91] If, like Gee, one defines literacy not merely as a skill but as a set of discourse practices that are taught along with that skill, literacy can easily be viewed not only as a means for popular emancipation, but simultaneously as a socializing tool for the poor and as "a possible threat if misused by the poor (for an analysis of their oppression and to make demands for power)."[92]

The attempts to socialize the peasant class, attempts that consciously capitalized on their ability to read, are illustrated in the bourgeois tradition of "peasant enlightenment" (*Bauernaufklärung*) and reflected in texts written by bourgeois authors and directed at the members of the lower orders.[93] Such texts, primarily Hans Caspar Hirzel's *Wirtschaft eines philosophischen Bauern* (Economies of a Philosophical Peasant, 1761), Rudolph Zacharias Becker's "Versuch über die Aufklärung des Landmannes" (Essay on the Enlightenment of the Rustic, 1785), and Hannah More's *Village Politics* (1792), invariably portray the peasant as the epitome of modesty, industry, piety, and submissiveness.[94] The declared goal of such literature, which develops a discourse of nature ideali-

---

[89] Thomas, 102–3.

[90] Cf. Thomas, 121, and Ferguson, "Introduction,"6–7.

[91] Cited in Stone, "Literacy," 83–84.

[92] Cf. Gee, 719–20, 734; the citation 734. On contemporary views of the dangers of lower-class literacy, cf. Christopher Hill, 229–30, Neuburg, 3–11, and Bridget Hill, *Servants,* 229–30.

[93] Cf. Goebel, 86; Götze.

[94] Cf. Baur, 69. Hannah More's pamphlet portrays Jack as the reasonable, contented, and submissive peasant persuading his revolutionary upstart neighbor Tom of the error of his ways (cf. Whitney, 304–5). On other bourgeois literature that teaches subordination to the poor, cf. Porter, 372–76; on the reception of such treatises among the reading peasant populace in eighteenth-century Germany, cf. Wittmann.

zation similar to the aesthetic treatises described earlier, was to increase the peasant's contentedness with his lowly condition,[95] thus forestalling discontent and unrest; in some cases, such bourgeois-authored moralizing tracts on the subject of happiness in poverty were published under the pretense of lower-class authorship.[96]

Even literature that was not overtly didactic was at times pressed into the service of suppressing potential unrest among the lower classes: Lessing praises Johann Wilhelm Ludwig Gleim's *Lieder für das Volk* (Songs for the People, 1772) particularly because they were written in such simple style that "even the stupidest among the people could understand them"; the declared goal of this collection, in Lessing's view, was not to distract the "people" through useless meditation from their work but instead encourage them to view their laborious occupation as "a source of principles appropriate to that class and simultaneously a source of gratification." Lessing cynically commends Gleim's portrayal of "that cheerful poverty, in which it is immaterial whether it is imposed or voluntary."[97] But not everyone was as adept as Lessing and Gleim at idealizing destitution: that same poverty had already become a problem in aesthetic discussions concerning bourgeois literature that portrayed the lower orders but was directed at a readership within its own class. The discrepancy between the ideal of the cheerfully and meekly toiling peasant and real-life poverty and oppression led to a long drawn-out debate on whether the portrayal of peasants in literature was admissible in principle,[98] a problem that resulted

---

[95] Dedner, *Topos,* 134, cf. also Dan Wilson, "Illuminatenideologie," 290–93. Pascal states that Johann Heinrich Merck, an atheist, was relieved that the increasingly philosophical and erudite attitudes toward religion had not yet affected the "productive classes" and that therefore "neither plow nor wheel are idle" ("Zum Glück daß der Theil der Welt, der dadurch verschlimmert ist, nicht in die producierende Klasse gehört, und deswegen weder Pflug noch Rad stille steht," quoted in Pascal, 46).

[96] Cf. Neuburg, 128; one example of this would be Hannah More's poem "The Ploughman's Ditty," authored ostensibly by "Will Chip the Ploughman," cf. More, *Poems,* 317–20.

[97] Quoted in Balet, 250–51: "Sich zum Volk herabzulassen [heißt] . . .: gewissen Wahrheiten . . . so leicht und fasslich vorzutragen, dass sie der Blödsinnigste aus dem Volk versteht. . . . Unter dieses Volk haben Sie sich gemengt: nicht um es durch gewinnstlose Betrachtungen von seiner Arbeit abzuziehen, sondern um es zu seiner Arbeit zu ermuntern, und seine Arbeit zur Quelle ihm angemessener Begriffe, und zugleich zur Quelle seines Vergnügens zu machen. Besonders atmen die meisten von Ihren Liedern das, was die alten Weisen ein so wünschenswertes, ehrenvolles Ding war, und was täglich mehr und mehr aus der Welt sich zu verlieren scheint: jene fröhliche Armut, bei der es wenig darauf ankommt, ob sie erzwungen oder freiwillig ist."

[98] Cf. Dedner, "Schäferdichtung," 57–62. In the English context, the question was posed, among others, by Pope and Crabbe, who, similar to Loen and Sonnenfels in the German context, polemicized against a literature that hid the miseries of rural existence behind poetic

in the division, mostly in early-eighteenth-century aesthetic works, of the rustic into the graceful Arcadian shepherd as an idyllic and the boorish dimwitted peasant as a comical character.[99] However, parallel to the aesthetic cult of the primitive and interest in folk literature, the mid- to late-eighteenth-century bourgeoisie did produce its share of literature in which the peasant (rather than the shepherd) is given a central part.[100] This literature frequently, as do works directly addressed to the lower classes, takes up the seventeenth-century tradition of usurping the rustic's voice to affirm bourgeois superiority: "God bless the squire and his relations / And keep us in our proper stations."[101]

Overall, bourgeois tactics proved fairly effective; the reasons for this are, for the most part, directly connected with the phenomenon of patronage, as discussed in the following chapter.[102] The assumption on which the entire structure of eighteenth-century bourgeois aesthetics rests — the idea that the seventeenth-century patronage system was supplanted, in the eighteenth century, by a "free" literary market — is oversimplified, as I have attempted to show, in relation to the bourgeoisie and not applicable to lower-class authors at all. To those authors, the "free" literary market was accessible *only* in a mediated fashion, through the intervention and protection of a (usually bourgeois, sometimes aristocratic) patron. On the heels of its own emancipation from aristocratic patronage — at least in the form of a literary existence as a "kept" court poet — the bourgeoisie discovered patronage as an opportunity to fashion literature in the practical as well as theoretical sense: through its control over the poetic production of authors from the peasant class, it simultaneously cultivated both the aesthetic and the ideological, categories that, in bourgeois writings as well as in peasant poetry, at times overlap. The peasants, in turn, frequently paid for their participation in literary life with a pathetic willingness to exemplify the rustic genius exalted in bourgeois aesthetics and by catering to bourgeois class ideol-

---

trappings. As Crabbe once pointed out in a poem, most bourgeois authors who praised the wholesome plainness of a peasant's meal would never touch it (cf. Williams, *Country,* 19–20, 87; the citation of Crabbe's poem, 20).

[99] Dedner, *Topos,* 5, 13–18, 161, and Baur 59–69; for the English context, cf. McClung, 26, and the discussion in Hauser, *Social History,* II, 515–19.

[100] Cf. Dedner, *Topos* and "Schäferdichtung"; Runge, 193–213, 221–28; Baur, 69–77; Schneider, 124–53; and Ehrenpreis and Robbins on the depiction of the poor and servants in English literature.

[101] The citation is taken from Herrick's poem *A Thanksgiving* and quoted in Williams, *Country,* 73.

[102] Cf. chapter 2 for a more extensive discussion of patronage and chapter 6 for an analysis of poetic responses by patronized poets from the lower classes.

ogy. Pastoral poetry, that genre in which many peasant poets were exhorted to write by their bourgeois patrons because their origins "in nature" seemed to suggest the analogy, already had a long history of propagating class harmony in the service of the upper classes by the time the first peasant tried his hand at the genre. Stephen Duck's "Gratitude, A Pastoral" (two words that "together, are the essential history," Williams claims)[103] and his later poems, which invariably portrayed blissful groves peopled with smiling swains, are certainly a far cry from his unforgiving depiction of harsh physical labor in *The Thresher's Labour,* written before he was blessed with (and muzzled by) Queen Caroline's patronage.[104] The cobbler and poet Robert Bloomfield was "reduced," in Williams's analysis, to similar "anxious obeisance"[105] under patronage.

One of the most revealing anecdotes illustrating the ways in which patronized peasant poets were induced to serve as representations of bourgeois aesthetics is the story of Ann Cromartie Yearsley, the "poetical milkwoman of Bristol," and her patron Hannah More. "Lactilla," as she was styled, was perceived — by her patron and by her readers — as the real-life manifestation of just such a "natural" genius as appears in countless aesthetic treatises of the age: originating in "Nature," spontaneously inspired, and unencumbered by education or reading of any kind. When More, understandably surprised by the frequent classical allusions in Yearsley's poetry, asked her how she had acquired these images, Yearsley "said she had taken them from little ordinary prints which hung in a shop-window."[106] It is this image that perhaps best describes the peculiar position in which publishing lower-class authors found themselves vis-à-vis their patrons and the bourgeois aesthetics that supposedly theorized their own existence: that of poetological window-shoppers, standing just outside the shop in which poetic inspiration, literary genius, and *authorship* was temptingly displayed, their noses pressed against the glass, simultaneously products of this poetology and excluded from it, simultaneously longing for reading, training, and an education that could lift them into the ranks of bourgeois authors, and forced to personify the "unlettered genius" which furnished the ideo-

---

[103] Williams, *Country,* 89.

[104] On Duck's poetic production under patronage, cf. Williams, *Country,* 88–90; Klaus, *Literature,* 4, and "Stephen Duck und Mary Collier"; and Zionkowski.

[105] Williams, *Country,* 134.

[106] The story is related by More in her introduction to Yearsley's first volume of poetry, *Poems on Several Occasions,* reprinted by Yearsley in More's "Prefatory Letter" to Yearsley's *Poems, on Various Subjects,* xii, and retold by Carter, 203–4, and Tompkins, 61, among others.

logical basis for their literary existence. It is, in this context, only seemingly a contradiction that the patron's function, to the extent that it transcended the largely mechanical task of procuring enough subscribers for the poet's work, often consisted of an attempt to force the natural poetic genius to *remain* "natural." Hannah More furnished her protegeé Yearsley with Ossian.[107] Sulzer proudly reports that fairy tales and Robinson's adventures made up almost the entire reading of his "natural genius," Anna Louisa Karsch.[108] Spence notes that Duck's reading consisted mainly of Milton, Addison, and pastoral literature.[109] Bürger expresses disappointment about the recent tendencies of the hatmaker apprentice and poet Städele to "erudition and imitation."[110] These examples echo the exhortations and prohibitions of the natural-genius aesthetic, thus showing the extent to which the "unlettered poet's" practice under patronage was steered by the nature and genius theories of earlier aesthetic treatises.

The dependence of practicing lower-class authors on the bourgeois aesthetic of the natural genius appears to have remained absolute well into the nineteenth century, where this dependence, paradoxically, occasionally expresses itself in protests against the new bourgeois aesthetic of classical education as a prerequisite for poetic practice. The shoemaker poet John Lucas's furious denial that poetic talent was limited to the educated elite and dependent on a classical education and his fervent assertion that poesy was inspired by those qualities that made man "godlike" and that were just as widespread among the poor[111] amount to an act of conformity with established aesthetic practice, his belligerent tone notwithstanding. His is just one example showing that bourgeois genius theory was adopted wholesale by many lower-class authors. Eighteenth-century peasant poets like Stephen Duck, although largely ignored by the

---

[107] Cf. Hopkins, 122. Yearsley's other reading was more or less limited to those texts that stood as exemplifications of natural genius in aesthetic treatises, including Milton, Virgil's Georgics (Hopkins, 122), Young's *Night Thoughts,* and Shakespeare's plays (Carter, 193); cf. also Tompkins, 61.

[108] Sulzer, "Vorrede," xv. In her autobiographical letters to Sulzer, which furnished the basis for his brief biography of her in his foreword, she cites as among her earliest influences two other names which make a frequent appearance in aesthetic treatises of the day: Albrecht von Haller and Edward Young ("Lebensbericht," 353).

[109] The notes are extensively quoted by Osborn, 128.

[110] Gottfried August Bürger in a letter to Boie, October 11, 1777: "If only he doesn't disappoint our hopes, as Thomsen did. I can already smell erudition and imitation" ("Wenn er unsere Hoffnungen nur nicht wieder, wie ehedem Thomsen, betriegt. Ich rieche schon Gelahrtheit und Nachahmung"; Strodtmann, II, 160).

[111] Cf. Ashraf, 48.

bourgeois readership, became symbols for great and unappreciated genius among nineteenth-century lower-class readers.[112] The proletarian poet John Lake, in 1834, complained bitterly about the tendency of modern reviewers to ravage those poets who attempted to write "inspired by Nature alone," and reviewers whose savage criticism prevented wealthy patrons from offering those poets their support.[113] In other words, although nineteenth-century bourgeois aesthetics had long taken leave of the eighteenth-century nature craze and genius ideology, now favoring a poetology that rested on erudition and training, the natural-genius model, originally supposedly developed by the bourgeoisie to cement its own independence from the aristocracy, was taken over by lower-class authors for whom this model, in either century, constituted the only possible poetological basis for a literary existence. And although nineteenth-century bourgeois authors had long left patronage behind, patronage remained, for their colleagues from the lower classes, the only means of access to the literary market. Historical incongruities like these — what Germans would call *Ungleichzeitigkeiten* — should make it impossible to generalize bourgeois literary history as universal literary history, as has been the predominant practice in both English and German scholarship,[114] and should induce us to re-examine both the merchandise displayed in the shop window of bourgeois authorship and the potential buyer standing outside.

---

[112] Ashraf, 156–57.

[113] Quoted in Ashraf, 157–58.

[114] There are, of course, some notable exceptions to this, particularly in scholarship on English literature. Cf., among others, John Barrell's and Raymond Williams's extensive work on the English peasant class; Harriet Guest's recent consideration of gender distinctions in her discussion of genius theories, and Fredric Jameson, Ian Watt, and Michael McKeon, who have extensively discussed class relations in their works on the English novel. John Barrell's work has shown to what extent the editing out of non-bourgeois contexts, such as the patronage context, has been essential to an understanding of literature as "universal"; cf. his essay "Editing Out: The Discourse of Patronage and Shakespeare's Twenty-Ninth Sonnet" in *Poetry, Language and Politics,* 18–43.

# 2: The Wild and the Civilized: Poet Making

## The Wages of Suffering and the Wages of Sin: Class Issues and Literary Patronage

LITERARY PATRONAGE IS worth reinvestigating with an eye to class issues, which are relevant for both patron and protégée. As discussed in the previous chapter, it is only possible to argue that patronage disappears from the eighteenth-century literary scene if one equates bourgeois literary history with literature in general.[1] Viewed differently, it would be just as easy to argue that the old-style system of patronage — consisting of a patron's direct protection and supervision of and control over his or her protégée — is retained, albeit with some significant changes, throughout the eighteenth century. One major shift taking place with respect to literary patronage in the eighteenth century would, following this argument, be one of class. The roles of both patron and protégée are passed down the ranks: in the patron's case, from royalty to the aristocracy and from there to the bourgeoisie, and in the poet's case, from the bourgeoisie to the lower classes. The fact that the first shift in the patron's class has been noted in scholarship on the history of literary patronage[2] while the second has been ignored can, again, be read as a testimony to the generalization of bourgeois literary history as literary history: patronage, by its very definition, necessitates a class difference between patron and protégée, and thus the recognition of the bourgeois patron's role would entail an acknowledgment of lower-class authorship — counterintuitively so, given the identification of bourgeois authorship with authorship in general.

This chapter examines the differences between seventeenth-century aristocratic patronage of bourgeois poets and eighteenth-century bourgeois patronage of lower-class authors, and looks at both mercenary and

---

[1] Cf. Gerth, 55–56, for the German context; Hauser, *Social History*, II, 547–48, Foss, 87, for the English context; critically, Rizzo, "The Patron as Poet Maker," 241. Korshin offers a somewhat more differentiated view of the situation when he describes the old system of literary patronage as on the decline and as coexisting with the bookseller-dominated system until about mid-century (455–56).

[2] Cf. Korshin, 457; Foss, 136.

poetological issues. In examining several patronage stories, my question is: To what extent did the *purpose* of literary patronage change along with the changes in class? Subscribing, for the moment, to a somewhat idealized view of literary patronage, let us assume that royal or aristocratic patronage of bourgeois authors (Friedrich II's patronage of Voltaire, Halifax's support of Congreve, etc.) was largely motivated by a desire to increase the court's luster and the patron's fame by peopling the court with the most shining examples of musical, literary, or Artistic brilliance. Patronage of this nature results in three related consequences for the poet, one financial, two poetological: it implies a degree of recognition, perhaps even admiration, of their work; it frees artists from the necessity of earning their bread in ways other than by the exercise of their art; and it imposes on artists the obligation of constant recognition of this bounty in song and story. In this way, art is simultaneously exalted (for it is, admittedly, art that adds radiance to the court, and presumably, appreciation of art is the driving force of the patron's generosity) and demeaned (since the resulting necessity to recognize that generosity takes precedence over other forms of artistic expression). Aristocratic patronage can thus be seen as invariably corrupting — the "wages of sin" that Korshin speaks of evokes the sycophancy-polluted art produced under patronage.[3] The idea that Art (and this term always infers bourgeois art forms alone) only became "divine" as it emancipated itself from patronage originates in this circumstance. The disappearance of literary patronage signifies the end of this subservience and thus — supposedly — the onset of Artistic independence, but it also marks the beginning of the Artist's meager subsistence on the "wages of suffering":[4] the "free" literary market never replaced the fixed income that poets enjoyed under courtly patronage, and the starving Artist becomes the dominant persona in the story of postpatronage Art, from Wolfgang Amadeus Mozart's brief career and tragic end to Allen Ginsberg's odd jobs as a dishwasher and night porter.

The relationship between aristocratic patron and bourgeois protégée cannot be transferred unproblematically to lower-class authors: few bourgeois patrons would have been in a position to settle an annuity on a poet or inclined to view that poet as personal entertainment. The deeper question, however, is whether the postpatronage bourgeois attitude toward Art as independent, "free" to follow its calling, and exalted beyond all petty obligations is applied, by the bourgeoisie, to the authorship of lower-class

[3] Cf. Korshin, 455.
[4] Like the "wages of sin," the term is Korshin's (455).

writers: Did bourgeois patrons consider the works of peasant poets, in particular those works produced under their patronage, Art in the sense by which they defined their own writing? Were that the case, one would have to assume two purposes behind the bourgeois patronage of lower-class authors: freeing these authors from the necessity of physical labor to enable them to write and granting them artistic autonomy. Successful patronage of lower-class authors would thus be closely linked to newly emerging aesthetic ideas about the sovereignty of Art (some of which were voiced within the genius movement), and it would imply deracination since it takes poets out of their original context — as a plowman, thresher, milkmaid, or cottager — and places them in an environment that enables their full-time dedication to their poetic vocation.[5]

But this, as other scholars have already noted,[5] has neither been the goal nor the result of bourgeois patronage of lower-class authors, which was not particularly concerned with the poet's autonomy over his or her writing or, for that matter, with enabling further poetic production. Most women peasant poets throughout the century published only one book of verse; *none* of them published more than one volume with the aid of the same patron. The story of the thresher-poet Stephen Duck (1705–56), frequently read as a model for peasant poets of the age, mirrors more closely the seventeenth-century aristocratic patronage of bourgeois authors than other patronage stories of his own era and class. Compared with other poets of his class, Duck was an exception in that he was patronized not by the bourgeoisie but by royalty; in that he was freed from physical labor and endowed with a house and an annuity; in that he was the only peasant poet in the century to become bourgeois, to the extent possible, via his ascent into the clerisy; and in that his patron employed him not only as a poetic entertainer and natural genius but also as a pawn in an effort to put down one of the most respected bourgeois poets of the age.[6] The first notable patronage story of any peasant poet of the age thus casts lower-class and bourgeois poets not as analogous (a conclusion that could then lead to the assumption of bourgeois poetic autonomy by lower-class authors) but as diametrically opposed, and this opposition can be traced along the two axes that are central to this chapter: the mercantile and the poetological. In pitting Stephen Duck against Alexander Pope, ostensibly as revenge for Pope's lampooning of her in the *Dunciad*, Queen Caroline demonstrated the superiority of natural genius over erudite authorship, but she also, in her lavish reward of Duck's complaisance, flaunted the advan-

[5] Cf. Rizzo, "The Patron as Poet Maker."

[6] On Duck's patronage story, cf., among others, Southey, 95–113; Osborn, 123–32; Klaus, "Stephen Duck und Mary Collier," 115–16.

tages of old-style patronage versus the new model of independent, unsupported publication.[7]

The reason Duck's story is central to the patronage story of other peasant poets is not because his is an example of theirs — as discussed later, subsequent patronage stories contain more differences than similarities to Duck's — but because Duck's story was subsequently *received* as paradigmatic for peasant poets *by the bourgeoisie*. His meteoric career and the Queen's unusual support of him was seen as both out of all proportion, given the quality of his work, and as opening the floodgates to a multitude of scribbling peasants who abandoned their honest livelihoods only to find themselves unable to make a living by writing. "When the late Queen patronized Stephen Duck, who was a wonder only at first, and had not genius enough to support the character he had promised, twenty artisans and labourers turned poets, and starved."[8] Duck's example did subsequently inspire some lower-class authors — the bricklayer Robert Dodsley and the washerwoman Mary Collier cited him directly — but there is hardly enough evidence to support the bourgeois assertion that "the slopes of Parnassus were cluttered with peasant-poets" as a result of Duck's career.[9] In 1778, barely fifty years after Duck's "discovery," this discourse was already so established that the reviewers of the *Monthly Review* could issue the following proclamation:

> Whereas it hath been represented to us, upon the oaths of several of our trusty and well-beloved booksellers, that certain journeymen taylors, shoemakers, barbers, Spitalfields-weavers, and other handicraftsmen, and that certain apprentices, shopmen, &c. have assembled in certain clubs, called Spouting-clubs, and, having there intoxicated themselves with porter and poetry, have presumed to make rhymes, and discharge them on the Public, under the title of *'Squires* and *Honourables*, &c. &c. to the great annoyance of said Public, and of us, the said Reviewers; We do hereby ordain and decree that every such journeyman taylor, shoemaker, barber, Spitalfields weaver, or other handicraftsman, and that every apprentice, shopman, &c. so offending in

---

[7] On the triangle-story between Duck, Pope, and Queen Caroline, cf. Rizzo, "The Patron as Poet Maker," 244–46.

[8] Letter from Horace Walpole to Ann Yearsley's patron Hannah More, dated November 13, 1784, quoted in Childers's supplement to Southey, 183. Cf. also the remarks of the writer cited by Spence, who blames Bloomfield and Clare for the "most injurious effect upon a very considerable number of rhyming tailors, cobblers, carpenters, and other handicraftsmen. Every *blockhead* who can jingle a few verses *neglects,* in these enlightened days, the business for which he may happen to have been educated, for the purpose of following the *idle* and unprofitable trade of a poet" (xi; the emphases are original).

[9] Childers's supplement to Southey, 182–83.

future, shall, for every such first offence, be chained to the compter, for a space, not exceeding twelve, nor less than six days; and that they and each of them shall, for every such second offence, be not only chained to the compter for the said space of time (more or less) but be obliged to wear hobwigs, and flapped hats without girdle or buckle, for the space of six months.[10]

The tone of this proclamation is intended to be humorous and good-natured, but the droll exaggeration cannot mask the serious message: that of the crucial difference between bourgeois poetry and lower-class "rhymes," between the poet's laurel crown and the fool's cap placed symbolically on the head of the peasant rhymer. To produce such rhyme is presented as a presumption on bourgeois privilege (a similar presumption as, say, assembling in clubs would be), to be punished by public exposure and ridicule. In effect, the proclamation constitutes a universal review, a unilateral condemnation of all poetic output by lower-class writers, issued by the appointed arbiters of literary taste, who thereby denied not only the possibility of the quality of any such work but also its autonomy as literature (in the withholding of individual reviews). Childers's view that "condescending patronage of any rhyming bricklayer or washerwoman has never succeeded in producing any fine verses, but has often converted an honest labourer into an unpleasant beggar"[11] echoes this sentiment in its sweeping denunciation of lower-class authorship and in the obviously implied contrast of their "rhyming" with bourgeois "poetry." The *inevitable* failure of the peasant poet is already prefigured in the end of Duck's career:

His end was an unhappy one; he became insane, threw himself into the water, near Reading, in 1756, and was drowned. Till that malady occurred he had been a useful parish priest, and approved himself every way worthy of the patronage which had been bestowed upon him. If the malady had shown itself earlier, it might have been ascribed to the transition from a life of great bodily labour to a sedentary one, and to excess in study; but as about thirty years had elapsed since he was taken from the barn, the cause is more likely to have been accidental, or constitutional.[12]

Southey, writing about seventy-five years after Duck's death, is too fair-minded to overlook the evidence of thirty years between Duck's transplantation and his suicide, but he is still clearly tempted to attribute Duck's insanity and death to his presumption of assuming a bourgeois

---

[10] Anonymous, "By the Reviewers, A Proclamation," 162.

[11] Childers's introduction to Southey, xv.

[12] Southey, 111–12.

lifestyle, a life defined, by virtue of its emphasis on intellectual and creative rather than physical labor, by the starkest contrast imaginable to his earlier life "in the barn," a life that was, in view of Duck's tragic end, the only life suited to the thresher. The simultaneous definition of Stephen Duck as the most successful peasant poet of the age *and* as an ignominious failure carries the same message as the reviewers' proclamation: the a priori devaluation of *all* poetry written by lower-class authors and the absurdity to regard them as authors in the sense of the emerging bourgeois definition of authorship.

So what was the purpose of bourgeois patronage of lower-class authors, if not to enable them to write and if not to establish their works as examples of the independent and autonomous Art that characterized the new bourgeois literature? To answer this question, I examine two kinds of patronage stories of peasant poets: the few who were successfully transplanted "from the barn" (Anna Louisa Karsch, Ann Cromartie Yearsley) and the many who were not (among them Janet Little, Ann Candler, Elizabeth Bentley, Molly Leapor, Christian Milne, Mary Collier, Susannah Harrison, Jean Glover, Elizabeth Hands, and Isobel Pagan). Not coincidentally, the best-documented patronage stories are those of successful transplantation, whereas little is known of the many poets who were left, postpublication, as they had been found. The two issues that define bourgeois patronage are the mercantile (both in terms of the financial arrangements made for the poets and in the extent to which their work was viewed as a financial commodity, as opposed to literature) and the poetological (to what extent the protégée was perceived *as* a poet, in the context of definitions offered in contemporary aesthetic treatises). It is important not only to examine the patronage story from the perspective of both patron and protégée but also to link the theoretical and aesthetic with the practical, since in some cases, the patrons of lower-class authors were also among the major bourgeois literary theorists of their day. A comparison of their theoretical or aesthetic writings with forewords, letters, and biographical texts in which they documented their discovery of "their" peasant geniuses might help us see both patronage and poetology in a new light, namely, as *mutually influential*.

## "Menial Maids, with No Release from Toil": Some Paradigms

The scant information we have about women peasant poets who were not transplanted into the bourgeois literary scene comes mostly either from their own prefatory statements to their volumes or from their patrons' introductions of them. These sources are worth re-examining in terms of patronage because the themes that reappear in most of them, frequently enough to be styled a discourse, touch on points central to our understanding of bourgeois patronage: the author's self-definition as a poet and a woman, the poet's definition from the outside as exemplifying natural genius, questions of authorship, and financial provisions and their purpose. Unlike "transplanted" peasants such as Duck, Karsch, or Yearsley, publication in these cases brought little remuneration and no relief from their existence as physical laborers; the poet remained, as Christian Milne (1773–after 1816) puts it in her rhymed preface, a "'menial maid,' with no release from toil."[13] The fact of these poets' continued postpublication poverty affords their patrons the opportunity to present them as the objects of charity, rather than patronage: whereas patronage would presumably be offered in support of the worthiness of the poet's verse, charity aims to relieve her from economic hardship, irrespective of her literary standing or achievements. Thus, Richard Gough, in his review of Elizabeth Hands's (no dates available) *The Death of Amnon,* could suggest good-naturedly that "her poetical talents, if they do not draw her out of obscurity, may make the remainder of her life comfortable to herself and her family."[14] The patron of the washerwoman Mary Collier (1689/90–after 1762) thought it "no Reproach to the Author, whose Life is toilsome, and her Wages inconsiderable, to confess honestly, that the View of her putting a small Sum of Money in her Pocket . . . had its Share of Influence upon this Publication."[15] The anonymous patrons of Christian Milne's poems earnestly exhorted the reader in the foreword, "(whatever be his sentiments of her merit as a poet) . . . to promote the object of the author, whose heart indulges an honest wish to be possessed of the pecuniary means of giving her children in early life [an] education"; the author, in this introduction, appears not as a writer but as a humble cottager "whom, though happy

---

[13] Milne, "Preface," 8.

[14] In *Gentleman's Magazine* 60 (1790): 540. Cf. also the anonymous letter to the *Gentleman's Magazine* of 1784, whose author claimed as the goal of support for Ann Yearsley that "her life be softened, and her own little family be brought forward" (897).

[15] From M. B.'s "Advertisement" prefaced to Collier's "The Woman's Labour," unpag.

even now, it is in the power of a generous public to make still more happy!"[16] Ann Candler's (1740–1814) poems were published, ostensibly, to enable her to "raise a sum sufficient to furnish a room, and place herself, in a state of comparative happiness, near her married daughter, where she might spend the evening of her days in peace, supported by her own industry": at the time of publication, Candler was living in a workhouse for the poor, and the "industry" with which she was to support herself in the future was clearly intended to be physical, not poetical.[17] Janet Little's (1759–1813) patron and employer Frances Dunlop outlines Little's modest ambitions in a letter to Robert Burns ("She says ten guineas would make her as happy as worldly circumstances could do") and from there seamlessly proceeds to the plan for publication: "I think were her rhymes properly put out . . . she might be made happy and indebted to none but herself, since her modest wishes are placed within such humble bounds. . . ."[18] The fact that the object of publication is, in every case, financial rather than literary preempts a possible reception of these poems as literature (cf. Dunlop's usage of the term "rhymes" as a descriptor for Little's poetry, which seems to indicate a similar devaluation of the work as contained in the *Monthly Review*'s proclamation), and of the poet as an author. Nowhere in the forewords or biographical introductions, whether written by poet or patron, does the poet appear as an author. This most central self-understanding of the publishing writer is not only subtly undermined in the alternative definition of the poet as a pauper or as a good, hard-working woman, aware of and happy in her humble station, it is often directly negated in the poet's presumed *rejection* of that role via the popular characterization of her as "entirely free from the egotism of authorship."[19] In reviews, the virtuous woman frequently cancels out the competent author; the mediocrity of the work appears side by side with the laudatory remarks on the excellent personal qualities of its author: "And indeed if the Poems will not recommend themselves to the Reader[s], . . . we beg leave to inform them, that her Conduct and Behaviour entirely corresponded with those virtuous and pious Sentiments which are conspicuous in her Poems. She was courteous and obliging to all, chearful, good-natured, and contented in the Station of Life in which Providence had placed her."[20] The empha-

---

[16] Cf. the "Preface" to Milne, 21 and 23, respectively.

[17] "Memoirs of the Life of Ann Candler," Candler, 17.

[18] Letter from Frances Dunlop to Robert Burns, September 23, 1790, in Burns/Dunlop, II, 103. Cf. Sales on a similar patronage story dating from the early nineteenth century.

[19] Paterson on Janet Little, 88.

[20] Bridget Freemantle, "To the Reader," in Leapor, *Poems,* unpag.

sis on the poet's feminine virtues,[21] the poet's claim that the poems were written "merely for my own amusement,"[22] and the assurance that the poet would never dream of neglecting her household duties to accommodate her writing are all strongly reminiscent of the discourse of modesty in bourgeois women's writings, thus showing that gender, as well as class, had a considerable impact on these poets' self-presentation to their readership. "Without her having e'er in duty fail'd / To parent, master, child or husband dear, / The following Compositions now appear".[23] Christian Milne's elegant "excuse" for writing could, the reference to her "master" subtracted, easily grace the forewords of countless bourgeois women's works.[24]

Parallel to the discourse of the poet as happy pauper, menial maid, and dutiful daughter, wife, and mother runs another discourse that seems to contradict it directly: in many forewords and prefaces, the poet is implicitly defined as a "natural" genius, with obvious references to the well-known contemporary discussion of originality and authorship in aesthetic treatises. The recurring themes that express this are the emphasis on the poet's lack of a formal education, her remarkable memory, and the presentation of the poet as a voracious reader and writer from childhood on, with reading and writing being presented as insatiable desires which could not be suppressed even by the most daunting obstacles. It is particularly the combination of the poets' strong desires to read and write and the attempts, mostly on the part of their parents, to discourage such activities, that points to a possible connection between their early fondness for writing and the natural-genius motif in aesthetic treatises, for there is, in these childhood stories, no possible model for literary activity: the desire to read and write appears as unbidden in their young lives as a poem supposedly springs into the mind of the spontaneously inspired natural poetic genius.

An early — and entirely unexplained, given the social circumstances — taste for books appears in the life stories of Molly Leapor (1722–46), Christian Milne, Mary Collier, Mary Masters (1694?–1771; some sources, 1706?–1759?), Elizabeth Bentley (1767–1839), and Ann Candler. In almost all cases, this appetite is presented more as an obsession than a leisure activity, in ways that bourgeois women writers of the age were careful to avoid for fear of being accused of pedantry. Mary Collier, for example, describes reading and writing as her only childhood

---

[21] Repeatedly in the "Preface" to Bentley, unpag.

[22] In "Memoirs to the Life of Ann Candler," Candler, 7.

[23] "Preface" to Christian Milne, 9.

[24] Cf. the conclusion for a brief discussion of the forewords of bourgeois women writers.

recreation.[25] Ann Candler "early evinced a fondness for reading"; when instruction in writing was not forthcoming, she took matters into her own hands and learned to write by imitating her father.[26] In a letter to the Reverend Walker, Elizabeth Bentley describes herself from childhood on as "naturally fond of reading" and relates that she early "discovered in myself an inclination for writing verses."[27] Tales of parental opposition to this passion evoke a sense of urgency that could well be intended to lead the reader to conclude that the act of writing constituted a "natural" and hence invincible vocation to the poet in question. Christian Milne, who read at an early age and tried to write poetry at six,[28] describes carrying a piece of broken slate around with her and secretly writing on it whenever she was unobserved; on that piece of slate, she copied anything and everything in the form of verses. Because her stepmother, "justly offended" by her scribbling, attempted to break her of her habit and even went so far as to hide her inkstand to prevent further excesses of this nature, Milne did her writing in the strictest secrecy.[29] The most prominent detail in the life story of Mary Masters, related in the preface to her poems, is that her desire to write "was always brow-beat and discountenanced by her parents."[30] Most famous is the following description of the early poetic attempts of young Molly Leapor, as told after the poet's death by her patron Bridget Freemantle following an interview with Leapor's father:

> He informs me she was always fond of reading every thing that came in her way, as soon as she was capable of it; and that when she had learnt to write tolerably, which, as he remembers, was at about ten or eleven years old, she would often be scribbling, and sometimes in rhyme; which her mother was at first pleased with: but finding this humour increase upon her as she grew up, when she thought her capable of more profitable employment, she endeavoured to break her of it; and that he likewise, having no taste for poetry, and not imagining it could ever be any advantage to her, joined in the same design: but finding it impossible to alter her natural inclination, he had of late desisted, and left her more at liberty. . . . she always chose to spend her leisure hours in writing and reading, rather than in those diversions which young people generally

---

[25] Cited in Landry, "The Resignation," 103.
[26] Cf. "Memoirs," Candler, 2–3; quotation 2.
[27] Elizabeth Bentley, "To The Rev. Mr. Walker, in Norwich," in Bentley, unpag.
[28] "Preface" to Milne, 12.
[29] In an autobiographical narrative by Christian Milne, quoted by Spence, 181–82.
[30] "Preface" to Masters, *Poems,* unpag.

chuse; insomuch that some of the neighbours that observed it, expressed their concern, lest the girl should over-study herself, and be mopish.[31]

Echoes of the natural-genius aesthetic abound in this description: writing is an obsession that manifests itself early and unbidden; it is an all-consuming passion throughout life; it occupies every free minute of the day, and it overcomes all obstacles and ignores public opinion. From Freemantle's depiction of Molly Leapor's "natural inclination" for writing, it is only a short step to the understanding of the "natural genius" as an unconscious and helpless medium in the grip of the muse that is so all-pervasive in aesthetic treatises. Because her family and her community, the only possible models for Leapor's literary interest, instead presented her with such formidable opposition, there can be no doubt in the reader's mind that her inclination for writing must indeed have been "natural," rather than educational or imitative. The fact that Leapor overcame all of these obstacles leaves the reader either to superimpose on her character that persona of the disobedient daughter that is so emphatically denied in the same treatise or, alternately, to suppose — analogous to the poet-as-helpless-medium discourse — that "choice" had nothing to do with her determination to continue writing.

The natural-genius aesthetic is only rarely evoked directly, but it is, in almost every case, alluded to in similar terms as were employed in aesthetic treatises. In both preface and poetology, the poet's lack of formal education serves as a guarantee for the naturalness and authenticity of her poetic output: "Elizabeth Bentley had no education; she read only by accident; but from the moment she did read, she felt in herself a power of imitation, and a faculty of combining imagery, together with a facility of poetical expression."[32] Likewise, Janet Little, to her patron, "betrays no one indication that I could discover of ever having opened a book or tagged a rhyme."[33] Christian Milne appears as a poet "who, without *external* aid from birth or education . . . Must look *within* to find / The secret turns of Nature in the mind."[34] Ann Candler's lack of schooling served as clear evidence to her patron "that her Poems are more the spontaneous productions of genius than the work of memory or education."[35] Molly Leapor's poems were presented to the reader "as a convincing Proof of the

---

[31] Cf. Bridget Freemantle's letter in the review of Leapor's *Poems* in the *Monthly Review* of 1751, 28–29.

[32] "Preface" in Bentley, unpag., cited also in Landry, *Muses*, 210.

[33] Frances Dunlop to Robert Burns, July 13, 1789, in Burns/Dunlop, I, 274.

[34] Preface to Milne, 10–11 (the emphases are original).

[35] "Memoirs," Candler, 3.

common Aphorism, *Poeta nascitur, non fit*,"[36] largely based on the unanswerable evidence of her lack of formal education.[37] John Duncombe, taking his cue from this image, wrote that Leapor had "lately convinced the world of the force of unassisted nature" and deliberately pitted her "natural" poetry against the "scholastic" writing of "learned" authors:

> Let cloister'd pedants in an endless round,
> Tread the dull mazes of scholastic ground;
> Brackley unenvying views the glitt'ring train,
> Of learning's gaudy trappings idly vain;
> For spite of all that vaunted learning's aid,
> Their fame is rival'd by her rural maid.[38]

The fact that Leapor was repeatedly compared with Shakespeare,[39] who served, together with Milton, as *the* exemplification of natural genius in aesthetic treatises on both sides of the channel, speaks volumes in this context. Natural genius, in Leapor's case as well as that of other women peasants, is defined in much the same way as it was in aesthetic treatises of the age, an analogy already suggested by the recurrence of the terms "Nature" and "Genius" in the forewords: because what is there is unfathomable and above criticism, it has to be largely defined by what is missing, namely, undue influence by "learning." For this reason, Freemantle insisted on Leapor's ignorance of dramatic rules[40] and Milne, in her foreword, stated somewhat defensively, "Let no stern critic . . . / talk of *rules*, when *rules* are all unknown."[41]

A further sign of the invocation of the natural-genius aesthetic that recurs in these introductory treatises is the emphasis on the speed and spontaneity of poetic production[42] and on the poets' amazing powers of

---

[36] Bridget Freemantle, "To the Reader," Mary Leapor, *Poems*, unpag.

[37] Freemantle took great care to present her in forewords as "destitute of the advantages of education" and as having had "so little advantage (or rather none at all) either from books or conversation"; cf. the review of Leapor's *Poems* in the *Monthly Review* of 1751, 24.

[38] Brackley in Northamptonshire was Leapor's home town; the introduction and the excerpt from the *Feminead* are both quoted in Harris, 250–51.

[39] In a review in the *Gentleman's Magazine*, Leapor appeared alongside Shakespeare as an uncultivated genius, warbling her native wood-notes wild; Duncombe likewise compared her with Shakespeare in the *Feminead*. Cf. Greene, 23 and 162.

[40] Review of Leapor's *Poems* in the *Monthly Review* of 1751, 30.

[41] Preface to Milne, 9 (the emphases are original).

[42] Cf., for example, the review of Leapor's *Poems* in the *Monthly Review* of 1751, in which she is said to have written a tragedy in a fortnight (23).

memory. Unusual memory is attributed to Mary Collier, Christian Milne, and Isobel Pagan (1741–1821), among others. (Isobel Pagan was supposedly capable of reciting the entire Bible from memory, word for word.[43]) What is interesting about this recurring theme is that in the depictions of the poet's mnemonic powers, her presentation as a natural genius clearly intersects with her characterization as a poor and disadvantaged cottager, for the way these powers are usually employed is to enable the poet to write *despite* the constant interruptions that are part and parcel of her life as a laborer. Like Stephen Duck, Christian Milne composed her poetry while employed at physical labor throughout the week and remembered it all, verbatim, until she finally had a chance to write down her compositions on Sunday evenings.[44] Milne described the creative process as follows:

> Though the profits of my little book and the patronage of the worthiest people have been very sweet to me; yet those blessings have been much embittered by the ridicule and contempt with which I have been treated, by those among whom I am obliged to live, because I have been so idle as to write rhymes. But those respectable ladies and gentlemen whose names I have mentioned can witness that I have not been the more idle on that account; for I have composed my poems, such as they are, when I was most busily employed about my washing, baking, or when rocking the cradle with my foot, the ink-stand in one hand, the pen in the other, and the paper on my knee, with my children about me. When busy at work, I laid the paper and ink-stand beside me, and wrote the stanza as it came into my mind, and then to my work again.[45]

In Milne's narrative, the discourse of the humble laborer and that of the natural genius inform each other: on the one hand, the statement is designed to protect the poet from accusations of "idleness" (by which is meant both the process of writing, which does not, in this narrative, count as real work, and the neglect of her household and wifely duties because of her writing). Her self-defense against this accusation, her failure to cite her creative occupation as *work*, and therefore respectable, indicates agreement with her accusers as to where her real duties lay and

---

[43] Cf. Paterson, 121.

[44] Milne's autobiographical statement, quoted by Spence, 182–83.

[45] Milne's autobiographical statement, quoted by Spence, 185–86. Milne's frequent complaints about the derision she encountered from people of her own class are clearly one of the most distinguishing features of poets who were not transplanted into the bourgeois context. Cf. her remarks in the "Preface" to her works, 13: "Having come to Aberdeen . . . when about fourteen years of age, I began to write down my little pieces; though, having no opportunity of shewing them to people of education, I had the mortification to find myself laughed at, and called idle by my fellow servants."

indirectly defines her as a peasant and housewife, rather than a poet. But the self-definition as a poet, and a poet modeled directly on the natural-genius theory of aesthetics, subtly injects itself into the narrative in her description of her writing as *unconscious:* poetic creation takes place at moments when she is "most busily employed," surrounded by either the wash or the children, at moments when her mind is clearly on other things. Milne's evocation of the unconscious creative process is strongly reminiscent of descriptions of the same process by Mary Collier, the first known eighteenth-century woman peasant poet, who conceived her verse "as on my Bed I lay, / Eas'd from the tiresome Labours of the Day" in a state between waking and sleep, during "moments of meditation that border on dream-work."[46]

It is not entirely clear from the introductory treatises whether the quality of the work constituted part of the authors' definition as natural geniuses or whether this definition rested purely on the unlikely fact that they wrote against all odds. Indirectly, however, the quality of the work is attested to in another recurring theme: denial of authorship. Mary Collier wrote an angry, rhymed retort to an exciseman from Gloucestershire who voiced his doubts as to the genuineness of her authorship and had to have her authorship confirmed in writing by her patrons;[47] both Jane Cave (c. 1754–1813) and Janet Little, whose poetry was frequently attributed to her father "because her genius was believed to be of the dwarfish kind,"[48] had to write a poem to one of their doubters for the expressed purpose of proving that they were capable of writing poetry.[49] Mary Masters, in a similar rhymed retort to the "Gentleman who questioned my being the Author of the foregoing Verses," evoked the *Poeta nascitur* paradigm in her defense, claiming that "Whate'er I write, what-

---

[46] The citation and analysis are Landry's, cf. "The Resignation," 102.

[47] Her response to the accusation: "there is none on Earth below / Nor yet above the Sky, / Can truly say, they made that Book, / But poor, despised I" (from "An Epistolary Answer to an Exciseman, Who Doubted Her Being the Author of the Washerwoman's Labour," in *Poems on Several Occasions* [1762], quoted in Klaus, "Stephen Duck und Mary Collier," 122). On her patrons' confirmation of her authorship, cf. Ferguson, *Eighteenth-Century Women Poets,* 12–13.

[48] Letter from Dunlop to Burns, August 20, 1789, Burns/Dunlop, I, 299.

[49] Cf. Cave's "A Poem, Occasioned By a Lady's Doubting Whether the Author Composed an Elegy," 46–48. On the inception of Little's poem, Dunlop reported to Burns: "The occasion on which she wrot it was to convince a young lady who doubted the authenticity of her having wrot something else she had shewed her, and asked her to write on a given subject" (Frances Dunlop in a letter to Burns, July 13, 1789, Burns/Dunlop, I, 275).

ever I impart, / Is simple Nature unimprov'd by Art."[50] Bridget Freemantle had to defend her protégée Molly Leapor posthumously against the charge of plagiarism.[51] Isobel Pagan's authorship of the now famous Scottish folk song "Ca the Yowes" was denied on no evidence but the song's quality.[52] Anna Louisa Karsch's patron Johann Wilhelm Ludwig Gleim asked her for a notarized statement asserting that her poems were really her work to forestall doubts of her authorship.[53] Toward the end of the century, Elizabeth Bentley's patrons were undoubtedly responding to a by-then-familiar discourse when they avowed it "necessary to assure the Reader, that the following Poems are the *genuine* and *sole* production of her pen."[54] These doubts as to the genuineness of the peasants' authorship can be understood in three (related) ways: as a commentary on the poets' social standing, which makes the very fact of their writing unlikely; as an implicit statement about the quality of their writing, which is viewed as impressive; and as a clearly implied *contrast* between author and work: what they wrote was simply too good to be attributed to them, given their social and educational background.

These recurring themes — the uneducated poet; the poet as inexplicably and irresistibly drawn to poetry as well as virtuous, unassuming, modest, and devoid of authorial ambition; the poet's amazing powers of memory; and the theme of unconscious poetic production — constitute a discourse whose context was more aesthetic than biographical. The *literariness* of these themes is clearly apparent in the fact that many of

---

[50] Masters, "To a Gentleman Who Questioned My Being the Author of the Foregoing Verses": "Sir, 'tis allow'd, as it has oft been said, / Poets are only *Born* and never *Made*," in *Poems*, 44–45 (emphases original).

[51] Cf. her letter appended to the review of Leapor's *Poems, Monthly Review* of 1751, 26: "Since the publication of her poems, I hear she has been accused of stealing from other authors; but I believe very unjustly. . . . I, that was so well acquainted with her way of thinking, dare venture to answer for her, that it proceeded from the impression the reading of those passages some time before happened to make upon her mind, without her remembering from whence they came; and therefore she can no more be reckoned a plagiary on that account, than a person could justly be accused of being a thief, for making use of a shilling or two of another's money that happened to be mixed with his own, without his knowing it."

[52] Cf. Paterson, 113: "This is a sweet little lyric; and its great superiority to the other known effusions of Isobel, is well calculated to raise a doubt whether it really be hers or not." McCue gives some further examples of the history of denial of Isobel Pagan's authorship of the song, including one instance in which the song was attributed to "a gentleman of the name of Pagan" (46).

[53] Letter from Gleim to Karsch, March 28, 1783, in Karsch, *"Bruder in Apoll,"* II, 176–77.

[54] Preface to Bentley, unpag. (emphases original).

them already appear in Duck's canonized biography;[55] at least in Molly Leapor's case, there are source materials that cannot be reconciled with the neat image of the natural poetic genius and virtuous cottager presented here. If Milne effortlessly produced poetry while concentrating on her "real" work, thus adeptly defending herself against accusations of privileging the poet over the servant, Molly Leapor failed miserably at the same task: "Her fondness for writing verses . . . displayed itself by her sometimes taking up her pen while the jack was standing still, and the meat scorching."[56] Leapor, whose lack of education furnished contemporaries with irrefutable proof of the adage of *Poeta nascitur,* is seen by modern critics as much better read than was then admitted: in modern interpretations, she appears as an admirer and imitator of Pope, someone who deeply regretted her lack of formal education, and who was on a lifelong mission to make up for it. She also tried to familiarize herself with the poetic conventions of her day and displayed her self-acquired learning proudly and purposefully in her work.[57] Leapor was also unusual in that she was the only poet in this group who tried to exercise some sort of control over the way in which she was patronized. For example, she refused to play the part of the humble cottager; instead, she ironically pointed to the humiliating aspects of patronage by referring to herself as a poetical court jester[58] and dismantled the familiar discourse of the hard-laboring peasant by describing her own poetic work, sarcastically and unapologetically, as "idleness."[59] Leapor went so far as to refuse a dedication to a noble patron, turn down a low offer for her poems,[60] and debate the process of patronage, including dedicatory practices, with her patron.[61] Posthumously, the story of the refused dedication is told by

[55] Among them are his humbleness and gratitude to his patrons, his mother's attempts to stifle his desire for reading when he was a child, his conscientiousness in never neglecting his "real" work for his studies, and his utter lack of authorial ambition of any kind; poetry in which Duck represented himself, undoubtedly under pressure to adjust to his patrons' expectations of him as a humble peasant happy in poverty, is quoted to obvious purpose in subsequent reworkings of his life (cf. Southey, 88–95).

[56] Anonymous, "Molly Leapor," in *Gentleman's Magazine* 54 (1784): 807.

[57] On Leapor's education, cf. Greene, viii, 9–11, 163, 169; Landry, *Muses,* 110; Rizzo, "Molly Leapor," 321, 332, 338; Harris, 253–54; Blunden, 67; and Lilley, 180–81. Greene emphasizes her familiarity with classical mythology (11); Blunden even entertains a suspicion that Leapor may have been familiar with a translation of Theocritus (65).

[58] Landry, *Muses,* 96–97.

[59] Cf. Freemantle's letter appended to the review of Leapor's *Poems, Monthly Review* of 1751, 27.

[60] Cf. Rizzo, "Molly Leapor," 322; Blunden, 80.

[61] Cf. Greene, 151.

Freemantle as a sign of Leapor's boldness and honesty,[62] but there can be no question that what Leapor is doing here is undermining the entire project of patronage. In one of her letters to Freemantle, she fantasizes herself a transplanted poet, an exaggerated success story of patronage containing more than one allusion to the saga of Stephen Duck:

> ... If our scheme succeeds, I intend to shew my public spirit: ... I shall erect a few Almshouses; and have some thoughts of founding a hospital for indigent or distracted poets. I presume this will take up as much of my superfluous wealth as I can spare from the extravagance of a gay retinue and splended equipage, in which I intend to abound. Amidst all this, I shall not be ingrateful, though perhaps somewhat haughty. Yet my chariot or landau shall ever be at your service, and ready to convey you to my country-seat, or to my house in *Hanover-square*.[63]

What Leapor skillfully lampoons here is the prejudice against which the common discourse of the humble cottager, content in her station, was intended to serve as defense: the bourgeois fear that elevating peasants above their "stations" would invariably result in their transformation into idle, haughty, luxury-loving, and ungrateful wretches. Simultaneously, Leapor's satire implicates the patron: her charitable intentions of erecting "almshouses" and hospitals for "indigent or distracted poets" are an unmistakable comment on the nature of patronage, here perceived precisely in the way in which it is presented in the forewords — as charity to the pauper rather than patronage of the poet.

Perhaps the most significant and consequential of Leapor's repudiations of the patronage game was her refusal to have her biography related in the foreword ("seeing myself described in Print," she argued, skillfully masking her subversiveness as modesty, "would give me the same Uneasiness as being stared at"[64]). As discussed previously, the introductory biography was essential to the project of patronage as the only possible means of instrumentalizing the poet as natural genius, dutiful daughter-wife-mother, and contented pauper worthy of patronage and support.[65] Without it, the entire project of presenting the work *as* peasant poetry collapses. Leapor's refusal may indicate a desire for her poems to be read

---

[62] Cf. Freemantle's letter appended to the review of Leapor's *Poems, Monthly Review* of 1751, 27.

[63] Letter from Leapor to Freemantle, quoted by Freemantle in the review of Leapor's *Poems, Monthly Review* of 1751, 30–31.

[64] Quoted in Landry, *Muses*, 98.

[65] Cf., for example, the statement of Elizabeth Bentley's patrons in the preface to her work, who deemed an introduction of the author essential for the success of the work (unpag.).

and critiqued on the same terms as the new bourgeois literature, that is, on their own terms and without any mitigating biographical or social circumstances. The fact that her patron published her work after her death prefaced by just such a representation of Leapor as dutiful daughter, humble servant, and natural genius states equally clearly either that Freemantle did not see Leapor's work on that level or that she thought it necessary to subordinate any possible poetic benefits (the potential of establishing Leapor's reputation as an author) to financial ones (the necessity of raising enough money to support Leapor's aging father).

Freemantle's dilemma is only one of many examples that could be used to demonstrate that the natural-genius aesthetic, translated into the practice of publishing peasant poets, appears to split into two rather contradictory discourses: on the one hand, the poet is defined as "virtuous" (a designation that entails the negation of all authorial ambition) and deserving pauper; on the other hand, the poet appears as an author in the natural-genius discourse, even, *ex negativo*, as a *good* author in the denial of authorship of poems that are simply too good to have been written by her. The collection must necessarily make claims to literary quality to justify publication; however, the purpose of publication is defined in every case as purely financial. The bourgeois patronage project, from its inception, seems to vacillate between patronage and charity, an apparent contradiction that I see as occasioned by a modern misreading of the patrons' adaptation of the genius aesthetic. For were one to take seriously the many claims in forewords that the purpose of publication was purely financial, one would arrive at a definition of bourgeois patronage not as patronage but as philanthropy. In contrast to the patronage of bourgeois authors of earlier ages, the goal was clearly not to enable poets to write but to secure their economic survival. The apparent contradiction lies in the fact that although the patron professes enormous respect for the poet's natural genius, there are no attempts to foster it beyond the first publication; as a result, few peasant authors ever had a chance to commit that "second offence" proclaimed in the *Monthly Review*. But the contradiction exists only as long as one equates the nature and genius discourse of aesthetic treatises with that in these forewords and overlooks the evidence that patrons, as well as critics, saw a substantial difference between a peasant's "rhyming" and bourgeois erudite poetry. The crucial difference is suggested in Leapor's refusal to permit her patron to insert a biographical introduction and in her patron's later dilemma: unlike bourgeois poetry, peasant "rhymes" were not seen as able to face their readership unaccompanied by a relation of the poet's life that could account for the defects in her verse. "Thus what the Author to the world presents, / Appears through numberless impediments; / And what of praise, or of dispraise, you view, / to Nature and the Muse is wholly due; / This, she presumes, will candid minds sufice, / And for her each defect apologise."[66] There is *no* review of any peasant's publication that does not refer to his or her life, and a good many that concentrate on the biography to the near-total or total exclusion of the work. Complimentary reviews usually add, already hinting at severe flaws in the writing, that the poet could have distinguished herself had she not been hampered by her modest circumstances.[67] The limitations of the life serve as an excuse for those of the work: "The short account which has been given of Mrs. *Leapor,* with the proposals for a subscription, it is hoped, will sufficiently apologize for the defects that shall be found in this collection."[68] Toward the end of the century, the assumption of the inevitable mediocrity of lower-class poetry was so universal that Elizabeth Bentley's patrons tried to forestall criticism of her poems by employing the discourse of mitigating circumstances of the peasant's life while comparing her poems favorably with the work of other poets of her class:

> . . . let a Critic consider, that no production of any Author was ever uniformly excellent, and that some of these pieces are occasional and temporary; there are also certain intensions and remissions of thought and imagination which must of necessity vary the energies of the mind; and after all, it may safely be asserted, that no Writer under the same disadvantages was ever less unequal. In general, Authors of this class have but a few brilliant passages to compensate for many a dreary page; it is not so with E. Bentley.[69]

---

[66] From "The Author's Plea" prefixed to the poetry of Jane Cave, 4.

[67] Cf. the following comments on Mary Masters ("And indeed there are few men, that would have wrote so well under the same discouragements, and disadvantages of education"; in Colman/Thornton, II, 146), Isobel Pagan ("What she could have achieved with a proper education and a decent standard of living we will unfortunately never know"; Stewart, 9), or Molly Leapor ("with so few advantages, she was capable of writing with so much credit to herself, there can be no doubt but, if her career had been prolonged, she would have greatly distinguished herself in the annals of female literature"; Anon., "Molly Leapor," in *Gentleman's Magazine,* 807). It is noteworthy that Leapor is here presented, at best, as potentially able to distinguish herself in the annals of *female* literature, clearly implying her obvious inability to compete with male bourgeois authors. On similar assessments of other poets, cf. the biographical essay in *Lexikon deutscher Dichter und Prosaisten,* 627 (on A. L. Karsch) and Ferguson's introduction to the re-edition of Collier's *The Woman's Labour,* xi.

[68] Review of Leapor's *Poems on Several Occasions* in *Monthly Review* of 1749, 14 (the emphasis is original).

[69] "Preface" to Bentley, unpag.

Degrees of more or "less unequal" were seen as the height of literary achievement possible for a poet of this class. There are few reviews that do not find some mitigating circumstance in the poet's life to excuse the poor quality of her writing, even fewer that take seriously the theme suggested by the patrons in the forewords — that these poems can be seen as the products of "untutored genius" and that this view speaks to the literary quality of the verse — and no reviews at all that consider these publications on par with works by acknowledged contemporary bourgeois authors. As the century progressed, there are even signs that reviewers began to resent the natural-genius discourse that was used to propel these authors onto the literary scene. The reviewers of Elizabeth Hands refused to review her poetry and instead reviewed her success in procuring subscribers:

> Whatever may be thought of the *character* of this poetry, we cannot but form the most favourable conclusions with respect to *that* of the writer . . . forming, as we do, our judgment from the uncommonly numerous list of subscribers: among whom are many names of persons of rank, and consideration. There could be no motive for extraordinary patronage, but a benevolent regard to merit — of some kind.[70]

The merit in the author's character can only be inferred from the number of her supporters, the idea that her writing could have any merit is scornfully ridiculed, if somewhat tempered in an attempt to avoid insulting the persons "of rank" among Hands's supporters. In a similar manner, the *Analytical Review* consigned Hands to well-deserved obscurity:

> As there is a respectable number of subscribers prefixed to this volume, we may be excused, if we do not lend a hand to support an humble muse, whose chief merit is a *desire* to please; — but, if we cannot praise the attempt of a servant-maid of low degree, to catch a poetical wreath, even after making due allowance for her situation, we will let her sing-song die in peace.[71]

It is not incorrect, but nonetheless misleading, to claim that according to bourgeois sensibilities rustics were predisposed to poetry,[72] or that the works of peasants made it into print because of the popularity of the cult of natural genius,[73] or even that bourgeois patrons entered into their

---

[70] Review of Hands, *The Death of Amnon, Monthly Review* of 1790, 346 (the emphases are original).

[71] Review of Hands, *The Death of Amnon, Analytical Review* of 1790, 96; the emphasis is original, presumably indicating the failure of Hands's "*desire* to please."

[72] Janet Todd, *Sensibility*, 57.

[73] Ashraf, 49.

relationship with lower-class poets because they valued their compositions as more genuine, spontaneous, original, or closer to nature. All of these motives may have played a part in the patrons' desire to promote their charges, but they are nonetheless misleading because all of these statements mistake the peasant's "rhyme" or "sing-song" for bourgeois "poetry" and confuse the aesthetic discourse of Duff, Gerard, and Sulzer with the practice of patronage, as it is outlined in the forewords. "Genius" and "nature" in these forewords may *allude* to the aesthetic discourse, but they are clearly meant to indicate an acknowledgment of the poet's unusual background, rather than her unusual talent. Whereas the aesthetic discourse, from mid-century on, pronounces natural inspiration superior to erudite composition, these forewords depict lower-class writings as far inferior to bourgeois and erudite literature. The nature and genius terminology that appears in forewords, and occasionally in reviews of peasant poets' works, is a borrowed discourse that makes use of the idiom and argumentative structure of aesthetic treatises and fills them with different content. It is doubtful that any bourgeois patron of the age ever saw their protégée's work as anything but a literary curiosity and an admirable sign of the poet's stamina in overcoming the odds. In some cases, their lack of respect for their charges' work, their inability to perceive it as the work of an *author*, can easily be demonstrated by the patron's assumption of the additional roles of muse and editor: at times, patrons suggested themes to their protégées, or edited or suppressed their work.[74] Both acts clearly suggest the patron's, not the poet's, autonomy over the work's inception as well as its publication. If reviewers marveled at the very existence of the work, given the social and educational limitations of its author, these limitations are equally frequently cited as detrimental to the sophistication of the writing, such as in reviews which hold lower-class authors incompetent to master stricter poetic forms.[75] The perceived difference between bourgeois "poetry" and lower-class "rhyming" persists in modern scholarship — for example, in Ashraf's confusion of peasant poetry with oral literature and her statement that "many of the best poems by working-class writers were (and

---

[74] Duck, Collier, and others wrote on subjects suggested by their patrons (cf. Southey, 95–96); Burns had to modify his initial sympathies for the French Revolution in order not to lose his patron's favors (Ferguson, *Eighteenth-Century Women Poets*, 94); Jean Adams, one of Burns's sources for folklore, did not include her poem "There's nae luck aboot the hoose" in her collection to uphold her reputation of piety and remain in her patron's good graces (Ashraf, 51).

[75] Peasant poets were frequently advised to write in free verse and considered incompetent to attempt the high literary pentameter couplet (cf. Landry, *Muses*, 211); for example, Duck was not thought competent to write in Miltonic verse (Southey, 105).

still are) more closely related to spoken rhythms than so-called elevated poetry. For this reason, . . . these verses should be 'heard' rather than read."[76] Ashraf's statement, although intended to compliment the literature of working-class authors, nonetheless reiterates what informs the discourse in the forewords and in most reviews: the essential *difference* between this literature and that of bourgeois authors, and its identification with a medium that precludes the long-term survival of the work (oral literature or the assertion that the peasant's first publication would also be her last), in contrast to the bourgeois author's work for posterity.

Ashraf's assessment is eerily reminiscent of the contemporary attitude toward the work of Anna Louisa Karsch, which was celebrated as long as it existed only in the form of spontaneously produced rhymes at court and severely criticized in reviews as soon as it appeared in print, and there were voices that claimed that she should have remained an oral performer. Karsch, however, was in a different league from the poets examined in this section: with Ann Yearsley, she was the only peasant poet of the age whose career can be said to parallel, in some ways, that of Stephen Duck, that first and supposedly most paradigmatic of all peasant poets. Unlike most of their colleagues, but like Stephen Duck, Karsch and Yearsley were taken from "the barn," enabled and encouraged to write, at least for a time, and the aesthetic natural-genius discourse that is employed by way of allusion in every other case became a sustained analysis in these two cases, an analysis that had consequences for the assessment of both poets' work and of aesthetic theory. It is thus worthwhile to re-examine the cases of Karsch and Yearsley, which represent the two best-documented and most often retold patronage stories of the century, with an eye to similarities to or differences from the patterns emerging in the patronage stories of their colleagues. Central to the two following sections are two questions: first, whether transplantation into the bourgeois context makes the crucial difference between patronage and charity, between poetry and rhyming, and between "menial maids" and authors; and second, to what extent a comparison between aesthetic treatises and texts relating directly to the practice of patronage (biographies and letters), written, in both Karsch's and Yearsley's cases, by their patrons, reveals the same incongruities between aesthetic theory and the practice of patronage as discussed previously.

---

[76] "Vielleicht ist das wesentlichste Merkmal darin zu sehen, daß viele der besten Dichtungen von Arbeiterschriftstellern enger auf dem Sprechrhythmus fußten (und noch fußen) als die sogenannte gehobene Dichtung. Aus diesem Grunde . . . sollten sie eher 'gehört' als gelesen werden" (Ashraf, 57).

## "The Poet's Silence is the Triumph of Taste": The Case of Anna Louisa Karsch

When Anna Louisa Karsch (1722–91) was spirited off to Berlin in the coach of Baron von Kottwitz in 1761, she began a literary existence that was, in many ways, a mirror of her earlier life in which she had toured the villages, providing impromptu occasional poems for weddings, funerals, christenings, and birthdays and made enough to live and support her children and her drunkard husband.[77] In Berlin, she was unencumbered by her husband, whom she had sold off to a Prussian army recruiter, and all children but her daughter Karoline. She exchanged the inns and farms for the court of Frederick the Great, where she astounded everyone with her ability to transform spontaneously words yelled out to her into poems that used these same words as rhymes. The parallel between this treatment of Karsch and that of other peasants by the same aristocracy, who flung coins among the peasants and were amused at the curious contortions the peasants made in picking them up, has been noted.[78] There can be little question that her aristocratic patrons, Frederick foremost among them, regarded Karsch as little more than a poetical court jester, and that his occasional engagement of her as evening entertainment had nothing at all to do with his patronage of authors he considered "true" geniuses, such as Voltaire. The story of Karsch's relationship with her royal patrons — initially Frederick, later his successor Frederick William II — contains possibly the most popular anecdotes of Karsch lore: Frederick the Great promised her a house and an annuity, such as Stephen Duck had received from Queen Caroline, but soon forgot all about it. Karsch's cheeky verse reminders to the King of his promise constitute an interesting counterdiscourse to the usual expressions in verse of the patronized poet's adulation and submissiveness. Ten years

---

[77] Karsch and Yearsley are by far the best-researched women peasant poets of the age, a fact that is, in large measure, due to the fact that they were also the only ones transplanted into the bourgeois literary scene. There is a vast body of secondary literature on Karsch; until the Karsch revival on the 200th anniversary of her death in 1991, however, much of it was largely biographical. On her biography, cf., among others, Klencke's and Chézy's biographies of her; Becker-Cantarino, "Belloisens Lebenslauf"; Anger; Menzel; Molzahn; and the biographical entries in *Lexikon deutschsprachiger Schriftsteller*, *Allgemeine Deutsche Biographie*, and *Lexikon deutscher Dichter und Prosaisten*. The most central critical and editorial texts on Karsch of recent years are Bennholdt-Thomsen and Runge's anthology, Nörtemann and Pott's edition of Karsch's correspondence with Gleim, Pott's analysis of that correspondence in *Briefgespräche,* and Schaffers's monograph.

[78] Cf. Schlaffer, 314.

after the promise was originally made, she returned Frederick's gift of two thalers with the following four-line poem:

> This gift is for a king unfit,
> And it does not my lot improve,
> No, it diminishes me a bit,
> Therefore, I send it back to you.[79]

This poem, as often as it has been quoted and discussed in Karsch scholarship, still raises questions about its exact meaning within the context of patronage.[80] Is Karsch, not unlike Leapor, attempting to exercise some control over the nature of her patronage, or at least indicating that she considers her poetic talent above such miserly recompense? Or does her proud refusal of the king's gift rest not on her estimation of her poetic talent, but merely constitute an insistence that he fulfill his promise? Her poetic response to the next sign of royal largesse (three thalers sent to her twenty years after the promise of house and annuity), which she wrote but did not send to the court, sheds some light on Karsch's attitude toward patronage:

> On orders of His Majesty
> Instead of building a house for me,
> Three thalers were paid out to me.
> The royal order was, indeed
> Promptly, genially obeyed,
> And my thanks I here convey.
> But this gift is not sufficient
> For a builder, however efficient
> To build me a house to stay.
> Else I would commission today
> Such a house in which one day
> Worms will feast on my remains,
> Giving their irritation the reins
> That the feast is such a shabby

---

[79] "Zwoo Thaler giebt kein großer König / Denn die vergrößern nicht mein Glük / Nein Sie erniedern mich ein wenig / Drumm geb ich sie zurük" (*"Bruder in Apoll,"* II, 397). The translations of all Karsch poems and letters are mine unless otherwise indicated.

[80] On Karsch and her patrons, cf. especially Scholz; Schlaffer; Mödersheim, "Igel oder Amor"; Krzywon, "Empfindung und Gesang"; Pott, "Berlin — Halberstadt — Berlin"; and Wappler, "Editionspraxis."

> meagre, sad, and worn out body
> An old woman's, whom her Sire
> Left ignobly to expire.[81]

These poems to Frederick already show a distinct interpretation of her relationship with her patrons: Karsch's argument is not the preservation of her poetic genius, but that of an old and destitute woman, a woman on the verge of starvation who lays claim to the king's *charity*, not his patronage.

Karsch untiringly applied to this charity to the end of her days, which became something of a controversy in her correspondence with one of her two most central bourgeois patrons, the Anacreontic poet and editor of her first volume, Johann Wilhelm Ludwig Gleim.[82] Gleim did his utmost to prevent Karsch from bothering the court with her requests,[83] criticized her supplications to the court,[84] and repeatedly flaunted his own aloofness toward royal favors or potential patronage.[85] How sensitive this subject must have been for Gleim is perhaps best demonstrated in the fact that Karsch's repeated appeals to him to consider editing a second volume of her poems[86] was taken up by him only

---

[81] The poem is entitled "Ann Quittungsstat im Jenner 1783": "Seine Maiestät befahlen / mir ann stat Ein Hauß zu baun / Doch drey Thaler auszuzahlen / Der Monarchbefehl ward Traun / Prommt, und freundlich ausgerichttet / Und zum Dannk binn ich verpflichttet / Aber vor drey Thaler kann / Zu Berlin kein Hubelman / mir mein lezttes Hauß erbauen / sonnst bestellt ich ohne Grauen / Heütte mir ein solches Hauß / Wo einst Würmer Taffel haltten / Und sich ärgern übern schmauß / bey des abgehärmtten altten / magren Weibes Cörperrest / Die der König seüffzen läßt" (in *"Bruder in Apoll,"* II, 450).

In other versions of the same poem, the final line reads "kümmern" (to waste away, cf. the version cited in *"Bruder in Apoll,"* II, 450) or "darben" (to starve, cf. the version published in Klencke's posthumous edition, *Gedichte,* 324–25).

[82] Pott and Nörtemann's edition of this correspondence, *"Mein Bruder in Apoll,"* is the first that does not correct Karsch's erratic spelling and includes the letters in a complete and unabridged form. Wherever possible, I cite from this edition; if quoting from letters that were not included in this edition, I cite either from Hausmann's or Beuys's editions of Karsch's letters. Karsch's correspondence with Gleim has been extensively analyzed by Pott (*Briefgespräche* and "Berlin — Halberstadt — Berlin"), Nörtemann ("Verehrung, Freundschaft, Liebe" and her "Nachwort" in the second volume of Karsch's *"Bruder in Apoll"*), Mödersheim ("Igel oder Amor"), Schaffers, and Nickisch.

[83] Cf. Gleim's continuous remonstrances not to petition the court in Karsch, *"Bruder in Apoll,"* I, 189, 220, and II, 125, 259, 268–69, and Karsch's response in II, 260–61.

[84] In Karsch, *"Bruder in Apoll,"* II, 136–37, 269.

[85] Cf. his letters to Karsch in *"Bruder in Apoll,"* II, 53, 131, and 320.

[86] Karsch, *"Bruder in Apoll,"* I, 198, 286; II, 6, 299; cf. also the letters in which she pleaded with others to "remind" Gleim of the second volume, for example in *"Bruder in Apoll,"* II, 479.

in answer to letters in which she threatens to supplicate the court, presumably as a form of appeasement:

> We will edit a collection of your *letters* and publish it on subscription, that is the main thing — but you, my dear, should not present us with any further reservations and hindrances; everything shall be done very swiftly, you shall receive so much of the yellow muck that you won't be obliged to intermingle with the ten thousand beggars who are bothering our most gracious king at the moment. . . .[87]

Gleim's obvious contempt of the fortune seekers around the throne ("beggars"), their mercenary attitude (conveyed in his disdainful wording, "yellow muck"), and his disgust at the thought that Karsch could meddle with such a crowd clearly convey a very different attitude toward royal patronage than Karsch's. Whereas she repeatedly and perhaps naively stated her firm intention to "weary the king with my pleas,"[88] he proudly refused, as he often stated, to "beg" at the throne;[89] whereas Karsch absolutely depended on the support of others for her livelihood, Gleim, who was comfortably off because of his employment as the canon of Halberstadt, could afford to judge patronage both tasteless and outdated. But Gleim's rhetoric aside, there are also indications that such patronage continued to hold its appeal both for him and for other poets of his class: Gleim himself had, at one time, applied to the royal generosity, a fact that he later denied emphatically in letters to Karsch;[90] and Karsch's attempts to secure her livelihood through royal generosity brought her into fierce competition with Karl Wilhelm Ramler. Karsch's envious reaction to the news that Ramler had received from the king that for which she had, for years, unsuccessfully applied — an annuity[91] — is perhaps more understandable than the fact that Ramler responded even

---

[87] In Karsch, *"Bruder in Apoll,"* II, 274: "Wir wollen eine Samlung Ihrer *Episteln* machen und auf Vorschuß herausgeben, das ist die hauptsache — Sie aber, meine beste! müßen uns keine hinderniße, keine Bedenklichkeiten mein' ich in den Weg legen; Alles soll rasch vonstatten gehn, sie sollen des gelben Koths so viel erhalten, daß Sie nicht nöthig haben sich zu mischen unter die zehntausend Bettler, die den besten König itzt umlagern. . . ." (The emphasis is original.) Cf. also Gleim's letters in the same edition, I, 201–2, and II, 125, 132, and 136. Neither the letter edition nor the repeatedly mentioned second volume of either poems or letters ever appeared.

[88] Karsch to Gleim, *"Bruder in Apoll,"* II, 18: " . . . ich hoffe das Er zulezt mit meiner Versart bekand werden soll, meiner bitten müde wird, und meine Geduld belohnet. . . ."

[89] Gleim to Karsch in *"Bruder in Apoll,"* II, 320.

[90] Karsch, *"Bruder in Apoll,"* II, 125.

[91] Karsch, *"Bruder in Apoll,"* II, 267.

more resentfully to Karsch's hopes of obtaining the king's patronage. As Karsch relates in a letter to Gleim,

> Mr. Ramler had another malcontent day yesterday. It is dreadful to be in his company on those occasions, everything anyone says offends him, and he gives continuous offence with his veiled bitter allusions. Someone, for example, tells him that I was received graciously by the Countess and saw the young Prince. This news gnaws at his heart. . . .
>
> Ramler took this as an occasion to make a remark on Insolence, always first to grab a hold of fortune, but ultimately destined to lose it again. He said he had finished an ode to Insolence. Tomorrow or the day after I'll write him a note and ask him for a copy of this ode, and I'll ask him whether he wouldn't also like to write a poem about Envy, and I'll tell him that Envy is a much bigger fool than Insolence or Forwardness could ever be.[92]

Karsch's poetic exchange of hostilities with Ramler not only illustrates her spirit and verve in answering back to a man who could, in some sense, also be regarded as one of her initial patrons — Ramler familiarized her with some rules of poesy when she first arrived in Berlin — but it also indicates the way in which Karsch's appeals to royal patronage were regarded by middle-class authors. In their response, they show themselves clearly torn between the advantages of royal patronage and the new bourgeois self-consciousness that defined literature as independent and the bourgeois author as "above" such "beggary." But the reasons behind both Gleim's attempts to prevent Karsch's supplications and Ramler's venomous reaction to their possible success are not only defined by a bourgeois attitude toward their own class but also toward hers. Gleim's attitude is best demonstrated in his comments on the potential deracination of another peasant who, in his account, represents the picture-perfect image of the rural laborer content in his lowly station: "One should not take the good man away from his plow — I would not do that, even if I were king — he is happy in his *current domestic pleasures,* if he stopped being a

---

[92] Karsch to Gleim, August 22, 1770, quoted in Beuys, 135–36: "Herr Ramler hatte gestern wieder seinen unzufriedenen Tag. Es ist übel, zu der Zeit mit ihm in Gesellschaft zu sein, alles beleidigt ihn, was man spricht, und er beleidigt durch versteckte Bitterkeiten unaufhörlich. Es muß ihm etwa jemand erzählt haben, daß ich von der Landgräfin wohl empfangen worden bin und den jungen Prinzen gesehen hätte. Diese Neuigkeit nagt ihm wieder am Herzen. . . .

Ramler nahm daher Gelegenheit, eine Anmerkung über die Unverschämtheit zu machen, daß sie ihr Glück am ersten erhaschen könnte, daß sie es aber endlich auch wieder verlöre. Er habe ein Gedicht über die Unverschämtheit fertig. Morgen oder übermorgen schreib ich ihm gewiß ein Billet und bitte mir das Gedicht aus und frage, ob er nicht auch eins über die Scheelsucht machen will, und sage ihm, daß dies eine viel größere Närrin ist, als die Unverschämtheit oder die Dreistigkeit sein kann."

peasant, he'd begin to be miserable —."[93] And although Karsch had long since been taken from her plow, and although he, as her patron, was ostensibly charged to enable her to make a living by writing, he transfers this attitude seamlessly to his protégée:

> Frau Karsch is quite right in not asking the King for an annuity. She wouldn't receive one; and kings should not provide poets with annuities; plow and spindle would stand idle if it was possible to earn one's bread through writing.
>
> One should offer this excellent woman employment as a governess in some public institution which would employ her talents. . . . She would make an outstanding governess in any institution that demands a woman's direction, and at the moment, there must be many of those in Berlin.[94]

Gleim's vagueness about what exactly Karsch could be employed to do indicates that the purpose of this letter is not actually to find her alternative employment, it is, rather, to express his sense of outrage that Karsch, a peasant born to laborious occupation, could not be made to *work*. Given her already complete deracination, bourgeois feminine employment (governess was one of the few possibilities of gainful employment open to bourgeois women of the time) suggests itself to him as the only option. Behind the entire scheme, which Gleim also repeatedly proposed to Karsch, is the by-now-familiar definition of writing poetry, if the act is performed by a peasant author, as *idleness* and therefore not only as morally objectionable but also as undermining the integrity of the state: Gleim's letter strongly evokes the discourse employed by Horace Walpole and others, who saw peasants, lured by the prospect of the fabulous riches with which their substandard verse would surely be rewarded, as deserting their plows and spindles in droves.

It is one of the paradoxes of Karsch's career that although a major part of her oeuvre consists of laudatory and appellatory occasional poems directed at royalty, her relationship with her bourgeois patrons was

---

[93] Letter dated March 7, 1784, in Karsch, *"Bruder in Apoll,"* II, 457: "Man muß aber den guten Mann nicht wegnehmen von seinem Pfluge — Das thät ich nicht, und wenn ich König wäre — Bey seinen *itzigen häußlichen Freuden* ist er glücklich, hört er auf ein Bauer zu seyn, so würd er anfangen unglücklich zu werden." (The emphasis is Gleim's.)

[94] Letter from Gleim to Rebelt, dated November 19, 1786: "Die Frau Karschin hat sehr recht, daß Sie den König um Gnadengehalt nicht bitten mag. Sie würde kein's bekommen; die Könige müßen auch den Dichtern Gnadengehalte nicht geben, Pflug und Spinrad würden still stehen, wenn Dichten Brod brächte.

Man sollte die vortrefliche Frau zur Aufseherinn machen, irgend einer öffentlichen Anstalt, die ihren Talenten Arbeit gäbe. . . . Aufsicht haben würde sie vortreflich über eine Anstalt, die eines Weibes Aufsicht fordert, wie dergleichen zu Berlin eine Menge seyn müßen" (Karsch, *"Bruder in Apoll,"* II, 494).

arguably much more significant for her writing. For while Frederick's patronage might have provided her with a financially secure existence, her bourgeois patrons also concerned themselves with her reputation as an author. To them, the phenomenon of Anna Louisa Karsch fulfilled the same function as that attributed to Leapor by her patron: she served as proof for the bourgeois theory of *Poeta nascitur*.[95] Two months after Karsch's arrival in Berlin, an awestruck Sulzer wrote to Bodmer:

> Here in Berlin, there has been an extraordinary apparition in circles of taste: a poetess formed by Nature alone, who, taught only by the muses, promises great things. . . . it is nothing to her to produce the finest thoughts on every subject and express them in excellent verse. I doubt very much that anyone has ever had language and rhyme as much in his power as this woman. She sits down in a large social gathering and amidst the chatter of twelve or more persons writes songs and odes of which no poet would need to be ashamed.[96]

Sulzer, who later claimed in his foreword to her poems that "poets are not formed through erudition and rules, but receive their calling and capacity from Nature alone,"[97] cites as proof of Karsch's natural genius and exemplification of this theory the same traits he mentions in his letter to Bodmer: the unconsciousness of her poetic production, her spontaneity and speed, her lack of formal education, and therefore her guaranteed lack of contact with poetic rules.[98] His assessment of Karsch also corresponds closely to his remarks in theoretical writings on the subjects of poetic inspiration, originality of invention, and poetic gen-

---

[95] On Karsch's instrumentalization in bourgeois definition of Art and authorship, cf. Mödersheim, "Fruchtbarste Bäume" and "Igel oder Amor"; Scholz; Bovenschen, 150–57; Schlaffer; and Schaffers.

[96] Letter to Bodmer, March 1761, cited in Hausmann, 74: "Es hat sich hier im Bereiche des Geschmacks eine wunderbare Erscheinung gezeigt: eine Dichterin, die blos die Natur gebildet hat und die, nur von den Musen gelehrt, große Dinge verspricht. . . . es kostet sie gar nichts, die feinsten Gedanken bei jedem Gegenstand zu erzeugen und in sehr guten Versen vorzutragen. Ich zweifle sehr, ob jemals ein Mensch die Sprache und den Reim so sehr in seiner Gewalt gehabt hat, als diese Frau. Sie setzt sich in einer großen Gesellschaft unter dem Geschwätz von zwölf oder mehr Personen hin, schreibt Lieder und Oden, deren sich kein Dichter zu schämen hätte."

[97] Sulzer's "Vorrede" to Karsch's *Auserlesene Gedichte* of 1764, vii-viii: "Es ist eine alte und bekannte Anmerkung, daß die Dichter nicht durch Unterricht und Regeln gebildet werden, sondern ihren Beruf und ihre Fähigkeiten blos von der Natur erhalten. . . . Das Beyspiel der Dichterin, von welcher wir hier einige auserlesene Lieder der Welt vorlegen, bestätiget die Wahrheit dieser Anmerkungen auf die unzweifelhafteste Weise."

[98] Sulzer's "Vorrede," vii-xxi.

ius.[99] Just as Sulzer views genius as a gift of nature, unattainable through training or education and closely linked with "physical circumstances"[100] in his aesthetic works, so he takes Karsch's biography as proof of the authenticity of her genius. In his foreword he writes,

> How indubitably our poetess has received her calling from Nature alone is evinced most clearly from all circumstances of her life. For in this life we find nothing, aside from natural inclination, that could possibly have instigated, artificially, her urge to write poetry, not a single circumstance that could lead us to surmise that erudite rules, in her case, take the place of genius.[101]

Karsch's literary career, in other words, depended on her continued ability to embody bourgeois theories of natural poetic genius, and she seems to have been quite aware of the role she played as an exemplification of genius aesthetics. Indications are that she did what she could to conform to this image by frequently emphasizing her humble origins and lack of formal education, and by minimizing her exposure to reading whenever she could.[102] "Art has no part of it," she claimed of her own writing, "and reading has only here and there added a touch."[103] After first hearing of Young's theory of natural genius, she professed herself a dedicated follower of his aesthetic and defined herself on his terms.[104] The

---

[99] Cf. Sulzer, "General Theory," 25–108, "Von der Kraft," and "Entwickelung des Begriffes vom Genie"; on Sulzer's genius aesthetic, cf. also Geitner, 285–88; Wolf, *Versuch*, 143–54; Gerth, 67; and Stüssel, 217–18; on the application of his theories to Karsch, cf. Schaffers, 68–79. There are also passages in his *General Theory*, however, in which he defines the ability to judge and edit as indispensable attributes of the great Artist, cf. the passages cited in Schaffers, 76–77.

[100] Sulzer, "Entwickelung": "Zuerst ist es klar, daß der innere Grad der thätigen Kraft der Seele, der dem Genie zur Grundlage dient, einzig und allein ein Geschenk der Natur ist, das durchaus durch keine Uebung erlangt werden kann: und wahrscheinlicher Weise hängt er größtentheils von der Beschaffenheit des Körpers ab" (319).

[101] Sulzer, "Vorrede," xi-xii: "Wie unzweifelhaft es sey, daß unsre Dichterin ihren Beruf allein von der Natur bekommen habe, erhellet am deutlichsten aus allen Umständen ihres Lebens. Denn darin finden wir nichts, das vermögend gewesen wäre, an statt des natürlichen Hangs einen künstlichen Trieb zur Dichtkunst in ihr zu erregen, keinen einzigen Umstand, woraus wir begreifen können, daß gelernte Regeln bey ihr die Stelle des Genies vertreten."

[102] Cf. her letters in *"Bruder in Apoll,"* I, 27, 148, 153, 169, 460, and II, 223; and her report of her meeting with Frederick the Great in a letter to Gleim: on that occasion, she introduced herself to the king as unerudite and inspired by "Nature" and Frederick's victories (cf. *"Bruder in Apoll,"* I, 182–85, reference 184).

[103] In her autobiographical letters to Sulzer: "die Kunst hat keinem Antheill daran, die belesenheit nur hat hier und da Einem Zug gethan" (*"Bruder in Apoll,"* I, 361).

[104] Cf. Karsch, *"Bruder in Apoll,"* I, 91–93.

story of her early and insatiable desire to read and write, which is so popular in the life stories of other peasant poets, appears in her biography as well, complete with a touching account of the strenuous parental opposition to her reading and writing (on the part of her mother and grandmother rather than her father and uncle, who supported her education but died too early to make much of a difference).[105] If Sulzer views the original impetus for her urge to write poetry as rooted in Nature, Karsch makes an effort to place it as closely to Nature as possible: according to her autobiographical letters, her love of poetry was first awakened by a young herdsman who read literature out loud to a circle of breathlessly listening peasant children.[106] In letters to Gleim, she frequently invokes the natural-genius theory and indirectly applies it to herself by emphasizing, as the primary traits of her writing, her speed,[107] spontaneity, the tremendous memory for which she was already famous, and the *compulsion* she felt to write poetry: her claim in one of her last letters that she wrote poetry in her sleep[108] directly echoes the mandate of unconscious poetic production issued in aesthetic treatises. Her letters to Gleim and others often contained verse passages, and she answered Gleim's objections to her rhymed letters[109] and his requests for proper prose epistles invariably with the comment that she could not help rhyming, and by advising him, with characteristic nerve, to read her verses as if they were prose.[110] To Hagestolz, she wrote, in apology for the rhymed beginning of her letter: "I notice I fell into rhyming again, as if I couldn't say everything that needs saying in prose. Rhyming has become such a habit for

---

[105] Cf. Karsch's autobiographical letters to Sulzer, which were intended to furnish the basis for his biographical foreword to her poems, *"Bruder in Apoll,"* I, 341–63; the story of her mother's and grandmother's opposition is on 343–44. Cf. also the account offered by Klencke, "Lebenslauf," 18.

[106] Letter to Sulzer, in *"Bruder in Apoll,"* I, 345; cf. also her letters to Gleim, in which she often claimed that she had learned to write by imitating "a shepherd's song" (e.g., in *"Bruder in Apoll,"* I, 148). On Karsch's construction of her own biography, cf. chapter 3.

[107] For example in her letter to Gleim in which she compared her muse with Hebrew women who "bear children without the aid of the midwife": "es gehet meiner Muse wie den hebräischen Weibern, Sie gebiehrt ohne den Geburtshelffer" (*"Bruder in Apoll,"* II, 19). Cf. also the same edition, II, 33.

[108] Cited in Hausmann, 381.

[109] Cf., for example, his letter in Karsch, *"Bruder in Apoll,"* II, 329.

[110] Cf. her response to Gleim's objections in *"Bruder in Apoll,"* II, 330–33, citation 332. The prose/verse debate was another longstanding controversy in the correspondence, cf. Nörtemann's "Nachwort" to the second volume of the edition, 541–42.

me, I cannot write any other way."[111] To Gleim, who was occasionally angered by her habit of writing verse letters, she once sent a similar apology, which was itself, cheekily enough, written in verse:

> Prose letters should I write, you say,
> But can I, with my wayward thoughts?
> Dear friend, your quarrel's not with me,
> My habit brings all pains to nought,
> Habit, this force of Nature strong
> Compels me to relentless verse
> And it's in verse that I, in my last song
> Will greet you even from my hearse[112]

In this depiction of herself as "compelled to verse," as literally unable to help it, she skillfully evokes the aesthetic discourse of the poet as medium, helpless in the grip of the muse. Paradoxically, Karsch, who insisted that her letters remain private documents and repeatedly refused to have them published, thus thwarted Gleim's attempts to make her letters appear more "private" and autobiographical (with an eye to potential publication) to forestall possible suspicions of the "literariness" of her letters that might be aroused by her rhymed interludes.

But if the phenomenon of Anna Louisa Karsch was instrumentalized, at least initially, as the exemplification of natural-genius theories, this image of her did not result in either poetological or financial autonomy for the actual poet. Although her first volume of poems was an unprecedented success, earning her the record honorarium of 2,000 thalers, she had no control over the capital, which was invested by her patrons Gleim and Sulzer, who acted as her legal guardians, on her behalf. When Karsch died in 1791, she left her children 3,600 thalers,[113] but during her lifetime, she meagerly subsisted on the interest of this investment and depended on the patronage of various supporters for her survival and the education of her children. As with other peasants, this financial dependence had poetological consequences because it defined the *reasons* for publishing her work as

---

[111] Quoted in Nickisch, 74: "Da binn ich nun schon wieder ins Reimen gekommen, als ob ich nicht In Prosa alles sagen könntte, was zu sagen ist, nu daß Reimen ward Mir einmahl so zur Gewohnheit, ich kanns nicht laßen. . . ."

[112] Karsch to Gleim, March 9, 1783, in *"Bruder in Apoll,"* II, 173: "Prosaisch schreiben soll ich dir / Kann ichs bey holprichtten Gedanken? / mein Herzfreund zannke nicht mitt mir / mitt der Gewohnheit must du zanken / die Nebengöttin der Natur / Zwinngt immer mich zum Sylbenmaaße / mir dünnkt daß ich derEinst nach Cahrons Überfuhr / Dich noch inn Verßen grüßen laße —"

[113] Cf. the commentary in Karsch, *"Bruder in Apoll,"* II, 377.

not literary but financial: the goal of the edition, as stated by Sulzer in the foreword, was to "rescue [Karsch] from the direst poverty."[114] Karsch herself, taking her cue from him, often defined her writing as occasional poetry written purely and exclusively for financial gain.[115] In letters to Gleim, she frequently tried to influence the manner in which her patrons provided for her financially and voiced her worries with respect to the security of the investment and frustration that her patrons consistently ignored her wish to use the capital for buying a house;[116] there are also indications that her patrons considered her financially unreliable and wasteful and controlled the capital, for this reason, all the more tightly.[117] Karsch's patrons, then, characterized their charge as an exemplification of natural genius and employed a rhetoric in which she appears as deserving of literary patronage, but also defined, via their firm control over Karsch's finances, that patronage as charity to the pauper, in much the same way as was the case for the poets discussed previously. The seemingly defining difference between Karsch and the poets discussed earlier, the central fact that Karsch was a deracinated poet and her permanent transplantation into the bourgeois literary scene, made no difference with respect to her authorial image: like her colleagues who were left in their original surroundings, she existed within this literary scene not as an autonomous poet but as a permanent pauper dependent on the charity of her patrons.

Her correspondence with Gleim, her only long-term patron (both Ramler and Sulzer withdrew their support immediately after publication of the first volume), bears this out. This correspondence documents an extraordinarily long-lived and complex relationship between patron and protégée, which begins with a misinterpretation of the poetological as the personal: Karsch, who swiftly fell in love with Gleim, mistook his Anacreontic discourse for an expression of real feeling.[118] She wrote him heartfelt love letters, he wrote her Anacreontic epistles that were designed to inspire her to write love poetry. "It is counterfeit feelings, not

---

[114] Sulzer, "Vorrede," xxiv: "Man hat Ursache, sich zu freuen, daß man diesen Weg eingeschlagen, eine Person von solchen Talenten, wenigstens aus der äussersten Dürftigkeit heraus zu reissen."

[115] For example, in Karsch, *"Bruder in Apoll,"* I, 276, 280–81.

[116] Cf. the letters in *"Bruder in Apoll,"* I, 263–64, 284, 289, 296, 315, and II, 9, 14, 253–54.

[117] Karsch reports resentfully in a letter to Gleim that Sulzer had claimed, supposedly in jest, that she would waste the entire capital if given the opportunity; cf. *"Bruder in Apoll,"* I, 289.

[118] Cf. the analysis in Nickisch, 75; Nörtemann, "Verehrung," 90–92; and Mödersheim, "Igel oder Amor," 30.

real ones, that make a poet," he claimed,[119] and described his "romance" with Karsch in a letter to Uz:

> Two lines will be sufficient to relate this romance. When I first saw her in Berlin last May, I told her she could be the German Sappho . . . but this would not be possible without a Phaon. She did me the honor of electing me to that position; if Phaon smiled, she sang the sweetest song, if Phaon frowned ever so slightly, the saddest poems issued from her pen; in all of our meetings we made use of every little circumstance, all kinds of affectations of love benefited her poetry. . . . In a manner of speaking, I experimented with her in various ways.[120]

What Gleim describes here is more than the Anacreontic love game that Karsch, presuming her ignorance of literary forms and conventions, would have had to mistake for reality: he is also defining himself in his new role as Karsch's patron, a role that transcends financial responsibilities. On the contrary, Gleim's concern here is entirely literary, expressed in his attempts to manipulate the situation to the effect of inducing Karsch to write her best love poems. The Anacreontic love game, the literary form he uses to that purpose, expresses itself in the letters in the assumption of various roles by both correspondents:[121] Gleim exists in his own letters as "Father Gleim," who defines himself primarily as a patron of younger and less experienced poets,[122] as the grenadier (his pseudonym for one of his early collections of patriotic poems), and as the shepherd Thyrsis, whose main role is that of the disdainful object of Sappho's affections; Karsch, in turn, is split between "Sappho," the poet-cum-melancholy-lover persona, and the light-hearted shepherdess Lalage, who functions as a counterrole to Sappho's part as tragic lover and shows herself more willing to participate in Thyrsis's Anacreontic game. Unlike Gleim, Karsch does not retain her own identity in this correspondence: for the first seven years, she signs her name almost exclusively "Sappho,"

---

[119] In a letter to Jacobi (" . . . die wahren Empfindungen nicht, sondern die angenommenen machen den Dichter"); cited in *"Bruder in Apoll,"* II, 446.

[120] Letter from Gleim to Uz, January 16, 1762, cited in Hausmann, 127–28: "Den Roman kann ich Ihnen in zwei Zeilen erzählen. Ich sagte, als ich zu Berlin im letzten Mai sie zum erstenmal sah, sie könnte eine deutsche Sappho sein . . . ohne einen Phaon zu haben, wäre es nicht angegangen. Sie tat mir die Ehre und wählte mich dazu; lächelte Phaon, so sang sie das süßeste Lied, hatte er eine kaum merkliche Wolke auf der Stirn, so hörte man den traurigsten Gesang; wir machten in unseren Gesellschaften uns alle kleinen Umstände zunutze, alle Arten von Affekten der Liebe bekam ihr Gesang . . . ich habe mit ihr gleichsam manche Versuche angestellt."

[121] On the role play in Karsch's correspondence with Gleim, cf. Nörtemann, "Verehrung, Freundschaft, Liebe."

[122] Karsch, *"Bruder in Apoll,"* II, 210, 458.

thus assuming the role assigned to her by Gleim. Essentially, what this means is that for several years of the correspondence, Karsch existed to Gleim *only* in her poetic roles, and that this fact was silently, in appellation, signature, and role-play in the letters themselves, acknowledged by both parties. Accepting the division between Gleim and Thyrsis, Karsch could, as either Sappho or Lalage, transfer her love and feelings of rejection to Thyrsis and complain to her friend Gleim about Thyrsis's coldness,[123] but there are also indications in the correspondence that she indirectly punished Gleim, her patron who exhorted her to write beautiful love poetry while refusing her love, by claiming that Sappho's love for Thyrsis had died and that Sappho's muse had fallen silent as a result.[124] In so doing, she withheld from Gleim the only thing he wanted from her: poems, preferably passionate love poems, and letters expressing the same sentiment. Conversely, Gleim occasionally refused to act as Karsch's patron by transferring his duties of editing to his shepherd persona — for example, in his statement that Thyrsis would take over the correction of Karsch's poems (indicating Gleim's refusal to have anything to do with them)[125] or, after an altercation with Karsch, in his (Gleim's) intention of following Thyrsis's advice to refrain from publishing a second volume of Karsch's poems.[126]

Gleim's "experiments" with Karsch thus appear manipulative in the extreme and clearly indicate the low degree of poetic autonomy that he granted his protégée: in other letters, he gave her concrete instructions for her writing,[127] criticized her "weak" love poems,[128] and insisted on his interpretive monopoly of her work. Ultimately, Karsch had as little control over her work as she had over her finances. Because she was a fast and prolific writer and extremely generous with her poems, her poems were widely distributed; when she attempted to collect some of them for the planned second volume, she often no longer had originals and had to either copy from published versions or appeal to others to provide her with copies.[129] Control over her work thus passed to others, and because Gleim was the principal collector of her work, he exercised almost total control initially over her writing and throughout her life over her pub-

---

[123] Karsch, *"Bruder in Apoll,"* I, 83.

[124] Karsch, *"Bruder in Apoll,"* I, 35, 77, 82, 169.

[125] Karsch, *"Bruder in Apoll,"* I, 89.

[126] Karsch, *"Bruder in Apoll,"* II, 182.

[127] Karsch, *"Bruder in Apoll,"* I, 63.

[128] Karsch, *"Bruder in Apoll,"* I, 80.

[129] Cf. her letters in *"Bruder in Apoll,"* I, 275; II, 24, 26, 280.

lishing.¹³⁰ Sulzer's designation of Karsch's poems as "odes," a designation she was uncomfortable with but unable to prevent;¹³¹ Karsch's unsuccessful attempts to influence the selection of poems for her first volume;¹³² Karsch's inability to prevent the publication of Ramler's "corrected" version of one of her poems — an alteration she was not shown before publication;¹³³ and Karsch's own frequent complaints that she was given no authority over her writing and publishing¹³⁴ all testify eloquently to the fact that she occupied, in the minds of her patrons, a different status from that of the autonomous bourgeois author.

The case that best demonstrates this fact was also the only case in which Karsch earnestly opposed her patron in her attempt to exercise influence over the fate of her work, and one that reveals the fundamental difference of interpretation of Karsch's work that divided patron and protégée. Following the 1768 publication of Gleim's and Jacobi's sentimental correspondence, in which there was also an account offered of Karsch's unrequited attachment to Gleim, Gleim approached Karsch with the plan of publishing her love letters and poems addressed to him, her "Sapphic poetry," as he termed it; how attached he must have been to this idea is evidenced by the fact that he frequently returns to it in later years, despite Karsch's vehement objections.¹³⁵ Karsch's reaction to this plan was prompt and unequivocal:

> I know that it is possible to love in such a way, but the better I know it, the more I feel the awkwardness of your ridicule of my platonic, pure and perhaps more sincere love for you, and why did Mr. Jacobi now have to inform the entire world of it? He could have saved himself the trouble of portraying the German Sappho's muse in this manner, how she sadly and tenderly pursues a poetic genius who grants her a glance of approval, but not of love, I am too honest to conceal the fact that your darling's pride insults me, even more insulting is the way in which he has been informed of all that which I, for the benefit of my tranquility, have already forgotten, he reminds me of it in an unpleasant manner, now it would be an open affront to me if the public should read the songs which were written for very few trusted friends / I forbid their publication, and if they were in my keeping I would even to-

---

¹³⁰ Cf., for example, his letter to Karsch in *"Bruder in Apoll,"* I, 305, in which he asks her for a copy of everything she writes.
¹³¹ Karsch, *"Bruder in Apoll,"* I, 129.
¹³² Karsch, *"Bruder in Apoll"* I, 163–64.
¹³³ Karsch, *"Bruder in Apoll"* II, 72.
¹³⁴ Karsch, *"Bruder in Apoll"* II, 67, 257, and 272.
¹³⁵ For example, in 1774 (Karsch, *"Bruder in Apoll,"* II, 66–67) and 1786 (II, 254).

day build a fire in my hearth and burn everything, for what interest of mine could it be to have posterity aware that Gleim was loved by me without returning my love, put yourself in my position and then answer me whether this would be a matter of indifference to you![136]

Essentially, Karsch's objections to the publication of her letters touch on two points: the fact that her patron not only assumed the right to publish her work as he saw fit but also the right to interpret it as he saw fit, regardless of her attempts to assume authorial rights over her work, which included, in this case, the right of proclaiming an authorial intention in creating the work that directly contradicted his interpretation. The works that the author defines as private documents (love letters from Karsch to Gleim) are interpreted by their first reader as literary compositions (Anacreontic epistolary effusions from "Sappho" to "Thyrsis," not unlike those exchanged between Gleim and Jacobi). The triangular love story that was clad by Jacobi in the customary antique trappings (Sappho in pursuit of her unwilling shepherd, as related by the shepherd's later friend and confidante) was read by Karsch as an embarrassing exposure of her feelings and as a sign of the insufferable pride of the real-life friend/lover who succeeded her in Gleim's affections. One could, of course, read this story, as has often been done, as evidence of Karsch's ignorance of poetic conventions and her personal naivete in mistaking fiction for reality, an interpretation that would again leave us with a view of Karsch as the naively inspired poetic genius and/or simple-minded country bumpkin. But perhaps more interesting is what this story indicates about the process of patronage as she experienced it, for in that context, her naivete was

---

[136] Letter to Gleim in *"Bruder in Apoll,"* I, 312–13: "ich weis es daß man auff diese Art lieben kann, doch je mehr ich diß weiß, je mehr ist es mir empfindlich daß Sie ehedem meine eben so platonische, reine und vieleicht auffrichtigerre Liebe zum Gelächter machten, und warum mußt es anietzt Herr Jacobi der ganzen Wellt erzählen? Er hätte sich die bemühung erspahren könen mit welcher die Muse der deutschen Sappho gemahlt wird, wie Sie Traurig und zärtlich einem dichtrischen Genius verfolgt, der Ihr einem blik voll Beyfall, aber nicht voll Liebe zuwirfft, ich Bin zu Ehrlich als daß ichs verhöhlen könnte, dieser Stolz Ihres Lieblings Beleidiget mich, noch mehr Beleidiget mich die Art mit der man Ihn von alle dem untterrichtet haben wird, was ich zu meiner Beruhiung schon vergeßen hatte, Er erinnert mich auff eine unangenehme Weise wieder daran, nunmehr würd es für mich eine öffentliche Beschimpfung sein wenn daß Publicum die Lieder lesen Soltte die nur wenig Vertrauten hörbar waren / ich verbitte die Bekantmachung davon, wären Sie in meiner Gewalt so würde noch heut ein Altar von feldsteinen auff meinem Heerd gebaut, und alles verbrannt, denn was kan mir daran liegen daß die Nachwellt weiß Gleim sey von mir ohne Gegenliebe geliebt worden, sezen Sie sich an meine Stelle, und dann antworten Sie mir ob es Ihnen gleichgültig sein würde!"

There was no attempt made to represent Karsch's erratic spelling in the translation; however, I have tried to approximate Karsch's scarce usage of punctuation.

first used to influence her writing and later to assume control not only of her publishing, but also of the creation of her authorial image.

Perhaps the most revealing indication of how Gleim as patron viewed Karsch as poet manifests itself in another recurring controversy in the correspondence: at its center was the fact that Karsch was unable, as Gleim charged and Karsch readily admitted, to edit her writing; she was "incapable of work," as Gleim once put it.[137] The reason this controversy goes to the heart of Karsch's authorial image is that Gleim's exhortation to edit and correct is inconsistent with the fiction of Karsch as Nature's Child on which the authority of the edition rested. Sulzer did his best to promote this view in the foreword — for example, in his definition of those poems "which she wrote in the first heat of her imagination" as her "best poems," whereas "those she produced with intent and calm reflection all show clear signs of constraint and lack of poetic inspiration."[138] Paradoxically, Karsch's poems had to be severely edited by Gleim[139] before they could be sold as the original, spontaneous, and "unlettered" effusions of "natural genius." To take the rhetoric of natural genius seriously by publishing her work as she wrote it obviously never occurred to Gleim: his requests that she rework her poems, clearly fuelled by his fear of negative reviews and Sulzer's report that there was hardly even a mediocre poem among the dozens she daily delivered to him for the edition, appear with increasing frequency and urgency as the publication date approaches.[140] To Gleim's chagrin, Karsch refused, and indirectly justified her obstinacy by recourse to the very image that her patrons had created of her. She once answered his angry exhortations to rework her poems with a long, flowery evocation of her rustic origins, complete with an idyllic description of her "Horatian" country home and surrounding scenery and a touching family portrait of contentedness in poverty.[141] Implicitly, her response is to point out that the Child of Nature cannot rework her spontaneous creations and that nature-inspired work, in its utter detachment from rule-based erudite poetry, is

---

[137] Gleim in a letter to Uz: "Arbeiten kan sie nicht; und so lieb ihr Horatz ist, so ist ihr doch nicht möglich, die Feile zu gebrauchen"; October 8, 1761, cited in Anger, "Nachwort" (1966), 9.

[138] Sulzer, "Vorrede," ix: "Die Lieder, welche ihr am besten gelungen, sind alle in der Hitze der Einbildungskraft geschrieben, da hingegen die, welche sie aus Vorsatz und mit ruhiger Ueberlegung verfertiget, allemal das Kennzeichen des Zwanges und den Mangel der Muse nicht undeutlich bemerken lassen."

[139] Cf. his remarks on editing her work in *"Bruder in Apoll,"* I, 44, 161, 240, and Karsch asking him to "correct" her poems in the same edition, I, 59.

[140] Karsch, *"Bruder in Apoll,"* I, 160–62, 181.

[141] Letter to Gleim, December 23, 1762, *"Bruder in Apoll,"* I, 168–70.

not subject to rule-based criticism. It is one of many indications in the correspondence that Karsch was quite aware of the role she was made to play in bourgeois poetology, and that she played it to the hilt in an attempt to gain a modicum of authority over her writing.

Karsch's consciousness of her role as patronized poet also finds expression in her correspondence with Gleim: she was keenly aware of the humiliation inherent in her financial dependence and occasionally associated this situation with her status as a recipient of bourgeois patronage. She once described the intense mortification she experienced on her birthday, which she had to celebrate with bourgeois and aristocratic supporters while her two brothers were dispatched to the servants' quarters,[142] and on another occasion compared the money doled out to her to the gift of a hand-me-down skirt, accompanied by strict instructions on how often she was permitted to wear it and where she was supposed to store it when not wearing it.[143] She even once wrote a satire on her beloved patron Gleim, as she ruefully confessed in a letter to Laurens van Santen:

> I very much regret the satire of which you have heard, I owe much to the man [Gleim], he has done much for me, and whether the basis of his actions was generosity, philanthropy and amiable good-will or vanity and ambition is immaterial because regardless of his motivations, I am being helped. . . .[144]

It is this and similar remarks that might induce us to re-evaluate the image of Karsch as the naive and unlettered rustic poet: if she was unable to distinguish, in the first years of her correspondence with Gleim, between Anacreontic fiction and reality, she later developed some lucid insights into the mechanisms of patronage. Her obvious affection for Gleim did not prevent her from attributing to him possibly selfish motives for his support of her (implied in her letter to van Santen is his ambition to present himself as her "discoverer"); she was keenly aware of her financial dependence and objected to it to the end of her days, and above all, she was quite conscious of the ways in which bourgeois patrons instrumentalized her in support of the aesthetic theory of natural poetic genius, a definition she quite deliberately adopted for herself because she knew that her entire career depended on this construction. Essentially,

---

[142] Karsch, *"Bruder in Apoll,"* I, 171.

[143] Karsch, *"Bruder in Apoll"* I, 263.

[144] Letter dated September 18, 1771, cited in *"Bruder in Apoll,"* II, 388: " . . . indessen reuet mich die Posse recht sehr von der Sie gehöret haben, ich bin dem Manne [Gleim] viel Verbündligkeit schüldig, Er that viel für mich, und die Quelle Seiner Handlungen mag nun Grossmuth, Menschenliebe, herzliches Wohlwollen, oder Eittelkeit und Ruhmsucht gewesen sein, So wird mir doch dadurch geholffen. . . ."

Karsch did her best to adjust to a poetological environment that gave her no chance at authorial self-definition, and while she herself reacted serenely to contemporary reviews and was not, she frequently insisted, in the least interested in posthumous fame,[145] how her contemporaries and posterity judged her should be of some interest to us, because these assessments attest both to the revision of the natural-genius aesthetic and to the consequences of its application to Karsch for her reception in the eighteenth century and later.

The reviews of Karsch's first edition are interesting not only with respect to Karsch's reception, but also show clearly that the genius aesthetic on which Karsch's publication rested was being revised *in light of this publication*. One example is the sudden distinction in reviews between the natural poet and poetic genius, in contrast to aesthetic treatises, which commonly identified the two. The *Journal Etranger* attested her "feeling" and "intuition" and professed great admiration for her gifts of "improvisation," but clearly distinguished between her talents and true poetic "genius."[146] Similarly, the *Journal Encyclopédique* defined her as a "natural" poet by referring to her unusual "imagination" and by repeating the relevant parts of her biography (she is presented as composing poetry while herding her cows), but claimed that she could not be considered a "genius," a term reserved for the "truly great" such as Ramler and Gleim (and it is, of course, significant that the review compares her unfavorably to two of her patrons).[147] The reviewer's central objection is the same as Gleim's, namely that Karsch did not rework her poems and dared publish them as impromptus.[148] It is this aspect that defined her reception from the earliest reviews to recent scholarly assessments: the *difference* between Karsch and "true" — that is, bourgeois and erudite — authorship. Two points are worth making here, one concerning Karsch's reception, the other regarding the ways in which her early reception in turn influenced the contemporary reading of the genius aesthetic. The first point has been forcefully made by Schlaffer and Scholz: as long as Karsch was content to inundate courtly and other societies with skillful occasional rhymes, the praise of her natural abilities continued unabated; as soon as she attempted to *publish* her poetry, her work became subject to the criticism of erudite bourgeois literati who, near-unanimously, voiced misgivings about the aesthetic quality of her

---

[145] Karsch, *"Bruder in Apoll,"* I, 81, 153.

[146] Cf. Gärtner, 55–56.

[147] Review of Karsch, *Auserlesene Gedichte, Journal Encyclopédique*, 76–86.

[148] Review of Karsch in *Journal Encyclopédique*, 83.

writing. The second point is that as soon as the genius aesthetic was directly applied to Karsch, it lost that aspect of *superiority* over erudite poetic production that is clearly implied in aesthetic treatises (cf. Young's remarks on the "original" [unerudite] versus the "secondary" poetic genius, who is defined as gaining his poetic inspiration from reading). On the contrary, the very attributes that defined Karsch as a natural genius — her speed, spontaneity, and lack of formal education — could be, and were, used simultaneously to justify her publication and to disqualify her from consideration as a professional author. The proclamation of Karsch's natural genius, in many reviews, leads seamlessly to the disqualification of her writing as mediocre — for example, in Heinse's remark that her handwritten poems were better than anything she ever published[149] or Herder's ambivalent description of her work as the "products of a rich poetic imagination," but nonetheless "flung together and displaying no plan, no economy of images, no knowledge of lyric periods."[150] Karsch's swift descent, postpublication, from natural genius to mediocre occasional poet can be paradigmatically traced in Mendelssohn's review of her work: at the outset stands an already ambivalent depiction of Karsch as Nature's Child, an inspired self-taught poet who "scribbled off" a collection of poems with miraculous speed.[151] But inspiration alone, he claims, does not make a poet: the fire of imagination, he claims in a theoretical treatise entitled *Genie*, must be tempered by reason and contemplation; genius, in other words, must edit after it writes.[152] In his review of Karsch, Karsch's "impromptu" poems appear not as manifestations of, but as counterexamples to, true poetic genius: "the best mind becomes unsuited to higher aspirations if it produces too many impromptu poems because it will become accustomed to speed and carelessness."[153] From reading Karsch's literature, he makes some central assumptions about Karsch's mode of writing, which in turn serve

---

[149] Heinse, 147.

[150] Herder, "Sappho und Karschin," 351: "so sind doch die Karschischen Gedichte damit [Dionysian poetry] nicht zu vergleichen, die ohne Plan im Ganzen, ohne Oekonomie der Bilder, ohne Känntniß des Lyrischen Perioden, hingeworfene Geburten einer reichen Dichterischen Einbildungskraft sind."

[151] Cf. Mendelssohn, 575: " . . . daß sie in einer kurzen Zeit diesen ganzen Band von Gedichten hingeschrieben, dem Wortverstande nach *hingeschrieben* hat. . . ." (The emphasis is Mendelssohn's.)

[152] Mendelssohn, 169–71.

[153] Mendelssohn, 577: "Man hätte ihr sagen sollen . . . daß . . . der beste Kopf, wenn er zu viel aus dem *Stegreife* dichtet, zu diesen höhern Schönheiten ganz untüchtig werden muß, indem er sich zu sehr an Eilfertigkeit und Nachläßigkeit gewöhnt" (emphasis original).

to disqualify her work: "More than once I thought to notice her pride of her own ability to write things down *quickly,* yet more mature consideration should cause her to be *ashamed* of this ability."[154] His advice to Karsch is, again echoing Gleim's demands, to show her respect for her readership and posterity by reworking her poems "countless times" before publication.[155] Like other reviewers, Mendelssohn claims that Karsch is principally not comparable with other poets,[156] but the aesthetic discourse that viewed this incomparability as a sign of the natural genius's superiority over erudite authorship is here inverted in the reassessment of unerudite writing as resoundingly mediocre.

In terms of Karsch's authorial position, Mendelssohn's review shows some interesting contradictions. On the one hand, he professes himself clearly aware of Karsch's position as a *patronized* poet: he repeatedly blames her patrons (rather than the author) for publishing her drivel, thus assuming (correctly) that she had no control over her own publication, and regrets her patrons' hasty proclamation of Karsch's genius, instead of, as they should have done, putting her in her place.[157] He himself metaphorically assumes this role by advising Karsch to "tremble" before her next publication and by stating that her future poetic career depended entirely on her *"obedience"* to her patrons.[158] But although the *author* in his review is clearly defined as worlds apart from the sovereign bourgeois author, her *work* is judged according to exactly the same standards that would be employed in judging his:

> As long as these poems were passed around in manuscript form, consideration of the poet's sex and circumstances helped cover up many a small flaw and augment many a little beauty. But as soon as the reader takes a *book* in his hand in order to read it, he will forget who the author was and what his circumstances were. A king, a woman, a Jew, what does it matter? Whoever has the ambition of becoming a writer must be judged as an author, all other considerations set aside. Without

---

[154] Mendelssohn, 599: "Mich dünkt mehr als einmahl bemerkt zu haben, daß sie sich auf das *hinschreiben* etwas zu gute thut, und sie solte es durch reifes Nachdenken dahin bringen, daß sie sich desselben *schämen* lernte." (The emphases are Mendelssohn's.)

[155] Mendelssohn, 598: "allein sie sollte nunmehr auch lernen, aus Hochachtung für das Publikum und für die Nachwelt, ein jedes Gedicht unzählichemale in die Hand nehmen, bevor sie es bekannt werden läßt."

[156] Mendelssohn, 576.

[157] Mendelssohn 577.

[158] Mendelssohn's repeated exhortation to Karsch to "tremble" on 578 and 600; on the subject of obedience to her patrons: "Wenn ich aber voraussetze, daß ihr einsichtsvolle Freunde den besten Rath geben werden, so wünschte ich auch recht sehr, daß unsere Dichterin *folgsam* seyn möchte" (599, the emphasis is Mendelssohn's).

considering the person, the impartial judge looks only at the thing, and his judgment will certainly be all the more severe, the higher his expectations were raised, and the greater the acclaim was with which a work was previously extolled.[159]

Mendelssohn's review is clearly informed by the new bourgeois attitude toward literature, an attitude that, I would argue, has gone on to influence the production, reception, and teaching of literature over the past 200 years. Literature, in this new assessment, is judged independently not only from patronage but also independently of its author. In Barthes's words: "the author is dead, long live the work"; the merit of the work is assessed irrespective of authorial circumstance, background, or biography. The new concept of *authorship* demands, somewhat paradoxically, a complete disregard of the author in favor of the supremacy of the work. But because the publication of peasant poetry, as the biographical forewords and reviews clearly attest and as Mendelssohn was also aware, *depends* on the biographical contextualization of the work, the ultimate conclusion of Mendelssohn's review is quite simply the exclusion of lower-class poets from the business of literature. Directly following his agreement with Sulzer's assessment that Karsch's best poems are those which she wrote "in the first heat of her imagination" and that her mediocre poems are the ones she wrote "with intention and calm reflection,"[160] he disqualifies what he claims are her best poems from publication: "The world does not demand of her the production of impromptu poems. To the reader of her poems, it is immaterial whether she has spent one hour or two months in their writing."[161]

Mendelssohn's review of Karsch's work can be considered more than a little disingenuous, for while proclaiming the new independence of

---

[159] Mendelssohn, 578: "So lange diese Gedichte nur noch geschrieben von Hand zu Hand herum giengen, half die Rücksicht auf das Geschlecht und die Umstände der Dichterin manchen kleinen Fehler bedecken, manche kleine Schönheit aufmutzen. So bald der Leser aber ein *Buch* in die Hand nimmt, um zu lesen; so wird er vergessen, wer der Verfasser sey, und in welchen Umständen er sich befunden. Ein König, ein Frauenzimmer, ein Jude, was thut dieses zur Sache? Wer die Ehrbegierde hat, Schriftsteller zu seyn, muß alle Nebenbetrachtungen bey Seite gesetzt, als Schriftsteller beurtheilt werden. Ohne Ansehen der Person siehet der unerbittliche Richter nur auf die Sache, und sein Urtheil wird ganz gewiß desto strenger ausfallen, je mehr man ihm versprochen, je grösser das Geschrey war, mit welchem man ihm ein Werk angepriesen hat."

For an analysis of this passage, cf. Barndt, 174.

[160] Mendelssohn, 599, quoting Sulzer: "in der Hitze der Einbildungskraft geschrieben" versus "mit ruhiger Ueberlegung verfertiget."

[161] Mendelssohn, 599: "Die Welt fodert von ihr keine Gedichte aus dem Stegreife. Dem Leser, der ihre Gedichte lieset, ist es einerley, ob sie eine Stunde oder zwey Monate mit der Verfertigung zugebracht hat."

literature from its author, he himself seems just as occupied with the author as with her work: his obsessively repeated indictments of Karsch for her obstinacy in refusing to make use of the "cultivation" she needed so badly and her insolence in approaching her critics without trembling[162] betray the primary purpose of the review as that of putting the peasant in her place. But his review is an excellent indication to what extent Karsch, even during her lifetime, was already caught in the controversy between the aesthetic image of the spontaneously inspired natural poet and the new bourgeois understanding of literature as independent of patron, author, or contextualization of any kind.[163]

Gerstenberg, in his spirited defense of Karsch against attackers like Mendelssohn, must have seen some of this broader context when he defined Karsch as a natural genius, very much in line with the aesthetic tradition, as documented in his comparison of Karsch with Dante and Shakespeare.[164] Gerstenberg's hesitant wish for an original and unedited volume of Karsch's poetry ("too much is lost, to observers of Nature, in the editing process"[165]) is immediately retracted because of his concern that such a publication would be savaged by Karsch's erudite critics. "The poet's silence is the triumph of taste":[166] perhaps not entirely unfairly, he saw Mendelssohn's devastating review as less concerned with Karsch's work than with silencing the poet, less as an honest review of a publication than a battle fought in the war of poetologies.

Posthumous assessments of Karsch, in both the nineteenth and the twentieth centuries, have been unable to divorce their analyses of her writing from the alternative assessments of her as either natural genius (that is, in contrast to contemporary bourgeois literature) or mediocre occasional poet (that is, in the context of contemporary bourgeois literature). Achim von Arnim, for example, speculated that her improvised poems must surely have been her best; he regretted that her poems were disfigured by her erudite editors and lamented the nonexistence of biographical poems, particularly poems describing her bucolic origins, thus

---

[162] Mendelssohn, 578, 600.

[163] On Karsch's contradictory treatment in contemporary reviews, cf. Barndt, 174.

[164] Heinrich Wilhelm von Gerstenberg, "12. Brief über Merkwürdigkeiten der Litteratur," cited in G. Wolf, 245.

[165] Gerstenberg, cited in G. Wolf, 245: "Ich war voreilig genug zu wünschen, daß die Dichterin den großen Vorrat ihrer Rhapsodien ohne Zurückhaltung ans Licht hervorziehen möchte, weil ich mir einbildete, daß den Beobachtern der Natur durch die Feile zu viel entzogen werden . . . dürfte."

[166] Gerstenberg, cited in G. Wolf, 246: "Die Dichterin schweigt, und der Geschmack triumphiert."

clearly legitimizing the reading of Karsch's oeuvre in light of her life.[167] Karsch's daughter Karoline von Klencke and her granddaughter Helmina von Chézy, both of whom published biographies of Karsch, presented her as a natural genius, defined largely through her rustic origins and ignorance of poetic rules and formal training; in both accounts, Karsch's contact with her erudite patrons is clearly presented as curbing her spontaneity and spoiling her poetic flight of fancy.[168] Notwithstanding recent assessments that the poet was much better read, more familiar with rules of prosody, and more willing and able to correct her work than admitted by either Karsch herself or her contemporary image makers,[169] the view of Karsch as Pure Nature has persisted into nineteenth- and twentieth-century criticism, where Karsch is either upbraided for her inability to revise her poems[170] — that is, for her failure to conform to Gleim's and Mendelssohn's image of a bourgeois author — or, alternately, for her failure to emancipate herself from the bourgeois influence which marred her "natural" expressions of "feeling" with parroted allusions to mythology and ill-fitting trappings of bourgeois erudition.[171] Such assessments are only possible by disregarding the context of patronage that enabled Karsch to write but also directed her writing, controlled her publication, and shaped her authorial image. Karsch was caught between conflicting models of authorship: between the nature poet of aesthetics and the occasional rhymer of criticism, between the patronized

---

[167] Arnim, 56.

[168] Cf. Klencke, "Lebenslauf," 28–29, 72–73, 91–92; Chézy, "Meine Großmutter," 14, 49, 72, 91–92; on the construction of Karsch's life in (auto)biographies, cf. chapter 3.

[169] Cf. Fell, 99; Kastinger Riley, "Anna Louisa Karsch," 143; Becker-Cantarino, "Belloisens Lebenslauf," 17; Krzywon, "Empfindung und Gesang," 342–43, and "Tradition und Wandel," 19, 32–33, 35; Schaffers, 39; Bennholdt-Thomsen and Runge, "Vorwort," 9; Mödersheim, "Fruchtbarste Bäume," 44–46 and "Igel oder Amor," 32; Scholz, 137. Krzywon provides evidence for Karsch's deliberate employment of those very literary forms the knowledge of which was consistently denied by her contemporaries in attempts to emphasize her ignorance of poetic rules, cf. "Tradition und Wandel," 32–33, 48, 56. On Karsch's corrections of her own work, based on her manuscript poems, cf. Schaffers, 173–74.

[170] For example, in Muncker, 297; Dawson, 142; Anger, "Nachwort" (1966) 8–9, "Anna Louisa Karsch," 245, and "Anna Louisa Karschin," 146; the biographical entries in *Allgemeine Deutsche Biographie*, 422, *Lexikon deutschsprachiger Schriftsteller*, 299, and *Lexikon deutscher Dichter und Prosaisten*, 625–27, 632.

[171] For example, in Blackwell, 330; Anger, "Nachwort" (1987) 189; Becker-Cantarino, "Deutsche Sappho," 121, and "Vorwort," 14; Hausmann, 79–80; and Menzel, 40; conversely, Kastinger-Riley and Nickisch assert her continued spontaneous and naïve poetic production in the face of all attempts at bourgeois influence (Kastinger-Riley, "Wölfin," 2 and 19; Nickisch, 71).

poet of earlier ages and the newly emancipated sovereign bourgeois author, between the supremacy of spontaneous inspiration and the necessity of bourgeois cultivation. The case of Anna Louisa Karsch has much to teach us about patronage, but also about the establishment of poetologies, since her case not only exemplified aesthetic theory but also shaped it. Some of the most contested and conflicting authorship models of the age were developed in direct response to the phenomenon of Anna Louisa Karsch and other poets like her,[172] and thus reviews of her work and the conflicting assessments of her in much scholarship tell us more about bourgeois definitions of Art[173] than they ever did about Anna Louisa Karsch and her writing.

## "Drive Your Cows from the Foot of Parnassus": The Case of Ann Yearsley

The patronage story of Ann Yearsley has received so much scholarly attention already[174] that my remarks on her are brief, but it is fitting to include her story here as both coda to and culmination of the phenomenon of eighteenth-century bourgeois patronage. Yearsley's authorial image and reception parallel that of Karsch and other peasant women in many ways: like them, she received no formal education, supposedly read only minimally and only texts appropriate for the "natural genius" (most notably, Milton, Young, Shakespeare, Virgil's *Georgics,* and, later, Ossian[175]). Her first patron, the writer and philanthropist Hannah More, decided to patronize Yearsley after being shown Yearsley's poetry by her cook. Like

---

[172] Cf., for example, Barndt's assessment of Sulzer's theories and Karsch's practice as mutually influential (167).

[173] To some extent, it can be argued that Karsch's critical reception was influenced by the canonization of some bourgeois poets over others: Glaser, for example, claimed simultaneously the destructiveness of Ramler's influence on Karsch's natural poetic production *and* upbraided her for not following Lessing's advice to have her poetry edited by bourgeois patrons (cited in Schaffers, 187–88). The blatant contradiction in Glaser's statements can obviously not be explained by the controversy over Karsch's "genius," but only by reference to the late nineteenth-century (and twentieth-century) canonization of Lessing (to whom Karsch should have listened) over Ramler (whom she was right to ignore).

[174] Most important, Tompkins; Demers; Landry, *Muses,* 120–85; Zionkowski, 98–106; Ferguson, *Eighteenth-Century Women Poets,* 45–89; and Waldron's works on Yearsley. Cf. also Hopkins, 121–29; Rizzo, "Patron as Poet Maker," 259–61; Carter, 192–232; Southey, 125–34, and 195–98; Franklin's introduction to Yearsley's *The Rural Lyre* and "An Historical Milkwoman."

[175] On Yearsley's reading, cf., among others, Tompkins, 61 and 70; Hopkins, 122; and More's letters cited by Mahl/Koon, 278 and 280.

Karsch's patrons, she approved of what she read less because of the work but because of the author's biographical circumstances: she found her poetry "extraordinary for a Milker of Cows, and a feeder of Hogs, who has never even *seen* a Dictionary."[176] Unlike Karsch, however, Yearsley was not a solitary phenomenon but one in a long line of peasant poets, beginning with Stephen Duck, all of whom had been published with the help of patrons. This meant that the class context in which Karsch's writing would ultimately come to be seen was established here from the outset.[177] More's patronage of Yearsley took the same form as Sulzer's and Gleim's of Karsch, the preparation of a volume of "Lactilla's" poems (Lactilla, Latin for milkmaid, was Yearsley's adopted pen name) and the securing of subscribers from among More's circle of acquaintances. When More wrote of her plans to Elizabeth Montagu, herself the patron of the shoemaker poet James Woodhouse, she received a warning: "It has sometimes happened to me," Montagu wrote back, "that, by an endeavour to encourage talents . . . by driving from them the terrifying spectre of pale poverty, I have introduced a legion of little demons: vanity, luxury, idleness, and pride, have entered the cottage the moment poverty vanished."[178] Horace Walpole similarly worried about the possible effect of the Stephen Duck phenomenon on the masses of hapless laborers, who might enter into unsuccessful publishing careers and starve as a result, and exhorted More to remind her charge that "she is a Lactilla, not a Pastora, and is to tend cows, not Arcadian sheep."[179] More's patronage of Yearsley, so it was perceived from the outset, could result either in vanity and luxury or starvation, but in no case produce a successfully publishing poet. And indeed, as More avowed in a letter to Montagu, nothing could have been further from her mind than the intention of turning her charge into a poet: "I am *utterly* against taking her out of her station. *Stephen* [Duck] was an excellent Bard as a *Thrasher*, but as Court Poet, and Rival of Pope detestable."[180] The lines between genuine poetic genius and peasant rhyming thus redrawn, More proceeded with the publication, which was — like Karsch's — highly successful. The immense interest in Yearsley's "uncultivated genius" is plainly apparent in the subscription list for the volume, which contained aristocratic supporters by the

---

[176] Letter from Hannah More to Elizabeth Montagu, October 22, 1784, cited in Mahl/Koon, 280 (emphasis original).

[177] In a letter to Montagu, More places Yearsley's writing in the context of other lower-class poetry; cf. her "Prefatory Letter," x.

[178] Letter from Montagu to More (1784), cited in Roberts, 368–69.

[179] Letter from Walpole to More, *Yale Edition* 31: 219.

[180] Letter from More to Montagu, September 27, 1784, cited in Mahl/Koon, 279 (the emphases are More's).

dozens, and Yearsley earned upwards of £500 for the edition, a respectable sum, even for bourgeois authors.

As with Karsch, Yearsley's patron did not consider this volume the beginning of her protégée's promising career, but as a purely financial venture designed to save the author from destitution — in More's own words: "it is not fame, but bread, which I am anxious to secure to her."[181] This interpretation of the venture as financial rather than literary manifests itself both in the financial provisions made for Yearsley and in the regard More professed for Yearsley's work. A *bourgeois* attitude toward Yearsley's writing, one that would have endowed her work with the transcendent qualities attributed to bourgeois writing, would have made it impossible for More to burn Yearsley's manuscript poems, including those not published, after the edition was complete;[182] it is an act that clearly defines Yearsley's poems as marketable wares and nothing else. Likewise, both More's consistent portrayal of Yearsley as a deserving pauper in her letters[183] and the financial provisions made for Yearsley, which ultimately led to the rift between patron and protégée, defined Yearsley as an object of charity rather than patronage: with Montagu, More invested Yearsley's earnings in such a manner that Yearsley could touch neither capital nor interest, under the pretext of keeping her and her husband from squandering the money. As soon as Yearsley demanded limited control over the interest, More withdrew her support, accusing Yearsley in letters of "the blackest ingratitude."[184] Finally, Yearsley's patrons made it more than clear that this volume was intended to be her first and last, that she was, after her economic situation was somewhat relieved, expected to "drive her cows from the foot of Parnassus and hum no more ditties,"[185] as Walpole rather crudely put it. Not unlike Gleim's plans for Karsch, More planned to put Yearsley to physical labor following the publication.[186] In the foreword to Yearsley's poems, she worried that the publication of her poems might "seduce her to devote her time to the idleness of Poetry . . . unsettle the sobriety of her mind, and, by exciting her vanity,

---

[181] More, "Prefatory Letter," xiii.

[182] Cf. Yearsley's prefatory "Narrative" to her *Poems, on Various Subjects,* xx; see also Tompkins, 73.

[183] For example, in her letter to Montagu, August 27, 1784, cited in Mahl/Koon, 277.

[184] Letter from More to Montagu, July 21, 1785, cited in Mahl/Koon, 283. Yearsley tells her side of the story in her prefatory "Narrative" to her second volume, *Poems, on Various Subjects* (xv-xxv); in that volume, she also appends the original deed of trust (xxvii-xxx).

[185] Letter from Horace Walpole to Lady Ossory, July 4, 1785, *Yale Edition* 33: 475.

[186] Letter from More to Montagu: "My present plan is, if Heaven blesses my endeavours, to put her into a small farm"; quoted in Demers, 139.

indispose her for the laborious employments of her humble condition";[187] thus again giving voice to the familiar bourgeois fears that the peasant, once raised above her "station," would refuse to return to the barn and aspire to the status of bourgeois authorship.

It should perhaps, in light of the cases discussed previously, no longer surprise us that despite the all-too-obvious fact that Yearsley's patrons flatly denied her such authorial status, they nonetheless employed the natural-genius aesthetic in marketing her poetic wares. Her patrons' as well as her readers' perception of Yearsley clearly centered on this image and on the eradication of everything that could undermine it: More introduced her to Ossian,[188] Walpole restricted her writing to the simplest forms,[189] and, like Karsch, she was instructed to stay away from classical mythology.[190] The topoi now familiar from earlier cases of "natural" and unassisted "geniuses" that reappear, near-verbatim, in Yearsley's presentation as "Muse-born wonder"[191] are as follows: her lack of formal education and the limitations of her reading,[192] her early and insatiable desire to read and write as a child,[193] the fact that her poetry was so good that authorship was at times attributed to others,[194] and the fact that she is repeatedly presented as unable to edit her work.[195] As with other poets, the first and last of these traits can be viewed alternately as testimony to the genuineness of Yearsley's genius or as evidence for the mediocrity of her work: Walpole once remarked contemptuously that More had "washed and combed the trumpery verses."[196] Yearsley's is the most obvious case of the *construction* of an authorial image, often in direct conflict with some of the available data. As with Karsch and

[187] More, "Prefatory Letter," xiii.

[188] Cf. More's letter to Montagu, September 27, 1784, cited in Mahl/Koon, 279.

[189] Cf. his correspondence in *Yale Edition* 31: 219, in which he recommended that she avoid blank verse; see also Carter, 209, and Hopkins, 122.

[190] Doody, *Daring Muse,* 130; Karsch reported her encounter with her critic who asked her to "remain natural" and avoid "the ancients" in a letter to Gleim, cf. *"Bruder in Apoll,"* I, 25.

[191] Cf. Waldron's title; the reference to Yearsley is taken from a letter of Anna Seward (Waldron, "Muse-born Wonder," 113); cf. also Seward's letters about Yearsley, I, 395–97; II, 32–33 and 364–65.

[192] Cf. More's letter to Montagu, August 27, 1784, cited in Mahl/Koon, 278.

[193] Cf. Tompkins, 60.

[194] Yearsley's prefatory "Narrative" to *Poems, on Various Subjects* states unequivocally that she saw her second volume as a means "to wipe away the suggestion of having been aided by other assistance" (xxiv-xxv), in other words, against the accusation that her earlier works had either been written or substantially edited by More.

[195] Cf. Tompkins, 72, 94.

[196] Cf. Tompkins, 72.

Leapor, modern critics regard Yearsley as hardly the Child of Nature as which she was presented but, on the contrary, as rather well read;[197] and Yearsley's image as a mother varies depending on the relationship with her patron. In early letters, More describes Yearsley as becomingly unambitious and aware of her laborious obligations ("she never allowed herself to look into a book till her work was done, and her children asleep"[198]); after her rift with Yearsley, Yearsley is turned into a profligate spendthrift who luxuriates in finery and has no qualms about wasting her children's money.[199] Another example of the obvious constructedness of Yearsley's authorial image is her patrons' view of Yearsley as religiously inspired, a derivative of the old discourse of natural inspiration: "Avaunt! grammarians"; Montagu exclaims in celebration of Yearsley's unerudite genius, "stand away! logicians; far, far away, all heathen ethics and mythology, geometry, and algebra, and make room for the Bible and Milton when a poet is to be made."[200] Shakespeare and Milton are exchanged for the Bible and Milton, and the familiar discourse, in its more pious incarnation, obliged Yearsley, who was thoroughly unreligious, to have her children hastily and belatedly baptized to conform to this image.[201]

From More's other writings, we do have some indirect evidence of how she viewed the natural-genius aesthetic which she employed so liberally in Yearsley's image construction, for it is a similar discourse that she applies to women writers of her own class in her treatise "The Practical Use of Female Knowledge." In this treatise, she fervently combats an idea that was all-pervasive in the assessment of lower-class geniuses as well as in the natural genius aesthetic of the age, namely, "that study is

---

[197] On recent assessments of Yearsley's level of reading, cf. Ferguson, *Eighteenth-Century Women Poets,* 60 and 69; Waldron, "Muse-Born Wonder," 118, and *Lactilla,* 29.

[198] Letter from More to Montagu, August 27, 1784, cited in Mahl/Koon, 278.

[199] Cf. the letter to Montagu, July 21, 1785, cited in Mahl/Koon, 284: "I hear she wears very fine Gauze Bonnets, long lappets, gold Pins etc. Is such a Woman to be trusted with her poor Children's money?" More's assessment was later repeated in Polewhele's *Unsex'd Females:* "Tho' soon a wanderer from her meads and milk, / She long'd to rustle, like her sex, in silk" (24). Cf. also Demers, 144.

[200] Letter from Montagu to More (1784), cited in Roberts, 364.

[201] Cf. Waldron, "Ann Yearsley and the Clifton Records," 303–5; Waldron provides convincing evidence that the first meeting between More and Yearsley, which More claims occurred in September 1784, must actually have taken place no later than July, and that More changed the date in an effort to conceal her influence on Yearsley's belated decision to baptise four of her children on August 1, 1784 (303). Yearsley, in her prefatory "Narrative" to her *Poems, on Various Subjects,* also claimed the first meeting occurred in September (xix).

an enemy to originality."[202] Her scathing portrayal of women writers' methodology, which is demonstrably rooted in the natural-genius aesthetic, could be just as easily applied to her own marketing strategy of Yearsley's unerudite genius:

> These self-taught and self-dependent scribblers pant for the unmerited and unattainable praise of fancy and of genius, while they disdain the commendation of judgment, knowledge, and perseverance. . . . To extort admiration, they are accustomed to boast of an impossible rapidity in composing; and while they insinuate how little time their performances cost them, they intend you should infer how perfect they might have made them had they condescended to the drudgery of application; but application with them implies defect of genius. They take superfluous pains to convince you that there was neither learning nor labour employed in the work for which they solicit your praise. . . . But . . . when the young candidates for fame are eager to prove in how short a time such a poem has been struck off, it would be well to regret either that they had not taken a longer time, or had refrained from writing at all.[203]

Similar to Mendelssohn's earlier review, More dismantles three of the most central aspects of unerudite genius — the tremendous speed and spontaneity of composition, the assumption that a poem springs into being full-blown and therefore cannot be improved on after its first inception, and the assumption that all learning is detrimental to original composition. And, like Mendelssohn's, her conclusion consists of the unilateral prohibition of such authors from writing and publishing, the silencing of the poet. The fact that More here dismantles a discourse that, applied to peasant poets, furnished the poetological basis for her publication of Yearsley's poems could well point to her employment of that discourse not as an aesthetic article of faith, as it sometimes appears in her letters, but as a marketing strategy to be applied to a lower-class author whose work, while extraordinary for a "Milker of Cows," could never aspire to the status of bourgeois authorship.

More's image of Yearsley is perpetuated in contemporary reviews and some posthumous research in which the author appears as *both* the natural genius of aesthetic theory *and* the good mother, wife, and daughter and entirely unambitious and humble servant of More's devising. The *Monthly Review* observed, employing now-familiar phraseology, "that the justness of the observation, *Poeta nascitur, non fit,* was never more pow-

---

[202] More, "The Practical Use," 290. Compare this with frequent claims in scholarship that More was a firm supporter of the genius aesthetic and convinced that genius was antecedent to rules, for example, in Carter, 197–200.

[203] More, "The Practical Use," 290–91.

erfully exemplified than by herself."[204] A letter published in the 1784 *Gentleman's Magazine* describes Yearsley simultaneously as a Shakespeare-type natural genius ("She warbles wild notes")[205] and as a "most pious" daughter and "a most excellent wife" characterized by "real humility."[206] The complimentary comparison to Shakespeare metamorphoses into a denigration of Yearsley's work in the 1791 *Monthly Review,* in which Yearsley, no longer considered a "genius" equal to the Bard, is demoted to the status of an imitator: "Mrs. Yearsley . . . endeavours to copy Shakespeare . . . but in this she is not fortunate."[207] But Yearsley's behavior as a recipient of charity was clearly more on the reviewers' minds than her authorial status as original genius or cheap copy. One reviewer in the *Monthly Review* worried that Lactilla might be seduced to exchange the milk pail for the pen and speculated how she would react to her success: "The moral qualities of her mind can only be known, when she hath felt the influence of public favour; and from her behaviour in *'that decent and comfortable situation'* . . . we may discover how far gratitude and humility may be reckoned among the other virtues of her character."[208] An answer to that all-consuming bourgeois concern is offered in 1787 by another reviewer who assured readers that "we still observe in *Lactilla* that modesty and decent humility which so particularly marked her character on her first emerging from obscurity. . . ."[209] By emphasizing the author's character rather than her work, Yearsley's reviews are reminiscent of Mendelssohn's review of Karsch, in which he demanded Karsch's "obedience" to her patrons, but also of the many forewords to volumes by early-to-mid-century peasant poets seeking to establish the author as a deserving pauper rather than a competent poet.

Whereas contemporary reviews were much more concerned with the author's character than her work, the evaluation of that work became one of the major themes in posthumous assessments. The central ques-

---

[204] Review of Yearsley's *Poems, on Various Subjects, Monthly Review* of 1787, 489.

[205] The reference to Yearsley's "wild wood-notes" already appears in a letter from More to Montagu; cf. More, "Prefatory Letter," x, and Carter, 198–99; Polewhele's satirical adaptation of this theme reads as follows: "And YEARSELEY [*sic*], who had warbled, Nature's child, / Midst twilight dews, her minstrel ditties wild" (23, capitalization original).

[206] Anonymous, "Copy of a Letter," *Gentleman's Magazine* 54 (1784): 897.

[207] Review of Yearsley's *Earl Goodwin, Monthly Review* of 1791, 348; cf. the more complimentary assessment of some speeches in her play as a "happy imitation" of Shakespeare's historical dramas in the same review (347).

[208] Review of Yearsley's *Poems on Several Occasions, Monthly Review* of 1785, 217 and 219, respectively. (The emphasis is original.)

[209] Review of Yearsley's *Poems, on Various Subjects, Monthly Review* of 1787, 485.

tion is essentially the same as that asked of Karsch's writing by her reviewer Mendelssohn — namely, whether it can justifiably be read as *literature* divorced from the patronage context. One of Yearsley's early reviewers already agonized over the quandary of being asked to review work that was not considered literature in the bourgeois sense:

> The productions of the *unlettered* Muse are generally esteemed for their rarity, more than their value; and in proportion as they take us by surprise, so we proportionably magnify their beauties, and overlook their faults.
>
> The world expects that criticism should suspend its rigour, when the *Thresher* and the *Milk-woman* leave the humbler occupations of the farm-yard, to pay court to the Muses, and bring offerings to Apollo....
>
> In strict justice, however, we must judge of a work by *itself*, and not by its Author; for the question is not so much, *who* hath written it, as *what* is written.[210]

The reviewer's fundamental dilemma is, of course, that the unlettered muse is not subject to criticism, either because of her natural superiority to erudite authorship — as proclaimed in the aesthetic tradition — or because of the considerations exacted by the disadvantages of the author's social status and education. The bourgeois model of independent authorship in which the work faces criticism by itself thus presents itself as objective because its "strict justice" is not swayed by such negligible considerations as authorial background; conversely, the passage clearly assumes the a priori inferiority of *all* peasant poetry by implying that it would never stand up to impartial and rigorous criticism. Both moves, the purported "objectivity" of criticism that ignores social circumstance and its simultaneous exclusion of most literature produced by lower-class (or, for that matter, women) authors have formed the basis of some highly influential critical traditions that shape our concept of literary interpretation to this day. Mendelssohn's point — a king, a woman, a Jew, what does it matter? — was reiterated in the early nineteenth century:

> There is in these prolific days so much admirable writing in prose and verse, that few readers will now allow the untoward circumstances under which a volume may have been composed to propitiate their favour for the author. It must possess intrinsic merits, or it will stand but little chance of success, for the times are past when circumstances purely adventitious might have been the means of ushering it into notice. A few years ago, a rhyming tinker or cobbler was regarded as a prodigy, and flattered, pampered, and caressed to an extravagant degree. Readers of

---

[210] Review of Yearsley's *Poems on Several Occasions*, *Monthly Review* of 1785, 215–16. The emphases are original.

the present day will not consent to waste their time in perusing a book, merely because they are told . . . "that it is a very extraordinary production, considering the limited education and habits of life of the author." If its merits are below a certain standard, no palliative that may be urged in its favour will avail in securing for it the indulgence it may require. If a new volume of poems now makes its appearance, the question is not, "Did the author compose it over his anvil or lapstone?" But, "Does it contain any thing calculated to repay the reader for the trouble of its perusal?"[211]

Two points, beyond the reiteration of the new bourgeois "standard," are important: first, the portrayal of the extraordinary goodwill that earlier ages supposedly showered on lower-class authors is surely, after a perusal of the relevant reviews, as greatly exaggerated as the panicked outcries over the "flood" of peasants leaving their farms in pursuit of a life of poetic idleness. The peasant poet's portrayal as "flattered, pampered, and caressed to an extravagant degree" moreover characterizes this attention as undeserved (thereby again evoking the assumed inferiority of the peasant's writing) and as benevolent and caring treatment bestowed on an inferior: these poets were not, for example, marveled at or esteemed, but pampered and caressed, as one might a child. The second point goes to the heart of the new bourgeois definition of literary Art: like Mendelssohn, but unlike the reviewer of Yearsley's work in the *Monthly Review*, the reviewer of Yearsley's poems views the new "objective" criticism and disregard of authorial background as a mandate not of the critic but of the *reader*. Literature is thus defined as emancipated from the patronage of earlier ages and from social considerations of recent memory, but also as subject to new pressures in the modern literary marketplace — namely, the necessity of pleasing its readership. The author is dead, long live the reader: it is here that the principal contradiction contained within the new bourgeois definition of Art reveals itself, for surely, "intrinsic merit" and the supremacy of the work are not the same thing as the work's need to pander to popular tastes, a need that can result in the same avoidance of controversial or unpopular forms and contents as that which characterized literature produced under patronage.

What this means is that the work of peasant poets was offered to its readership assuming a different mode of interpretation than that under which it subsequently came to be judged: the presentation or interpretation of the peasant poet as natural genius, deserving pauper, tender mother, and humble servant linked the poet's literary raison d'être inextricably with her social background. The author mattered; social identity

---

[211] Cited in Spence, xiii-xiv.

was central. The title page of Stephen Duck's first volume contains practically his entire biography,[212] and Achim von Arnim postulated such a close relationship between the life and work of Anna Louisa Karsch that he saw the work as incomprehensible without recourse to the life: "It is easily predictable that the life of the famous poet . . . will, in the future, have to sustain her poems, after she herself was forced to write poems in order to sustain her life."[213] It is not my intention here to advocate one concept of literary Art over another, but I suggest three related points: first, that the bourgeois view of literature as "independent" and judged purely on its "intrinsic merit" was developed *in direct response* to lower-class art forms (not only, as is frequently supposed, in response to the end of aristocratic patronage); second, that lower-class art forms, in their reinterpretation according to these new standards, are inevitably devalued because their inception as *patronized* art directly contradicts that new definition; and finally, that the new bourgeois understanding of literary Art, with its purported objectivity and simultaneous devaluation of nonbourgeois art forms, became a cornerstone of nineteenth- and twentieth-century literary criticism, which is largely characterized by its concentration on the work of bourgeois male writers and its disregard for works by women and lower-class authors.

Modern readers of lower-class literature, then, are faced with two fundamentally unappetizing alternatives: either to read the work of peasant authors in terms of the new bourgeois discourse which substantially influenced the history of nineteenth- and twentieth-century literary criticism, but which would result in an unavoidable reading of this work as "inferior" to bourgeois Art forms, or to employ the discourse suggested by the natural-genius aesthetic and the poets and patrons themselves, which, however, terminates in a view of lower-class literature as static and unchanging. For, as Landry has pointed out, the uncultivated

---

[212] "POEMS on Several Subjects: written by *STEPHEN DUCK,* Lately a poor *Thresher* in a Barn in the County of *Wilts,* at the Wages of Four Shillings and Six Pence *per* Week: which were publickly Read by The Right Honourable the Earl of *Macclesfield* in the Drawing-Room at *Windsor* Castle on *Friday* the 11th of *September,* 1730, to Her MAJESTY: who was thereupon graciously pleased to take the Author into her Royal Protection, by allowing him a Salary of Thirty Pounds per *Annum,* and a small house at *Richmond* in Surrey, to live in, for the better Support of Himself and Family. London: Printed for J. ROBERTS, near the Oxford Arms in Warwick-*Lane:* and SOLD by the Booksellers of *London* and *Westminster,* M.DCC.XXX. (Price Six Pence)." (quoted in Southey, 187–88, all capitalizations and emphases original).

[213] Arnim, 260: "Es läßt sich leicht voraussagen: daß das Leben der bekannten Dichterin . . . ihre Gedichte künftig erhalten muß, nachdem sie selbst ihr Leben mit ihren Gedichten zu erhalten gezwungen war."

genius is of literary interest because it *remains* uncultivated,[214] and the point of the insistence on the poet's continued "naturalness," as expressed in the recurring statement that her first (crude, original, unedited, unerudite, etc.) work was her best[215] seems to be simply to deny the poet the capacity for development: "she was finished as she was, incapable of becoming more than she had always been."[216] Neither the bourgeois patrons' view nor the bourgeois critics' view has ever resulted in a fair assessment of the work of lower-class authors. The bourgeois definition of Art, as it was developed partly in response to the work of lower-class authors, is inadequate for a balanced interpretation of their work. Modern readers of this work should therefore regard this bourgeois aesthetic with skepticism, an attitude that might also be useful when applied to time-honored interpretive strands such as the insistence on the death of the author, which survives today in the near-unanimous view of "biographical" readings as outdated and methodologically primitive. But the author's biography, in the case of peasant poets, is inextricably intertwined with the inception, substance, development, publication, and reception of their writing; and patronage constitutes the most central nexus linking life and literature. No work that was so fundamentally implicated in and framed by patronage can be understood without that context, and for that reason, I regard an interpretation of patronage a central precursor to any and all interpretations of work produced under patronage. Such an interpretation must certainly acknowledge patronage as the principal foundation on which this entire body of literature rests. But this interpretation can also, as Landry has recently done, show patronage as a fundamentally conservative mechanism, as an "inoculation" of "the social body, neutralizing the threat of an epidemic of social

---

[214] Landry, "The Resignation," 116.

[215] Cf., for example, Klencke, "Lebenslauf," 95–96; Hausmann, 297; Anger, "Nachwort" (1966) 14–15, on Anna Louisa Karsch; Tompkins, 95; and Waldron, "Clifton Records," 321, on Ann Yearsley. Cf. also Southey's assessment of Stephen Duck's writing: "he was incapable of imitating what he clearly saw was best; and that it was not likely he could produce anything better than his first efforts" (113).

[216] Hausmann in her assessment of Anna Louisa Karsch's writing: "Sie aber war fertig, so wie sie war. Mehr als sie von Hause mitbrachte, konnte aus ihr nicht werden" (75). Sulzer already claimed the impossibility of Karsch's becoming "more" in a letter to Bodmer written in 1761, Karsch's first year in Berlin: "nothing more will become of her than what she already is. They [her poems] are *impetus ingenii vividissimi* [the impromptus of a most quick-witted genius], and she is now too old to learn anything or to think according to principles" (quoted in Pott, *Briefgespräche*, 41: " . . . es wird nichts mehr aus ihr, als was sie gegenwärtig ist. Es sind impetus ingenii vividissimi, und sie ist zu alt, um noch zu lernen und nach Grundsätzen zu denken.").

change,"[217] and it can further reveal that a nonpejorative inclusion of lower-class art forms in the literary scene would constitute just such an "epidemic." "To-day," as Childers wrote of the poems of John Jones, a servant in Southey's household, "his poems are remembered from no merits of their own but solely because of 'the embalming power of Mr. Southey's pen.'"[218] Childers's metaphor of the patron as the "embalmer" of peasant poetry constitutes perhaps the aptest description yet of the patron's role with regard to the poet's work: to make it smell more sweetly (by referring to the natural-genius aesthetic and touching depictions of the poet as contented pauper and devoted mother) and, simultaneously, in the unequivocal presentation of the volume as a financial rather than literary venture and as the poet's first and *last* publication — to prepare it for burial.

---

[217] Landry, "The Resignation," 115; the term "inoculation" and its social application are Barthes's, its application to the bourgeois patronage context, Landry's.

[218] Childers's introduction to Southey, xi.

# 3: The Life As the Work: Counterfeit Confessions, Bogus Biographies, Literary Lives

THE CONTINUED EXISTENCE of patronage throughout the eighteenth century and its near-exclusive application to lower-class poets resulted, as discussed in the previous chapter, in two far-reaching consequences. First, the phenomenon of patronage not only drastically influenced how lower-class literature was produced — through near-total control over publication in terms of access to the literary market and, consequently, significant control over writing in terms of form, content, and authorial perspective — but also how it was *read*. Second, the way literature was read differed significantly from new conceptualizations of the bourgeois literary enterprise: the phenomenon of patronage essentially results in a fundamental rift between the reception of bourgeois and that of lower-class literature. In effect, postpatronage bourgeois literature, with its new aspirations to transcendence, was, ideally at least, judged on its "intrinsic merit," whereas biographical background was deemed as indispensable for an assessment of lower-class literature as it was for the presentation of the lower-class "genius" in the foreword. Some poetological treatises already suggest a connection between biography and poetry as central to the products of natural genius — for example, Alexander Gerard's *Essay on Genius* postulated an *inevitable* literary (auto)biographism on the part of both author and reader. The (auto)biographical aspects of the literary text, in his theory, are automatically inferred by the reader: when reading a poem about war, soldiers revel in the glory of death, ladies sympathize with the wives of the fallen, and merchants note the ways in which trade is affected by war. Analogously, "a poet of real genius will always draw his images from that state and face of nature which occurs in the places he is acquainted with," and poetic themes are invariably "suggested by a man's own situation."[1] Gerard, and other genius theorists of his age, did not have lower-class authors in mind as exemplifications of natural genius, but their aesthetics are nonetheless significant in this context because they provided

---

[1] Gerard, 131, on the analysis of the war poem; the quotations are on 128 and 191, respectively.

the theoretical basis for the presentation of peasant poetry and the depiction of the author's life in forewords by both poets and patrons.

Some modern scholars, as well, have postulated the importance of an author's biography in the context of natural-genius theory. For in this context, as Kerstin Stüssel has argued, literary traditions are nothing but paradigms to be referred to *negatively*, in distinguishing the nature-inspired work from traditional erudite literature. The new literary organism consists of single works whose intertextual connection is no longer guaranteed by recourse to the erudite tradition. The new context, Stüssel argues, is provided by the lives of geniuses. In the production of the "original" work, imitation is no longer imitation of other works, but, obliquely, imitation of the author, and less of his writing than of his *life:* "If you must imitate, imitate the man and not his work: . . . have courage, as he did, to show your unadulterated and unobscured self."[2] If the poet's life assumes the function of *contextualizing* the works of genius, thereby replacing the context formerly provided by the erudite tradition, if "the man" rather than the work furnishes the new source of inspiration for aspiring geniuses, then the life furnishes more than merely essential background for an understanding of the work: it has, in effect, *become* the work which then merely functions as an expression of the author's "unadulterated self."

The following analyses of peasant poets' life stories rest on two presuppositions that are indebted to this theory: first, that of the absolute importance of the lives of lower-class authors for an interpretation of their work, in contrast to the bourgeois position that literature can or should be judged on a rather indeterminate "intrinsic merit." I further presuppose that the life is, in fact, the work, or at least *a* work, that it is a literary construct that defines itself not by adherence to historical or biographical fact but through its employment of literary tropes, images, characters, structures, and genres. My concern in highlighting the difference between historical "truth" and biographical construction is not the recovery of biographical facts: if one postulates, with Montrose, the "textuality of history" along with the "historicity of texts," one would have to regard historical or biographical "truth" as irrecoverable in any case.[3] But I do, as already expressed in my confrontational title, consider

---

[2] From an anonymous author quoted by Stüssel: "Wollt ihr nachahmen, so ahmt den Mann und nicht sein Werk . . . wagt es wie er euer unverfälschtes und unverwischtes Selbst zu zeigen" (116). For Stüssel's discussion of the connection between autobiography and poetological theory, cf. 113–17.

[3] The "historicity of texts" presupposes that every text arises from a specific cultural and social climate; the "textuality of history" assumes that it is impossible to gain "access to an 'authentic' past, unmediated by the texts we use to interpret that past, and by the

it crucial to investigate to what extent these life stories are indeed "bogus" or "counterfeit"; to what extent peasant poets adjusted their own biographies, in letters, poems, and forewords, to participate in the project of patronage; and to what extent their life stories were edited, modified, falsified, or reinterpreted by patrons and, later, scholars, to institute or uphold poetological and interpretive traditions. My primary interest in this chapter is in the *literariness* of these lives, in the question to what extent the poets, as well as their later biographers, saw the necessity for autobiographical or biographical representation as an opportunity to turn the life into literature, and which literary genres and topoi were employed in that enterprise.

The literariness of the peasant poet's biography has often been acknowledged in scholarship, where these life stories, while being read as trustworthy biographical material, have simultaneously been likened to fairy tales, romances, novels, morality plays, comedies, Greek tragedies, or trivial literature.[4] An indication of the extent to which some biographers have subordinated biographical data to fiction is provided by Hilton Brown, who invents a love story for Janet Little that is entirely unsupported by the available data: "It is a pretty little romance; I make a present of it to the romantic."[5] But fictionalizing and mythologizing

---

process by which those texts have been compiled, preserved, and effaced" (French, 19). As French has shown in her application of Montrose's theory to the epistolary works of German women writers, the problem of the inaccessibility of the past is aggravated in the interpretation of texts that vacillate between the public and the private, such as letters. The same would seem to apply to an interpretation of seemingly "personal" texts like autobiographies and biographies which nonetheless fulfill a function transcending the personal — for example, the social and poetological implications contained within the autobiographies and biographies analyzed later.

For recent accounts of (middle- and upper-class) German women's autobiographies, cf. Ramm and Davies, Linklater, and Shaw. See also Holdenried for an overview of the research on women's autobiographical texts.

[4] Zionkowski speaks of More's fictionalizations of Yearsley's life and Yearsley's counterfictions in her subsequent foreword (100–103); Southey defines Yearsley's life alternately as a tragedy and a comedy (195). Menzel describes Karsch's biography as "the Fairy Tale of her Life" (14), Gärtner as a "novel" (55), Molzahn as an "idyll" (76); Gerhard Wolf casts it alternately as a morality play, trivial literature (referring to the episode in which Karsch, pregnant with her fourth child, is abandoned by her husband, 273) or a Greek tragedy (275), and quotes a passage from *Faust* to emphasize the literary qualities of her life story (270). Schlaffer speculates that Karsch may have invented her celebrated encounter with the herdsman who first exposed her to literature (316); although Karsch's correspondence disproves this assumption (Johann Christoph Grafe, the herder boy in this story, manifestly existed and later corresponded with Karsch, cf. his letter to her in *"Bruder in Apoll,"* I, 405–6), Schlaffer's biographical error is of analytical value, since it points to the pastoral and fairy tale–like qualities of this story.

[5] Hilton Brown, 19.

their lives is also an aspect that is used by the peasant poets themselves: ironically, they, who were supposedly innocent of all literary or mythological background, and who usually took great care to depict themselves as such in their autobiographical works, take the terms of that description straight from literary and mythological sources. Their usage of literary paradigms, forms, and genres in their autobiographical material is perhaps the best indication of the immense rift that separates their self-presentation as unlettered geniuses from the level of reading and literary awareness that many of these poets displayed in their writing. Life stories, as related by the poets themselves, their patrons, and subsequent biographers, center on characters taken straight from sagas, pastorals, myths, and fairy tales, among them Arcadian shepherdesses, the legendary poetess Sappho, war heroes, princesses, and witches. The concentration on mythical and fairy tales, not coincidentally those genres situated *furthest* from historical "reality," already reveals the authors' attitude toward the biographical text: the poet's life, masquerading as both empirical reality and indispensable background for her work, is also clearly the stuff of which legends are made.

## Arcadian Shepherdesses and Toiling Peasants: On Poetry and Poverty

Given that the natural-genius theory furnished the theoretical basis for their literary existence, it is not altogether surprising that many poets used autobiographical poems, letters, and prefatory material as a chance to define themselves as natural and unerudite geniuses consistent with both the aesthetic mandate and the patrons' marketing strategies. Thus, these sources invite, to some extent, the criticism that these poets jumped on the bandwagon of the nature craze[6] and uncritically adopted the image presented of them by their patrons. Although the poets' self-representations undeniably signify their participation in the project of patronage, many of them also treat themes that are not prefigured in their patrons' writings. The two most frequently recurring themes in these

[6] Cf., for example, Pott, *Briefgespräche,* 17, Schaffers, 39, Becker-Cantarino, "Vorwort," 17, and Schlaffer, 315 (all on Karsch), the biography of Karsch in *Lexikon deutscher Dichter und Prosaisten,* 632, and Carter's criticism of Yearsley's "shrewd awareness of the contemporary vogue" (233) and her "flaunting" her natural genius (192; the quotation 195; for a similar line of reasoning, cf. Whitney, 105). The problem with criticisms such as Carter's is, of course, that they ignore the context of patronage as well as the fact that other contexts of authorial self-definition were not available to lower-class authors, thus positing the poet's response to the natural-genius aesthetic as voluntary rather than coerced.

poetical and prose autobiographies center on poetology, the element that declares the writer a poet, and poverty, that which defines her as a lower-class poet. The Arcadian shepherdess, in her idyllic surroundings, is thus played off against the hard-working peasant pauper, hungry and trembling with cold: "half sunk in snow, / *Lactilla*, shivering, tends her fav'rite cow."[7] In Karsch's most famous autobiographical poem, "Belloisens Lebenslauf" (Belloise's Life Story), she romanticizes her surroundings as well as her poetic infancy: "Belloise" (Beautiful Louise; the name itself is an idealization for Karsch who was famed for her ugliness[8]) grows up in a pastoral landscape, amidst lambs and doves, singing along with lark and nightingale, simultaneously inspired to poetry and moved to faith by the beauties of Nature.[9] The purpose of this imagery is obviously to align the poet's biography with the pastoral genre and to define her impetus for writing in line with the aesthetic mandate of the naturally inspired poet. Karsch, and other poets, emphasized this aspect frequently in letters and in poetry: nature imagery not only serves as a highly literary evocation of the pastoral landscape in the description of her surroundings[10] but is also repeatedly employed in the creation of a metaphorical self-image. The recurring metaphorical comparison of the poet with a tree, moss, or "wild and unpruned vine"[11] evokes, as it does in aesthetic treatises of the age, Nature both as idyllic Arcadian locus and as an idealized opposition to Art and Culture. Thus, the lack of a formal education

---

[7] Yearsley, "Clifton Hill," originally in *Poems, on Several Occasions* (1785), in Fairer/Gerrard, 443–49, the citation 444.

[8] Becker-Cantarino has read the appellation less as a depiction of Karsch's exterior than a poetic signal for her beautiful poetic naiveté and therefore as part of Karsch's self-stylization as unlettered "naïve" poet, cf. "Belloisens Lebenslauf," 15.

[9] Karsch, "Belloisens Lebenslauf," *Gedichte*, 197–98, reprinted in *O, mir entwischt nicht*, 9–10, and *Gedichte und Lebenszeugnisse*, 69–70. A similar idealization of her surroundings occurs in her poem "Ueber die Vergleichung, An Nantchen," in *O, mir entwischt nicht*, 110–11 (reprinted in *Gedichte und Lebenszeugnisse*, 121–23, and as "An das stolze Nantchen" in *Das Lied der Karschin*, 113–14). For an extensive interpretation of "Belloisens Lebenslauf," cf. Becker-Cantarino, "Belloisens Lebenslauf."

[10] Cf. her letter to Gleim, December 23, 1762, in *"Bruder in Apoll,"* I, 168–70, in which she evokes a Horatian idyll in the description of her home village. On Karsch's self-definition as an unlettered poet, cf. also Schaffers, 47 and 54–57.

[11] Cf. Karsch's letter to Gleim, December 23, 1762, in which she likens herself to a linden tree (*"Bruder in Apoll,"* I, 168–70, the citation 170) and her poem "Das Harz-Moos," where she compares herself to the moss on a tree (*Auserlesene Gedichte*, 339–40; reprinted in *Das Lied der Karschin*, 82–83, and *Gedichte und Lebenszeugnisse*, 71). The comparison of herself with a wild and unpruned vine occurs in her autobiographical letters to Sulzer (*"Bruder in Apoll,"* I, 348: "unbesorgt wegen meines künfftigen schiksaals wuchß ich gleich Einer willden unbeschnittnen Weinrebe herrauff").

serves as a guarantee for spontaneous inspiration: "My learning it can soon be told, / Ten weeks, when I was seven years old."[12] Karsch, in her poem "An einen jungen Freund" (To a Young Friend), likewise invokes the aesthetic discourse in attributing her poetic talent to Nature:

> You praise my skill, and claim Nature the donor.
> Nature deserves your praise: to her is due all honor.
> All inspiration, strength, and force, that stir
> My song into existence, I owe her.
> Never did art enrich my own production,
> And ne'er did I from masters take instruction.[13]

Karsch's self-presentation as a natural poet is rather inconsistent with much of her writing, but the fact that she reiterated it so insistently in autobiographical material shows that she viewed it as fundamental, if not for her writing, then at least for her success. Although she frequently critiqued works by many contemporary bourgeois authors, including Gleim,[14] she also insisted on her status as virtually unread and therefore incapable of adequately judging literary works.[15] Elsewhere she referred to Young's theory of original composition, particularly the aspect of its independence from and debilitation by erudition and imitation, as her own poetic model.[16] Karsch's image as unlettered genius later recurs in most biographical accounts of her, most prominently in those written by her

---

[12] Cf. Pagan, "Account of the Author's Lifetime," *Songs and Poems*, 3.

[13] "An einen jungen Freund": Lobst mein Talent, schreibst der Natur es zu. / Sie ist es werth, und ihr gebührt die Ehre, / Ihr dank ich Einfall, Ausdruck, Geist und Schwung; / Mir gab die Kunst niemals Bereicherung, / Und nie nahm ich von einem Meister Lehre. (Gedichte, 76–77, the citation 76).

Cf. also her letter to Gleim's niece, Sophie Dorothea Gleim, in which she essentially makes the same points (cited in Karsch, *"Bruder in Apoll,"* I, 460–61, the reference 460).

[14] For example, in *"Bruder in Apoll,"* I, 65, 247, 269–70, 288, 313–14, and II, 47–49, 117, 128–30, 211–13, 216, 245–47, 337–38, and 464; cf. especially II, 130 and 214–15, where Karsch rewrote two of Gleim's poems.

[15] Cf. Karsch's autobiographical letters to Sulzer, *"Bruder in Apoll,"* I, 361, and her letters to Gleim in *"Bruder in Apoll,"* I, 27, and *Die Karschin*, 139.

[16] Letter to Gleim, March 28, 1768, in *"Bruder in Apoll,"* I, 91–92; particularly revealing seems her resolution to "forget" that there was ever a poet before her, a passage in which she also invokes two of Young's most central terms, "genius" and "original poet": "I want to forget that ever a poet lived before me, I want to make peace with my genius, as soon as you, my dearest friend, will make peace between Thyrsis and myself, but when? On the day that an original poet was born?" ("Ich will vergeßen daß außer mir noch Ein Dichter gelebt hat, Ich will mich außsöhnen mit meinem Genie so bald Sie mein liebster Freund mich mit Tyrsis außsöhnen werden wenn denn? An dem Tage da Ein Originaldichter gebohren ward?" Karsch, *"Bruder in Apoll,"* I, 93.)

daughter Karoline von Klencke and her granddaughter Helmina von Chézy.[17] Both Klencke and Chézy fervently avowed the superiority of Karsch's "natural" poems over the work she produced under the "erudite" influence of her patrons, lamented her use of "mythological hodgepodge," and either claimed that Karsch's "natural genius" happily emancipated itself from her patrons' influence or was greatly impaired by such harmful manipulation:[18] "[Ramler] paralyzed her imagination and forced it to walk on stilts."[19] Klencke's assessment of Karsch's minimal education is, in essence, a reiteration of the natural-genius aesthetic in which lack of formal training guarantees the poet's genuineness and spontaneity: "If the poet had, instead of her life as a herder girl, enjoyed an artificial education and access to modern books, her talent would never have achieved the heights for which it is now generally acknowledged."[20] Klencke's judgment of Karsch's writing is diametrically opposed to that of bourgeois critics: whereas Mendelssohn, for example, viewed Karsch's speed and the massive number of poems she produced as a sure sign of her work's mediocrity, the Karsch of Klencke's account was blessed with an inexhaustible and undiminished genius, regardless of the quantity of her output.[21] Perhaps the most substantial biographical change Klencke made to Karsch's authorial image as natural genius was to make permanent the initial bourgeois fascination with the unerudite phenomenon of Anna Louisa Karsch and to erase Karsch's subsequent more critical reception. "Critics considered only her genius, appreciated her as a work of Nature, and did not insist on a sophistication that she could not provide. . . . They were patient and indulgent towards her and wished to see her happy. . . ."[22] By trans-

---

[17] For a contrastive analysis of Klencke's and Chézy's biographies of Karsch, cf. Schaffers, 150–90, Heuser, "Stationen," and Niethammer, 235–54.

[18] Cf. Klencke, "Lebenslauf," 91–92, and Chézy, "Meine Großmutter," 14, 49–50, 72, 91–92, and 104; cf. especially Chézy's extremely negative depiction of Ramler's influence on Karsch in 49–50, 72, and 104. The term "mythological hodgepodge" ("mythologischer Wust") appears in Chézy's account, 72 and 91.

[19] Chézy, "Meine Großmutter," 49: "Er lähmte ihre Schwungkraft und machte sie auf Stelzen einherschreiten."

[20] Klencke, "Lebenslauf," 28–29: "Hätte statt dieses Hirtenlebens die Dichterin das Glück einer gekünstelten Erziehung genossen und die Bücher unserer Tage gehabt, so würde sie kaum ihr Talent zu der Höhe geschwungen haben, in welcher es allgemein bekannt ist."

[21] Klencke, "Lebenslauf," 99: "her genius lost nothing due to the quantity of its output" ("ihr Genie verlor nichts durch die Menge seiner Geburten").

[22] Klencke, "Lebenslauf," 106–7: "Man sah nur auf ihr Genie, schätzte an ihr das Werk der Natur, und forderte nicht von ihr was ihr an Lebenston mangelte . . . Man hatte Geduld und Nachsicht mit ihr, man wünschte sie glücklich zu sehen. . . ."

forming Karsch's rather unforgiving critics into a crowd of well-wishers, even claiming that experts unilaterally considered Karsch's impromptu poems her best work,[23] Klencke deletes the critical context in which her mother's work ultimately came to be seen — namely, the controversies that demonstrate how problematic the natural-genius theory later became for bourgeois critics. In her account, the natural genius enjoys the same undiminished enthusiastic acclaim in the 1790s as it had during its brief vogue in the 1760s, simultaneously fuelled by and expressed in Karsch's enthusiastic reception.

Karsch's self-definition as naturally inspired and untouched by learning recurs in the autobiographical works of many other peasant women.[24] One notable exception is Molly Leapor's "Epistle to a Lady," in which she identifies herself as "learned," a term that most contemporaries would have considered antithetical not only of lower-class authors but also of bourgeois women writers of the age. In Leapor's "Epistle," Mira, her autobiographical persona in poems, experiences poetry and poverty as warring realities, one defined by books and art, the other dominated by drudgery:

> You see I'm learned, and I shew't the more
> That none may wonder when they find me poor.
> Yet *Mira* dreams, as slumbring poets may,
> And rolls in treasures till the breaking day:
> While books and pictures in bright order rise,
> And painted parlours swim before her eyes:
> Till the shrill clock impertinently rings,
> And the soft visions move their shining wings:
> Then *Mira* wakes, — her pictures are no more,
> And thro' her fingers slides the vanish'd ore.
> Convinc'd too soon, her eye unwilling falls
> On the blue curtains and the dusty walls:
> She wakes, alas! To business and to woes,
> To sweep her kitchen, and to mend her clothes.[25]

---

[23] Klencke, "Lebenslauf," 95–96; compare this with Mendelssohn's deprecation of Karsch's impromptu work (559).

[24] Cf. chapter 5 for a more extensive discussion of poems on the subject of poetic inspiration.

[25] Leapor, "An Epistle to a Lady," in Colman/Thornton, II, 30–32, the quotation 31 (emphases original). The poem was republished in Lonsdale's *Eighteenth-Century Women Poets*, 215–17, and is briefly discussed in Lilley, 179–81.

The life of the mind, in Leapor's poem, is relegated to a dream world, which emphasizes both its desirability and its unattainability for someone of her class: books and pictures are only available to those living in painted parlors. For all others, the life of the mind is inevitably precluded by the reality of physical labor; poetry is thwarted by poverty. Poverty plays a prominent role in the works of other peasants as well, where it takes both idealized and more pragmatic forms. Karsch wrote several poems in which she seems to echo bourgeois treatises of the meekly and cheerfully toiling peasant — for example, her depiction of her own contentedness in poverty[26] or her many poems in praise of simple rustic fare over the more refined cuisine required to satisfy the upper-class palate.[27]

But elsewhere, Karsch found harsher words for the drudgery and humiliations of her life as a pauper: in her dedicatory poem to Baron von Kottwitz, she referred to the life from which he had saved her as "unworthy business . . . a plebeian and restless existence."[28] The pastoral landscape of some of her autobiographical poems is replaced elsewhere by harsh winters, during which the poet went out, clad in thin rags, to collect firewood,[29] by hungry children clamoring for food,[30] and domestic miseries caused by an abusive spouse.[31] Other peasant poets, as well, were much more open about the conditions in which they lived than were bourgeois women writers: Ann Candler's "Memoirs," for example, not only describe the extremity of her poverty and her absolute dependence on charity, but also elaborately relate her difficult relationship with her drunkard husband, who plunged her and her children into destitution

---

[26] "An den Reichs-Grafen zu Stolberg-Wernigerode," *Auserlesene Gedichte*, 89–91.

[27] Among them, "Die Abendmahlzeit auf dem Lande" (*Das Lied der Karschin*, 61–62; republished in *O, mir entwischt nicht*, 55–56), "Das Lob des Essens" (in *O, mir entwischt nicht*, 53–54, and *Gedichte und Lebenszeugnisse*, 81–82), and "Lob der schwarzen Kirschen" (from *Gedichte*, 125–26; republished in *O, mir entwischt nicht*, 51–52, and *Gedichte und Lebenszeugnisse*, 82–83; this poem was translated by Walter Arndt as "In Praise of Black Cherries"; cf. Blackwell/Zantop, 143–44).

[28] "Zueignungsgesang an den Baron von Kottwitz": "Der mich aus unanständigen Geschäften, / Aus einem pöbelhaften Leben ohne Ruh / Herausgerissen, mit des Menschenfreundes Kräften, / Mein *Teurer Kottwitz!* der bist Du" (*Auserlesene Gedichte*, unpag., reprinted in *Gedichte und Lebenszeugnisse*, 79–80; emphasis original).

[29] "Der Winter hauchet Frost," *Das Lied der Karschin*, 78–79.

[30] "Morgen-Gedanken," *Auserlesene Gedichte*, 21–22; reprinted in *Gedichte und Lebenszeugnisse*, 60–61.

[31] Cf., for example, the poem Karsch wrote using rhymes provided by others and published in *Gedichte*, 313, and *O, mir entwischt nicht*, 147–48. Karsch also describes her miserable marriages, one to an indifferent, the second to an abusive husband, quite openly in her autobiographical letters to Sulzer, cf. *"Bruder in Apoll,"* I, 348, 351–52.

and ultimately deserted her.[32] That such conditions are less than conducive to poetic inspiration is, on occasion, admitted: in some autobiographical poems, it is poverty rather than Nature that directs the process of writing, either by stifling all creativity or by forcing the Muse to stoop to the business of begging for bread: "Thus hunger often forced me to compose trivial songs, / my feeble tribute to contemptible men."[33] Apparently unaware of the contradiction, the description of extreme poverty and its destructive effect on poetic inspiration stands side by side with Arcadian imagery in which the poet wanders her native groves, nature-inspired and blissfully content in her modest state. At times, both themes appear in the same poem, for example, in Christian Milne's "Introductory Verses," in which she defines her poetic talent as innate rather than acquired:

> At six years old I felt my artless Muse
> Begin her rays of fancy to diffuse;
> Even then I felt my inclination strong
> To pour my feeble, infant thoughts, in song.[34]

Poetic genius, in her depiction, is marked by the same traits that distinguish it in aesthetic treatises: spontaneity, a denial of all formal training, and an unusual memory that separates this poetry from even the most rudimentary connection with the erudite context, namely, *writing*: "Clear was my memory, and retentive then, / The aid it wanted not of ink and pen."[35] But far from flourishing in her natural surroundings, inspiration wanes in the face of poverty and menial drudgery: "For servitude, with its incessant toil, / Harsh damp'd my Muse, when she inclin'd to smile."[36] Similar to Leapor's "Epistle," physical labor appears as a severe impediment to poetic inspiration; like Karsch, Milne relates her humble circumstances *both* to the naturalness, and therefore genuineness, of her poetic inspiration *and* to the impediments confronting her poetic practice.

In Karsch's autobiographical writing, there are two important encounters in which poetry and poverty intersect: the first with the young herdsman who provided her with books, the second with another poet

---

[32] Candler, "Memoirs," 1–17.

[33] Karsch, "Als sie krank lag," *Das Lied der Karschin*, 86–88: "also trieb / Mich Nahrungskummer oft, daß ich zu kleine Lieder / Matt sang und an Unedle schrieb" (87).

[34] Milne, "Introductory Verses," 33–35, the citation 33.

[35] Milne, "Introductory Verses," 34.

[36] Milne, "Introductory Verses," 34.

of her own class, Maria Catharina Dippen (ca. 1737–62). Her encounter with the herder boy, related in her autobiographical letters to Sulzer,[37] is an important poetological statement because it attributes not only Karsch's initial poetic inspiration but also her continued development to "Nature," or at least as close thereto as possible. The herder boy, himself a rustic and uneducated, may have provided her with books, but would not have been capable of directing her reading, increasing her understanding of what she read, or providing her with an "education" of any kind. Thus, reading, in this context, serves an inspirational function by feeding the young poet's fantasy life, as she relates in her letters, but it does not lead to an intellectual or analytical attitude toward literature. What Karsch takes from her reading, as she emphasizes time and again, is *themes* ("I found Robinsons, errant knights, dialogues in the realm of the dead, ah, there were new worlds for me!"[38]), not increased knowledge of literary forms, genres, or traditions. Thus, Karsch, who was both better read and more conversant in literary traditions than she ever let on, actively tried to obscure that knowledge in an effort to conform to the image of the unlettered genius.

More important is her description of her brief acquaintance with Dippen, because Dippen's biography, in Karsch's account, mirrors her own in more ways than one. Like Karsch's, Dippen's "natural genius" manifested itself mainly through the tremendous speed and spontaneity with which she wrote; as a woman endowed with similar impromptu talents as Karsch possessed, she was capable of engaging Karsch in a spontaneous verse dispute.[39] In Karsch's depiction, Dippen simultaneously personifies physical labor and poetic inspiration:

> A moment later she sat down beside me and wrote verses to me with incredible speed, Imagine, if you can, the two of us sitting there, see directly to my left, clad in a cap, black skirt and bodice and in a snow-white shirt this tall-grown peasant woman, how she throws verses onto paper with a copyist's speed, her hand as strong and coarse as the hand of a thresher who binds sheafs of wheat in the fields or threshes the full-

---

[37] In *"Bruder in Apoll,"* I, 344; for an English translation of this letter, cf. Prandi's translation in Blackwell/Zantop, 131–39, reference 134.

[38] Karsch's autobiographical letter to Sulzer, September 1, 1762, trans. Julie Prandi, in Blackwell/Zantop, 131–39, citation 134. In the original, the passage reads: "Da waren Robinsons, irrende Ritter . . . Gespräche im Reiche der Todten, o da waren neue Welten für mich!" (*"Bruder in Apoll,"* I, 345)

[39] The story is related in Karsch's letter to Sulzer of June 10, 1762, *"Bruder in Apoll,"* I, 426–30; the verse dispute appears on 429–30.

grained corn, her hard hand, roughened from field work, effortlessly and swiftly manages the pen, and equally effortless is her inspiration. . . ."[40]

In this story, Dippen is more than merely the ideal peasant of bourgeois treatises, content in her lowly station, although that is part of her character: Karsch reports that Dippen, modest and unassuming, had to be dragged away from her occupation of planting cabbages into a society eager to hear her poetry.[41] More important, however, Dippen also represents a model that many self-representations of peasant poets pronounce unworkable, namely, the successful combination of physical and creative labor. The shift from planting cabbages to writing poetry that seemed so unthinkable to poets like Leapor and Milne (and, elsewhere, to Karsch herself) is effortlessly performed by Dippen, whose hands are equally skilled at threshing and writing. The image of Dippen that Karsch presents to Sulzer thus performs a feat that no other peasant poet ever managed to accomplish: she conforms to the aesthetic mandate that views her *origins* in "Nature" (by virtue of her lack of erudition, speed, spontaneity, and originality of composition) and to the bourgeois mandate that the poet remain in "nature" (by virtue of Dippen's complete lack of authorial ambition and Karsch's refusal, in her description of her, to privilege the creative aspect of her work over the physical). Dippen thus represents the best of both bourgeois images: the poet who is both innocent of all learning *and* modestly disinterested in acquiring such erudition, the rural songstress who delights her listeners with spontaneously composed lays *and* thereafter contentedly returns to her cabbages. Clearly, Karsch's presentation of Dippen is more inspired by bourgeois images of the ideal peasant than by her own real-life experience of village life or even by her undoubtedly intense identification with Dippen. Even Karsch's enthusiastic report on Dippen's considerable local influence seems affected by bourgeois anxieties about the epidemic of writing among the lower classes:

---

[40] Karsch to Sulzer: "Den Augenblick sas Sie neben mir und schrieb mit Einer unglaublichen Geschwindigkeit Verße an mich, Mahlen Sie sich wan Sie können in Ihrer Einbildung uns ab, und sehen dicht an meiner linken Hand in Einer Trauerkappe[?] schwarzen Rok und müder [soll heißen: Mieder] und Einem schneeweißen Hemde diese hochleibichte baurenfrau sizen wie Sie mit der fertigkeit Eines Abschreibers Verße auffs Papier wirfft Ihre Hand so Stark und so grobhaüticht als die Hand des Knechtts der im fellde Waizengarben bindet oder auff dem Tenn vollkörnerichte Ähren außklopft, Ihre gehärtette Hand von der Arbeit des felldes ganz rauh führt mit Leichtigkeit die fortschreibende feder und eben so leicht ist Ihr Gedanke" (*"Bruder in Apoll,"* I, 428).

[41] Karsch to Sulzer in *"Bruder in Apoll,"* I, 427.

She is the glory of the village of Eimersleben, all the girls take to the pen on Sundays to emulate her. A whole village full of poetesses, no, the Father of the Muses could not wish for that....[42]

Where the patron's image of natural, unlettered genius is transformed into a self-image in autobiographical or biographical writing (as in Karsch's portrayal of Dippen), where that image takes literary shape in the form of the Arcadian shepherdess, it is invariably confronted with the poet's approximation of lived reality in the form of servitude and destitution. The shepherdess and the peasant women who, side by side, people the autobiographical statements of peasant poets, signify not only an assessment of the poet's origins but also a projection of her future as a poet. Some of these autobiographical personae, like "Sappho" (Karsch) and "Lactilla" (Yearsley), exclusively and perhaps defensively engage in autobiographical retrospective; others, like "Mira" (Leapor), foresee clearly a return to that state in which "nature," that fabled locus of poetic inspiration, turns out to be nothing but the hovel in which the rural laborer lives and performs her endless rounds of menial tasks. The juxtaposition of the singing shepherdess, the poetic stand-in for the autobiographical figure, and that figure herself who, more often than not, turns out to be the closer-to-life figure of the hard-working peasant, distraught mother, and abused wife points to the poets' clear understanding that their literary existence was embodied in the pastoral creature rather than their more realistic autobiographical persona. Whether or not this constitutes a critical reflection, on the poets' part, of the patrons' images and the aesthetic mandate, it does indicate the poets' awareness of their low chances for long-term survival as writers. Where the authorial self-image is trapped in the pastoral, the literary survival of the real-life poet seems unlikely. Where a literary *context* cannot be established — the village of poetesses remains unthinkable — such survival can only be purchased at the price of deracination and transplantation; it can, at best, be imagined as a temporary existence as a solitary marvel, the lone sensation permitted to exist briefly within a literary tradition shaped by the predilections and aesthetics of a different class of writers.

---

[42] Karsch to Sulzer: "Sie ist der schmuk des Dorffes Eimersleben und alle Mädchens ergreiffen am Sonttag die feder Ihr nachzuEiffern Ein ganz Dorff voll Poettinen, nein daß wolle der Vatter der Musen nicht" (*"Bruder in Apoll,"* I, 430).

## The German Sappho: Controversies Surrounding a Legend

Sappho, originally a Greek poet of considerable fame (ca. 610–ca. 580 B.C.), represented for many centuries virtually the only acknowledged woman poet of any nation or age and thus became a symbol for female poetic creativity and simultaneously a standard appellation for women poets. But in the eighteenth century, when only a few lines of Sappho's work had been recovered,[43] the poet's reputation rested less on her work than on her authorial image, an image that was far less concerned with Sappho's poetic talent than with her intriguing personality. More than the great poet, Sappho appears as the great tragic lover; her entire oeuvre, which forbids generalizations of this nature since so little of it has been recovered, is reduced to love poems and thus pressed into the service of that image. Her character comprises a reputation for beauty, a tragic flair (because of her unhappy love for Phaon), intensity of passion (because of her suicide after Phaon abandoned her), and lasciviousness (possibly because of her love for other women; her lesbianism, however, conflicts with the Phaon story and is therefore suppressed in most eighteenth-century accounts of her[44]).

One discrepancy that is perhaps indicative of the varying reception of bourgeois versus lower-class authors is that although Sappho has served as a common appellation for bourgeois women poets,[45] her name was not applied to poets from the lower classes. The only notable exception is Anna Louisa Karsch, who was originally assigned the appellation by her patron Gleim and soon became widely recognized as the "German Sappho" in criticism. In her letters to Gleim, she signed herself "Sappho" from 1761 until 1768, thus demonstrating that at least for the initial seven years of their thirty-year correspondence, she was willing to identify with the persona Gleim had assigned to her. But there are indications that the role was interpreted differently by patron and poet: Gleim saw Sappho primarily as a love poet and the epitome of tragic and unrequited passion, and he clearly intended to cast Karsch in the same role. His

---

[43] Cf. Landry, *Muses*, 85, and the sources she cites on 299 on the recovery of Sappho's texts for an eighteenth-century audience in Britain.

[44] On Sappho as lesbian or possibly bisexual in the works of eighteenth-century British writers, cf. Harris, 248.

[45] Cf. Harris, 247, for a list of English women writers who were called Sappho or claimed descent from her and Schaff on the common attribution of the name to English women writers, which she views as condescending (135); similarly, Gärtner on the German tradition of Sappho appellations (56).

application of the name to Karsch thus signifies more than a complimentary pen name, it essentially articulated both his demands on her writing and his interpretation of her work. For Karsch, on the other hand, Sappho was merely a designation of a woman poet, a designation which did not necessarily proclaim the nature of her work or her choice of genre or theme. When she speaks of the death of Sappho or the death of her muse in letters, she indicates at times a refusal or inability to write love poems, but just as frequently a more general lack of inspiration;[46] at the outset of her daughter's writing career, she easily transferred the appellation to her,[47] thus indicating that, in her mind, Sappho was not a distinctive but a general designation applicable to any woman writer.

As Nörtemann has shown, the use of the Sappho persona in the correspondence between Karsch and Gleim and its eventual abandonment in Karsch's letters is highly informative not only with regard to Karsch's participation in the construction of her authorial image but also with respect to the question to what extent that image differed from that of her patrons.[48] Karsch's self-stylization as Sappho contains two important deviations from Gleim's model: it does not infer Sappho's exclusive role as a love poet and it is not supplemented by a casting of Gleim in the role of Phaon, a character that he suggested to her for himself when he first styled her as Sappho,[49] and a part that both might have seen as roughly reflective of Karsch's unrequited attachment for Gleim. Instead, Karsch casts Gleim in the role of the Virgilian shepherd Thyrsis and creates a counterimage to her own Sappho persona in the persona of the shepherdess Lalage (Karsch herself, interestingly enough, does not enter into the equation, although Gleim exists side by side with his fictitious stand-in Thyrsis). In Nörtemann's analysis, Karsch's two personae represent different responses to the rejection of Sappho's/Lalage's love on the part of Thyrsis/Gleim and simultaneously different responses to the poetological directive of Karsch's patron Gleim: Lalage accepts his mandate that *counterfeit,* rather than real, feelings make a poet; Sappho does not.[50] Not only does this imply Karsch's adoption of Sappho's role of the tragically unrequited lover, but also a poetological statement of her own

---

[46] Cf. Karsch's letters to Gleim in *"Bruder in Apoll,"* I, 35–36, 77, 103, 108, and 169.

[47] Cf. her letter to Gleim, June 10, 1772, in *"Bruder in Apoll,"* II, 33.

[48] On the image of Sappho in the correspondence between Karsch and Gleim, cf. Nörtemann, "Verehrung, Freundschaft, Liebe" and her "Nachwort" to their correspondence, particularly Karsch, *"Bruder in Apoll,"* II, 529–32.

[49] Cf. his letter to Uz cited in Hausmann, 127–28; see chapter 2.

[50] Cf. Nörtemann, "Verehrung, Freundschaft, Liebe," 85–86. Gleim's mandate is taken from a letter to Jacobi and cited in Karsch, *"Bruder in Apoll,"* II, 446.

that differs radically from that of her patron: Sappho's poems are based on and express feelings that are not counterfeit, but real.[51] It is this autobiographical aspect of Karsch's poetic production that forbade, to her mind, publication of her "Sapphic"[52] letters and poems to Gleim and led to the controversy with her patron over their circulation among his friends and his plans to have them printed. The disappearance of the Sappho character from Karsch's letters, the sudden emergence of "A L Karschin," "A L Dürbach," or simply "K" in signatures as of 1769, signals not only Karsch's abandonment of her self-image as unrequited lover but also the death of a poetical persona whose entire oeuvre was supposedly inspired by tragic love. And finally, Karsch's ultimate repudiation of the role could be seen as an act of passive resistance against her patron, who exhorted her to write love poetry and love letters that were based on counterfeit feelings and hence publishable:[53] Karsch's repeated laconic comments on Gleim's acquisitiveness, particularly of her love poems, suggest that, in part, the death of the Sappho character amounts to a refusal on *Karsch's* part to supply her patron with the coveted material that *Sappho* had willingly provided.[54] Indications are that Gleim as

---

[51] Cf. Nörtemann, "Verehrung, Freundschaft, Liebe," 90.

[52] The term "Sapphic" is used throughout this chapter in the sense that both Karsch and Gleim used it in their correspondence, designating a genre (love poems) and the author's gender as female; the now-common association with lesbianism was not part of the discussion in this correspondence and can therefore not be applied to Karsch's work as discussed by Karsch and her patron.

[53] Cf. Gleim's comment in a letter to Karsch: "When, my dear Sappho, have I ever forbidden you to sing songs to Thyrsis? O he likes them far too much, the excellent songs of his Sappho, to permit so much as the appearance of a prohibition to creep into his letters. No, in songs he is quite partial to her sincere, anguished melancholy love, but in her eyes, no, in her eyes he cannot bear to see heartache, no Sapphic odes there; he wants his friend Sappho to be cheerful always, if he sees heartache in her eyes, be its cause what it may, he will fancy her unhappy and he could not bear to think her unhappy." (Gleim to Karsch, November 23, 1761, in Karsch, *"Bruder in Apoll,"* I, 45: "Wo, meine l. Sapho, wo habe ich Ihnen verbothen dem Thyrsis keine Lieder mehr zu singen? O er hört sie allzu gern, die fürtreflichen lieder seiner Sapho, als daß er nur einen Schein eines Verbothes sich hätte können entwischen laßen. Nein, in den liedern kan er die ernsthafte gramvolle melancholische liebe nur alzu wohl leiden [über gestr.: vertragen], aber in den Augen, nein in den Augen kan Er keinen Gram, keine saphische Ode sehen, er will, daß seine Freundin immer aufgeräumt sey, sieht er Gram in ihren Augen er entstehe woher er wolle, so hält er sie nicht [für] glücklich, u sie nicht glücklich zu wißen das kan er nicht ausstehn.")

[54] Cf., for example, her early suspicion that Gleim loved merely Sappho's poems rather than Sappho herself (Karsch, *"Bruder in Apoll,"* I, 29), her laconic comment that "Thyrsis" had lost interest in her when he had collected enough of her poems (cited in Beuys, 83; cf. also the letter cited in Hausmann, 134), the many letters in which Karsch as Sappho tries to woo or placate Gleim in verse form (e.g., *"Bruder in Apoll,"* I, 334, 336–

patron had a greater stake in the continued existence of Sappho than Karsch, as poet: Gleim continued to refer to her as Sappho in letters long after she herself had stopped using the name.[55]

Where Karsch criticism discusses the Sappho image, it adopts Gleim's perspective of Sappho as a love poet rather than Karsch's broader interpretation of the character. In some cases, the Sappho discourse is conflated with the natural-genius theory: Heinse, in his "Sappho" essay of 1775, postulates that "the ladies of Myrtilene [Sappho's home] and in the other cities of Lesbos lived as Children of Nature, almost like the girls of Otaiti."[56] In Heinse's essay, the defining characteristic of Sappho's image is her intensity of passion, a trait that Heinse locates in her biography rather than her work: Sappho appears as an ardent and jealous lover who intensely resents being "imprisoned in the too narrow confines of the female body," who longs to "conquer Nature, to break out, to hurl herself from the precipice and perish like a stream in a sea of ecstasy."[57] Sappho's lesbianism is turned into the quintessential female inferiority complex: Sappho's female lover abandons her for a man, thus demonstrating that a woman's love cannot compete with a man's, "as even the brightest star must perish before the rays of the rising sun."[58] Thus, Sappho appears as a highly controversial character, "unfeminine" in both the extremity of her passion and because the object of that passion is not men, but women — so controversial, in fact, that Heinse inserts an apology to his women readers for treating the theme.[59] When Heinse, at the end of his essay, presents Karsch as the second Sappho, he essentially assigns to her Sappho's extremity in matters of love. Heinse considers Karsch's work comparable to that of Sappho because it is "replete with the most ardent and sweetest Sapphic fire" and quotes one of her love

---

37), and Gleim's repeated requests to her to send him her occasional poems (*"Bruder in Apoll,"* I, 89) and her "sapphic songs" (*"Bruder in Apoll,"* II, 190, 254).

[55] For example, in his letter to her dated May 27, 1783, in Karsch, *"Bruder in Apoll,"* II, 184.

[56] Heinse, "Sappho," 121: "Die Damen zu Myrtilene, und in den anderen Städten von Lesbos lebten wie Kinder der Natur, beynahe wie die Mädchen von Otaiti."

[57] Heinse, 128: "Ihr Herz war eine Quelle von Feuer . . . das die Natur, die es in dem zu engen Raum eines weiblichen Körpers verschlossen hielt, zu überwältigen kämpfte, um auszubrechen, sich hineinzustürzen, und wie ein Strom in einem Meere von Wonne zu vergehen."

[58] Heinse, 128: "Sie zitterte, das zärtliche Wohlwollen, die Freundschaft ihrer Freundin gegen sie, möchte, in der Liebe des schönen iungen Mannes verlöschen, wie auch der hellste Stern vor den Strahlen der aufgehenden Sonne — ."

[59] Heinse, 128.

poems as evidence.⁶⁰ Viewed in the context in which Heinse places her work, Karsch's "Sapphic" poetry could well be seen as contravening propriety: the reason Heinse gives for the rarity of contemporary Sapphos is that "men and women tend to disrespect . . . girls and ladies who sing much about their love. One of the main virtues which we, appropriately, demand of women is modesty; unfortunately, this is often understood to mean duplicity, and this attitude is incompatible with the creation of Sapphic odes."⁶¹ In this manner, Karsch's Sapphic predilections could be related both to the aesthetic mandate and Heinse's awareness of her class background: as a Child of Nature, she is not bound by society's rules; her status as a peasant frees her from consideration of bourgeois decorum which would surely extinguish the Sapphic fire in her work. Thus Karsch can only function as Sappho if she is cast *outside* of the bourgeois class context as well as the bounds of feminine propriety.

Nine years before Heinse published his Sappho essay, Herder had flatly denied the applicability of the name to Karsch: Karsch, in his brief analysis, is "a poet who often, and at times inappropriately, styles herself Sappho."⁶² Herder's argument upholds the image of the Greek Sappho as an exclusive love poet, but places her work firmly within the bounds of bourgeois propriety, and it is precisely this act of taming Sappho that no longer allows Herder to equate Karsch's work with that of the ancient poet. Karsch's "Sapphic fire," in his assessment, burns *too* unbridled for her to be worthy of the name: "the German Sappho, whose fire rages unchecked rather than burning gently, whose work is more tempestuous than melting, can be considered more androgynous as far as her work is concerned than a tender companion of Venus like the Greek Sappho."⁶³ Herder's judgment of

---

⁶⁰ Heinse, 147–48: ". . . kann folgendes Gedicht beweisen, das voll des stärksten und süssesten sapphischen Feuers ist, welches eine Dame aus der Fülle ihres Herzens schrieb . . ." followed by the quotation of Karsch's poem "An Mirtill" on 148–50.

⁶¹ Heinse, 147: " . . . weil . . . Männer und Frauen die Mädchen und Damen . . . nicht sehr hochzuachten pflegen, die viel von ihrer Liebe sangen. Eine der Haupttugenden, die wir mit Recht von dem Frauenzimmer verlangen, ist die Schaamhaftigkeit; leider aber versteht man gewöhnlich darunter: nicht wahr zu seyn; und dieß verträgt sich nicht mit sapphischen Oden."

⁶² Herder, "Sappho und Karschin," 350–51: " . . . eine . . . Dichterin . . . die sich oft, und manchmal am unrechten Ort den Namen Sappho gibt." Herder was not alone in this assessment; cf., for example, Grillo's doubts that Karsch was capable of upholding the Sapphic tradition (in his "Idyllen aus dem Griechischen des Bion und Moschus" [1767], cited in the commentary to Karsch, *"Bruder in Apoll,"* II, 374).

⁶³ Herder, "Sappho und Karschin," 351: "allein die Deutsche Sappho, in ihrem Feuer mehr wild als sanft, mehr stürmisch als schmelzend, dörfte eher in ihren Werken Androgyne seyn, als eine zärtliche Freundin der Venus, wie die Griechin war." Schubart agreed with Herder as to the inappropriateness of the Sappho appellation for Karsch, but for the

Karsch, although opposed to Heinse's concerning the applicability of the Sappho label to Karsch, does arrive at some similar conclusions: both writers judge Karsch's work as untamed, unbridled, and extreme. The bulk of Karsch's published work at the time both Sappho essays were written, abounding, as it does, with highly decorous poems of praise addressed to God, King, members of the royal family, and various other patrons and supporters, hardly supports such an interpretation, suggesting that Herder's and Heinse's image of Karsch is either indebted (as Herder's definition of Karsch as "androgynous" already hints) to a reading of Karsch's war poems in light of the author's gender or based on those rare love poems whose publication Karsch was unable to prevent. "The German Sappho" as the ardently tragic lover is obviously *Gleim's* image of Karsch, the one he assigned to her at their first meeting in 1761 and later tried to publicize via publication of her love letters, and simultaneously the image that was at the heart of Karsch's most bitter and prolonged battle with her patron. Viewed in this fashion, the image of Karsch as the German Sappho not only blatantly negates her own authorial image and results in a reduction of her oeuvre to a fraction of her work, but also implies the expulsion of the poet from bourgeois society and from the society of women. The Sappho image thus results in the removal of another potential contextualization for Karsch's work: as both Heinse's apologies to "the ladies" and Herder's assessment of Karsch's work as "androgynous" make abundantly clear, even the inferior context of "women's" literature cannot appropriately frame the extreme effusions of the German Sappho, just as the peasant's work cannot be placed in the context of bourgeois culture. Sappho, then, remains exceptional, a solitary marvel similar to the spontaneously inspired and breathtakingly quick-witted — but ultimately short-lived — peasant sensation of the age.

## A Man or a Mother? Anna Louisa Karsch Forgets Her Gender

Herder's designation of Karsch as "androgynous" takes up a recurring theme in auto/biographical writings on Karsch, whose autobiographical letters and poems and later representation in biographies are rife with conflicting gender images. Stüssel has already shown that Karsch herself endowed her autobiography with motifs that later furnished the quintessential metaphors of *male* individuation.[64] In her autobiographical letters

---

opposite reason: he viewed Sappho's suicide and her emotional extremity as incompatible with Karsch's long-suffering patience, feminine gentleness, and love of life (cf. his letter to Karsch, February 23, 1787, cited in Chézy, *Aurikeln*, 42–45, the reference 44).

[64] Cf. Stüssel, 220–22.

to Sulzer, Karsch emphasizes her boyish predilections as a little girl and relates these incidents with a clear awareness of the gender conflict she establishes in her writing. One prominent trait that defines the boyishness of Karsch as a girl in her life story is her great fondness for books, which were forbidden her as a girl: "Beloved books became my sole refuge and I had again forgotten that I was a girl. . . ."[65] Karsch's "forgetfulness" of her gender effectively defends the girl, to Karsch's readers, from the accusations of deliberate stubbornness and disobedience that her mother and grandmother reportedly heaped on her; the fact that it is a frequent occurrence makes it one of the defining aspects of Karsch's autobiography. It is a trait that expresses itself in the girl's extraordinary dislike for traditional feminine occupations, such as needlework and knitting,[66] and her equally unusual fondness for boyish games. "I built sandcastles, shored the walls up with pebbles and then razed my castles to the ground with wooden missiles. In my right hand I bore a staff, and in conversing with myself I became the head of an army! All the thistles were my enemies and with martial valor I slashed all their heads off."[67] An image that, as Stüssel reminds us, became the prototypical reflection of adolescent masculine self-ideation when Goethe used it in "Prometheus" and Moritz employed it in *Anton Reiser* appears here in a woman's work written years before the publication of either of these texts.[68] Both Goethe's and Moritz's use of the image is commonly attributed to their borrowing the image from Macpherson's Ossian epic,[69] but Karsch's letter *precedes* both the first German translation of *Fingal* and its first publication in the original.[70] There are, of course, other possible

---

[65] Karsch's autobiographical letter to Sulzer, in Blackwell/Zantop, trans. Julie Prandi, 131–39, the quotation 134. "Meine einzige Zuflucht war das geliebte Buch und schon hatt ich wieder vergeßen, daß ich ein Mädchen war. . . ." (Karsch, *"Bruder in Apoll,"* I, 345).

[66] Cf. Klencke, "Lebenslauf," 18, and Chézy, "Meine Großmutter," 7, 13; the motif is later taken up in Karsch's brief biography in *Lexikon deutscher Dichter und Prosaisten*, 608.

[67] Karsch, autobiographical letter to Sulzer, in Blackwell/Zantop, 133–34: "Ich bauete Thürme von Sand, und maurte sie mit Steinen, und stürmte sie mit hölzernem Geschoße darnieder. Ich führte in meiner rechten Hand einen Stab und indem ich mit mir selbst redete, war ich das Haupt einer Armee! Alle Disteln waren meine Feinde und mit kriegerischem Muth hieb ich allen die Köpf' ab" (*"Bruder in Apoll,"* I, 345). Cf. Schaffers, 34–36, for an analysis of this passage.

[68] Cf. Stüssel, 221.

[69] Cf. Gaskill, "Blast," 109; the scholarship cited by and discussion in Stüssel, 221, for the Goethe reference; and Gaskill, "Joy of Grief," 110 and 113–14, for Moritz.

[70] Karsch's first autobiographical letter to Sulzer is dated, by the recipient, as September 1, 1762, but must have been written as early as the autumn of 1761: Sulzer refers to her first three autobiographical letters in a letter to Karsch written on December 15, 1761, in which

explanations for Karsch's use of the image — Stüssel speculates, based on Jördens's biography of Karsch, that she may have borrowed it from an unverifiable biblical source[71] — but more important is the question of the function of this image in Karsch's autobiographical writing. Particularly given her "unfeminine" fondness for books, it would make sense to infer that Karsch was well aware of the inappropriateness of her martial fantasies in light of her gender, and that she is, in establishing a masculine biographical persona whose assumption of the roles of reader/writer and war hero does not conflict with his gender, indulging in an autobiographical act of "forgetting" her gender. Karsch's martial fantasies as a girl are mirrored in much of her later writing, particularly her war poetry:[72] even her sternest critic Mendelssohn attested her a "masculine" imagination and wondered how a woman who had no first-hand experience of war could have imagined such graphic battle scenes.[73] The image of the boy decapitating thistles with his staff recurs in her autobiographical poem "An die Chartenspieler" (Addressed to Players at Cards), where it is linked with other central aspects of Karsch's autobiographical persona, including her self-stylization as formally untaught:

> Shuffle your cards and play on, lost in thought
> Your hopes to win with countless joys are wrought
> Joys that you savor in a blissful trance.
> But stern and stoic I, who, from such joys pre-empted,
> Was never once by any card-game tempted,
> And never did I leap in joyous dance.

---

he refuses to return them to her for fear they might get lost in the mail (cf. Pott and Nörtemann's introductory commentary to the letters in Karsch, *"Bruder in Apoll,"* I, 341). Macpherson's *Fingal* did not appear in the original until December 1761; the first German translation of the work appeared in 1762 in the *Bremisches Magazin* as "Zwei Fragmente der alten Dichtkunst von den Hochländern in Schottland, aus der alten Gallischen oder Ersischen Sprache übersetzt," an anonymous translation of the pieces that had appeared in the *Gentleman's Magazine* in June 1760. Macpherson's *Fragments of Ancient Poetry* first appeared in English in 1760, *Temora* in 1763; his work was not generally known in continental Europe until the appearance of the two-volume *Works of Ossian* in 1765, which was republished in 1996 (cf. Gaskill's "J. M. R. Lenz und Ossian," forthcoming in the *Lenz-Jahrbuch*, vol. 8). The thistle motif appears in Macpherson's *Fragments* as well as in *Fingal* and *Temora*. I thank Howard Gaskill for his valuable help in tracing this motif and in dating Macpherson's work in its original edition and German translation.

[71] Stüssel, 221–22.

[72] Margaret Ives is the most recent scholar to have written on Karsch's war poetry ("A Brave Woman Goes to War"); I would like to thank her here for providing me with that essay in manuscript before it was published as well as her unpublished lectures on Karsch.

[73] Cf. Mendelssohn's review of her first edition, 335 and 337, respectively.

Too stiff to move my feet in meter and in time,
And too uncouth to contemplate a game,
I thus remained untutored in both skills.
Card's names to me are strange mysterious things,
Nothing I know of jacks and queens and kings
And nothing of the trick that wins the spoils.

When I was young, books were my sole affection,
To read and think my only predilection,
I even wrote a book, bad as it may be.
Dances and games were no concern to me,
I read of the hero's reward for bravery,
Fought battles and braved dangers in my dreams.

Walls of defense I built with brick and pile
I ordered armies march in rank and file
And as their general I acted proudly,
Erected barricades, fired bits of peat
And never did I order a retreat
And when I called "attack!," my voice rang loudly!

And when a fortress had declared surrender,
I ordered swift pursuit of its defenders,
And bravely did I conquer enemy lands.
I marched my armies shrewdly to and fro,
Vanquishing many thousands of my foes
In the form of nettles killed with my own hands.

And thus their little bodies were laid low,
Struck down by my fearsome and mighty blow,
Thousands cut down before me, brave and bold!
Proudly, I thought myself invincible,
I was a child, and by life's principle
We often act like children when we're old.

O, my imagination, it runs wild,
As it did then, when I, a herder child,
Still drove my herd from valley, hill, and glen.
But now, it sees a different battlefield,
It thinks of all who once the sword did wield,
And him who grew immortal by his pen.[74]

---

[74] Karsch, "An die Chartenspieler," in *Auserlesene Gedichte,* 190–91:

Amidst the multitude of authorial constructions we have from Karsch with regard to her own inspiration, this poem is perhaps the most interesting because it links and contrasts Nature and Nation, war and reading, male and female, and her own origins and the educated bourgeois/aristocratic elite. Initially, the narrator of the poem rejects two facets of a bourgeois/aristocratic girl's background — namely, learning to dance and playing at cards — as irrelevant for her own life, which was spent herding unspecified animals. (Read with reference to the author's actual biography, those animals would have been cows; however, one could surmise that the author refused to make the autobiographical connection explicit, assuming that the reader would infer sheep and thereby neatly supplying a pastoral context). Significantly, in her reference to dancing and card games, Karsch singles out those very trappings of the bourgeois/aristocratic background that had come under heavy attack in contemporary moralistic writings as wasteful, immoral, profligate, and encouraging women to neglect their households, accumulate debts, and squander their days in uselessness and self-indulgence. The speaker's claim that she remained *"ungelehrt,"* or "untutored" in these arts and her repetition of key words such as *"wissen"* in the second stanza, perhaps an oblique allusion to the near-universal distaste for *gelehrte Weiber* (erudite women), indicate that these trappings are viewed as part of an upper-class *education*. The heroine's opposing self-representation as hard-working and simple evokes a pleasing contrast of virtue, which the author needs, of course, for she is about to endow her heroine with the most unfeminine traits imaginable: a predilection for reading and a taste for battle.

Mischt immer eure Blätter, spielet / Gedankenvoll, und hoffend fühlet / Die Freuden des Gewinnes ganz; / Mein Geist, zu stoisch und zu trocken, / Ließ nie die Charten sich verlocken, / Und hüpfte nie zu einem Tanz! // Zu steif den Fuß im Tact zu lenken, / Zu roh, beym Spiele was zu denken, / Blieb ich in beyden ungelehrt; / Ich kenne nicht der Blätter Nahmen, / Weiß nicht, was Buben sind und Damen, / Weiß nichts vom Blatt, dem Sieg gehört. // Nur Bücher hab ich liebgewonnen, / Darum gelesen, nachgesonnen, / Selbst eins gemacht, so schlecht es war! / Nichts fragt ich da nach Spiel und Tänzen, / Ich las, wodurch sich Helden cränzen, / Und träumte Schlachten und Gefahr! // Ich ging, auf selbst gebauten Wällen, / Ließ sich mein Volk in Ordnung stellen / und that, als wie ein General; / Warf Schanzen auf, schoß Ziegelstücke, / Zog schlechterdings mich nicht zurücke, / Sprach laut wenn ich den Sturm befahl! // War eine Vestung eingenommen, / Dann ließ ich meine Völker kommen / Drang tapfer ein in Feindes Land, / Marschirte listig hin und wieder / Hieb viele tausend Feinde nieder, / In allen Nesseln die ich fand. // Da lagen dann die kleinen Leichen, / Gefällt von meinen starken Streichen, / Bey tausenden gestreckt vor mir; / Stolz dacht ich mich als Ueberwinder / Ich war ein Kind, und wie die Kinder / Thun gar zu oft im Alter wir! // O meine Phantasie ist heftig, / Schon dazumahl war sie geschäftig, / Als ich noch meine Herde trieb; / Itzt aber sieht sie andre Schlachten / Denkt die, die sich unsterblich machten, / Und den, der sich unsterblich schrieb!

War and reading are intimately connected, for it is dreams of war that inspire the reading, and, as she admits, her writing. The fourth, fifth, and sixth stanzas could have been versified straight from her autobiographical letter to Sulzer, in which her transition from general to reader/writer is expedited by her encounter with the herder boy: "After many important battles," during which General Anna Louisa valiantly decapitates thistles by the thousands, her imagination finally received an impetus beyond these childish fantasies.[75] As is the case in Karsch's autobiography, this poem not only closely links war and reading and, ultimately, war and authorship, it also removes the speaker from the image of femininity and instead evokes two counterimages: that of a man — the valiant hero in battle, the commanding officer, the proudly victorious general — and that of the child mentioned in the penultimate stanza, burdened with the monotonous occupation of herding sheep (or cows) and with an overactive imagination. That Karsch imagines her heroine in the role of a man in authority and views this authority, and masculinity, as a precondition for writing at all is not that unusual: these traits became standard topoi in the writing of many women writers of the late eighteenth century, particularly in their forewords.[76] What is unusual in this poem, though, is her reduction of the concept of poetic inspiration to the level of childish fantasies and turbulent daydreaming. *Ungelehrt*, uneducated, endowed with nothing but excessive fantasies, she is empowered to write: Karsch's model deliberately reverberates bourgeois theories on "natural" poetic production. In Karsch's adaptation of the genius aesthetic, there is only a short distance from wild fantasies, a childish imagination, and a love for books unencumbered by formal education to the enduring recognition that can only be the reward of poetic genius, awarded to "Him who grew immortal by his pen."

Karsch's self-image as masculine plays an important part in biographies of her, beginning with those of her daughter and granddaughter, where this self-stylization immediately comes into conflict with another image that was central to the poet's biography, that of Karsch as a mother.[77]

---

[75] Karsch links these two experiences closely in her autobiography, where the encounter with the boy follows immediately on the martial fantasy: "After many important battles I was sitting one autumn day on the edge of a narrow stream when I caught sight of a boy on the other side of the water. . ." (Karsch, autobiographical letter to Sulzer, in Blackwell/Zantop, 134). "Nach vielen wichtigen Schlachten saß ich an einem Herbst-Tage am Rande eines kleinen Flußes und ward jenseits des Waßers einen Knaben gewahr. . . ." (*"Bruder in Apoll,"* I, 345).

[76] See the conclusion.

[77] On Karsch's portrayal as wife and mother in autobiographies and biographies, cf. Schaffers, 153–59.

Motherhood is femininity condensed and, as such, an important aspect of any woman poet's biography, as the many rather defensive forewords that highlight the poet's excellent qualities as a wife and mother, written by both poets and patrons, attest. In Klencke's biography of Karsch, the contrast between writing and femininity that Karsch had already illustrated in her self-stylization as a boy assumes more significant proportions, for, in Klencke's account, the boy does not grow into a good woman. The story of Karsch's early self-identification as a boy and her adamant rejection of the girl's role is related much as Karsch herself told it:

> She was given a doll at a fair which she threw into the crown of a pear tree, and along with it she threw away all inclination for childish games. When she was not reading or studying, she went into the garden, took a stick from a hazel tree and with it attacked the nettles as if they were a legion of enemies. She hacked off the heads of entire fields of them, and in the course of this daily warlike pursuit the nettles were demolished before the summer was over. Her warlike disposition changed with the seasons. Instead of the nettles, armies of peas and beans were lined up on the table and ordered to attack. Or outside she would collect little pebbles, arrange them in rank and file, and fire upon them with larger stones.[78]

Like Karsch's self-descriptions, Klencke's description of Karsch's childish amusements emphasizes her predilection for serious reading ("studying") and boyish war games, and by directly preceding this characterization with Karsch's scornful rejection of the doll, she makes certain that the reader understands these proclivities not merely as childish but as expressly masculine. Far from abandoning such masculine traits in adulthood, Klencke expands on the theme in her occasional portrayal of Karsch as rather mannish — for example, taking snuff[79] — and in her repeated assertion that Karsch failed miserably at the traditionally feminine roles of wife and mother. As a young wife, she is portrayed as clumsy, incompetent at housework, and exasperating to her first husband

---

[78] Klencke, "Lebenslauf," 17: "Man hatte ihr zum Jahrmarkt eine Puppe gekauft, diese warf sie in den Wipfel eines Birnbaums, und mit ihr jede Neigung zu kindischen Spielen. Wenn sie nicht las oder lernte, so ging sie in den Garten, nahm ein Haselstrauchstäbchen, und zog damit auf die Nesseln, wie auf eine Legion Feinde los. Ganzen Feldern voll hieb sie die Köpfe ab, und durch diesen täglichen kriegerischen Zeitvertreib waren die Nesseln ausgerottet, ehe noch der Sommer verging. Mit den Uebergängen der Jahreszeit veränderte sich auch ihre kriegerischen Dispositionen. Statt der Nesseln wurden nun Armeen von Erbsen und Bohnen auf den Tisch gestellt, welche aufeinander losgehen mußten. Oder draußen im Freyen wurden kleine Kiesel gesammelt, in Reihe und Glieder gestellt, und mit größeren Steinen darauf losgefeuert."

[79] Klencke, "Lebenslauf," 83.

(an ominous beginning in view of the fact that he later divorced her);[80] her second husband, Daniel Karsch, who appears in Karsch's letters as an abusive drunkard, is transformed in Klencke's account into a loving husband and father with a regrettable weakness for alcohol who merely defended himself, at times not entirely verbally, against his wife's incessant nagging.[81] Karsch's role as a mother is portrayed in even more problematic terms, since it is linked with her poetic activity: in a direct reversal of the many forewords by poets and patrons avowing that the poet would never neglect her children over her writing, Klencke relates an episode in which Karsch's poetic occupation is held indirectly responsible for the death of her newborn daughter, reputedly the poet's favorite child. Karsch, still nursing, undertook a journey on foot to a distant village where she had an engagement to supply impromptu poems at a wedding. On the long walk through a February ice storm, which Karsch had to endure in her thin summer dress, she caught a fever which she passed on to her baby through her mother's milk after her return and which killed the child within days.[82] Later, Karsch goes on to ruin her son's chances to obtain a university education and forces her daughter Karoline into a marriage with an abusive uncle, Karsch's brother Hempel.[83] Klencke's assertion that Karsch would have been far happier if she had been freed from husband and children[84] is a rather loaded statement, for it implies Karsch's active rejection of her role as wife and mother, rather than merely an inability to fulfill it. In Klencke's depiction of Karsch's disastrous failure as a parent, her account functions simultaneously as biography and autobiography, for although she never expressly states that she herself was the child mistreated or neglected by Karsch and consistently refers to herself in the third person, she delivers her judgment with all the authority of first-hand experience: "She lacked all capabilities which are necessary for raising children, for her condition was one of dependence and her spirit much too agitated to confine itself to

---

[80] Klencke, "Lebenslauf," 41–42; cf. also Hausmann's negative assessment of Karsch's qualities as a housewife (34).

[81] Klencke, "Lebenslauf," 63–64; on Klencke's depiction of Karsch's husband Daniel, cf. also Schaffers, 139.

[82] Klencke, "Lebenslauf," 69.

[83] Klencke, "Lebenslauf," 108–12; but compare Karsch's letter to Gleim, in which she denies having arranged this marriage (March 14, 1770, in Karsch, *"Bruder in Apoll,"* II, 12).

[84] Klencke, "Lebenslauf," 72.

the rules of educating children."[85] Klencke's ambiguous statement subsists on the contrast of Karsch the poet and Karsch as a mother: on the one hand, Karsch is clearly portrayed as an incompetent mother (she lacked *capabilities*); on the other, her unsuitability to the task is rooted in her existence as a patronized poet (her *dependence*) and in the energy attributed to her spirit, which, in an allusion to the natural-genius discourse, cannot *confine* itself or adhere to *rules*.

In Helmina von Chézy's biography of Karsch, the story of little Anna Louisa throwing her doll away is retold unchanged, the episode of the girl's martial games copied verbatim from Klencke.[86] But Karsch's portrayal as an incompetent housewife and mother is subtly changed. The story of the death of Karsch's newborn is repeated, but the element of blame that is clearly implied in Klencke's account is here modified by the stronger emphasis on the "hunger and wretchedness"[87] that compelled Karsch to her fateful journey. In Chézy's account, Karsch's husbands appear as considerably more abusive than in Klencke's,[88] and there is no hint that Karsch might have neglected her son's education or forced an abusive husband on her daughter: what sounds in Klencke's biography like brute force exerted jointly by Karsch and Hempel[89] is muted, in Chézy's account, into an act of persuasion by which Karsch was taken in,[90] so that Karsch's choice of a husband for her daughter is presented as an act of bad judgment rather than deliberate cruelty. Whereas motherhood in Klencke's account is subtly juxtaposed to poetry, it serves here as the source of poetic inspiration *in extremis,* in the touching image of Karsch's love for her fourth child, born soon after her abandonment by

---

[85] Klencke, "Lebenslauf," 93: "Ihr selbst fehlten nun schlechterdings alle Kräfte, welche zur Erziehung erfordert werden; denn ihr Zustand war abhängig, und ihr Geist viel zu unruhig, als daß er sich in die Regeln der Erziehung eines Kindes hätte einschränken können."

[86] Chézy, "Meine Großmutter," 12.

[87] Chézy, "Meine Großmutter," 42: "Hunger und Elend hatten sie zu dieser Wanderung getrieben."

[88] For example, Chézy's depiction of Hirsekorn in "Meine Großmutter," 23–24 and 29, and Daniel Karsch, 43.

[89] Klencke, "Lebenslauf," 111: "The daughter was not asked for her opinion: because she was not a dazzling beauty, both [Karsch and Hempel] thought they were not doing her an injury. To say more of this would sound vengeful and be inappropriate here" ("Die Tochter wurde weiter nicht um ihren Willen gebeten: weil sie nicht blendende Reize hatte, so glaubten beide, daß sie kein Unrecht thäten. Mehr davon zu sagen, würde wie Repressalien klingen, und hier am unschicklichen Orte stehn").

[90] Chézy, "Meine Großmutter," 63: " . . . after she had heard that Karsch had been persuaded to betrothe her to her uncle . . ." (" . . . nachdem sie erfahren hatte, daß sich die Karschin habe bereden lassen, sie ihrem Oheim zu verloben . . .").

and divorce from her first husband: "she delighted in the child, blossomed like a rose, and sang like a bird on the green bough."[91] At the point at which Karsch is portrayed at her most dejected — destitute, homeless, and shamefully abandoned by her husband — it is motherhood that sustains her: "With tender tears she softened her meager piece of bread, embraced her child on her hard cot and found renewed courage in his cheerful mien."[92] Whereas Klencke ended her assessment by pronouncing Karsch *principally* unsuited for motherhood, Chézy obviously felt compelled to turn her into a loving mother.

The gradual development of Karsch's gender identity in autobiographical and biographical writing — from her masculine self-image to Klencke's depiction of her as a failed woman to the alignment of her image with traditional notions of femininity in Chézy's account — can, in part, be attributed to the historical time lapse that separates these three accounts. As Hausen, Duden, and many others have shown,[93] a woman's "natural calling" (*natürliche Bestimmung*) to wifedom and motherhood was a notion that was not extensively propagated in philosophical and literary texts until the late eighteenth century, and it began to exhibit a pervasive influence on the presentation of women writers, particularly with respect to their gender, around the turn of the nineteenth century.[94] Karsch's autobiographical works, written in the early to mid-1760s, and even Klencke's biography, written in the early 1790s, were almost certainly still unaffected by the far stricter nineteenth-century notions of feminine propriety that began to manifest themselves in philosophical and literary works around the turn of the century and that may well have directed Chézy's writing in 1858.[95] Because these

---

[91] Chézy, "Meine Großmutter," 33: "Doch sie freute sich des Kindes, blühte wie eine Rose, und sang wie ein Vogel auf grünem Zweige."

[92] Chézy, "Meine Großmutter," 34: "Mit sanften Thränen netzte sie ihren kargen Bissen Brot, schloß auf ihrem harten Lager ihr Kind in ihren Arm, und sog neuen Lebensmut aus seinen heitern Blicken."

[93] Cf. particularly the essays by Hausen, Duden, Dotzler, Cocalis, and Frevert ("Bürgerliche Meisterdenker").

[94] Pertinent turn-of-the-century texts include Humboldt's "Plan einer vergleichenden Anthropologie," "Über den Geschlechtsunterschied," and "Über männliche und weibliche Form"; Kant's "Anthropologie" and "Metaphysik"; Knigge's *Über den Umgang mit Menschen;* and Pockels's *Versuch einer Charakteristik des weiblichen Geschlechts,* among others.

[95] See Niethammer for a brief discussion of the increasing definition of the family and motherhood in terms of emotionality as of the turn of the century (71–76); for a more extensive treatment of motherhood throughout the ages, cf. Badinter.

notions of feminine propriety were manifestly *bourgeois* concepts,[96] Chézy's act of taming the wild boy into a tender and conscientious mother constitutes simultaneously an act of *Verbürgerlichung* of the peasant Karsch, one that is all the more significant since it deviates so extensively both from Karsch's autobiographical material and from Chézy's immediate source, her mother's biography, which was easily the most extensive, influential, and best known of all Karsch biographies at the time of Chézy's writing. The difference between Chézy's account vis-à-vis Klencke's or Karsch's own letters and autobiographical material is that whereas all three writers clearly saw writing as in conflict with contemporary notions of femininity, Chézy could not, as did Karsch and Klencke, let that conflict stand unresolved without fatally damaging the poet's reputation. The cleansing of Anna Louisa Karsch in her granddaughter's biography from the assumption of the masculine role, her transformation from wild boy to tender mother, can be read as a forcible, albeit posthumous, reminder of the poet's gender. Simultaneously, that transformation, which relegates Karsch's rejection of the girl's role, her penchant for war games, in fact her entire "boyhood," to the status of mere childish games, is yet another illustration that biography was understood not as providing a history of the poet's life but rather as an opportunity for authorial image construction, and many biographical writers felt entirely justified to adjust biographical data to this purpose.

## Beauty and the Beasts: Fairy Tale Imagery

Fairy tale motifs and characters are possibly the most persistently recurring images in biographies of peasant poets. Unlike the Child of Nature or the Sappho role, this tradition is nowhere prefigured in the poets' autobiographical material but originates with later biographers — for the most part, biographers who wrote about their subjects posthumously. The first biography on record to transform the poet's life into a fairy tale is Karoline Luise Klencke's life story of her mother, Anna Louisa Karsch. Klencke introduces her theme by speculating that Karsch might have been the last descendant of an aristocratic family,[97] a fact that, together with her wretched poverty, provides the ideal frame for a Cinderella story. The idea of Karsch's noble origins is further compounded in the depiction of the poet's mother: blue-eyed, pale-skinned, black-haired like Snow White, she is endowed with a beautiful singing voice and portrayed as an extraordi-

---

[96] For a discussion of these concepts and their consequences for the authorial self-image and image of bourgeois women writers, cf. the conclusion.

[97] Klencke, "Lebenslauf," 3.

narily accomplished dancer. "Whoever saw this wonderful woman dance in her sixty-fifth year of age is still charmed by her. Like a bird above water, she seemingly floated above the ground. . . ."[98] The grace and elegance of Karsch's mother provides an obvious contrast to the image the reader would be likely to infer: instead of the clumsy and heavy-set laboring peasant woman one might expect, one encounters a swan among the village geese. The Karsch-as-Cinderella motif recurs in the story of Karsch's mistreatment in the service of the miller's wife[99] and, most prominently, in the account of Karsch's escape from her lowly existence: the coach of Baron von Kottwitz spirits her away to his "magical castle" (*Zauberschloß*), where she spends three nights and is regaled with delectable food from magnificent plates,[100] all seemingly negligible events that are nonetheless told with the same descriptive concreteness they would be accorded in fairy tales. The transformation from peasant maid to princess, or, as Menzel puts it, from "ugly duckling" into a swan,[101] takes place in the traditional manner, in the clothing of the maiden in rich and luxurious robes.[102] The story of Karsch's wedding also is told using the vocabulary and style of the fairy tale genre,[103] clashing strangely with Karsch's own harsh descriptions of her miserable experiences in marriage, which Klencke's account, paradoxically, does not suppress but juxtaposes to both the fairy tale model and bucolic motifs:

> The bride was a slender, not yet sixteen-year-old girl with a radiant face, a rural-friendly mien and fiery blue eyes. Her indescribably beautiful forehead bore no powdered curls; instead, her thick chestnut brown hair was put up in braids, similar to the fashion among the girls

---

[98] Klencke, "Lebenslauf," 6: "Wer diese wunderbare Frau in ihrem fünf und sechzigsten Jahre hat tanzen sehen, der ist noch bezaubert von ihr. Sie hat, wie der Vogel über dem Wasser, gleichsam nur über dem Boden geschwebt. . . ."

[99] Klencke, "Lebenslauf," 30–31. Klencke later repeats this story nearly verbatim, casting herself in the lead role; cf. Klencke's relation of her years of servitude at her uncle's house ("Lebenslauf," 110–11).

[100] Klencke, "Lebenslauf," 84–87, the citation 85: "Zwei Tage und drei Nächte brachte sie hier wie in einem ihr gehörigen Zauberschlosse zu." The number three, like the numbers seven and twelve, makes a regular appearance in the fairy tale tradition and is liberally employed by Klencke as well. The fairy tale imagery in the story of Karsch's rescue through Kottwitz, including the reference to Kottwitz's "magical castle," is repeated in Chézy's "Meine Großmutter"; cf. 46–48, the reference 46.

[101] "Like the ugly duckling that was nonetheless destined to be a swan. . . ." ("Wie das häßliche junge Entlein, das später doch ein Schwan werden sollte," Menzel, 14).

[102] Klencke, "Lebenslauf," 89.

[103] This is the case in both Klencke's and Chézy's biographies of Karsch; cf. Klencke, "Lebenslauf," 40–41, and Chézy, "Meine Großmutter," 22–23.

of French Switzerland. . . . Thus she stood before the altar, where she was consecrated into sorrowful wedlock.

After the wedding celebration, which lasted three days, she was brought home by her husband and chained into her yoke.[104]

Klencke's account is clearly indebted to several literary discourses, among them the aesthetic of the simple and natural, complete with an allusion to Switzerland, which, since Haller's famous poem, "Die Alpen," had come to represent many of these qualities to contemporaries, and the fairy tale in which weddings last three days (it is highly unlikely that a poor rural household would have indulged in such expense, particularly for the wedding of a daughter). The vocabulary employed in the depiction of the fairy tale wedding, culminating in the bride being "brought home" (the word *heimführen* is an easily recognizable circumscription for marriages in literature and commonly used in fairy tales), keeps seemingly unproblematic company with the brief but sinister glimpse of the married life that follows. And it is surely significant that although the *wedding* is portrayed in terms of the fairy tale, the *marriage* and its attendant misery is symbolized in an allusion to the rustic: marriage begins with the newlywed wife, like an ox or a plowhorse, being chained into her yoke.

Fairy tale imagery not only abounds in later biographies of Karsch, many of which were indebted to Klencke's account and some of which copied lengthy passages verbatim from her, but also in pictorial representations. Two portrayals that seem clearly indebted to the turn-of-the-century and early-nineteenth-century understanding of the "folk," which finds its truest expression in folk songs and fairy tales, are W. Arndt's 1790 engraving of Karsch and the herder boy and Karoline Leonhardt Lyser's portrait of Karsch in the woods. Both are visual interpretations of her early biography: Leonhardt Lyser's painting (fig. 1) shows Karsch as a girl, clad in a thin dress, walking through the snowy forest under a pale moon, her body hunched over and hands clasped against the cold. It is a representation that could well serve as an illustration for any of the abandoned girls of the Grimms' tales, from Sterntaler wandering the freezing forest to Little Red Riding Hood about to encounter the wolf.

[104] Klencke, "Lebenslauf," 40–41: "Die Braut war ein schlankes, noch nicht voll sechzehnjähriges Mädchen mit blühendem Gesicht, ländlich-freundlichen Mienen und feuervollen blauen Augen. Ihre unbeschreiblich schöne Stirn trug keine gepuderte Locken, sondern ihr stark kastanienbraunes Haar war nach der Art der Köpfe französischer Schweizermädchen, in Flechten aufgeschlagen. . . . So stand sie vor dem Traualtar, wo sie für einen unglücklichen Ehestand eingesegnet wurde.

Nach dreytägiger Hochzeitfeyer wurde sie von ihrem Manne heimgeführt, und in ihr Joch gespannt."

*Fig. 1: Karoline Leonhardt Lyser (1811–99), "Anna Louisa Karsch, geb. Dürrbach."
Ink and water color painting. Courtesy of Städelsches Kunstinstitut und
Städtische Galerie Frankfurt.*

In a similar manner, Arndt's engraving (fig. 2) maps a motif from a folk song onto Karsch's biography in his interpretation of a seminal moment in Karsch's life, her first encounter with the herder boy. In Karsch's autobiographical letters to Sulzer, the encounter is described as follows: "I was sitting one autumn day on the edge of a narrow stream when I caught sight of a boy on the other side of the water who was surrounded by several other herder children. He was reading to them and I flew to his side to augment the number of listeners."[105] Arndt's engraving deletes the other children and with it Karsch's depiction of the reading as an experience shared by a group, thus both privatizing and intensifying the moment of inspiration: in the engraving, the boy is portrayed alone, his attention as fixed on the girl as hers is on him. The body postures of both figures, her kneeling by the side of the river, him

---

[105] Karsch, autobiographical letter to Sulzer, in Blackwell/Zantop, 134: "Nach vielen wichtigen Schlachten saß ich an einem Herbst-Tage am Rande eines kleinen Flußes und ward jenseits des Waßers einen Knaben gewahr, welchen einige Hirten-Kinder umgeben hatten. Er war ihr Vorleser und ich flog hin um die Zahl seiner Zuhörer zu vermehren" (*"Bruder in Apoll,"* I, 345).

*Fig. 2: "Encounter with the herder boy." Etching by W. Arndt, ca. 1790. From: Gisela Brinker-Gabler, Deutsche Literatur von Frauen, vol. 1 (1988).*

standing in the boat, their hands desperately outstretched toward each other, resonates with a melancholy image gleaned from a folk song: that of the unhappy prince and princess who "could not reach each other, the water was far too deep."[106] The reduction of Karsch's biography to a "folk" motif in both pictures makes it difficult not to see them as making an aesthetic of poverty, as making "nature" idyllic in the Arcadian sense, despite the fact that the overt *themes* of these pictures are Karsch's physical destitution, as in Lyser's painting, and intellectual deprivation, as in the engraving by Arndt.

Of all predictable fairy tale images, it is the story of the girl's rescue from such poverty and deprivation that most lends itself to a literary representation of the patronage theme. Hannah More, who, like Klencke, did not hesitate to edit Yearsley's biography in the service of image construction,[107] likewise played on fairy tale motifs in her relation of Yearsley's miraculous rescue from starvation in the stable.[108] Later adaptations of More's depiction of the stable scene were quite conscious of the literary nuances of this story. The following rendition makes good use of the sentimental value of the story, simultaneously hinting that such a scene could not possibly be real:

> It is said that the scene he encountered in the milkwoman's home, though familiar to the pages of fiction, has, happily, not often been realized, even in the annals of the poor. Her cows, the main dependence of a large family, had gone to satisfy the landlord's claims; the cottage, denuded of its humble plenishing, scarcely afforded a bed; before a fireless hearth sat the famished, dispirited husband; scattered around were six children crying and clamorous for bread; in one corner, on a heap of dirty straw, lay the aged grandmother, bedridden; while at the opposite side, struggling in the throes of childbirth, was she who bore the relation of daughter, wife, and mother to all these wretched beings. It is almost needless to say that succor came promptly and liberally; to

---

[106] "Es waren zwei Königskinder, / Die hatten einander so lieb, / Sie konnten zusammen nicht kommen, / Das Wasser war viel zu tief." The original folk song was based on Ovid's tale of Hero and Leander and first published in its entirety in a Nuremberg chapbook in 1563. Around the turn of the nineteenth century, several versions of this song appeared in collections, including, in 1804, in Friedrich Heinrich Bothe's *Frühling Almanach*, the version published in 1807 in Büsching and von der Hagen's *Deutsche Volkslieder*, and Werner von Haxthausen's transcription of the song (cf. http://ingeb.org/Lieder/eswarenz.html). I thank Howard Gaskill for his help in tracing eighteenth-century versions of the song.

[107] Cf. especially Waldron, "Ann Yearsley and the Clifton Records."

[108] Cf. her letter to Montagu, August 27, 1784, cited in Mahl/Koon, 277–78, the citation 277.

one alone it came too late. The grandmother, overcome with joy at knowing that relief was secured, sank back and died.[109]

What is familiar from the "pages of fiction in the description of this scene is not only the pathos of the situation but also more concrete allusions to contexts both magical (in the miraculousness of the rescue, an effect so extreme that it proves fatal for one of the paupers) and mystical (in the biblical parallel established in the tale of Yearsley giving birth in a stable). Unlike Klencke's story, this rendition shows less interest in the tale's Happy Ending than in the depiction of the sheer despair from which the poet was saved through generous intervention. More, too, reputedly showed herself particularly responsive to poems in which Yearsley professed her wretchedness,[110] and demonstrably did what she could, in her description of the poet's situation, to augment her misery: in More's version, Yearsley was "sacrificed" in marriage to an oaf when she was barely seventeen (Yearsley was twenty-two when she married); in the stable scene, Yearsley's fate of near-starvation was shared by six children (Yearsley only had four).[111] The fact that even such elementary biographical data as the poet's age and family circumstances could be falsified once more points to the fact that these life stories were not primarily intended to provide readers with actual biographical background but rather to establish an authorial image, an act that occasionally demanded the subordination of biographical and historical fact to carefully designed fiction.

Perhaps not surprisingly, the most frequently recurring fairy tale character representing the poet in biographical material is neither the princess nor the pauper but the witch. Outward appearance played a highly significant part in the establishment of authorial image, a fact that is reflected in the circumstance that virtually *all* peasant women poets were famed for their ugliness. Janet Little[112] and Maria Catharina Dippen[113] are portrayed as masculine, coarse, and swarthy; Isobel Pagan is depicted as clubfooted, tumorous, and squinting[114] — a woman of "very unearthly appearance" who was described by a contemporary clergyman as "the most perfect

---

[109] "An Historical Milkwoman," 395.

[110] Cf. Southey, 125, and "An Historical Milkwoman," 395.

[111] Cf. Waldron, "Ann Yearsley and the Clifton Records," 306.

[112] Cf. the description of Little in Paterson, 87; on Little's outward appearance, cf. also Dunlop's letter to Burns, July 13, 1789, in Burns/Dunlop, I, 274. Hilton Brown suspects Little's unprepossessing exterior as the main reason why Burns refused all contact with her (15–16).

[113] Cf. Karsch's description of Dippen in her letter to Sulzer, *"Bruder in Apoll,"* I, 427.

[114] Cf. Stewart's description of her (9) and Paterson, 115–16.

realization of a witch or hag that I ever saw."[115] Most of Pagan's biography consists of anecdotes of "wicked Tibbie Pagan" indulging her extraordinary fondness for whisky, "scrieching out poetic verse," and wildly swinging her crutch about in the process.[116] Molly Leapor is described as "extremely swarthy, and quite emaciated, with a long crane-neck, and a short body, much resembling, in shape, a bass-viol";[117] the success of her work has been sardonically attributed to her early death: Leapor as a person, "ungainly, unlovely, uncharming, and proletarian," would have been difficult to sell to a patron;[118] thus, the success of her work was greatly abetted by the removal of its least prepossessing aspect, its author, from the scene.[119]

As the depiction of Pagan as the witch screeching out her verse already suggests, the ugliness of the witch is inextricably intertwined with her status as a poet: ugliness, in many biographical accounts, *connotes* poetic genius. It is this symbolic value that often results in depictions of the poet not merely as homely but as shockingly, implausibly hideous. Klencke describes Karsch as so repulsive at birth that her mother spontaneously expressed a wish to have the child drowned in the river[120] and has this to say about Karsch's later physical development:

> Nonetheless, it must be noted that the poet later grew up nothing less than ugly, and if she had had any control over her body and her facial expression, she could almost have been considered beautiful, even to her dying day. She had a regular and fine figure of middle stature, a beautiful and lasting skin color, the most beautiful forehead ever seen on a human being on which lay fully the light of her great spirit; the most brilliant, brightest and most expressive blue eyes, unchangingly red lips, and when in a good mood warm cheerfulness in her expression. But when she displayed that searching gaze that predominated in her face most of the time, she was difficult to bear, and one could not have borne to be in her company if her thoughts and occupations had not been easily distracted by diversions such as the moment often afforded. Her eyelids contracted in this gaze, her eye became smaller, and like the sun concentrated through a burning glass its rays shot towards the object of its contemplation. It was an all-consuming gaze.... The

[115] The quotations are in Paterson, 115 and 117, respectively.

[116] Paterson, 115–20, the quotations are on 120 and 117, respectively.

[117] In the *Gentleman's Magazine* of 1784, 807.

[118] Rizzo, "Molly Leapor," 317.

[119] Rizzo, "The Patron," 251.

[120] Klencke, "Lebenslauf," 12. The story is later repeated in Chézy's biography of Karsch, where Karsch's mother is reported to have screamed in horror on first looking on her child ("Meine Großmutter," 5).

poet, who was not aware of her own facial expression, was subject to innumerable aggravations because of it, and at bottom, this gaze can be considered the source of all of her misfortunes.[121]

Klencke's description is obviously not limited to Karsch's physical exterior: in her account, Karsch is only fearfully ugly at moments of intense concentration; as soon as she is distracted, she drops her penetrating gaze and reverts to "Belloise," her normal, "almost beautiful," self. That the intensity of Karsch's gaze, her all-consuming absorption, is related to her poetic activity would be obvious even if Klencke had not stated elsewhere that Karsch "rarely, due to the poetic fire raging within her, looked straight with her eyes, but was nearly cross-eyed."[122] Karsch's all-consuming gaze is defined in terms that point negatively to its intellectual component (*Forschblikk*); apparently this constituted a recurring subject in Klencke's interaction with Karsch, who reported repeatedly to Gleim that her daughter had exhorted her to "think less."[123] Klencke's assessment of Karsch's poetic nature, distilled in her description of Karsch's frightful gaze, is highly pejorative — surprisingly so, given that it appears in the introductory biography to an edition of Karsch's poems — but it also evokes the nature aesthetic in defining Karsch's poetic activity as involuntary: Karsch was not in control of her horrifying expression, she could not help it, and the implication is that had she been able,

---

[121] Klencke, "Lebenslauf," 12–14: "Indeß ist anzumerken: daß die Dichterin nachher nichts weniger als häßlich aufwuchs, und hätte sie ihren Körper und ihr Mienenspiel in der Gewalt gehabt, so würde sie bis zu ihrem Tod beinahe für schön haben gelten können. Sie hatte einen wohlgeordneten feinen Wuchs mittlerer Größe, schöne und daurende Gesichtsfarbe, hellbraunes Haar, die schönste menschliche Stirn, welche jemals gesehn worden ist, auf welcher ganz das Licht ihres großen Geistes ausgebreitet lag; die strahlenvollsten, hellsten, sprechendsten blauen Augen, beständig rothe Lippen, und bei guter Laune herzlichen Frohsinn in den Mienen. Allein, wenn sie ihren Forschblikk hatte, welcher die meiste Zeit in ihrem Gesichte herrschte, so war sie schwer auszuhalten, und man würde nicht mit ihr haben Umgang pflegen können, wenn ihre Gedanken und ihr Thun nicht leicht wären abzulenken gewesen, durch Zerstreuung, welche oft der Augenblick würkte. Die Augenlieder zogen sich bei solchem Blikk zusammen, das Auge wurde kleiner, und seine Strahlen schossen, gleichsam wie die Sonne in einem Brennpunkt, auf seinen Gegenstand, zusammen. Es war ein verzehrender Blick. . . . Die Dichterin, welche nichts von diesem Mienenspiele wußte, hat sich unzählige Verdrüßlichkeiten dadurch zugezogen, und eigentlich kann man es die Grundlage aller ihrer Unglüksfälle nennen." For an analysis of this passage, cf. Schaffers, 163–64.

[122] Klencke, "Lebenslauf," 36: ". . .weil sie damals, vermöge ihres in ihr wirkenden Dichterfeuers selten mit den Augen gerade sah, sondern beinahe schielte."

[123] Karsch's letter to Gleim, November 14, 1788: "my daughter asks me to think less and write almost nothing at all, but that means not to live" ("meine Tochter bittet ich Sol weniger dennken, sol fast gar nicht mehr schreiben, daß heißt nicht mehr leben"; *"Bruder in Apoll,"* II, 304).

she would have discarded her poetic gift to live a normal life. For her poetic talent, condensed in the horrific gaze, disfigures the poet's usually congenial appearance, repels human companionship, and is held responsible for every misfortune that later befell the poet. It is a theme later taken up by Klencke's daughter Helmina von Chézy in her description of her grandmother on her deathbed: in this episode, the dead Karsch appears as more beautiful than she had ever been in life.[124] Like Klencke's, Chézy's biography links the poet's ugliness with her poetic talent; beauty can only be attained by relinquishing this gift — in Klencke's account, momentarily through distractions, in Chézy's, permanently in death. In both accounts, poetic inspiration comes at a cost: the "innumerable aggravations" and "misfortunes" that make up the poet's life reach their pinnacle in the portrayal of other humans recoiling from the poet whose image becomes bearable only in death.

Karsch's fabled hideousness was a recurring theme not only in posthumous biographical writing but also during her lifetime, partly because it contrasted with that other authorial image of her, beautiful Sappho.[125] Her first letter to Gleim, written before they met in person, warns him not to expect a beautiful Sappho,[126] and she repeatedly had to contend with readers' conjectures of her beauty based on her pen name.[127] All portraits that we have of her portray her as intensely ugly: Georg Friedrich Schmidt's 1764 engraving (fig. 3) shows her in profile, a simple, rounded face, unadorned and well nourished, more evocative of rural plenty than Karsch's extreme poverty, but certainly descriptive of Karsch's bucolic origins. Daniel Chodowiecki's drawing (fig. 4) draws attention to her double image by portraying her as an aging Sappho with an unmistakably masculine demeanor: hollow-cheeked, clad in a peasant's dress, but hair coifed *à la Greque*. Hempel's drawing of Karsch at her desk (fig. 5) and Karl Christian Kehrer's painting for Gleim (fig. 6), painted in the year of Karsch's death, complete the circle from peasant maid via androgynous Sappho to writing witch. The legend on the back of Kehrer's painting may emphasize Karsch's virtues over her talent ("painted for Gleim, more on account of her virtue than of her genius"), but the painting itself evokes different images: the gaunt face and the long spindly fingers tell of

[124] Chézy, "Meine Großmutter," 96–97.

[125] Cf. Heinse's essay for an analysis of Sappho's beauty and seductiveness (122–23). For an analysis of Karsch's exterior in biographical writing and physiognomic analysis, cf. Schaffers, 159–64.

[126] Karsch's letter to Gleim, May 14, 1761, *"Bruder in Apoll,"* I, 7.

[127] Cf. Nörtemann, "Verehrung, Freundschaft, Liebe," 81, and Klencke, "Lebenslauf," 78.

deprivation and are unmistakably reminiscent of the image of a witch. The painting thus returns Karsch to the original image of the woman "from the people" and echoes both Gleim's and Uz's appellation of Karsch as "poetic witch"[128] and her own repeated statement that people were so astonished by her speed and spontaneity of poetic production that they claimed she "must have produced these verses by magic."[129] Most significant in the history of Karsch portraiture as a witch and its exploitation as indicative of Karsch's poetic genius is Johann Heinrich Lips's engraving (fig. 7) of 1777: to both Gleim's and Karsch's dismay, Lavater included this portrait in his *Physiognomische Fragmente* (Physiognomic Fragments) and began his analysis of her poetic gift, based on her features, by anticipating the viewer's shock at Karsch's appearance: "Much better not to write verse than to look like this!"[130]

Fig. 3: Anna Louisa Karsch. Etching by Georg Friedrich Schmidt, 1764. Frontispiece to Karsch's Auserlesene Gedichte (1764).

Fig. 4: "Meierei auf dem Hammer bei Schwiebus." Drawing by Daniel Nikolaus Chodowiecki. Archiv für Kunst und Geschichte, Bildarchiv Preußischer Kulturbesitz, Berlin.

[128] Cf. Gleim's letter to Karsch in Karsch, *"Bruder in Apoll,"* II, 461; Uz's letter is quoted in Barndt, 174.

[129] In her third autobiographical letter to Sulzer: "alle sagten ich müste den Gesang gezaubert haben" (*"Bruder in Apoll,"* I, 357). Cf. also her remark in her second autobiographical letter, in which she is called a "sorceress" (*Zauberrin*) by her admiring listeners (I, 352).

[130] "Lieber keine Verse machen, als so aussehen!" Lavater, Abschnitt 11, Fragment 14, 315. Cf. Niethammer, 249, for a brief discussion of Lavater's physiognomic analysis of Karsch.

Fig. 5: *Anna Louisa Karsch at her desk.*
Drawing by Ernst Wilhelm Hempel.
Courtesy of Societätsverlag Frankfurt.

Fig. 6: *Anna Louisa Karsch. Oil painting by Karl Christian Kehrer, 1791.* Notation on back: "Painted for Gleim, more on account of her virtue than of her genius." Courtesy of the Gleim-Haus, Halberstadt.

Fig. 7: *Anna Louisa Karsch.*
Etching by Johann Heinrich Lips.
In: Johann Kaspar Lavater,
Physiognomische Fragmente, *1777.*

It is hardly useful to speculate how close these portraits of Karsch came to an accurate representation of the author, but it is nonetheless worth noting — without intending to present Karsch's self-image as more "accurate" than the many pictorial representations of her by others — that Karsch herself considered her ugliness in paintings greatly exaggerated. In 1761, she complained about the disfigurement of her image in Adam Friedrich Oeser's portrait of her;[131] in 1784, she attributed her portrayal in Stubinitzki's sculpture of her to his envy and his deliberate and malicious intent to portray her as a witch.[132] Six years earlier, she had this to say about the inclusion of Lips's portrait of her in Lavater's work:

> I am indebted to Lavater for introducing me to him [Chodowiecki], although my botched portrait in his Physiognomics seems to frighten away visitors so that nobody calls on me or greets me anymore sinceced that my face could scare off children.
> 
> I don't put much store in such honors, but nonetheless, I liked it when young men from foreign lands wanted to see me. You know that I don't have such a piercing, wild and fiery owl's eye as that given to me by Lips. . . .
> 
> But what's the use, dear Gleim? In general, I don't think much of this deeply analytical Lavaterizing, since I find it very untrustworthy.[133]

Karsch's critique encompasses not only Lavater's entire methodology,[134] but also, applied specifically to Lips's portrait of her, singles out

---

[131] Cf. her letter to Gleim, December 27, 1761, in *"Bruder in Apoll,"* I, 55–57, the reference 56.

[132] Cf. her letter to Gleim, April 6, 1784, in *"Bruder in Apoll,"* II, 207–9. Her granddaughter Helmina von Chézy, on the other hand, claimed that Karsch's image in paintings was not true to life because she was usually portrayed as more beautiful than she actually was ("Meine Großmutter," 110).

[133] Letter from Karsch to Gleim, February 24, 1778, in Beuys, 181–82: " . . . ich danks dem Lavater, daß er mir zu seiner Bekanntschaft verhalf, obgleich mein mißlungenes Porträt in der Physiognomik die Fremden abzuschrecken scheint, daß keiner mich mehr aufsuchen und grüßen will, seitdem die Welt glauben muß, mein Kopf könnte Kinder scheuchen. Ich mache mir endlich nicht viel aus dieser Ehre, dennoch war mirs lieb, wenn die Jünglinge aus fremden Ländern mich sehen wollten. Sie wissens, ich habe kein solches stieres wildflammendes Eulenauge, als mir Herr Lips gegeben hat. . . .

Doch was kanns helfen, lieber Gleim? Ich halte überhaupt wenig von der tief forschenden Lavaterei, weil ich sie sehr unzuverlässig finde" (the quotation 182).

[134] Geitner has recently analyzed Lavater's analytical methodology as presupposing the opposition of a "natural language" of pure expression with the spoken or written language of deception (239–70, especially 250–51 and 256); "Lavaterizing," in other words, assumes a close connection between the study of physiognomy and the search for the "natural" in which aesthetic theory was also engaged (cf. also Geitner's chapters on the naive, 284–301). Richard Gray has persuasively argued that Lavater's search for the "natural" is, by definition, a bourgeois undertaking comparable to Herder's and Bürger's

that one facet that was at the center of Lavater's analysis of her poetic talent: the eye. For it is that same eye in Lips's portrait, an eye whose existence in reality Karsch emphatically denied, that Lavater's physiognomic analysis diagnosed as the abode of Karsch's poetic talent. Regardless of Karsch's objections, the points of agreement between contemporary analysis and posthumous portrayal are significant: both in Karsch's interpretation of Lips's portrait and Klencke's later biography, Karsch's eye is described as "piercing," a quality that is deemed intensely repellent in both cases. Both Lavater and Klencke identified the eye as the central and *exclusive* focal point expressing Karsch's poetic gift (Lavater analyzed the remainder of her face as that of "a coldly probing thinker" and claimed that while the eye clearly defined her as a poet, the rest of her face suggested predilections for philosophy rather than poetry[135]). Both Karsch's reading of Lips's portrait and Klencke's later biography involve the image of others recoiling in horror from Karsch's repugnant exterior. Given that Klencke's biography must have made at least some use of her mother's letters, these parallels suggest that Klencke's depiction of Karsch's repulsive gaze may have been based on Karsch's *denial* of both the actual existence of this eye and its symbolic significance as interpreted by Lavater. However one may read the relationship between these three texts, there can be no question that these visions of the poet's eye, from the piercing eye to the shockingly repulsive eye to the eye as the center of poetic inspiration, were still under debate and open to interpretation at the time of Karsch's and Lavater's writing; it was Klencke's biography, which owed its credibility largely to the author's intimate knowledge of her subject, that solidified them into biographical fact.

Physiognomy seems to have been a fairly common method of dissecting the natural genius: Yearsley, as well, was the subject of physiognomic analyses linking her homely exterior to her poetic genius.[136] To Leapor, we owe a splendid poetic parody of the science: in "The Visit," she attacks physiognomy head on, describing the speaker's frantic flight into the most remote recesses of the wilderness

---

search for the *Volk:* he defines Lavater's physiognomics as part of the most basic project of "bourgeois ideology . . . to develop a unifying theory of the human — i.e., bourgeois — subject" (132).

[135] Lavater, vol. 3, Abschnitt 11, Fragment 14, 315.

[136] Cf. Tompkins's report on Cottle's analysis of her outward appearance (69).

> Where careless creatures, such as I
> May 'scape the penetrating eye
> Of students in physiognomy;
> Who read your want of wit or grace
> Not from your manners, but your face;
> Whose tongues are for a week supplied
> From one poor mouth that's stretched too wide;
> Who greatly blame a freckled hand,
> A skinny arm, full shoulders; and,
> Without a microscope, can spy
> A nose that's placed an inch awry.
> In vain to glaring lights you run,
> Their eyes can face a mid-day sun:
> You'll find no safety in retreat,
> Like sharks they never mince their meat;
> Their dreadful jaws they open throw,
> And, if they catch you, down you go.[137]

Leapor's poem transfers the "penetrating eye" to the practitioner rather than the object of physiognomy and skillfully juxtaposes the unbearable intensity of its vision with the superficiality of its interpretation. What the eye sees (everything) is hugely overread in pseudoscientific analysis, where the gain in understanding is nil. Leapor, moreover, asserts that the purpose of the analysis is disingenuous, that it is not to see but to obliterate the object of contemplation. Given the close link between the appearance of the poet and the criticism of her work that was characteristic of physiognomic analysis, Leapor may be pointing to an aspect that Karsch later pointed out as well: the notion that physiognomy replaces in-depth engagement with the poet's work by superficial contemplation of the poet's exterior, misreads surface as content, and thus relieves the viewer from any engagement with its object of criticism, either her personality or her work.

Central to physiognomic analyses of lower-class women is their indescribable hideousness, and this shocking exterior of the "natural" woman poet — the witch, the hag, the "coldly probing thinker" described by Lavater and Klencke — circumscribes, among others, the unusualness of the poet, who is, in many of these accounts, not fit for human companionship (Karsch repels others with the intensity of her gaze, while Pagan chases them off by wildly swinging her crutch about). It is more than obvious that these representations served a purpose in the construction

---

[137] Leapor, "The Visit," reprinted in Lonsdale, *Eighteenth-Century Women Poets*, 212–13.

of the poets' authorial image: intense ugliness, in pictures as well as textual descriptions, guarantees the poet's originality, authenticity, simplicity, and coarseness, and simultaneously, in the recourse to fairy tale motifs, serves as a class denominator: the witch in this discourse is nothing but an intensification of the woman "from the people." Some peasant poets were quite conscious of these connections, as Molly Leapor's satirical self-description in her poem "*Mira's* Picture" shows. In Leapor's "Pastoral," the discussion of two shepherds about the most beautiful nymphs of the valley is interrupted by Mira's appearance:

> *Phillario.* But who is she that walks on yonder hill,
> With studious brows, and night-cap dishabille?
> That looks a stranger to the beams of day;
> And counts her steps, and mutters all the way?
>
> *Corydon.* 'Tis *Mira,* daughter to a friend of mine;
> 'Tis she that makes your what-d'ye-call — your rhyme.
> I own the girl is something out o'th'way:
> But how d'ye like her? good *Phillario,* say!
>
> *Phillario.* Like her! — I'd rather beg the friendly rains,
> To sweep the nuisance from thy loaded plains;
> That —
>
> *Corydon.* — Hold, *Phillario*! she's a neighbour's child:
> 'Tis true, her linen may be something soil'd.
>
> *Phillario.* Her linen, *Corydon*! — Herself, you mean.
> Are such the dryads of thy smiling plain?
> Why, I could swear it, if it were no sin,
> That yon lean rook can shew a fairer skin.
>
> *Corydon.* What tho' some freckles in her face appear?
> That's only owing to the time o'th'year.
> Her eyes are dim, you'll say: Why, that is true:
> I've heard the reason, and I'll tell it you.
> By a rush-candle (as her father says)
> She sits whole ev'nings reading wicked plays.
>
> *Phillario.* She read! — She'd better milk her brindled cows:
> I wish the candle does not singe her brows,
> So like a dry furze-faggot; and, beside,
> Not quite so even as a mouse's hide.[138]

---

[138] Leapor, "*Mira's* Picture, A Pastoral," Colman/Thornton, II, 123–26, the quotation 124–25. (The emphases are original.)

The main theme that permeates Leapor's satire is the same that appears in Klencke's biography of Karsch, Lavater's physiognomic theories and contemporary descriptions of Pagan and other poets: the poet's ugliness is not merely coincidental to her poetic inspiration, it is *caused* by it. Mira's appearance as a *poetical* witch, dim-eyed due to her reading, muttering to herself presumably because she is counting out the meter to a poem, is as popular in biographical representations of other poets as the suggestion that the poet had best return to milking her cows.

*Fig. 8: Ann Cromartie Yearsley, 1787, from a reprint of 1814.*
*Engraving by [Wilson?] Lowry (1762–1824).*
*Courtesy of British Library.*

Like Pagan's sarcastic sobriquet on her own deformity, "Pistol Fit,"[139] Leapor's satire is essentially defensive, a barb directed at the critic's view of the peasant poet which not only wildly exaggerates her physical repulsiveness but simultaneously undermines her continued existence as a poet. With the possible exception of Ann Yearsley, no peasant poet was in a position to provide a counterimage to the writing witch. Yearsley, whose depiction as "plain, but by no means disagreeable"[140] is by far the most complimentary physical description available of any of these poets, was consistently portrayed by others as a milkmaid, her face shaded in to indicate the rural laborer's sunburn, surrounded by flowers to complete the bucolic image (fig. 8). These images, used as the frontispieces to her collections, reiterated the notion that Yearsley's career as a poet would be rather short-lived by implicitly announcing her return to that which was visually defined as her *true* vocation, her existence as a milkmaid. But the engraving produced by her son William and proudly displayed as the frontispiece to her classical collection *The Rural Lyre* suggests an entirely different context, regardless of whether the picture is intended to portray Yearsley.[141] For this engraving (fig. 9) represents a significant departure from the depiction of the poet as Child of Nature/Woman from the People that permeates most biographical accounts and visual representations: the engraving relies heavily on a classical education that Yearsley was not supposed to possess, let alone flaunt in this manner, and that is similarly on display in many poems in *The Rural Lyre*. The engraving has been interpreted in terms of its obvious political significance, as a representation of "the divinely sanctioned mediation between the ideal of national liberty and the British public."[142] Although this reading is undoubtedly valid, one could also, given that the picture adorns the collection of a lower-class author, infer an aesthetic meaning. Perhaps Yearsley, in the only pictorial representation over which she had any control, uses this image to hint at an aesthetic compromise that few of her patrons were willing to consider: in this scene, representing the discovery of the native Britons by Brutus, Liberty mediates between Jove and the Britons — perhaps alluding to the obvious parallel to Yearsley's "natural talent," which could, rather than be extinguished by a forced return of the poet to physical labor, be developed by cultivation "from above."

---

[139] Cf. Paterson, 121.

[140] Cf. the *Gentleman's Magazine* 54 (1784): 897.

[141] Landry recognizes Yearsley herself in the image (*Muses*, 173), whereas Tompkins claims that the picture resembles Mrs. Siddons (94).

[142] Landry, *Muses*, 173.

*Fig. 9:* "British Liberty." *Etching by William Cromartie Yearsley, 1796. Frontispiece to Ann Cromartie Yearsley,* The Rural Lyre. *Courtesy of the British Library.*

Physical portrayals, in pictures and tales, often represent a central aspect of the poet's biography: the poet's ugliness can only assume the tremendous importance accorded it in most accounts — as in Klencke's attribution of Karsch's every misfortune to her forbidding gaze — because it stands as symbolic of the poet's vocation. Understanding ugliness as a symbol for poetic creativity could well explain why virtually *all* lower-class poets appear as witches or hags in the works of their biographers. Among all the beasts peopling the biographies of lower-class women authors, there is only one beauty, the Scottish poet Jeanie Glover (1758–1801). But although Glover manifestly constitutes an exception to the rule, her brief biography can, to some extent, be seen as paradigmatic in its linking of her outward appearance to her poetic inclinations and in the assumption that these two aspects determined the entire course of her life: "She was remarkable for beauty — both of face and figure — properties which, joined to a romantic and poetic fancy, had no doubt their influence in shaping her future unfortunate career."[143] Glover's biography reads less as a fairy tale than a morality play: "in an evil hour,"[144] she eloped with an actor, ran away to the stage, became an adventurer and traveling singer of dubious repute (Burns described her as "not only a — — , but also a thief" and claimed that she "in one or other character has visited most of the correction houses in the west"[145]). Unsurprisingly, Glover's beauty and depravity are punished by a sudden and untimely death.[146] Glover's biography is highly significant in comparison to the others because she is not only the only reputedly beautiful woman among them but also the only peasant poet whose poetic work is almost entirely suppressed in her biography. Although she did write,[147] her biography portrays her as a *performer* rather than composer of songs: she was "seen at a fair in Irvine, gaily attired, and playing on a tambarine at the mouth of a close, in which was the exhibition-room of her husband the conjurer."[148] Glover's brief and perfunctory appearance as an author is overlaid by her much more extensive and colorful portrayal as circus performer, vagabond, and petty criminal.

---

[143] Paterson, 36; cf. also Greig, II, 10–11: "As may be too easily guessed, however, her subsequent career was that of an unfortunate." Glover has recently been briefly discussed in McCue, "Burns," 43–45.

[144] Paterson, 36.

[145] Burns's characterization is taken from his "Remarks on Scottish Songs and Ballads" and quoted in Paterson, 34.

[146] Paterson, 37.

[147] Burns attributed to her the song "Owre the Muir amang the Heather"; cf. Greig, II, 148–49; Stewart suspects that Glover "must have composed many more songs" (unpag.).

[148] Paterson, 37.

The erasure of Jeanie Glover, the only beauty in a herd of beasts, as an author seems to confirm the existence of a relationship between the poet's authorial image and her legendary ugliness. Extreme ugliness as the poet's defining characteristic in biographies, then, serves essentially four related functions: it symbolizes the poet's creativity; it sets the poet apart from humanity; it distinguishes her from others of her gender — in the implicit depiction as unfeminine, the witch's ugliness fulfills the same function as Sappho's intensity of passion; and casts doubt, from within the biographical text, on the biography's historical and biographical accuracy. The popular portrayal of the poet as a witch and the employment of other fairy tale motifs and characters not only point to the literariness of the biographical tale, they fairly *emphasize* it, an aspect that has not prevented later scholars and biographers from reading these tales quite straightforwardly as biographical background. Taking the fairy tale imagery seriously would obviously compromise such a reading, which, in the absence of more reliable biographical information about these authors, is difficult to acknowledge. But read with an eye to aesthetics rather than history, the fairy-tale-as-biography affords us intriguing insights on poetological traditions. It indicates, particularly for nineteenth-century writers and painters, the conflation of the eighteenth-century "folk" discourse, which manifested itself primarily in an interest in unlettered geniuses, with that of the nineteenth century, which found popular expression in the recovery of folk and fairy tales. Nineteenth-century biographies of peasant poets thus make precisely that link that aesthetic treatises of the eighteenth century had refused to contemplate: the identification of the natural genius, which in eighteenth-century aesthetics was primarily represented by Shakespeare and Milton, with the lower-class writer. But as the ending of the tale demonstrates, the "magic" wrought by the peasant "genius" is not to be confused with the transcendent and enduring work of the bourgeois author: like the ending of the fairy tale, the ending of the peasant poet's biography is often spectacular and transparently moralistic.

## Unhappy Endings: Biographical Punishment

Tragic endings, whether supported by the biographical data or not, inevitably conclude the biographical tale of the peasant poet; the commentator's tone often suggests that this ending was no less than deserved.[149] That the

---

[149] Cf., among others, the remarks on Jeanie Glover in Greig, II, x; Isobel Pagan in Paterson, 122; Anna Louisa Karsch in Klencke, 118; Molzahn, 80; Menzel, 50; and, as an ironic commentary on this biographical righteousness, Rizzo's remarks on the timeli-

unhappy ending in most cases is linked with the poet's response to patronage suggests an act of biographical punishment: what the poet is punished for is her ultimate incompatibility with the bourgeois image of the happy pauper, gratifyingly obliged to her patrons yet content in her station. Molzahn, for example, hints darkly at the "gloomy and desolate last years" of Karsch's life;[150] her untimely death (of consumption) is frequently attributed to the fact that she moved into the house finally provided her by the king while the house was still wet, stubbornly ignoring the counsel of her bourgeois patrons and supporters advising her to wait.[151] Karsch's obstinacy, her act of *disobedience*, as Mendelssohn would have said, results in the fact that she only enjoyed for two short years that boon of royal generosity for which she had applied for nearly thirty years.

Possibly the most drastic case of biographical punishment appears in life stories of Ann Yearsley, where the poet's unhappy life and dismal end is frequently directly explained by her "disobedience" to her first patron, Hannah More.[152] "Without the business and influence of Hannah More, Ann Yearsley never prospered. Her books continued to sell for a few years, but interest waned, just as it had with her predecessors, and as Walpole had predicted it might with her. For a while she ran a circulating library near Bristol, grew penurious again, and died, probably insane, in 1806."[153] Waldron has since established that neither Yearsley's insanity nor her financial destitution were supported in the original records; on the contrary, there is every indication that Yearsley's library flourished. Certainly, Yearsley herself continued to publish successfully and was favorably reviewed to the end of her life.[154] Despite biographical facts, there were few disasters that were not visited on Yearsley's later life in the accounts of her biographers. Cottle's report of Yearsley's calamities reads as follows:

---

ness, in terms of the reception of her work, of Leapor's death at age 24 ("The Patron," 251).

[150] Molzahn, 80: "Gequält durch die Lieblosigkeit ihrer Tochter Karoline, ist ihr Lebensabend dunkel und trübselig." Cf. also Palm's biographical entry, which culminates in the "end of her disordered and sorrowful existence" (" . . . in welchem sie am 12. Oktober 1791 ihr unruhiges und leidvolles Leben endete," 422).

[151] First in Klencke, "Lebenslauf," 118, and later repeated by Chézy, "Meine Großmutter," 78; Menzel, 50; Muncker, 296; and the Karsch biography in *Lexikon deutscher Dichter und Prosaisten*, 631.

[152] Cf. the interpretation in Waldron, *Lactilla*, 273–75.

[153] Unwin, 80; the story of Yearsley's insanity and her financial distress recurs in Southey, 134. Cf. also Cottle's critical appraisal of her disobedience toward More (50).

[154] Cf. the source materials and interpretation in Waldron, "Ann Yearsley and the Clifton Records," 315, and Franklin's introduction to *The Rural Lyre*, x.

Gloom and perplexities in quick succession oppressed the Bristol milk-woman, and her fall became more rapid than her ascent! The eldest of her sons . . . prematurely died; and his surviving brother soon followed him to the grave! Ann Yearsley, now a childless and desolate widow, retired, heart-broken from the world, on the produce of her library; and died many years after, in a state of almost total seclusion, at Melksham. An inhabitant of the town lately informed me that she was never seen, except when she took her solitary walk in the dusk of the evening![155]

Cottle seamlessly transitions Yearsley's meteoric rise, buoyed by the generous support of Hannah More, to her swift fall into death and desolation, by erasing her entire life between 1784, the year of her discovery, and 1806, the year of her death, from his account. Neither Yearsley's life during these years nor the publications that appeared independently of More's support, comprising two further poetry collections, a drama, a novel, and several poems published individually,[156] are mentioned in his story. Similar to accounts of Yearsley's financial destitution, a motif that forcibly returns the pauper to her "station," Yearsley's loneliness and childlessness in old age is greatly exaggerated: she was survived by three children and died, as another report has it, "in the bosom of her family."[157] Nonetheless, the dire version of Yearsley's end became the critical standard: Spence, writing in 1833, already refers to a well-known tale when she comments on the "too ardent muse and hapless fate of Lactilla, the Bristol milk-woman, whose short sunshine of patronage only gave place to deeper clouds of adversity, and plunged her in more hopeless misery."[158]

If the many disasters visited on Yearsley by her biographers are not rooted in her actual life, which has to be severely edited or, in Cottle's case, even deleted to maintain these fictions, it stands to reason to assume that at the bottom of these tales lies a bourgeois response to Yearsley's unwillingness to conform to the bourgeois image of the grateful pauper: "She was not amiable. She lacked altogether the docile subservience that makes charity a pleasure."[159] Yearsley's character is here described as the exact reverse of the deeply thankful and deferential pauper of the biographical forewords, where

---

[155] Cottle, 51; cf. also Carter, 196–97, who quotes and affirms Cottle's tale, and Hopkins, who claims more generally that Yearsley's later life was "shadowed by domestic griefs as well as by disappointed expectations" (125).

[156] Cf. Waldron's list of Yearsley's publications, which also lists the owning libraries, *Lactilla,* ix-xiii.

[157] On Yearsley's surviving children, cf. Waldron, *Lactilla,* 272–73, and Tompkins, 100–101; John Evans's report of Yearsley's death appeared originally in *The Ponderer* in 1812 and is cited in Tompkins, 100.

[158] Spence, 179.

[159] Tompkins, 82.

the poet's biography also serves less to describe her life than to prescribe her behavior, a genre exemplified in Hannah More's prefatory letter to Yearsley's first edition. Just as the poet in the foreword is lifted from poverty and obscurity as a reward for her subservience, so Yearsley is punished for her obstinacy and pride by her return, in biographical writing, to her former wretchedness and destitution. But whereas More, like other patrons, insisted on the reception of her fictionalization of Yearsley's life as historical truth, later biographers of Yearsley were at times quite willing to hint at their own act of fictionalization in allusions to the literariness of Yearsley's life, and it is surely nothing short of ironic that the *purpose* of some of these fictionalizations was the denigration of the bluestocking Hannah More, Yearsley's first fictional biographer:

> The life of Mrs. Ann Yearsley, "the milkwoman of Bristol," is a most unsavoury tragedy if her career is seen as the rise of a woman, who, from collecting "hog wash," suddenly became the chief literary exhibit of the year; but if one views the mud splashed by Lactilla upon certain dainty blue hose, there is no more delightful comedy in the history of English literature.[160]

Biographical punishment in posthumous biography is perhaps one of the most consequential biographical traditions, for it constitutes the most easily recognizable symptom for the notion that the life not only frames the work, but *substitutes* for it, in this case by predetermining its reception. The unhappy ending of the poet's biography-as-fairy-tale institutes a tradition of reading the life that precludes a reading of the work, for biographical punishment is meted out for the poets' inadmissible assumption of the author's role beyond that of the temporarily relieved and grateful pauper which was accorded them by their patrons. The poet's tragic end essentially not only turns the life into text but transforms it from pre-text (a text to be consumed *before* a reading of the work, suggested by its placement in the foreword) to a pretext. The deservedly unhappy ending of the poet's life defines the poet both as a failed author (by pointing to her lack of financial and critical success) and as a fake author (for the crime for which she is punished is her illegitimate assumption of the authorial role), thus turning the poet's biography into the pretext that relieves the reader from the responsibility of engaging her work.

Conversely, the necessity of biographical punishment alone suggests that bourgeois image construction of the peasant author was not necessarily successful, that the authorial image of the peasant poet was contested territory, both during the poet's lifetime and in posthumous assessment. But

---

[160] Cf. Childers's supplement to Southey, 195.

the relationship between poets' autobiographical texts and the biographical work of their patrons and later writers is too complex to be reduced to a paradigm of image construction on the part of patrons and resistance on the part of poets. Such resistance did occur, as is obvious from Karsch's refusal to permit Gleim's publicization of her as a love poet in his planned edition of her love letters and poems and Leapor's opposition to the biographical preface to her edition. Certainly, Karsch's and Leapor's protests against their visual oversimplification as hags and their critique of the *analytical* tradition that saw their ugliness as symptomatic of their poetic genius could be read as the poets' repudiation of what they considered a distorted authorial image. But more often, such resistance is embedded in and undermined by acts of conformity to the authorial images generated by their patrons and other bourgeois theorists, as evidenced by the consistent and calculated self-presentation as Nature's Child on the part of Karsch, Yearsley, and others. At times, this act of conformity to bourgeois images of the peasant author is buttressed through the invocation of bourgeois literary traditions. The poets' juxtaposition of the Arcadian shepherdess and the peasant in their autobiographical writing, for example, mirrors the bourgeois debate surrounding the alternate portrayal of the rustic as either graceful Arcadian shepherd or bumbling comical peasant. Just as the bourgeois debate specifically addressed the question of the principal admissibility of the klutzy peasant as a character in literature (cf. chapter 1), the poets' identification of the authorial persona with the Arcadian shepherdess, rather than the peasant, in their autobiographical texts can be read as an ironic reminder of the principal inadmissibility of the peasant as a producer of literature. The patrons' definition of the purpose of patronage in the biographical foreword, outlined as *temporarily* relieving the poet in financial terms and enabling her to make a future living by *physical* labor, is revisited in some poets' depictions of their forcible return to poverty following a brief and blissful dreamlike encounter with the world of poetry (Leapor's "Epistle to a Lady") or, satirically, in the mocking self-portrayal as a rich, popular, and successful poet glancing haughtily down from her coach-and-four (Leapor's epistle to her patron discussed in chapter 2). Although such ironic perversions of bourgeois notions of lower-class authorship can easily be read as a form of protest, it would be an exaggeration to claim that peasant poets' autobiographies and biographies are universally, or even predominantly, characterized by such resistance. The case of Anna Louisa Karsch demonstrates this the most clearly, for Karsch, who is the only poet in this group who functioned both as autobiographer (in poems and letters to Sulzer and Gleim) and as a biographer (of Maria Catharina Dippen), demonstrates a complete and uncritical adherence to bourgeois desires in her biography, desires which she *both* answers and repudiates in different autobiographical texts and letters.

Biographies of peasant authors and, to the extent that they were influenced by their patrons, the poets' autobiographical texts as well can be viewed as predetermining the poets' reception in two important ways: on the one hand, the *literarization* of the poet's life and the *substitution*, in the critical process, of the life for the work; on the other hand, the *decontextualization* of the poet's oeuvre. In the act of writing biography, biography as a genre is redefined not as a life story rooted in historical fact but as a pre-text with a gatekeeping function that initially backgrounds the literature and ultimately precludes all nonbiographical interpretations of the work. The life, itself turned into literature not merely through liberal adjustment of biographical data but in the frequent evocation of literary genres, by reducing the poet to a fairy tale or mythic character (the rescued princess, Arcadian shepherdess, or, most prominently, the witch) or her folkization and mythologization in visual representation, no longer functions as a frame for the work but as its proxy. Not surprisingly, this was the defining aspect of the scholarly reception of eighteenth-century lower-class writers until at least the 1980s, a reception that can be characterized both by lack of interest in the poet's work and by exclusive emphasis on the poet's life.

The second consequential predetermination of the poet's reception in biography occurs in the deletion of possible literary contexts for her work: if the life constitutes the central contextualization of the work, an assumption stated in every contemporary foreword, it becomes impossible to judge this literature by its "intrinsic merit," however defined, thus deleting the context of the new bourgeois literature as a possible interpretive frame. The alternate contextualization of their work as "women's literature" is thrown into doubt by the recurring juxtaposition of authorship and femininity, achieved, for example, in the definition of Sappho, that symbol of female poetic creativity, as essentially unfeminine, or in the consistent identification of poetic genius as male (in Karsch's depiction of her "boyhood," in Klencke's portrayal of Karsch as absent mother, even in Chézy's compensatory counterimage of Karsch as a kind of supermom). Although some modern scholars have contextualized the work of eighteenth-century peasant poets as "workers' literature,"[161] such a denomination is accurate only in the most basic biographical sense (the poets were indeed workers), but inaccurate in its mapping of nineteenth-century historical circumstance like the industrial context and the common understanding of "workers'

---

[161] Ashraf, for example, applies the term to eighteenth- as well as nineteenth-century literature.

literature" as literature of protest onto eighteenth-century conditions. In the eighteenth century, such a community of poets united against their (political or poetological) oppressors, a "village of poetesses," remains unthinkable. Eighteenth-century peasant poetry by women can thus only be defined *negatively*, as *neither* bourgeois literature *nor* women's literature *nor* workers' literature, and this aspect, the fact that it is deprived of all context, makes it inaccessible to interpretation of any kind except the biographical. Read in this fashion, the relation of the author's life stands not only as "history" and literature but also as poetology, as the primary context of interpretation *and* symptomatic of the erasure of all other contexts, as the beginning of an interpretive tradition as well as the end of interpretive possibilities.

# 4: A Literature of Labor: Poetic Images of Country Life

## Physical Labor and Poetic "Idleness"

> *And few amid the rural tribe have time*
> *To number syllables and play with rhyme.*
> — George Crabbe, "The Village"

LABOR IS A significant aspect in considering the poetic work of peasant women, and in more ways than merely the thematic or biographical. Labor as a feature in the poets' lives and a theme in their works is of obvious importance, given that this is literature produced by laborers, that many of them viewed their poetic endeavors as antithetical to or a potential escape from (physical) labor, and that either the description or avoidance of labor constitutes a defining characteristic of some of their literature. Although I consider these contexts in this chapter, the chapter's focus is, as with previous chapters, on the social and the aesthetic. It is the representation or absence of labor as a theme in their poetry that best indicates the degree to which laboring poets either tried to write social history from below or, alternately, adapted aristocratic genres, such as pastoral poetry, simultaneously conforming to the bourgeois injunction to write pastorals because the genre was seen as expressive of the rural poets' background. And finally, labor as a concept figures significantly in analyses of the process of writing. What Weinstein has stated for nineteenth-century American literature can equally be applied to this context: "Writing was supposed to appear effortless, natural, and easy.... Simply put, writing was not supposed to look like work...."[1] Writing was viewed as antithetical to labor, and the writing of peasant poets was no exception. Not only are the two occasionally contrasted in their work — Leapor's Mira, as previously discussed, awakes from her poetic dream "To sweep her kitchen, and to mend her clothes"[2] — but the principal opposition of writing and labor is consistently stated by bour-

---

[1] Cf. Weinstein, 13.

[2] Leapor, "An Epistle to a Lady," in Colman/Thornton, II, 30–32, the quotation 31; cf. the discussion of this and other poems on the same theme in the previous chapter.

geois patrons and critics in their interpretation of the writing process, where writing poetry is not considered work, but "idleness" in pronounced contrast to physical labor, and where those poems that are produced spontaneously and apparently effortlessly, such as Karsch's impromptu poems, are received with the highest degree of enthusiasm. The aesthetic context that furnished the justification for the publication of peasant poetry assumes the same incompatibility of writing and work, for the characterization of the work as the result of spontaneous inspiration obviously denies the concept of labor as part of the writing process. The assumed opposition of writing and labor thus not only defined the process of writing but also imposed a choice of genre on the poet: the general assumption was that peasant poets were particularly well qualified to write in the pastoral genre. In part, this injunction can be seen as the result of a simple equation between the poet's rustic origins and the pastoral's evocation of an idealized rural landscape. Gleim, for example, firmly believed that the pastorals of Anna Louisa Karsch were so convincing because of the poet's first-hand knowledge of the pastoral idyll, rather than her knowledge of Virgil.[3] Labor is an additional consideration in this regard, for the pastoral distinguishes itself from other literary genres partly through the pronounced absence of labor in the text. Literature of labor, written by eighteenth-century laborers, was thus produced in a poetological context that impacted both the writer and the work: it obliterated authorial agency through suppression of the understanding of writing as labor and made taboo the appearance of labor in the text.

## Rural Realities I: Pastoral Landscapes and Village Scenes

> *Yes, thus the Muses sing of happy swains,*
> *Because the Muses never knew their pains*
> — George Crabbe, "The Village"

The correlation of the rural poet's origins with an assumed predilection for the pastoral is already partly prefigured in the aesthetic tradition, where innocent rural pleasures are frequently viewed as conducive to poetic genius. William Duff, in his *Essay on Original Genius*, defined the natural poet as one who

> Happily exempted from that tormenting ambition, and those vexatious desires, which trouble the current of modern life . . . wanders with a serene, contented heart, through walks and groves . . . unfrequented des-

---

[3] Cf. Mödersheim, "Fruchtbarste Bäume," 50.

ert, along the naked beach, or the bleak and barren heath. In such a situation, every theme is a source of inspiration, whether he describes the beauties of nature, which he surveys with transport; or the peaceful innocence of those happy times, which are so wonderfully soothing and pleasing to the imagination. . . . Such a situation . . . is particularly favourable to a pastoral Poet.[4]

Duff's treatise thus defines a predominantly aristocratic genre,[5] later adapted by the bourgeoisie, as particularly appropriate for the "natural" and rural poet, that poet later epitomized by lower-class writers.[6] Simultaneously, Duff establishes a new context in which the pastoral genre, no longer limited to evoking a mythical Golden Age, is empowered to describe an experienced reality of nature observation and nature inspiration. The later popular identification of peasant poets with the pastoral genre relies on many ideas already expressed in Duff's treatise, including the removal of the natural/pastoral poet from civilized life and the implicit equation of the "country" that is the origin of the rustic poet with the idealized landscape of the pastoral. Duff's text already envisions that this identification of the peasant with the pastoral both mandates the poet's choice of genre — as Runge has stated, "the business of the true poet is and will be to sing of Nature"[7] — and regulates his or her authorial self-image. For authorial ambition and other "vexatious desires" are identified with a troubled modernity to which the pastoral serves as both contrast and antidote.[8] As Messenger has observed, women writers were particularly likely to be caught in the "pastoral trap" since pastorals were considered "especially suitable" for women:[9] a critic in the *Monthly Review*, for example, considered pastoral poetry one of the rare poetic genres in which "the Ladies . . . seem qualified

---

[4] Duff, 271–72.

[5] On the pastoral as an aristocratic genre, cf. Hauser, *Social History*, II, 517–19.

[6] The connection between the natural-genius aesthetic and the popularity of pastoral poetry has already been established by Waldron in "This Muse-born Wonder": "This belief in the existence of mysteriously endowed 'primitive' writers was related to the critical preoccupation with pastoral poetry which was a feature of much of the century" (113).

[7] Runge, 131.

[8] On this aspect in Duff's work cf. also Waldron, *Lactilla*, 33–34.

[9] Messenger, "Daughter of Shenstone," 464; cf. also her "Women Poets" and *Woman and Poet*, 2–3. In Mary Whateley-Darwall's case, as Messenger shows, this poetological injunction determined the poet's entire career (*Woman and Poet*, 61–67). On Whateley-Darwall's belittling reception as a "virtuous lady who wrote nice pastorals," cf. "Daughter of Shenstone," 481. Tebben, in "Soziokulturelle Bedingungen," makes the same point for the German context (14).

to excel."[10] Thus, the identification of the pastoral with the writing of lower-class authors and women speedily led to a declassification of the pastoral as an inferior poetological genre.[11]

Labor becomes a significant consideration in this context, for pastoral poetry is largely defined by the conspicuous absence of labor. Crabbe writes in "The Village" that the muse can sing precisely *because* the muse does not work.[12] Thus, the idealized landscape of the pastoral, peopled by shepherds rather than peasants,[13] is one in which no labor takes place: since Theocritus, an unworked-for abundance of riches, the fertility of a land that needs no farming, has been one of the essential features of both the traditional pastoral and its derivative, the country house poem.[14] The excision of labor, or, for that matter, of laborers, from the land — peasants in this genre appear, if at all, as "rurall folke" who benefit from the lord's charity[15] — is complemented by a vision of rural life in which the earth yields its fruit without labor or stint and birds and beasts offer themselves freely for consumption at the lord's table.[16] As Williams has shown, both the pastoral and the country house poem thus not only present a social vision in which the happy swain lives free from ambition, in which his subordination is presented as the "natural order," and in which class relations are seen as harmonious,[17] but they also describe a view of nature

---

[10] Cited in Messenger, "Women Poets," 96–97, the quotation 96.

[11] On pastoral literature as a lesser genre appropriate for women writers, cf. Tebben, "Soziokulturelle Bedingungen," 14, and Messenger, "Women Poets," 94–95; see also Fagan, 10, on the devaluation of the pastoral.

[12] On the discrepancy between labor and the pastoral mood, cf. Greene, 105–9 (Crabbe's poem is cited on 105) and Charles/Duffin, 144–55.

[13] As Dedner has outlined, mingling the pastoral landscape of the shepherd with the rural landscape of the peasant would have been considered a breach of style in the pastoral; cf. "Vom Schäferleben zur Agrarwirtschaft," 45–47 and *Topos*, 2, 5.

[14] Williams, *Country*, 14, 17, and 23–32, and Dedner, *Topos*, 9 and 141, on some German texts. On the English country house poem, cf. especially Hibbard, Fowler, and McClung; Radcliffe's essay usefully comments on the social and formal distinction of genres.

[15] Williams, *Country*, 32; cf. also Dedner, *Topos*, 141. Fowler rejects Williams's theory that labor is commonly deleted from pastoral and country house poems (Fowler, 6–9), but his citation of incidents of "overseeing" and "mental labour" as the sole examples of representations of labor in these works (8) seems to support Williams's point rather than refute it.

[16] Williams, *Country*, 14 and 30; Fowler, 2 and 8; McClung, 118–20; and Hibbard, 164–65; cf. also Runge, 192 and 209; McClung, 124, on the country house poem; and Dedner, *Topos*, 9–11, on the German context.

[17] On class relations in the pastoral, cf. Hibbard, 167, and the introduction by Barrell and Bull to *The Penguin Book of English Pastoral Verse*, 4.

and its exploitation as equally free from antagonism: nature is presented as — willingly — on its way to the table.[18]

To lower-class writers, the bourgeois injunction to write pastorals must have presented a social, aesthetic, and biographical paradox: social because it is a traditionally aristocratic genre recommended to them by mostly bourgeois critics as particularly expressive of lower-class existence. Aesthetic because this recommendation simultaneously constitutes an explicit invitation to "imitate," issued to poets whose entire literary existence was predicated on their supposed spontaneity and originality. And biographical because although the life that the pastoral was deemed so fit to symbolize was defined almost exclusively by physical labor, there is no room for descriptions of labor in the traditional pastoral. Nonetheless, traditional pastorals do appear in the work of many peasant women. Elizabeth Bentley and Anna Louisa Karsch wrote extensively in the genre;[19] other important lower-class poets of the pastoral include Elizabeth Hands, Molly Leapor, Jane Cave, and Janet Little.[20] Some of their work, such as Hands's pastorals, emulates the artificial world of courtship of shepherds, swains, and maidens, untroubled by class antagonism;[21] others reiterate the concept of unworked-for rural bounty. In Leapor's "The Month of August," unpruned fruit trees rain bushels of fruit on the plenteous table;[22] Bentley's

---

[18] Williams, *Country*, 26–30.

[19] On Bentley's pastorals, cf. Landry, *Muses*, 215–16; Karsch wrote a number of pastorals or nature poems that incorporated traditional pastoral motifs, including "Auf den Mai und den Dichter des Frühlings" (*Das Lied der Karschin*, 59–61), "An die jüngste Demoiselle St*hl" (in *Gedichte*, 257–59), "Dorimön und Amariethe" (in *Gedichte*, 276–78), "Phillis, die Helferin, eine Idylle an Damon" (*Gedichte*, 279–86), and "Lied der Lalage" (in *"Bruder in Apoll,"* I, 16–17). In addition, Karsch wrote a number of poems of praise of rustic simplicity, including "Die Abendmahlzeit auf dem Lande" (*Das Lied der Karschin*, 61–62), "Lob der schwarzen Kirschen" (in *Gedichte*, 125–26; *O, mir entwischt nicht*, 51–52; and *Gedichte und Lebenszeugnisse*, 82–83; in English in Walter Arndt's translation in Blackwell/Zantop, 143–44), "Das Lob des Essens" (*O, mir entwischt nicht*, 53–54, and *Gedichte und Lebenszeugnisse*, 81–82), and "Der Unterschied eines Schmauses und einer kleinen vergnügten Mahlzeit" (*O, mir entwischt nicht*, 57).

[20] Elizabeth Hands, "A Pastoral," in *Death of Amnon*, 69–71; Molly Leapor, "Colinetta," in Colman/Thornton, II, 24–27; "The Beauties of the Spring," *Poems Upon Several Occasions*, 15–18; "Florimelia, the First Pastoral," *Poems Upon Several Occasions*, 183–87; and "Florimelia, the Second Pastoral," *Poems upon Several Occasions*, 187–92; Jane Cave, "Credulia's Complaint," in *Poems*, 18–21, "From Eusebia to Fidelio," 25–27, and "The Garland," 68–70; Janet Little, "Damon and Philander," in *Poetical Works*, 50–57.

[21] For example, Hands's "A Pastoral," in *Death of Amnon*, 69–71; on Hands's pastorals, cf. Franklin's introduction to her *Death of Amnon*, x-xiii. To date, Landry has written most extensively on Hands's pastorals; cf. her *Muses*, 186–209.

[22] In Colman/Thornton, II, 27–30, the reference 28–29.

"On A Summer Morning, 1786" evokes human "labour" not as work but as part of the happy swain's untroubled and virtuous character:

> Man to his daily labour takes his way,
> With sweet contented face and healthful brow;
> That health and peace can all his toils repay,
> Which exercise and temperance bestow.
>
> These are the pleasing scenes of rural life,
> These the blest joys the country e'er displays;
> Who would not wish, remov'd from noise and strife,
> Amid such scenes to spend their tranquil days.[23]

In the traditional pastoral, what appears as backbreaking labor in other poems is muted to healthful exercise performed in a serenely peaceful environment: labor is, as Bentley's poem expresses, "remov'd from strife."

Given the close connection between the pastoral and the aesthetic, it comes as no surprise that the genre was occasionally also used as a reflection on aesthetics. Karsch's pastoral tale "Der Sänger bey der Heerde" (The Singing Shepherd Tending His Flock)[24] draws the same connection between the pastoral and the peasant that was expressed in the bourgeois advocation of the pastoral as a suitable genre for lower-class authors: Karsch incorporates facets of her own biography into her shepherd's life and draws explicit autobiographical parallels in the final lines of the poem. Her tale exemplifies the bourgeois aesthetic that mandates spontaneous inspiration for the natural poet, but it is also a sign of her awareness of the role she was made to play in its establishment. "Der Sänger bey der Heerde" is a rhymed pastoral tale in which poetic genius is personified in an illiterate Italian shepherd, who, unaware of his gift, is awakened to his destiny when a farmer reads Tasso to him. The next day the shepherd's copious poetic production begins, and he writes, as is repeatedly emphasized, "without a master teaching him / Of beauty of expression."[25] His unerudite verse gains him the love of his shepherdess and a fame within the rural community that eventually reaches the court. At this point, the patronage story unfolds: the duke invites the shepherd to become his court poet, the shepherd accepts and proves his poetic genius, not through the

---

[23] In Bentley, *Genuine Poetical Compositions*, 3–4. On Bentley's pastorals, cf. Landry, *Muses*, 209–16.

[24] For a brief interpretation of the poem, cf. Dawson, "Selbstzähmung," 135–36.

[25] "Ohn daß ein Lehrer ihm die Wahl / Des schönen Ausdrucks wieß"; Karsch, "Der Sänger bey der Heerde, in Welschland, eine Erzählung," *Auserlesene Gedichte*, 311–14, the citation 312.

quality of his work but through the prodigious quantity of his output: "And it is said that within sixty days / He wrote two hundred songs, all in his praise."[26] But then the success story changes: the shepherd, unable to bear the intrigues and vices of the court, asks the duke's permission to return home to the countryside. The duke gives the poet leave and rewards him with a "Meyerey," a farmhouse (an obvious allusion to Horace); the poet returns home, continuing to write but not to publish, and dies happily after a long life — "His grey head crowned with a fresh myrtle wreath."[27] Karsch ends the poem with a direct application of the shepherd's situation to her own: "How happy I will be, when I thus, at life's end / Shall walk my final steps, supported by a friend!"[28]

"Der Sänger bey der Heerde" traces not only the traditional patronage story but also outlines the conditions on which a peasant poet could become a success in the elite (bourgeois or aristocratic) community. Karsch's hero, innocent of any formal education, is initially inspired by a chance reading of great literature, inadvertently supplied by another rustic, a scenario that is certainly reminiscent of the story of Karsch and the herder boy. Like her hero's, Karsch's own poetic production was extolled as exemplary for poetic genius mainly based on the tremendous speed and spontaneity with which she wrote. The breach between the autobiographical and the pastoral, a connection the author draws in the final lines of the poem, occurs in the patronage story: biographically, the breach consists of her hero's rejection of the king's largesse (for which Karsch herself unrelentingly applied) and in his return to the countryside (nothing could have been further from Karsch's mind, who viewed her entire village existence, her life before she came to Berlin, as "misery survived"[29]). It is at this point that the poem becomes a pastoral tale that confirms the bourgeois expectations of Karsch as Pure Nature, shown in its indictment of the vice-ridden and deceitful aristocracy, in its rather simplistic characterization of the shepherd as "zu redlich"[30] (too honest) for such a corrupt environment, and, most important, in the hero's self-contentedness and modesty, in his rejection of any kind of professional ambition and his voluntary

---

[26] "Und, wie man sagt, hat er in zweymal dreißig Tagen / Zwey hundert Lieder ihm gemacht"; "Der Sänger," 313.

[27] "Sein graues Haupt bekränzt mit frischgebrochnen Myrten"; "Der Sänger," 314.

[28] "Wie glücklich, wenn ich einst bekränzt, und mit Gesang, / Aus meiner Freunde Arm, geh meinen letzten Gang!" "Der Sänger," 314.

[29] "Auf überlebtes Elend blick ich nieder"; the reference is taken from her autobiographical poem "Zueignungs-Gesang an den Baron von Kottwitz," in *Auserlesene Gedichte,* iii-iv, the reference iv.

[30] Karsch, "Der Sänger," 313.

return to the simple life. In this, there are several allusions to Karsch's possible awareness of the nature of patronage. The topos of the corrupt aristocracy, for example, was common in bourgeois writings and has often been cited as *the* distinguishing factor in the establishment of a bourgeois aesthetic: politically powerless, the eighteenth-century bourgeoisie establishes itself as the ruling intellectual and Artistic class via dissociation from the aristocracy.[31] Karsch's indictment of aristocratic corruption and intrigue thus rather ostentatiously aligns her work with bourgeois predispositions. The second indication of Karsch's awareness of her place in bourgeois aesthetics is the hero's voluntary abdication of any kind of authorial ambition or professional future, in conformity with William Duff's view of the natural poet's laudable lack of all "tormenting ambition." Although this move clashes strangely with remarks Karsch made elsewhere about her own poetic ambitions and goals, it does correspond precisely to the upper- and middle-class view of the peasant poet as a short-lived literary wonder, a perception that, as we have seen, also played a significant role in Karsch's own reception.

Karsch's pastoral tale is not a straightforward pastoral, but an adaptation that, despite all expressed conformity to generic form and aesthetic theory, ends in inadvertently questioning some expectations central to the bourgeois marketing of the peasant sensation: her hero's life answers these expectations, her own does not. Her unsuccessful attempt to align her biography with that of the shepherd emphasizes the discrepancy rather than masking it. The discrepancy between pastoral idyll and rustic reality persists in the face of the bourgeois reading of the pastoral as expressive of the peasant's origins.

In the work of other poets, that discrepancy is frequently expressed in adaptations of the pastoral genre. Mock pastorals, antipastorals, and satires on the genre considerably outnumber traditional pastorals in the work of peasant women. In many of these texts, the poets deliberately return to that aspect most notably *absent* from the traditional pastoral — antagonism of any kind — and reintroduce it into the genre. Molly Leapor's "Mistaken Lover" Strephon, on marrying his nymph Celia, promptly falls out of love with her; following his discovery that Celia is equally unenamored with him, "They part — and thus the story ends."[32]

---

[31] See the introduction and chapter 1 for a more extensive discussion and critique of this concept.

[32] Molly Leapor, "The Mistaken Lover," in Colman/Thornton, II, 54–60, the citation 60; also published in *the Monthly Review* (November 1749): 16–20. The poem is briefly interpreted in Landry, *Muses*, 89–90, and Doody, "Swift," 79–80. A similar scenario is

Strephon's "modern love-letter" to Celia already makes it obvious that his courtship is motivated less by her charms than by her wealth.[33] In the mock-pastoral tradition of women peasant poets, the graceful courtship of the traditional pastoral tale either terminates in rejection[34] or it is parodied as the inept wooing of the country bumpkin.[35] If nymphs in traditional pastorals pine for the love of their shepherd, Hands's heroine in "Perplexity" finds it impossible to decide between her two suitors.[36] Mary Masters's "Morning Frolick" may start out as a traditional good-natured romp as the swains take their nymphs out for a joyride in the coach, but it ends with the swains in the ditch as the coaches are overturned and the damsels daintily stepping through cow dung.[37] Such pastoral burlesques are indeed, as Landry has stated, a sign of "trouble in paradise,"[38] but they also consciously conflate two spheres that many bourgeois theorists of the pastoral sought to isolate: Arcadia and the village, the graceful shepherd and the clumsy country bumpkin, strictly separated in bourgeois aesthetics,[39] appear here sometimes side by side, at other times as one and the same. Not entirely dissimilar to the bourgeois view of the pastoral as epitomizing the peasant's background, the pastorals of women peasants are clearly literary adaptations, but what is being adapted, in many cases, is not life but literature. Rather than aestheticizing the peasant's background through its redefinition as a pastoral idyll, the infiltration of village life into the Arcadian landscape often results in undermining the pastoral.

Molly Leapor's "Crumble-Hall"[40] is a good example of the satirization of a literary tradition — in this case, the country house poem — through

---

found in Janet Little's pastoral poems "The Fickle Pair" and "The Month's Love," in *The Poetical Works*, 40–41 and 47–49, respectively (cf. also Bold's brief interpretation, 26).

[33] Leapor, "Strephon to Celia, A *modern* Love-Letter," in Colman/Thornton, II, 65–67 (emphasis original); brief interpretation in Doody, "Swift," 80.

[34] Ann Yearsley, "The Indifferent Shepherdess to Colin," *The Rural Lyre*, 139–42; Janet Little, "Celia and Her Looking Glass," *Poetical Works*, 86–90.

[35] Elizabeth Hands, "Lob's Courtship" and "The Widower's Courtship," in *The Death of Amnon*, 86–87 and 104–5, respectively.

[36] In Hands, *The Death of Amnon*, 78–79.

[37] Mary Masters, "The Morning Frolick," *Poems On Several Occasions*, 211–28.

[38] Landry, *Muses*, 202.

[39] Cf. chapter 1 for a discussion of the traditional division in bourgeois poetics between the Arcadian shepherd as an idyllic and the boorish dim-witted peasant as a comical character; see Dedner, *Topos*, 5, 13–18, 161, and Baur, 59–69; for the English context, cf. McClung, 26, and the discussion in Hauser, *Social History*, II, 515–19.

[40] In Colman/Thornton, II, 126–32; an excerpt from the poem was republished by Lonsdale in *Eighteenth-Century Women Poets*, 210–11.

the insertion of a lower-class viewpoint.[41] It is, as Landry has stated, a rarity, a "class conscious plebeian country house poem" that mocks not only the genre but also the values of the gentry on which it rests.[42] Whereas other country house poets such as Alexander Pope and Ben Jonson find refuge in the house from the pressures of the new society,[43] Leapor takes the conflict into the house itself. The traditional country house poem, a panegyric to the house and its owners and a celebration of their hospitality, is satirized here in the depiction of guests feasting excessively on spoiled food — "tainted ven'son," "hunted hare" and "simp'ring ale" — until "their stretch'd girdles would contain no more."[44] Traditional facets of the country house poem, such as the elaborate description of furniture, carpets, tapestries, and heraldry, are cut short:

> Gay *China* bowls o'er the broad chimney shine,
> Whose long description would fatigue the Nine:
> And much might of the tapestry be sung:
> But we're content to say, the parlour's *hung*.[45]

Instead, the reader is afforded a house tour through unlit halls adorned with grim-looking statues, up the stairs through a storage room that boasts such treasures as old shoes, sheep ticks breeding in discarded wool, and the wheel spokes of a tattered plow,[46] a tour during which the speaker more than once envisions the possibility of hapless visitors taking a tumble down the rickety stairs or bumping their heads on low beams: "Back through the passage — down the steps again; / Thro' yon dark room — Be careful how you tread / Up these steep stairs — or you may break your head."[47] Rather than concentrating on the estate's wealth and opulence, for which the spectacular abundance at the table stands as paradigmatic in the traditional country house poem,[48] Leapor's Mira

---

[41] For first interpretations of the poem, see Landry, *Muses*, 107–19, and Greene, 137–42; Doody ("Swift," 82) and Blunden, 63–64, also mention the poem. On Leapor's other antipastorals, cf. Greene, 92–103. Jane Cave, to my knowledge the only other lower-class woman poet to engage the genre, wrote a traditional country house poem; cf. her "Written To a Friend, on going to Itchen, About Five Miles from Winchester: To see a Country Seat belonging to the Duke of Chandos," *Poems*, 41–45.

[42] Landry, *Muses*, 107.

[43] Williams, *Country*, 29.

[44] Leapor, "Crumble-Hall," Colman/Thornton, II, 126–32, the citation 127.

[45] Leapor, "Crumble-Hall," 128 (emphasis original).

[46] Leapor, "Crumble-Hall," 129.

[47] Leapor, "Crumble-Hall," 129.

[48] On this aspect of the genre, cf. McClung, 124–25.

shows us the estate seen through the eyes of a servant girl: in the dank and dusty halls she describes, spiders and mice are safe from persecution by "the hated broom."[49] Mira takes us where no visitor to the country house has ever gone before, into the scullery, kitchen, and servants' quarters; the objects of her song are not the lord of the manor, as is customary, but the cook and her cheesecakes, the stablehand and his oxen, the servant and his jug of beer.[50] The tale focuses briefly on the domestic drama between the servant Roger, who snores off his too-ample meal of cabbage, and his wife, Ursula, who bemoans his neglect of her with all the tragic sentiment appropriate to the pastoral courtship, but has to interrupt her speech because the kettle is boiling.[51] Leapor's tale ends with a glance out of the window; however, the observation of nature offered here again differs markedly from the idyllic landscape that provides the setting in traditional country house poems.[52] Mira's initially equally idyllic view of Nature is rudely interrupted by a shriek: the "rev'rend oaks" surrounding the house are torn "ignobly from their roots" to make room for a new parlor, leaving "The *Dryads* howling for their threaten'd shades."[53] Destruction without is matched by decay within: just as opulence and wealth in the traditional country house poem express the lord's generosity and hospitality, Leapor's deconstruction of the genre indirectly shows up the greed and thoughtlessness of the (otherwise unsung) lord of the manor.

As in Karsch's pastoral tale, the subtext of the patronized poet and the lower-class poet subtly inserts itself into the text. Mira, our guide on the metaphorical house tour, functions within the poem as one of the servants responsible for the upkeep and cleaning of the estate. But she is also a deprived reader who describes the holdings of the lord's library with considerable longing, a library that is unused and unappreciated by its owners:

> Here *Biron* sleeps with books encircled round;
> And him you guess a student most profound.
> Not so — in form the dusty volumes stand:
> There's few that wear the mark of *Biron's* hand.[54]

---

[49] Leapor, "Crumble-Hall," 128.

[50] Leapor, "Crumble-Hall," 130.

[51] Leapor, "Crumble-Hall," 131.

[52] On landscape in eighteenth-century poetry and the rural working class, cf. Barrell, *Idea of Landscape*.

[53] Leapor, "Crumble-Hall," 132 (emphasis original).

[54] Leapor, "Crumble-Hall," 129 (emphases original).

Mira's remark already defines her as a character who is socially barred from an existence that would grant her access to literature or reading of any kind, privileges in which those who have access show no interest. At the outset of the poem, Mira presents herself as a poet who is similarly torn between her own aspirations and social reality: she "repents" her poetic occupation and "vows to quit the darling crime,"[55] her muse is hurled precipitously from the highest spire of the palace and, as a punishment for getting "above herself," is dragged down into the "nether world" of the kitchen and the scullery.[56] The punishment for the poet who oversteps her social boundaries is the same as that preemptively outlined in patrons' forewords to peasant poets' first volumes, the forcible return of the poet from her poetic "idleness" to "real" (physical) labor. But the violent death, the *fall*, of Mira's muse, can also be read as a reversal of the success story Karsch outlines in her pastoral, which makes clear that the patronized poet's success is predicated on the poet's acceptance of patronage, the dedication of the poet's work to the patron's praise, and the poet's unswerving compliance with such bourgeois mandates as the poet's lack of ambition, his humble renunciation of his poetic occupation, and his willing return "to the country."[57] The danger that Leapor alludes to here, in Landry's analysis, is that the poet could give in to "that treacherous attraction to the aestheticizing language of the pastoral," that she could, in other words, "write like a traditional country-house poet."[58] For that poet is by definition a panegyrist whose praise of the lord's wealth and hospitality was either directly commissioned by the lord of the manor or at least rewarded by his hospitality.[59] "Of this rude palace might a poet sing / From cold *December* to returning spring":[60] Leapor's mocking tribute can easily be read, as Landry has done, as an allusion to the panegyrist's attempt to "seek shelter during these particularly inhospitable months by singing for supper at the gentry's table."[61]

---

[55] Leapor, "Crumble-Hall," 126.

[56] Interpretation and quotations in Landry, *Muses*, 112.

[57] I am intentionally using the masculine form in reference to Karsch's male hero; the relevance of her story to women peasant poets seems obvious.

[58] Landry, *Muses*, 112.

[59] Hibbard describes this relationship as "sound and wholesome" rather than coercive, deleting the social hierarchy contained within the relationship in his depiction of the poet as "an honoured friend and guest" at the lord's table (159); on his similarly idealized view of the relationship between the lord and his peasants and servants, cf. 164. On the panegyric as the central aspect of the genre, cf. also McClung, 165–67.

[60] Leapor, "Crumble-Hall," 127 (emphasis original).

[61] Landry, *Muses*, 109.

Another prominent example of the destabilization of the pastoral through the insertion of a lower-class viewpoint is Elizabeth Hands's "Written, originally extempore, on seeing a Mad Heifer run through the Village where the Author lives."[62] The scene set at the outset of the poem is recognizably that of the pastoral:

> When summer smil'd, and birds on ev'ry spray,
> In joyous warblings tun'd their vocal lay,
> Nature on all sides shew'd a lovely scene,
> And people's minds were, like the air, serene. . . .[63]

The heat-crazed cow breaks into this idyll and turns it briefly into a "bovine comedy"[64]; her mad dash through the village ends in the village pond where she finally cools off. The mock heroic that Landry has diagnosed in the poem shows itself in the depiction of masculine valor in overcoming the beast and in the humorously exaggerated danger to the women and children of the village: while the heifer's dash through the village is enough to send gentle nymphs into paroxysms of terror, and screaming mothers snatch their infants off the road, the men valiantly tackle the cow with flails and rakes. It is at this stage that darker images are suggested; the "broken rakes," the "rotten stakes," and "half rails" that serve as the village farmers' weapons of defense constitute, as Landry notes, a surreptitious introduction of another theme that usually finds no place in either the pastoral or the georgic traditions — that of rural poverty.[65] Hands's traditional pastorals have elsewhere been analyzed as reclaiming "the pastoral for the rural laborer,"[66] but her "Mad Heifer" poem makes a different use of the genre: it introduces a traditional pastoral that is already contravened by the poem's burlesque title, demolishes the genre in the same way in which the heifer disturbs the peace of village life, shows us a brief glimpse of the reality behind the village idyll (destitution and decay), and ends in a reinstitution of village peace that seems to restore the mood set at the outset of the poem, that of the languid contentment evoked by the pastoral introduction. The village, briefly disrupted, is now permitted to return to its sleepy routine. The mock happy ending pre-

[62] In *The Death of Amnon*, 115–16; republished by Lonsdale in *Eighteenth-Century Women Poets*, 424–25.

[63] Hands, "Written, originally extempore," *The Death of Amnon*, 115–16, the citation 115. Landry has interpreted this poem as an antipastoral and countergeorgic in the mock-heroic mode; cf. *Muses*, 192–93.

[64] Landry, *Muses*, 193.

[65] For Landry's interpretation of this theme, cf. *Muses*, 193.

[66] Cf. Landry, *Muses*, 202.

sented in the cow's cooling off in the water — "No more she'll fright our village"⁶⁷ — invites the reader to reimpose the pastoral idyll onto rural life, a perception that can, however, only be upheld at the price of blindness to the rural poverty glimpsed in the poem.

Poverty is a frequent theme in the work of women peasant poets:⁶⁸ Christian Milne's "The Wounded Soldier"⁶⁹ describes a starving family in heart-rending terms; Ann Candler's "Reflections on my Own Situation" provides a glimpse of the author as a pauper living on meager alms "with the dregs of human kind."⁷⁰ Karsch's untitled impromptu poem, inserted seamlessly into a letter to Gleim, depicts similar circumstances:

> oh dearest Gleim see fathers hurry, in vain to work for just a little bread, meanwhile beset by cold and hunger's dread, the children cry, redoubling his worry, they cry like dogs deprived of mother's breast, their mothers roam the streets full of despair, the children are abandoned everywhere, like little ravens flung out of the nest, they hope for bread from morning until night, and many sick and poor lie on the straw, not even granted water in their plight, whereas the rich do shove into their maw, the most delicious foods till they are ill, I see this sadly, much against my will, my spirit bids me forget nevermore, that I myself was hungry, cold and poor⁷¹

Such stark descriptions of poverty, frequently, as with Karsch and Candler, autobiographically anchored, stand side by side with poems that place the theme in a literary context. Janet Little's "Poem on Contentment,"⁷² addressed to the pauper Janet Nicol, contrasts Nicol's "contentment" in poverty with the many vexations experienced by amorous shepherds (an allusion to the pastoral tradition), ambitious writers (an autobiographical allusion), and vain courtiers (employing the traditional contrast of court and country). Karsch's "Meine Zufriedenheit" (My

---

⁶⁷ Hands, "Written, Originally Extempore," *The Death of Amnon*, 115–16, the citation 116.

⁶⁸ Cf. also Ehrenpreis's account of the portrayal of poverty in (bourgeois) Augustan literature in England.

⁶⁹ In her *Simple Poems*, 101–9.

⁷⁰ In her *Poetical Attempts*, 53–57; the citation 53.

⁷¹ Anna Louisa Karsch in a letter to Gleim, December 17, 1768: "ach liebster Gleim die Väter eilen, umsonst nach Arbeit um die Kost, indeßen plagt der Hunger und der frost, die Kinder daß Sie kläglich heülen, wie Hunde wenn die Hündin fehlt, viel Mütter lauffen durch die Straßen, und ihre Kleinen sind verlaßen, wie junge Raben, sind gequält, und hoffen brodt vom Morgen bis zum Abend, viel arme Kranken liegen mat, auff altten Stroh kaum Waßer habend, wenn sich die Reichsten dieser Stadt, an Lekerspeisen Ekel Eßen, mein Geist blikt Traurig auff Sie hinn, und rufft mir zu nicht zu vergeßen daß ich auch arm gewesen bin" (*"Bruder in Apoll,"* I, 333–34).

⁷² In her *Poetical Works*, 173–79.

Contentment) uses the theme of poverty as a personal experience, remembered with disgust but now thankfully in the past:

> My fingers now no longer tear the flax,
> I, now so used to wine, am never parched
> With thirst, laboring under the distaff's arch,
> And never does the sun melt me like wax.
>
> When Sirius's flame in vale and glade
> Burns up the thresher, tires the walking boy,
> Then I sit bless'd with bounty and with joy,
> In plenty do I rest, and in the shade.
>
> O friend! and when the spinner's hand
> Laboriously tears and rents the cotton wool,
> Then I now play my undemanding role
> Which often wins me praise throughout the land![73]

Whereas Candler and Milne allow poverty to stand undiluted by invocations of literary traditions or moralistic admonitions of "contentment," both Little and Karsch in "My Contentment" contrast poetry and poverty, Karsch in her interpretation of poetry as a ticket out of poverty, Little in her contrastive treatment of the "contentment" in poverty with the miseries of Arcadian existence, exemplified, in a pointed reversal of the pastoral tradition, by unhappy marriages and unrequited love. Poetry, in all cases including the "contentment" poems, contextualizes poetry in such a way that negates bourgeois claims of the transcendence and divinity of literature: poetry written from within poverty, past or present, accentuated or submerged, can make no such claim; like the pauper it depicts or disowns, the rustic Muse appears, as Little states in her poem, "in tatter'd low condition."[74] The business of poetry is rather prosaically downgraded to easy (rather than arduous) labor performed in the shade rather than under the scorching sun. But this depiction of writing as easy work is predicated on the understanding of writing *as* work, a simultaneous violation of four mandates: the pastoral tradition that excludes labor from literary represen-

---

[73] Karsch, "Meine Zufriedenheit": Mein Finger zerrt an keinem Flachs / Nie wird an einem kümmerlichen Rocken / Der weingewohnte Gaumen trocken, / Nie schmilzt die Sonne mich wie Wachs. // Wenn der beflammte Sirius / Den Schnitter brennt, den Wandrer müde machet, / Dann sitz ich, wo die Freude lachet, / Im Schatten und im Überfluß! // O Freundin! wenn die Spinnerhand / Mühselig zieht an baumgewachsner Wolle, / Dann spiel ich meine leichte Rolle, / Die oft des Kenners Beifall fand! (Gedichte und Lebenszeugnisse, 124–25).

[74] Little, "Poem on Contentment," *Poetical Works*, 173–79, the citation 173.

tation, the new bourgeois understanding of bourgeois literature as "divine," the simultaneous bourgeois interpretation of lower-class poetic occupation as "idleness," and the aesthetic/critical view of the peasant poet as spontaneously inspired and therefore, as Gleim once said of Karsch, as *incapable* of (poetic) work.[75] Peasant poets' literary aspirations, at least as presented in their poetry, are often neither prompted by a sense of themselves as natural "geniuses" nor inspired by bourgeois-style dreams of posthumous fame, but simply by a desire for an improvement in their working conditions. "While in laborious toil I spent my hours, / Employ'd to cultivate the springing flowers: / Happy, I cry'd, are those, who leisure find / With care, like this, to cultivate their mind. . . ."[76] Similar to Karsch's poem on "contentment," Leapor in this poem defines intellectual labor as more "like this," as comparable to physical work, than as its antithesis. The difference, as both Karsch and Leapor knew, lay in the kind of labor and in the circumstances under which it was performed, not in an opposition of (physical) work and (poetic) idleness. Unlike the cultivation of a garden, the cultivation of a mind may be performed in the shade; it may, as Leapor states, sport the appearance of "leisure." The poet thus employed may, as Karsch said, seem to be merely "resting," but writing is nevertheless, in a marked deviation from the bourgeois and pastoral discourses, recognized as labor. Although this is not a consistent rendition — examples contrasting poetry and physical labor or describing poetry as "idleness" can certainly be found in the poetic works and forewords of peasant women[77] — the occasional portrayal of poetic labor *as* labor seems worth emphasizing because it answers the bourgeois obliteration of lower-class authorial agency, as their mock pastorals and antipastorals can be read as a response to the traditional pastoral, that literary paradise from which laborers of any kind are expelled.

---

[75] Gleim in a letter to Uz, October 8, 1761, pronounced Karsch unable to edit her poems: "Arbeiten kan sie nicht" ("for she is incapable of work"; cited in Anger, "Nachwort" [1966], 9); cf. my discussion of this letter in chapter 2.

[76] From Molly Leapor, "The Rural Maid's Reflexions," in *The London Magazine*, 45.

[77] Cf. the examples and discussion in the previous chapter.

## Rural Realities II: The Rustic at Work

> *I assure you that there are moments when Art almost attains to the dignity of manual labour.*
> — Oscar Wilde, "The Model Millionaire"

Poetic representations of physical labor constitute the tradition that most obviously contravenes the pastoral, a tradition that ousts the shepherd from the poem to make room for the laboring peasant. In contrast to the rather overdetermined pastoral tradition, these poems are characterized by a marked absence of literary context: unlike the pastoral, they portray physical labor; unlike the georgic, they do not present a positive or heroic view of labor; unlike the nineteenth-century tradition of workers' literature, these earlier poems, although they depict the living and working conditions of the lower classes in the harshest possible terms, do not draw political or social consequences; they cannot be considered "protest" literature in a sense that would align them with the later "proletarian" tradition. Critics have at times been unable to classify this literature according to genre or to fit it into a literary tradition: in the absence of a "satisfactory title for their genre,"[78] it becomes difficult to conceive of this literature *as* literature. In light of the traditional taboo against labor in literature, one could argue, of course, that these works are not perceived as literature because they depict physical labor, and in ways that do not conform to the terms of established literary genres, but that is only half the story. The critics' inability to perceive and classify these labor poems as literature is largely rooted in the bourgeois theory that moves "by definition, from the 'creative' to the 'fictional,' or from the 'imaginative' to the 'imaginary'," thus defining "fiction" as "an account of 'what did not (really) happen'," a definition that, in Williams's analysis, "depends . . . on a pseudo-positive isolation of the contrasting definition, 'fact.'"[79] Williams has regarded this dichotomy between fact and fiction as "the theoretical and historical keys to the basic bourgeois theory of literature," a theory that limits our perception of literature to that of a genre representing an "inner" truth, reserving the expression of "external" truths for nonliterary genres and thus restating the bourgeois separation of individual and society.[80] Applied to the labor poems of women peasants, a critical reading of their works in terms of bourgeois

---

[78] Goodridge on Duck's poem "The Thresher's Labour" and Collier's response "The Woman's Labour": "A satisfactory title for their genre has not been formulated" (6).
[79] Williams, *Marxism*, 148.
[80] Williams, *Marxism*, 148–49.

literary theory would thus result in their interpretation as mere fictionalizations of historical or biographical fact. But Williams's assertion that actual writing surpasses the "reduction of 'creative imagination' to the 'subjective'"[81] could not describe any poetic genre more accurately than these poems. In the absence of a bourgeois interpretive framework for these works, I would like to attempt a reading of three poems in another context: one that refuses to use the fact/fiction dichotomy as a means to classify the works under discussion as "fiction" in the sense of "what did not (really) happen," but to infer what Williams has identified as "the more complex series: what really happened; what might (could) have happened; what really happens; what might happen; what essentially (typically) happened/happens."[82] I analyze these works against the backdrop of contemporary agricultural and labor history not to reiterate the fact/fiction dichotomy but to probe the documentary value of these works. My reading of these poems as poetic documentaries does not perceive them as personal in the sense of "this is what happened to me" — a reading that would, as Williams has stated, reduce the creative to the subjective — but in the broader sense of "this is what essentially (typically) happens," as *class* documentaries. In this sense, I consider these poems rare exemplifications of that "realism" in the poetic portrayal of rural life that Mendelssohn called for — and for which he claimed he did not know a single instance.[83]

The three poems in this section, one from each national context (England, Scotland, and Germany), all consider physical labor or rural life in a way that can neither be considered "literary" (if literary implies "fictional" as opposed to "fact") nor "personal" (if personal implies an opposition to broad and class-related applicability and relevance). To be sure, Mary Collier's "The Woman's Labour," Christian Milne's "Written at Fourteen," and Anna Louisa Karsch's "Schlesisches Bauerngespräch" (Silesian Peasant Talk) use a literary form (meter and verse), place themselves in a literary tradition (Collier's "Woman's Labour" is ostentatiously a response to another poem, Stephen Duck's "The Thresher's Labour"), and at times employ the subjective "I" (Milne's poem), but all three nonetheless document experiences that transcend "fiction" in three major ways: by depicting rural labor or working/living conditions that cannot be contained in either the pastoral or the georgic traditions, by refusing to limit themselves to the "subjective" that has its place in

---

[81] Williams, *Marxism*, 148.
[82] Williams, *Marxism*, 148.
[83] Cf. Dedner, "Schäferleben," 49–50.

"fiction" and can comfortably be contrasted with "objective fact," and finally by their clear positing of the individual not as separate from or opposed to society but as its symbol and representative.

All three texts were written at a time when culture, as Williams has reminded us, "was still a noun of process: the culture *of* something — crops, animals, minds,"[84] a concept defined more by the process of cultivation than by its current sociological and anthropological meanings. Not unlike aesthetics, that process underwent significant changes in all three countries during the eighteenth century. Throughout the century, the majority of the people in all three countries — between 80 and 90 percent — lived in the country and worked in agriculture.[85] In England and Scotland, enclosure created a new landless class of disinherited farmers by eliminating open-field villages and common rights to farming and grazing and raising rents on property in some areas of England between 300 and 400 percent; much of the peasantry was displaced in the process of building large estates.[86] In Scotland alone, the number of people thus evicted has been estimated at about 200,000 in the 140 years between 1739 and 1880.[87] One of the main consequences of enclosure was the pauperization of the population by turning thousands of former owner-occupiers into day laborers dependent on a wage and seasonal labor.[88] Although the effect of pauperization was general, even impoverished England seemed wealthy compared to Scotland, attracting wave after

---

[84] Williams, *Marxism*, 13.

[85] Christopher Hill, 203; in 1700, 80 percent of all Britons lived in the countryside, with 90 percent of the population employed either in agriculture or in the production of raw materials; cf. Porter, 25, and Bridget Hill, *Women, Work and Sexual Politics*, 19. Between 85 and 90 percent of eighteenth-century Germans lived in the country or in unincorporated villages with fewer than 5,000 inhabitants; most of them drew their living from the land (Vaughan, 33; Marion Gray, 173). On English and Scottish demographics in the eighteenth century, cf. also Thirsk, *English Peasant Farming*, 197–204, and *Rural Economy*, 17; Bridget Hill, *Women, Work and Sexual Politics*, 16–23, and Cole/Postgate, 14–22; on German demographics, cf. Schissler, 72–78, Achilles, 138, Barkhausen, 218, and Frevert, *Women*, 22.

[86] In mid- to late eighteenth century England, there were 4,000 parliamentary acts passed enclosing six million acres of land, which constituted approximately a quarter of all cultivatable acreage; cf. Williams, *Country*, 96–97, 66. On enclosure and its consequences for small farmers in England and Scotland, see also Ashton, 37, 39, 46 (on rent increases); Christopher Hill, 223; Hecht, 15; Porter, 229; Pinchbeck, 29–30, 43–45; Hobsbawm, 81–82; Patton, 27–28; Thirsk, *English Peasant Farming*, 212–13; and Cole/Postgate, 122–25, 49 (on enclosures in Scotland). In Scotland, enclosure could be achieved by fiat of the landlord without the sanction of an Act of Parliament (Cole/Postgate, 49).

[87] Johnston, 194, and the tables on 190–93.

[88] Porter, 110, 230–31.

wave of comparatively well-educated Scottish emigrants.[89] Eighteenth-century agriculture in Germany, which had likewise been defined by common use of farm and grazing lands (*Kollektivismus*),[90] also experienced a decrease in small-scale farming and an increase in large leaseholding, escalating the indebtedness and pauperization of the rural population.[91] In contrast to the massive displacement and disappropriation of small farmers in England and Scotland, however, the majority of German farmers were bound either to the land by hereditary dependence (*Erbuntertänigkeit*) or to the lord by personal servitude (*Leibeigenschaft*) and thus infinitely exploitable in the physical as well as the judicial sense.[92] A peasant's release from hereditary dependence could only be effected by relinquishing his land, which was then added to the landlord's estate without compensation for the peasant.[93] Repeated attempts throughout the century to repeal the system of hereditary dependence failed, largely because this would have meant that the state would have had to support impoverished peasants whose support under the old system was the landlord's responsibility.[94]

Although the rural laborer's pay is difficult to quantify because so much of it was paid in goods and services either in place of or in addition to the wage,[95] two facts appear unilaterally applicable to each national context. First, the pay of women laborers in all categories of employment was substantially lower than that of men, ranging between 40 and 65

---

[89] Currie, I, 7; on the coexistence of widespread literacy with widespread poverty in eighteenth-century Scotland, cf. also Young, *Women*, 37.

[90] Schlumbohm, 65–66.

[91] Vaughan, 33; Schissler has estimated the landless rural population in Prussia ca. 1800 as 36 percent (92). On the increasing pauperization of the German rural population throughout the eighteenth century, cf. Jacobeit/Nowak, 17; Marion Gray, 174; Abel, *Geschichte*, 275, and *Massenarmut*, 46–54.

[92] Vaughan, 33–35. On the legal position of eighteenth-century peasants under hereditary dependence or servitude, cf. Schissler, 89–90; Brandt, 23–28 and 33–35; Marion Gray, 29–36; and Balet, 24–26.

[93] Schissler, 93.

[94] Schissler, 54–55, and Vilfan; but cf. Stadelmann, 76, on the repeal of hereditary dependence in East Prussia in 1723.

[95] Comparative pay scales for eighteenth-century unskilled workers can be found in Ashton, 220–23 and 232; for rural laborers' pay, cf. Gilboy, 8, 24; Porter, 101–2; Cole/Postgate, 69–77; Pinchbeck, 54–55, 138–50, 173; on rural wages in Scotland, cf. Gibson/Smout, 286, 289–90; for domestic servants' wages, cf. Hecht, 69, 142–56; Kent, 118–19, 121–25. For the German context, cf. Schissler, 98–99, on the pay of Prussian peasants; on the pay of rural workers in eighteenth-century Hanover, see Achilles, 8, 126–33, 138.

percent of the average wage for men.[96] In some cases, a woman's wage was simply subsumed into the man's, who was paid one sum for the "family's" labor.[97] Second, most sources available for all three countries document that laboring families, as a rule, did not earn enough to live at subsistence level.[98] In Scotland, stable wages in conjunction with unstable food prices affected both laborers who worked for a monetary wage and small tenants or farm servants working for payment in food and goods.[99] During the final third of the century, the same was true for Germany, where grain prices rose steeply due to increased demand: much of German grain was exported to England, which, now in its first stage of industrialization, was forced to import basic foods that had formerly been produced within its own agriculture.[100] In marked contrast to the pastoral idyll, eighteenth-century rural life, in all three countries, became increasingly defined by poverty[101] and a more pronounced class struggle, which expressed itself in the continuous displacement of small farmers by large landholders, a widening wage gap, and frequent riots.[102] Women laborers were particularly affected by these developments, for the

---

[96] On women's wages in agriculture, cf. Simonton, 35–36; Bridget Hill, *Eighteenth-Century Women*, 195–96; on women's pay scale compared with men's, cf. Simonton, 35–36, 45–46; Kussmaul, 37, 144; Porter, 101; Pinchbeck, 19; in Scotland, Gibson/Smout, 289–90, 297; in Germany, Jacobeit/Nowak, 17.

[97] Pinchbeck, 1–2.

[98] Cf. the sources and tabulations cited in Bridget Hill, *Eighteenth-Century Women*, 165–72; Gilboy, xix-xx, 117–21; Christopher Hill, 212; Porter, no pag., 386–92; and Cole/Postgate, 83–84. Mr. Davies, Rector of Borkham in Berkshire, worked out the yearly incomes and expenditures for farming families in 1787 and came up with a deficit in almost every case (Pinchbeck, 46–48). Cf. also Thirsk's tabulation of eighteenth-century agricultural wages and their purchasing power (*Agrarian History*, V, 4–5). For figures on the purchasing power of wages in eighteenth-century Hanover, cf. Achilles, 126–28; on the income of the eighteenth-century German peasantry, cf. the works by Henning. Schlumbohm estimates that in eighteenth-century Germany, approximately 80 percent of peasants were forced to find extra employment in addition to their agricultural labor to support their families (64–65).

[99] Gibson/Smout, 11; on food prices in England, cf. Porter, no pag., and Beveridge, I, 237, 240, 290–95; in Scotland, cf. the tabulations and discussion in Gibson/Smout, 16–17, 193, 196, 343.

[100] Schissler, 59–65, and Brandt, 99.

[101] Contemporary testimonials to poverty and statistics regarding relief for the poor in the Warwick parish in the late eighteenth century are cited in Bridget Hill, *Eighteenth-Century Women*, 162–73; on the poor laws in England, cf. Pinchbeck, 68–69; on relief for the poor in England, cf. Christopher Hill, 212; in Scotland, cf. Young, *The Rousing*, 56.

[102] On various incidents of mutinies, uprisings, and other manifestations of lower-class discontent in England, Scotland, and Germany, cf. Young, *The Rousing*, 44–55; Gilboy, 25; Thirsk, *English Peasant Farming*, 214; and Schissler, 54.

gender difference in rural wages alone must have made them even more vulnerable to pauperization than were men.

Sources on women laborers of any category are not only comparatively rare[103] but also at times problematic: although domestic servants, for example, have attracted some scholarly attention,[104] some of these newer investigations tend to be based either on documentation provided by employers or on contemporary fiction. It thus seems hardly surprising that some of these histories of domestic servants concentrate, in large measure, on the (idealized) working conditions of the domestic and omit the same aspect that is also excised from the portrayal of the rural nymph or swain in the pastoral: that of the servant as a laborer.[105] Whereas the rarity of representations of women's work in historical and social scholarship[106] mirrors the absence of labor in literary representations, some women laborers passionately took up the theme in their poems, thus vacillating between literature and social history and defying all attempts at literary classification.

Mary Collier's poem "The Woman's Labour" (1739), written in response to Stephen Duck's "The Thresher's Labour" (1730), is the first published documentation of women's rural labor written by a woman laborer,[107] provoked in part by Duck's depiction of women field laborers sitting idly by while the men toiled in the field, busily employing their tongues rather than their hands.[108] Collier's objective, then, is not merely

---

[103] Cf. Simonton for the most concise history of women's work to date.

[104] Cf. Kussmaul, Kent, Hecht, Charles/Duffin, 157–60, and Frühsorge/Gruenter, Schröder, and Wierling for German servants. For a portrayal of the servant in English literature, cf. Robbins.

[105] This is true particularly for Hecht's account, based largely on documentation provided by masters (some with easily discernible grudges).

[106] Depictions of labor that I have found include the following: of dairymaids, cf. Pinchbeck, 10–15; of cottagers, Pinchbeck, 19–23; spinners, Bridget Hill, *Eighteenth-Century Women*, 199, and Schlumbohm, 78–79; domestic servants, Bridget Hill, *Eighteenth-Century Women*, 229–31; and agricultural laborers, Bridget Hill, *Eighteenth-Century Women*, 187–95.

[107] Collier worked as a field hand, washerwoman, and beer brewer; cf. her "Some Remarks," in Ferguson, *First Feminists*, 264–65, and Klaus, "Stephen Duck und Mary Collier," 117. The poem was reprinted by the Augustan Reprint Society (publication number 230 [1985]) and anthologized in excerpts in Lonsdale, *Eighteenth-Century Women Poets*, 172–73, and Vivien Jones, 154–57. For interpretations of Collier's poem, cf. Ferguson's introduction to the "Woman's Labour" and the passages in her *First Feminists*, 257, *Eighteenth-Century Women Poets*, 12–16, and "Feministische Polemik," 294; Klaus, "Stephen Duck und Mary Collier"; Landry's article "The Resignation," which was also included as a chapter in her *Muses*, 56–77; and Charles/Duffin, 146–47.

[108] Stephen Duck, "The Thresher's Labour." The relevant passage is Duck's depiction of women haymakers as "prattling Females" (19) who "sit still on the ground" while the men

the depiction of women's labor but the depiction of women's labor as unnoticed and scorned (by men in general and Duck in particular). The opening lines draw a clear distinction between herself and Duck: whereas Duck, formerly a laborer, has already ascended to the status of "Immortal Bard" and "Fav'rite of the Nine," not to mention favorite of the Queen who granted him her patronage, Collier herself "ever was, and's still a Slave," her life "always spent in Drudgery."[109] It is a response written by a laborer during her rare minutes of leisure between the endless rounds of physical work she describes in the poem, addressed to someone for whom physical labor is, at most, a remembered experience; implicit in this initial drawing of the lines is Collier's distrust of Duck's selective remembrance, even the suspicion that he may have deliberately falsified the facts to embroider his fiction: "on our abject State you throw your Scorn, / And Women wrong, your Verses to adorn."[110] Duck's concern, Collier asserts, is clearly no longer with labor (its accurate representation as experienced reality) but with his verse (its embellishment for the benefit of his bourgeois and aristocratic readers); in stating this, she defines his poem not as an honest representation of actual labor but as fiction produced for a nonlaboring audience. An answer to this, which she sets out to provide in "The Woman's Labour," would therefore have to eradicate this discrepancy between fact and fiction, and it is this aspect of Collier's poem, the dissociation of her work from Duck's, that makes it possible to read it as a self-conscious documentary of labor rather than a "poem" in the literary sense.

Collier documents a series of women's tasks performed in the fields, washhouse, scullery, and in their own homes; hers is the first description of women's double shift as full-time worker and housewife/mother, which continues to be a subject of public debate to this day.[111] Emphasized throughout her elaborate depiction of haymaking, raking, prowing, reaping, gleaning, charring, washing, brass-, pewter-, and iron-cleaning, beer brewing, cooking, bed making, swine feeding, and child and husband tending are the length and hecticness of a woman's work day, general work conditions (extremes of heat and cold), the physical injuries women undergo in the performance of labor (raw and bleeding hands), and the exploitation of women by the masters who underpay them and the men

are working, "so they may chat their Fill. / Ah! were their Hands so active as their Tongues, / How nimbly then would move the Rakes and Prongs!" (20)

[109] Collier, "The Woman's Labour," 5–6.

[110] Collier, "The Woman's Labour," 7.

[111] For a view of Collier's rendition of women's "double burden" in and outside of the home, cf. Simonton, 70–75.

of their own class who profit from but underappreciate their labor. Repeatedly, a man's work conditions are contrasted with a woman's: the men, coming home from the fields, are finished for the day, waiting to be fed and go to sleep, whereas women returning from the fields "find our Work but just begun; / So many Things for our Attendance call, / Had we ten Hands, we could employ them all."[112] Charwomen regularly get up at midnight to do the lady's washing, "While you on easy Beds may lie and sleep, / Till Light does thro' your Chamber-windows peep."[113] Collier's repeated instances of women's work performed while the men are asleep is, of course, a direct refutation of Duck's accusation of women's idleness; her summing up — "Our Toil and Labour's daily so extreme, / That we have hardly ever Time to *dream*"[114] — again emphasizes to what extent the longer workday of women encroaches on their sleep and simultaneously takes up Duck's statement that work follows the laborer into his dreams.[115] Although Collier's description of field labor is comparatively brief, she elaborates on those areas of work that are specific to women, such as washing: in this, as well, she deliberately pits the woman's work against the man's ("So many Hardships daily we go through, / I boldly say, the like *you* never knew").[116] A washerwoman's day begins in the middle of the night when "O'ercome with Sleep; we standing at the Door / Oppress'd with Cold, and often call in vain, / E're to our Work we can Admittance gain":[117] the arduous work of scrubbing, washing, laying out, and bleaching, and the treatment of sensitive materials like ruffles, lace, and fringes, is interrupted only by the mistress's admonishments to save on soap and firewood. This work goes on

> Until with Heat and Work, 'tis often known,
> Not only Sweat, but Blood runs trickling down
> Our Wrists and Fingers; still our Work demands
> The constant Action of our lab'ring Hands.[118]

Collier's poem ends on a grim note: the laborer is paid off with "Sixpence or Eight-pence"[119] (the difference in pay could well, as Landry has

[112] Collier, "The Woman's Labour," 9–11, the citation 10.
[113] Collier, "The Woman's Labour," 12.
[114] Collier, "The Woman's Labour," 11 (emphasis original).
[115] Duck, "The Thresher's Labour," 25; cf. the interpretation in Klaus, "Stephen Duck und Mary Collier," 120–21.
[116] Collier, "The Woman's Labour," 12 (emphasis original).
[117] Collier, "The Woman's Labour," 12.
[118] Collier, "The Woman's Labour," 14.
[119] Collier, "The Woman's Labour," 15.

assumed, allude to the gender wage gap);[120] the future holds nothing for the laborer but "*Old Age* and *Poverty*"[121] and continuous exploitation by "sordid Owners [who] always reap the Gains."[122] Her concluding image of women laborers as the daughters of Danaus, with which she answers Duck's comparison of the male field hand with Sisyphus, evokes the poem's author simultaneously as a poet and as a washerwoman: a literary allusion to Greek mythology in a poem about labor by a laborer who, in its opening lines, describes herself as completely uneducated[123] could be considered a rather incongruous motif. But paradoxically, it is this highly literary image of the eternal washerwomen, endlessly employed in filling the bottomless tub, that most succinctly reiterates Collier's description of women's labor as never-ending and thankless.

Collier's poem, concerned with gender as well as class, answers Duck's in another way as well: whereas Duck, in his elaborate description of women as uselessly prattling gossips, can be said to accentuate traditional views of femininity, Collier's response obscures the femininity of the woman laborer. Her laboring women, covered with soot, dirt, and filth at the end of their workday, are hardly recognizable as women, again a depiction of male laborers that she takes over from Duck's poem but trumps in her portrayal:

> Colour'd with Dirt and Filth we now appear;
> Your threshing *sooty Peas* will not come near.
> All the Perfections Woman once could boast,
> Are quite obscur'd, and altogether lost.[124]

Collier's elimination of femininity from the image of rural womanhood is reiterated in the comments of bourgeois observers, who frequently voiced their irritation at the indistinguishability of peasant men and women, objected specifically to the fact that many rural women looked like men, and bemoaned the loss of morals and ladylike reticence in the female sex as it appeared walking behind the plow.[125] When objections were voiced to women's work in the fields, they did not, as a rule, grow out of

---

[120] Landry, "The Resignation," 106.

[121] Collier, "The Woman's Labour," 15 (emphases original).

[122] Collier, "The Woman's Labour," 17.

[123] Collier, "The Woman's Labour," 6: "No Learning ever was bestow'd on me; / My Life was always spent in Drudgery." Cf. also her "Some Remarks," reprinted in Ferguson, *First Feminists*, 264.

[124] Collier, "The Woman's Labour," 16 (emphasis original).

[125] Cf. Frevert, *Women*, 27, and Armstrong, 20, for the traditional portrayal of women as masculine in nineteenth-century analyses of the working classes.

a concern for the woman's well-being, but rather concern for her appearance as feminine. An observer of women's field labor in 1794 found it

> painful . . . to behold the beautiful servant maids of this country toiling in the severe labours of the field. They drive the harrows, or the ploughs, when they are drawn by three or four horses; nay, it is not uncommon to see, sweating at the dung-cart, a girl, whose elegant features, and delicate, nicely-proportioned limbs, seemingly but ill accord with such rough employment.[126]

How laboring women appear to men is also a substantial part of, indeed furnished the provocation for, Collier's poem, where the elimination of femininity serves a distinct purpose: it negates the male view of women (either as beautiful and delicate or as useless, lazy, and gossipy) and identifies labor as the defining aspect of a woman's existence. The woman in her description is no longer recognizable as a woman but merely as a laborer. Nevertheless, and this seems to be Collier's implicit conclusion, the view of this laborer as a woman persists, must persist, for it is this distinction that makes it possible to pay her even less for her labor than the already insufficient wage for men and to saddle her with a workload that is described as double that of the male laborer. Collier's poem is thus, as Landry has stated, a protofeminist work;[127] it is class-identified in its clear indictment of the exploitation of the laborer through upper-class employers, but it simultaneously furnishes one of the earliest examples for a gendered critique of the exploitation of laboring women not only by the upper classes but also by men of their own class.

Christian Milne, in "Written at Fourteen Years of Age, on an Elderly Lady Whom I Then Served" (1787, published in 1805), takes up Collier's theme of the servant's exploitation by her mistress. The long hours Collier describes are also part of the domestic servant's labor: Milne's autobiographical servant persona describes how she unweariyingly tends to her sick and elderly mistress, sitting up with her until deep into the night. Her mistress, in turn, takes revenge for her own helplessness and dependence on her servant by putting her in her place whenever possible:

---

[126] From Pringle's *General View of the County of Westmoreland*, 1794, cited in Bridget Hill, *Eighteenth-Century Women*, 186.

[127] Cf. Landry's interpretation and problematization of Collier's protofeminism in "The Resignation," 117.

> She cannot move without my aid,
> Nor turn without her little maid;
> Yet she must shew her pride and spleen,
> She cries "I'm great, and you are mean!"[128]

Whereas Collier describes the harshness of the work itself, Milne broaches a subject that must have been particularly relevant to the domestic servant, a laborer who was frequently perceived as having the easiest labor and the best working conditions available to the lower-class worker:[129] the incarceration of the domestic in the house of her master or mistress. The servant, "Excluded from the world that's gay," depicts her life as one dominated by "Confinement, and a brawling tongue, / My spirits curb'd, and I so young!"[130] The feeling of imprisonment that permeates the entire poem is intensified through the depiction of the stuffy atmosphere of the sickroom, that room in which the servant spends her entire working life and into which neither the sun nor fresh air are ever permitted.

Milne's poem, although clearly intended to describe her own working life, of necessity also alludes to what could be considered a literary topos — namely, the comic motif of the servant tending to her sick mistress in the hopes of being remembered in her will. Milne's poem treats this theme straightforwardly: her mistress, her servant persona claims, has indeed promised her a legacy "To pay my care of her when ill."[131] Although she asserts that this care is bestowed from unselfish motives ("Conscience and a feeling heart"[132]), she admits her secret wish to be rid of her difficult mistress with astonishing frankness:

---

[128] Milne, "Written at Fourteen," *Simple Poems*, 36–38, the citation 37. Karsch describes the same process of exploitation and humiliation of the domestic from the mistress's perspective in her "Lied einer alten reichen Wittwe, die gern Dame werden will" (Song of an Old Rich Widow Who Fancies Herself a Lady), *Gedichte*, 254–55 (reprinted in *Gedichte und Lebenszeugnisse*, 123–24).

[129] Cf. Kussmaul, 40–42, and Hecht, 22, 97–101, 109, 111–12, 115, 123, 125–26, 158–77, 198, who describes domestic service as "a comfortable and protected existence, and an opportunity to acquire a competence, it also functioned as a path for social ascent" (177). In her description, many servants entered the profession in hopes of economic and social advancement (22).

[130] Milne, "Written at Fourteen," *Simple Poems*, 36.

[131] Milne, "Written at Fourteen," *Simple Poems*, 38.

[132] Milne, "Written at Fourteen," *Simple Poems*, 38.

> If Fate would send a blacken'd barge,
> To rid me of my fretful charge,
> And she embark'd in it, I'd pray
> That e'en to bliss she'd find her way:
> For her I'd mourn with outward show,
> Equipp'd in black from top to toe.[133]

Milne's puzzling final lines can be read as a commentary on the servant's divided position in her mistress's household as *both* subordinate and, if the ideological discourse is to be credited, family member. Unlike that of the agricultural laborer, hers is a position that requires not only physical labor but also psychological and emotional qualities such as loyalty, gratitude, and love, unquestioningly bestowed, no matter how exploitative and abusive the relationship. It is this emotional "duty" to her mistress that is commented on in the final lines of the poem: the servant's relief at finally being rid of her "fretful charge" is unmistakable even as she dutifully prays for the soul of the departed, dons her black clothes, and goes through the "outward show" of mourning her mistress.

Anna Louisa Karsch's "Schlesisches Bauerngespräch zwischen Vetter Hanß und Muhm Ohrten, gehalten zu R . . . bei Großglogau im November 1758" (Silesian Peasant Talk between Cousin Hans and Aunt Ohrte, Which Took Place in R . . . Near Großglogau in November 1758) takes us back to the country, where two peasants discuss the impact of the Seven Year's War on the rural population.[134] The conversation progresses from complaints about heavy taxation and the mistreatment of peasants in times of war to a praise of rural life in peacetime, finally ending in a panegyric on Frederick the Great. The poem deliberately mixes both the public and the private spheres (in its intertwining of larger political and social concerns and personal matters) and the literary sphere with rural reality. Written in the Silesian dialect, it is one of the earliest dialect poems in the German language[135] and clearly attempts to emulate real-life conversation in other ways as well, particularly in the unmotivated changes of subject and the interspersing of seemingly irrelevant news, such as the news of Cousin Lehne who is preparing for a visit from her brother at the end of the

---

[133] Milne, "Written at Fourteen," *Simple Poems*, 38.

[134] The poem has been briefly interpreted or mentioned in Krzywon, "Empfindung und Gesang," 339; Kastinger-Riley, "Wölfin," 13–14, and "Anna Louisa Karsch," 142. The most extensive interpretation so far is in Krzywon's "Tradition und Wandel," 47–56.

[135] Cf. Kastinger-Riley, "Anna Louisa Karsch," 143.

poem.[136] In addition, the exact designation of time and place in the poem's title establishes a claim to realism by anchoring the conversation in a specific historical context: the reader's position as a consumer of didactic literature is obscured by the intimated role of someone listening in on a private conversation. At the same time, the employment of alexandrine meter throughout the poem equally obviously places the poem into a literary tradition: Krzywon has read the poem as a typical example of the political poetry of the German Baroque (*Bauernklage*)[137] and has linked Karsch's usage of literary form to both Opitz and Gottsched.[138] Although the deliberate (mis)use of the "heroic" alexandrine meter would seem to hint at a subversive evocation of literary traditions,[139] both the panegyric on the king and the portrayal of peasant life in peacetime evoke other literary traditions, including both pastoral and georgic, without a trace of irony. Rural reality, as it appears in Hanß's description, is characterized by health, piety, hard work, a loving family life, and a delight in plain rustic fare, all of which are elaborately contrasted with the city dweller's corruption, hypocrisy, lavish eating habits, and frequent illnesses. Although labor supposedly dominates this idyllic life, only four of sixty-two lines in his speech even mention labor;[140] the rest of Hanß's report is given over to philosophical and religious ruminations about the virtues and pleasures of country life. As far as labor is concerned, one might be inclined to read this poem as indebted to the traditional pastoral and/or georgic, and not, as Kastinger-Riley has read it, as a "mirror of the true rural milieu"[141] or as based in any way on Karsch's "vivid personal experience."[142] But if Karsch, rather than describing labor as she knew it, fell into the "pastoral trap" discussed earlier, she simultaneously negates a literary tradition: in claiming the pastoral for the peasant, she defies the bourgeois depiction of the literary peasant as coarse, unrefined, and ridiculous, the comic character of rural literature.[143] She does this not only by usurping the Arcadian shepherd's space for the peasant, but also by hinting at an — albeit imagined — reality. For Hanß's initial complaints about the heavy taxation

---

[136] Karsch, "Schlesisches Bauerngespräch," *Gedichte*, 376–88, the citation 388.

[137] Krzywon, "Empfindung und Gesang," 339.

[138] Krzywon, "Tradition und Wandel," 48.

[139] Cf. Krzywon, "Tradition und Wandel," 48.

[140] Plowing (Karsch, "Schlesisches Bauerngespräch," 379) and threshing (381) are accorded two lines each.

[141] Kastinger-Riley, "Wölfin," 13.

[142] Kastinger-Riley, "Anna Louisa Karsch," 142.

[143] Kastinger-Riley has made this point in "Anna Louisa Karsch," 142, and "Wölfin," 14.

during wartime — peasants in times of war paid between 30 and 45 percent of their total income in taxes directly to the armies[144] — are trumped by Ohrte's account of the unimaginable suffering visited on the peasant under enemy occupation. Ohrte's fiction within a fiction, her act of imagining potential disasters destroying the pastoral idyll that poses as "fact" within the poem, is paradoxically the passage that comes closest to evoking rural reality: the peasant's farm is burned down, his seeds destroyed, his grain, livestock, and household goods stolen. Where this attempt to represent real suffering disintegrates is at the point where the suffering is perceived as so extreme that it can no longer be contained in the pastoral or georgic form that provides the poem's frame. Whereas Karsch manages to convey highly affecting images of the peasant being beaten by troops and his barn and stables being emptied, the experience of rape in wartime is irresolutely hinted at:

> And many a man has had to witness, stand amazed
> As soldiers treat his wife in most improper ways
> One does not like to speak of it. But really, it's a fright
> To hear of things the Russians do to young women at night.
> One listens to these things, it is no laughing matter,
> And your wife, Hans, is pretty, the village has none better,
> Cossacks would gladly take her, their hours to while away,
> And you'd be spitting mad, and there'd be hell to pay.[145]

At this point, Karsch's attempt to convey rural reality in the pastoral form breaks down, the form proving woefully inadequate for the content. For the same reasons that labor is omitted or aestheticized in literary traditions, the unsuitability of the literary form to a description of the actual experience is expressed in euphemisms that demote a crime to "improper" behavior, helplessness and despair to a childish tantrum ("spitting mad"; in the original: "Du argertest Dich närsch"), and the destruction of lives to "no laughing matter." In a literary world that is engaged, as Hanß is in the elaborate description of his workday, in an

---

[144] Balet, 26; cf. also the chapter on the Seven Years' War in Brandt, 45–60.

[145] Anna Louisa Karsch, "Schlesisches Bauerngespräch," 377–78: Und mancher Man der muß mit seinem jungem Weibe / Su was beginnen sahn was sich nu gar nich schickt, / Man redt nich gern davon. Und wirklich man erschrickt, / Wenn man die Dinge hört, es iß gar nich zum lachen, / Sie solns a wing zu arg mit jungen Frovolk machen. / Du Vetter Hans du hast och noch a hübsches Weib, / Die wär für den Cosack a bißel Zeitvertreib, / Du argertest Dich närsch, und das in einer Stunde.

I have tried to emulate Karsch's use of meter, rhyme, and style in my translation. No attempt has been made to convey her use of dialect in the original.

aestheticization of rural reality, such experiences are beyond the words available to the genre, a fact that expresses itself inadvertently in the painful inappropriateness of the terms employed to describe what is, within this genre, indescribable.

Karsch's "Schlesisches Bauerngespräch" is a good example of what happens when the pastoral meets rural reality in a work that is primarily concerned with the latter rather than the former: her poem tries to adapt the traditional pastoral and georgic to a different purpose, and one that is not, as is a mock pastoral, strictly literary. The didactic purpose of the poem is essentially conservative, as is expressed in both Hanß's idyllic view of rural life and the elaborate apotheosis of the king. Nonetheless, Karsch attempts, as Kastinger-Riley has noted, to give the peasant his due: in contrast to bourgeois portrayals of the peasant as the klutzy comical character, peasants in this conversation appear as the backbone of rural society as well as of Frederick's war: "As provider of food and supplier of troops and horses, the peasant is vital to the nation's well-being and defense."[146] Without question, Karsch portrays it that way; at the same time, it is difficult to overlook the aestheticization inherent even in this acknowledgment of the peasant's vital role: parallel to the denial of labor and the depiction of unworked-for rural bounty in the pastoral, the peasant's forced contributions (in both Karsch's poem and Kastinger-Riley's interpretation) appear as voluntary offerings. Karsch's poem thus seems essentially torn between its employment of literary forms (pastoral and georgic) and their purpose (the aestheticization of rural life and the apotheosis of the king), as opposed to its social purpose (the realistic portrayal of lower-class concerns) and its literary form (the employment of dialect, the attempts to emulate real-life conversation in the frequent jumps, non sequiturs, unmotivated subject changes, and relation of seemingly unimportant details). Where rural reality threatens the pastoral idyll, as it does in the rape story, the pastoral is quickly reasserted in the refusal to engage reality ("One does not like to speak of it") and in the conformist conclusion that compared with such horrors, peasants should recognize their current hard lives as a veritable bed of roses[147] and stop complaining about such negligible annoyances as war taxes: "That pittance of a tax is all you suffer now / And trifle that it is, you whine and make a row."[148]

[146] Kastinger-Riley, "Anna Louisa Karsch," 142.

[147] This is Muhme Ohrte's conclusion: "We still sit here as if in a garden full of roses" ("Wir sitzen hier gewiß noch wie im Rosengarten"; "Schlesisches Bauerngespräch," 378).

[148] "Das bißel Liefern ist nu alles was ihr traget / Worüber ihr nu gar a su abscheulich klaget"; "Schlesisches Bauerngespräch," 382.

Despite her radically different perspective, Karsch's poem can be read from within the tradition of women's labor poems, because she attempts, as do Collier and Milne, to describe rural reality from within a literary form. Whereas the labor theme is somewhat downplayed in her poem, the lower-class experience of exploitation emerges as a major theme in the depiction of "what might happen" if war came to the village, even if her conformist conclusion differs radically from Collier's and Milne's depiction of the servant's resigned view of her physical (Collier) and emotional (Milne) exploitation. The reality of exploitation is the common denominator in all three poems, the quintessential lower-class experience represented in three different forms, with Collier speaking in the class-encompassing "we," Milne in the subjective "I," and Karsch offering an exchange between two different people with two distinct perspectives (Hanß complains, Ohrte appeases). Whereas Collier's and Milne's works demonstrate both class consciousness and class solidarity in the depiction of the servants' exploitation, Karsch tries to find a way to map the pastoral sense of contentment onto the rural reality she describes, accordingly downplaying and negating the fact of exploitation that Hanß, at the outset of the poem, protests so vigorously, and turning this protest into praise of the king in the peasant's mouth. In its conclusion, her poem is closer to the bourgeois conservative tradition of "peasant enlightenment"[149] epitomized by texts such as Hannah More's *Village Politics* than to the labor poems of other women writers. This alliance can, to some extent, be explained by the fact that of the three poets under discussion, she was the only one who was transplanted from the rural environment she describes in her poem into a bourgeois literary context. Although her poem must be acknowledged as a pioneering effort in terms of its innovative use of dialect and style, it is less successful as a class documentary than either Collier's or Milne's poems, for the simple reason that she does not, unlike Collier and Milne, employ a literary tradition in the service of the documentary but subordinates rural reality to the pastoral purpose of the aestheticization of the country and the deification of the king.

---

[149] For a brief discussion and examples, cf. chapter 1.

## Pastorals and Power:
## Social and Aesthetic Considerations

The implications behind the bourgeois identification of the pastoral as particularly expressive of the peasant poet's background are, as many contemporaries readily admitted, as much social as they are aesthetic. W. Richardson, in his attempt to analyze the source of the bourgeois pleasure in reading pastorals, cites all the reasons already outlined in the work of thinkers like Duff and others, paramount among them a delight in nature and the bourgeois longing for a return to simplicity and tranquility. But he also expands the argument from the aesthetic to the social when he adds that part of the attraction of the shepherd as a character is that "he seems to be entirely in oure power.... I am somewhat inclined to think, that the idea of our own superiority, conveyed by the representation of simplicity of manners, may constitute a part of the pleasure."[150] The superiority of which Richardson speaks here is partly aesthetic: as he was well aware, "The pastoral muse sports in the vales and the meadows; she does not ascend olympus."[151] But simultaneously, the pleasure the bourgeois reader experiences in reading pastorals is in no small measure triggered by that feeling of *social* superiority that Richardson succinctly summarizes in the formula of the shepherd "in oure power." The implicit parallel between the shepherd, the quintessential character of the pastoral, and its peasant author whose circumstances are supposedly epitomized in the genre, is more than obvious: the same power relation applies to the peasant poet under bourgeois patronage. In Richardson's ruminations about the pastoral genre as well as the work of women peasant poets, thematic and generic choices are largely determined by social relations coupled with aesthetic concerns.

If there is a unifying theme connecting the pastorals, mock pastorals, antipastorals, and labor poems by women laborers, it is the exploitation of labor, a theme significant not only for the way in which it is treated in their labor poems, but even more so for its notable absence in their pastorals. Of these varied forms, pastorals, mock pastorals, and antipastorals far outweigh labor poems in their work, and even the latter, as we have seen, at times reiterate the concerns of the ruling rather than the working class. This circumstance can be linked to the status of individual authors as being patronized and deracinated or largely ignored — cer-

---

[150] Richardson in a letter to William Craig, June 3, 1765; original manuscript in the National Library of Scotland (MS 9931, f. 81).

[151] Richardson's letter to Craig (unpag.).

tainly, such a link would seem to be suggested by the fact that the most critical labor poems were written by poets who were not transplanted into the bourgeois context, or, as in the case of Stephen Duck, written at a time before this relocation took place. But the predominance of pastorals, particularly mock and antipastorals, rather than labor poems, in their writing could also indicate a greater readiness on the poets' part to fight aesthetic battles rather than social ones.

Although labor documentaries thus remain a comparative rarity, it would be difficult to establish clear-cut political allegiances in the work of any one peasant poet. Molly Leapor, for example, wrote both traditional pastorals in which labor is superfluous because fruit falls readily from the tree and highly satirical poems mocking the lifestyle and arrogance of the wealthy. Anna Louisa Karsch wrote poems describing the wretchedness of poverty and physical labor and poems in which, as in her "Schlesisches Bauerngespräch," the same conditions are sublimated and aestheticized. The coexistence of pastorals and labor poems, of aristocratic art forms and lower-class concerns in their writing indicates both the amount of literary experimentation permeating their work and that their writing, of necessity, reflected both aesthetic and social conditions. Clearly, the public acknowledgment and survival of their work simultaneously hinged on its lower-class origins — a social fact with aesthetic implications — and its ability to adhere to upper-class paradigms. This conformity was, paradoxically, proscribed in aesthetics, where the "original" genius reigned supreme, but nonetheless insisted on in the social realm. Whereas the skillful adaptation of the pastoral genre in the writing of many peasant poets could be seen as countering the myth of the unerudite natural poet, a pastoral written by a peasant was not, in the aesthetic sense, viewed as an imitation of an aristocratic art form but as the result of natural inspiration: a case of nature imitating art. In addition, peasant-produced pastorals provided the bourgeois reader with a pleasing affirmation of bourgeois superiority. Thus, the reception of the peasant's pastoral was, like its production, governed by aspects that touch on both the aesthetic and the social, for the bourgeois superiority demonstrated in the pastoral could be experienced in the aesthetic sense — in the difference between the low-lying pastoral meadow and the dizzying heights of Mount Parnassus — as well as in the social sense, via the gratifying subordination of both the shepherd in the pastoral and its peasant author in the practice of patronage.

# 5: Inspired by Nature, Inspired by Love: Two Poets on Poetic Inspiration

TWO IDEAS HAVE predominated both the contemporary reception of peasant women's poetry and later scholarship: the assumption that the author's work must have been inspired by Nature (presumably because she was a peasant) and that the work must have been inspired by Love (presumably because she was a woman). The first idea is, as discussed in previous chapters, closely linked with conjectures voiced in aesthetic treatises about the nature poet and his or her predilections, themes, and genres;[1] the second is a notion that is not particular to the work of women peasant poets but has demonstrably influenced the reception of bourgeois women writers as well. In this chapter, I try not to diminish the centrality of either concept for the writing of lower-class women: Anna Louisa Karsch, for example, was a prolific love poet, even though many of her most ardent love poems, which were inserted into letters to Gleim, were never published during her lifetime.[2] Most peasant poets discussed in this book wrote some love poems, and Nature or nature imagery is undeniably central to their work. But whereas verse that uses love and nature as themes clearly constitutes a significant portion of these poets' oeuvre, my focus is not on these poems, which could be read as responding to bourgeois expectations, but rather on works that thematize these expectations more directly. Concentrating on the work of Anna Louisa Karsch and Ann Cromartie Yearsley, I discuss poetry in which the authors expressly respond to the bourgeois reception of their writing as *inevitably* inspired either by Nature or Love or in which they discuss the phenomenon of poetic inspiration and the process of writing specifically with respect to these two themes. Without claiming their representativeness for the overall work of peasant women poets, in

---

[1] Cf. chapters 1 and 4.
[2] Cf. her poems to Gleim in *"Bruder in Apoll,"* I, 11, 16–17, 269–70, and II, 34–35, 87–88, 93–94, 138. Some of these poems were later edited out of her letters and published in posthumous collections. Examples are her poem "Freund, zeichne diesen Tag," published in abbreviated versions in *Das Lied der Karschin*, 64, and *Gedichte und Lebenszeugnisse*, 91–92 (originally in her letter to Gleim, June 22, 1761, *"Bruder in Apoll,"* I, 12–14) and her poem "Sappho ist traurig bei Thyrsis" (Sappho Sad in Thyrsis's Company [not Karsch's title]) published in *Gedichte und Lebenszeugnisse*, 104.

which nature poems considerably outnumber poems on poetic inspiration, I concentrate specifically on works by Karsch and Yearsley that can be considered intertextual in the sense that bourgeois aesthetics are expressly reflected in the poetic response. Some of these poems can be read as a kind of preemptive reader response: as discussed in chapter 6, many poets developed a clear awareness of how their work was likely to be received and, accordingly, transformed their poetry from a bourgeois object of critique into a vehicle capable of preempting this critique from an authorial perspective. On the aesthetic level, a similar authorial response to the bourgeois Nature poetology takes place in some of these poems. This aspect, the authors' explicit response to the bourgeois aesthetic and its impact on their own writing, makes these comparatively rare works as central for an understanding of their overall oeuvre as the many nature poems that simply reflect this aesthetic, although the latter outnumber the former considerably. For in the absence of aesthetic treatises or letters, diaries, or other extensive self-reflective writings, which do not exist for any of these authors except Anna Louisa Karsch, such poems constitute virtually the only commentary we have by peasant authors on the subject of aesthetics in general and bourgeois aesthetics as applied to peasant poets in particular. Together with some passages in letters and forewords, these poems are the only indication to what extent peasant poets defined literary Art differently from their bourgeois patrons and critics, and to what extent they attempted or refused to participate in the bourgeois project of Art.

## The Rural Muse:
## On Nature Inspiration and Book Learning

If Nature inspiration is understood in the sense in which it is postulated in bourgeois aesthetics, meaning the poet's total and exclusive inspiration by nature and the prohibition of any formal education or training, two diametrically opposed poetic traditions can be cited as responses: one in which the poet states her exclusive indebtedness to Nature and one in which she, conversely, emphasizes her extensive reading in both contemporary and ancient traditions. Unsurprisingly, the former is far more common in the work of peasant women, where the statement of exclusive nature inspiration often also assumes a biographical function.[3] The

---

[3] For some examples, cf. chapters 2 and 3.

emphasis on "Nature's strong Impulse,"[4] the "artless Muse,"[5] the "rural Muse," or the "Muse Ungovern'd" roaming the rustic scenery "Wild, as the tunefull Lark that loves the grove"[6] is virtually ubiquitous. The rural muse, as Jane Cave describes it, enters the author's humble cottage spontaneously, unbidden;[7] as Karsch stated, "three Muses leap up when I beckon to one."[8] Karsch explicitly places her poetic production in the realm of nature by frequently comparing her own poetry with birdsong or the simple songs of rustics at work.[9] Poetic inspiration is thus presented as much in line with the bourgeois aesthetic mandate of the original author as both spontaneously and nature inspired. True to the bourgeois adage of *Poeta nascitur non fit*, which is occasionally cited directly,[10] the subject of Nature inspiration often expands into an explicit rejection of formal learning of any kind: the rural muse sings "Unskill'd in Converse, and in Schools untaught, / Artless my Words, and unrefin'd my Thought."[11] Poetic inspiration "in schools untaught," or, in Milne's words, "Without the school's instructions,"[12] assumes synonymity with the "natural" since formal education is invariably identified with rule-based poesy. The poets' self-representation as "One who has had Nature only for her Tutor"[13] thus necessitates the explicit declaration

[4] Mary Masters, "To a Gentleman who questioned my being the Author of the foregoing Verses," *Poems*, 44–45, the citation 45.

[5] Milne, "Introductory Verses," *Simple Poems*, 33–35, the citation 33.

[6] Ann Yearsley, "To The King On His Majesty's arrival at Cheltenham 1788," in Ferguson, "Unpublished Poems," 37–38, the citation 36. The poem is briefly discussed in Ferguson, *Eighteenth-Century Women Poets*, 79–81.

[7] Cave, "The Author's Plea," *Poems*, 1–4, the citation 3.

[8] "Drei Musen hüpfen auf, wenn ich nur einer winke"; Anna Louisa Karsch, "Drei Musen hüpfen auf," *Das Lied der Karschin*, 67–68, the citation 67. Other poems in which Karsch presents her poetic work as rooted exclusively in nature include "An Mademoiselle Sack," *Gedichte*, 266–67, and "An einen jungen Freund," *Gedichte*, 76–77 (for a brief discussion of this poem, cf. chapter 3). The same theme frequently appears in her letters, cf. her letters to Gleim in *"Bruder in Apoll,"* I, 91–93, 98.

[9] For example, in her "Lied an gefangene Lerchen," originally in *Auserlesene Gedichte*, 95–98 (republished as "Gefangene Lerchen," *Das Lied der Karschin*, 87–88); "Der Frühling, an die Frau von Wrech," in *Auserlesene Gedichte*, 33–35, the citation 34 (republished in *Gedichte und Lebenszeugnisse*, 62–64); "Der unnachahmliche Pindar, an Herrn Ramler," in *Auserlesene Gedichte*, 167–72, the citation 169.

[10] Mary Masters, "To a Gentleman," *Poems*, 44–45: "Sir, 'tis allow'd, as it has oft been said, / Poets are only *Born* and never *Made*," the citation 44 (emphases original).

[11] Masters, "To the Right Honourable Earl of Burlington," *Poems*, 5–7, the quotation 6.

[12] Milne, "To a Gentleman, Who Sent Me a Present of Pens," *Simple Poems*, 139.

[13] Yearsley, billet to Lord Courtown accompanying her tributary poem "To the King," cited in Ferguson, "Unpublished Poems," 39. In the dedication of her second volume to

that she remains "Wholly unpractis'd in the learned Rules."[14] As Candler exclaims, "Ah! What am I? — — A stranger to the rules / Observ'd by those instructed in the schools; / Unskill'd, unpractis'd. . . ."[15] Poetic inspiration takes place in a realm

> Where strong Idea may on Rapture spring:
> I mount! — Wild Ardour shall ungovern'd stray:
> Nor dare the mimic pedant clip my wing.
> 
> *Rule!* what art *thou?* Thy limits I disown!
> Can thy weak law the swelling thought confine?
> Snatch glowing Transport from her kindred zone,
> And fix her melting on thy frozen line?[16]

This last question is purely rhetorical, posed for the sole reason and in the secure knowledge that Young and other aestheticists had already answered it. What masquerades as a question is thus revealed to be a poetological credo, clearly discernible in the contemptuous relegation of the unoriginal author (in Young's sense) to a "mimic" and the erudite author to a "pedant." But whereas bourgeois authors are free to avow their independence from rules and literary models, such assertions on the part of the lower-class author lead straight into the irresolvable paradox of patronage: the fact that her declaration of independence is founded on a new allegiance, that to the bourgeois aesthetic model of the "original," nature-inspired author.

Alongside poems that assert the poet's originality and independence from formal learning can be found, at times in the work of the same author, poems that state the author's indebtedness to earlier poets or

---

the Earl of Bristol, Yearsley describes herself as "Unadorned by art, unaccomplished by science" and her poems as "the effusions of *Nature* only" (*Poems on Various Subjects,* vi; the emphasis is original). On Yearsley's self-presentation as an untutored genius, cf. Carter, vii, 192–93, 207–8, 212–22; Tompkins, 87; and Landry, *Muses,* 124.

[14] Masters, "To a Gentleman," *Poems,* 44–45, the citation 44. The same claim is made by Karsch in her poem "Ihr Freunde von den Wissenschaften" (cited in Chézy, "Meine Großmutter," 41) and in her report on her audience with Frederick II, in which she denies the existence of any formal education or training in connection with her poetic productivity; cf. her description of her audience with the king in *"Bruder in Apoll,"* I, 183–85, the citation 184. Karsch also versified her encounter with Frederick; cf. her "Bei Friedrich dem Großen," *Das Lied der Karschin,* 134–37 (as "Antwort der Dichterin" in *O, mir entwischt nicht,* 106–10). Chézy republished this poem in her biography of her grandmother ("Meine Großmutter," 56–58).

[15] Candler, "To the Rev. Dr. J — — n," *Poetical Attempts,* 58–60, the quotation 58.

[16] Ann Yearsley, "Written on a Visit," *Poems on Various Subjects,* 139–43, the citation 142 (emphases original). For a brief discussion, cf. Landry, *Muses,* 53–54.

emphasize the extent of their own reading. One of the most obvious examples is the double-edged discourse in Yearsley's *Rural Lyre,* a classical collection in which Yearsley simultaneously flaunts her knowledge of literature, mythology, and history and reaffirms her authorial image as an "Untaught, unpolish'd . . . savage mind."[17] Molly Leapor, posthumously held up as an example of exclusive nature inspiration,[18] entreated Pope's spirit in a poem to "teach my soul to reach the seats divine," thus invoking Pope simultaneously as idol, model, and inspiration.[19] Elizabeth Hands, in her "Critical Fragments on Some of the English Poets," demonstrates the extent of her reading in her brief stylistic ventriloquies of such greats as Milton, Shakespeare, Young, Swift, Pope, Prior, and Butler.[20] Such erudition is similarly displayed by Ann Yearsley in her poem "To Mr. ****, an Unlettered Poet, on Genius Unimproved," in which she recommends that the natural poet ignore all poetic rules and give imagination the rein, claiming that "untaught Minds" are the most receptive to poetic genius, only to demonstrate her knowledge of the "Mythology" she disowns in references to both Eastern and Western traditions, from Zoroaster to Pythagoras.[21] Similarly, Mark Anthony, Julius Caesar, Apollo, Jupiter, and other gods and heroes from the Greek and Roman traditions appear rather incongruously in Karsch's rhymed account of her audience with Frederick the Great, in which she claims exclusive nature inspiration and a complete lack of formal education.[22]

Such poetological double-talk has its roots in the principal incompatibility of erudition and poetic genius proclaimed in bourgeois Nature aesthetics: the bourgeois mandate that limits the lower-class author to "natural" inspiration simultaneously pronounces him or her incapable of acquiring the learning necessary for an existence as an erudite poet. Anna Louisa Karsch, in her poem "An den Freyherrn von Kottwitz, als er ihr Gemählde zeigte, und sie fragte, ob die Blumenstücke nicht schön wären"

---

[17] Cf. Ferguson, *Eighteenth-Century Women Poets,* 68–69; the quotation is taken from Yearsley's "Brutus: a Fragment," *The Rural Lyre,* 1–27, the quotation 17.

[18] Cf. Waldron, *Lactilla,* 39.

[19] Leapor, "On Mr. Pope's Universal Prayer," in Colman/Thornton, II, 72–73, the citation 72.

[20] Hands, "Critical Fragments," *The Death of Amnon,* 126–27. Landry briefly discusses the poem in *Muses,* 193–95. Both Leapor's and Hands's poem can be read in a long tradition of works in which women, including lower-class women, acknowledge a debt to masculine bourgeois authors; cf. Landry, *Muses,* 47–49.

[21] Yearsley, "To Mr. ****," *Poems on Various Subjects,* 77–82, the quotations on 81 and 79, respectively (republished in Fairer/Gerrard, 450–51). The poem is briefly analyzed in Waldron, *Lactilla,* 150–52; Zionkowski, 104; Tompkins, 79; and Landry, *Muses,* 127.

[22] Karsch, "Bei Friedrich dem Großen," *Das Lied der Karschin,* 134–37.

(To the Baron von Kottwitz, When He Showed Her Paintings and Asked Her Whether She Did Not Find the Floral Paintings Beautiful) implicitly confounds this expectation when she dutifully states her admiration for the flowers and immediately thereafter expresses her greater interest in paintings representing motifs from history and mythology.[23] For the nature poet to reject the bucolic in favor of the formal knowledge on which bourgeois poesy rests can be considered nothing short of a poetological statement, and one that stands in direct contrast to that expressed in bourgeois aesthetics. In Karsch's case, her inconsistent statements on the subject of nature inspiration — she considered herself a nature poet but at the same time laid claim to some aspects of bourgeois erudition — were posthumously smoothed into an unbroken image of Karsch as Pure Nature: in the first and most influential Karsch biography, written by her daughter Karoline von Klencke, Karsch is presented as a student of Nature, not books. Whereas Karsch describes reading as one of the most central early experiences while she was employed herding cows, Klencke does her utmost to downplay this influence and emphasize aspects that are more congruent with the bourgeois concept of nature inspiration:

> Perhaps the three summers during which she herded cows became the source which nourished and expanded her poetic inclinations; for here her curiosity was not merely satisfied by books but she also acquainted herself with the subjects of Nature. She learned about the various kinds of birds and rural insects; she studied differences between trees, plants and flowers, and the most obscure little herb was stored by name in her incomparable memory. In the same way, she became acquainted with the changes of the seasons, the elements, and the stars in the sky. From this she collected all the beautiful colors for her splendid portraits of Nature which adorn her masterpieces in a manner that can, perhaps, be considered unique. If the poet had, instead of her life as a herder girl, enjoyed an artificial education and access to modern books, her talent would never have achieved the heights for which it is now generally acknowledged.[24]

---

[23] Karsch, "An den Freyherrn von Kottwitz," *Auserlesene Gedichte*, 273–77.
[24] Klencke, "Lebenslauf," 28–29: "Vielleicht wurden die drei Sommer ihres Hirtenstandes die Quelle, welche ihre Dichterader so weit ausdehnte und so stark anfüllte; denn hier begnügte sich ihre Wißbegierde nicht nur an den Büchern, sondern machte sie auch mit den Gegenständen der Natur bekannt. Sie lernte die mannichfaltigen Arten der Vögel und der ländlichen Insekten kennen; sie erforschte den Unterschied der Baumarten, der Pflanzen und Blumen, und in ihrem unvergleichlichen Gedächtnisse fand das vergessenste Kräutchen seinen Namen wieder. Auf gleiche Weise wurden ihr die Veränderungen der Jahreszeiten, so wie der Elemente bekannt, und der gestirnte Himmel mit ihrem Geiste vertraut. Daher sammlete sie alle die schönen Farben zu den herrlichen Bildern der Natur, welche ihren Meisterstücken einen Vorzug geben, den sie vielleicht in ihrer Art einzig hat.

What Klencke describes here is a classic case of Nature inspiration, unaided by outside influences, books, schooling, or teachers. In this account, Karsch does not learn anything, nor does anyone teach her; precisely how she "acquaints herself" with the basic elements of botany, zoology, and astronomy that Klencke lists as the sum total of her knowledge remains unclear. The image evoked here is not unlike that presented by Duff in his description of the nature poet in search of poetic inspiration; Karsch's course of "study" is one limited to personal observation and expressly contrasted to a formal "artificial education." Two statements are central to Klencke's account in terms of defining Karsch as a nature poet in the sense in which s/he appears in bourgeois aesthetics. First is the implied statement that Karsch's knowledge, acquired as spontaneously and unconsciously as she would later write her poetry, is not knowledge for its own sake, but rather to serve as the foundation of her poetic work, a statement that not only describes Karsch's mode of writing but also limits her themes and preempts her reception (in the proclamation that her nature poetry is by far her best work). The second is the articulated notion that Karsch would never have become a poet if she had been exposed to an unnatural (artificial) education. It is worth noting that Karsch herself, while citing the influence of nature on her work in numerous poems, does not anywhere in her letters or autobiographical writings relate the intense interest in plants, trees, flowers, or insects that Klencke describes; in her autobiographical letters to Sulzer, the presence or absence of books is instead presented as by far the most significant aspect of her early literary life.

Klencke's account ends, unsurprisingly, in a series of poetological statements that are more or less copied directly from Sulzer's aesthetics in general and his foreword to Karsch's first edition in particular.[25] Subsequent Karsch scholars, as well, have chosen to concentrate on the many passages in Karsch's letters and poems in which she defines herself as a nature-inspired poet or rejects rule-based poesy and have interpreted her statements as conforming to the bourgeois definition of the rustic poet as a nature poet. And although this interpretation is indeed securely anchored in Karsch's work — numerous examples could be cited in support of her adherence to this model — it is equally necessary to consider the occasional deviation, the small body of work in which Karsch refuses the offered flowers in favor of forays into bourgeois erudition, because these odd

---

Hätte statt dieses Hirtenlebens die Dichterin das Glück einer gekünstelten Erziehung genossen und die Bücher unsrer Tage gehabt, so würde sie kaum ihr Talent zu der Höhe geschwungen haben, in welcher es allgemein bekannt ist."

[25] Cf. Klencke, "Lebenslauf," 29.

examples elucidate Karsch's awareness of the limitations of the bourgeois understanding of her own writing, as well as her consciousness that, compared with the erudite bourgeois author, she was being cast in an inferior role. Perhaps the best example of her awareness of the connection between bourgeois erudition and the presumed creativity of the peasant author is contained in her poem addressed to her mother, in which she accused her mother of refusing to permit her to learn Latin. It is a regret that at times appears in Karsch's letters as well: "I am still upset that my mother did not leave me with my old uncle; he would have taught me Latin and I could now read Flacchus and Virgil."[26] The same indictment is levied in her poem "Ann meine Mutter in jene Wellt geschrieben den dritten Juny 1785" (To My Mother, Written to Her in the Other World on the Third of June 1785), but in this poem, she sarcastically turns blame into gratitude for the ignorance in which she was kept:

> But upon further contemplation
> I am quite certain that your daughter
> Would not be seen as a sensation
> If you had more than German taught her
> For if you had, then folks would say
> That I pilfered from him, or him
> Who wrote poetry in the ancient days
> That must be why it was your whim
> To save me from Latin and erudition,
> Accept, dear Mother, my contrition,
> Your nagging thus my thanks has earned
> 'Tis my good fortune I'm unlearned[27]

Karsch's observation draws a link between the bourgeois reception of the peasant "sensation" as an "original" author and the assumption that the poet's originality is guaranteed by her ignorance, particularly of those aspects of learning (Latin, Greek, ancient history, and mythology)

---

[26] Karsch to Gleim, May 1762: "ich bin noch böse daß mich meine Mutter nicht dem alltten Vetter da lies, Er hätte mich Lateinisch gelernt und da könt ich iezt den Flacus und den Virgill lesen"; *"Bruder in Apoll,"* I, 112. Cf. also her letter to Gleim, June 12, 1785, in which she voices the same regret (cited in Beuys, 127–28).

[27] Anna Louisa Karsch, "Ann meine Mutter": Doch wenns recht wird überdacht / Würde wol aus deinem Kinnde / Kein solch Wunnderding gemacht / Wenn es mehr als Deutsch verstünnde / Denn da sagtte mann wol gar / Daß ich den und den bestohlen / Der vor Zeiten Dichtter war / Drum ward dirs gewis befohlen / Vom Latein mich abzuziehn, / Liebe Mutter laß dir danken / mir zur Ehre warst du kühn / vom Latein mich wegzuzanken ("Bruder in Apoll," II, 469–70, the citation 470). The poem was included in a letter to Gleim; cf. her letter in *"Bruder in Apoll,"* II, 230.

that constituted the basis of a bourgeois Classical education. The bourgeoisie's ban on education for the lower-class author constitutes an obvious conundrum: in her letters, Karsch regretted her limited education, particularly her ignorance of foreign languages, to the end of her days; simultaneously she was well aware that it was this ignorance that enabled her entire career as a "natural" poet.

Yearsley's poem "Addressed to Ignorance, Occasioned by a Gentleman's desiring the Author never to assume a Knowledge of the Ancients" refutes both the assumption that holds the nature poet ineligible for bourgeois erudition and the poetological mandate that limits her to nature-inspired poetry.[28] For the lower-class poet, the pretense of ignorance serves as a protective cloak, or veil, as Yearsley has stated — a veil that shields the poet from the penetrating gaze of bourgeois critics and simultaneously pulls the wool over their eyes:

> Lend me thy dark veil. — Science darts her strong ray;
> In the orb of bright Learning she sits:
> Haste! haste! Cloth'd by thee, I can yet keep my way,
> Still secure from her Critics, or Wits.
>
> All slight thee; no Beauty e'er boasts of thy pow'r;
> No Beau on thy Influence depends;
> No Statesman shall own thee; no Poet implore,
> But Lactilla and thou must be friends.
>
> Then come, gentle Goddess, sit full in my looks;
> Let my accents be founded by thee:
> While Crito in pomp, bears his burden of books,
> On the plains of wild Nature I'm free.[29]

Yearsley's poem moves between two opposites: ignorance, which is paraphrased as "Nature" and juxtaposed to "Science," and the "freedom" the poetic "I" gains by her pretense to be ignorant juxtaposed to the unstated alternative. The speaker's embracing of ignorance is presented as both deliberate and coerced: it is a safety measure, a way of hiding beneath a dark veil, the only way to "keep my way" — to continue writing, the reader is led to assume — and it is simultaneously

---

[28] For brief interpretations of the poem, cf. Ferguson, *Eighteenth-Century Women Poets*, 54–55; Zionkowski, 103–4; Waldron, "Ann Yearsley," 317–18; Landry, *Muses*, 162–65; and Doody, *The Daring Muse*, 130–31.

[29] Yearsley, "Addressed to Ignorance," *Poems on Various Subjects*, 93–99, the citation 93–94.

recognized as an unusual mandate, one not imposed on any other figure of public life, be it statesman, poet, or beau. The speaker's stated obedience to the gentleman's desire that she, the Nature Poet, assume no knowledge of history and mythology — "I am blind to the Ancients"[30] — is sarcastically undermined in the remainder of the poem, in which Yearsley parades a long sequence of characters from Greek and Roman history and mythology past the reader. "Addressed to Ignorance" is thus more than "Occasioned" by the unnamed gentleman's mandate that Yearsley stay away from formal knowledge, it is both an adamant refutation of his prohibition and a clear statement that obedience to his demand constitutes the only "freedom" to write and publish granted the author. Her solution is to "assume" her ignorance in the same manner in which she is desired "never to assume . . . Knowledge"; she wears it like a veil, both dimming her own view of "bright Learning" and obscuring the stern critic's gaze.

In the work of some peasant poets, most prominently Yearsley and Karsch, nature inspiration and erudition are not perceived as mutually exclusive, the way they appear in bourgeois aesthetics, but rather complementary. Their repeatedly stated scorn for poetic "rules" does not, as it does in the bourgeois estimation, translate into a rejection of reading or formal knowledge or into a repudiation of this knowledge in the process of writing. Karsch, in her "Ode an Freund Bachmann" (Ode to My Friend Bachmann), describes her poetic talent as a gift from heaven, but elsewhere she defines this gift as one that, despite its divine origins, could stand to benefit from human refinement. In the poetic reinvention of the story of her birth, one of heaven's angels finds her at birth and, moved to compassion by her abject poverty, pleads with God to make him the baby's guardian angel: "Contemptible dust now covers / The forehead which was made / By you for contemplation."[31] When God grants his wish, the angel endows his charge with a lyre and one of the muses. The heavenly inspiration that Karsch claims here as the background for her own writing can be considered a radicalization of the concept of nature inspiration, but it does not carry with it the same prohibition on formal learning that is an integral part of the bourgeois interpretation. On the contrary, her choice of words ("contemplation") seems to hint at the cerebral qualities of her writing. In her dedicatory poem to the Baron von Kottwitz, Karsch goes so far as to claim that left in the "wild," left in that Nature which, accord-

[30] Yearsley, "Addressed to Ignorance," *Poems on Various Subjects*, 94.
[31] "Es decket schmählicher Staub / Die ernstgefaltete Stirne, / Von dir zum Denken gebaut." Karsch, "Ode an Freund Bachmann," *Gedichte und Lebenszeugnisse*, 134–35, the citation 134.

ing to bourgeois aesthetics, furnishes the ideal surrounding for the natural poet, her talent would not have flourished but withered:

> For without you, this gift that is my own
> It would have perished on the Oder's strand
> Just as a flower seed dies, thrown upon the stone
> Unable to draw roots in barren sand.
>
> A plant dies in the sun, if neither clouds
> Nor gardener afford it irrigation,
> A noble fruit tree, unkempt, wilder sprouts
> If growth remains untamed by cultivation.
>
> Thus would I have gone wild; but then your hand,
> Steered by a God, led me from this rough land,
> And brought me to the city of the King
> whose praise and glory evermore I sing.[32]

In Karsch's dedicatory poem to Kottwitz, nature plays a dual role: shown here is a sinister barren landscape that furnishes a deliberate contrast to the idyllic landscape of the pastoral and from which the speaker escapes to "magnificent Berlin."[33] Fertility, one of the central themes of traditional nature poetry, is here countered both in the barrenness of the landscape, in which not even a seed can sprout and plants shrivel up for want of care, and in the transformation of the fertile plain into an untamed and threatening wilderness. Likewise, metaphoric Nature, poetic Nature, is presented as savage, as wild and unkempt, but whereas many peasant poets, Yearsley foremost among them, proudly employed epithets like "wild," "savage," and "uncontrolled" in the circumscription of their own poetic talent,[34] Karsch points to the limitations of this model. In an aesthetic context in which plants are frequently utilized as

---

[32] Anna Louisa Karsch, "Zueignungs-Gesang an den Baron von Kottwitz": Denn ohne Dich wär, an dem Oderstrande / Mühselig unterdrückt mein glückliches Genie; / Ein Blumen-Saame stirbt in unbetautem Sande, / Keimt auf des Steines Rücken nie. // Die Pflanze stirbt, von Wolken unbegossen, / Vom Gärtner unbesprützt, wenn Erndte-Sonne glüht; / Der edle Fruchtkern treibt zum wilden Apfelsprossen, / Wenn nicht die Kunst den Baum erzieht. // So wär auch ich verwildert; aber Deine, / Von einem Gott gelenkte, rechte Freundes Hand, / Zog mich zum grossen Sitz des Königes, der seine / Gecrönte Schläfe grün umwand (*Auserlesene Gedichte*, iii-vi, the citation iv-v, reprinted in *Gedichte und Lebenszeugnisse*, 79–80, the citation 80).

[33] Karsch, "Zueignungs-Gesang," *Auserlesene Gedichte*, vi: "Du machtest mir in sorgenlosen Tagen / Zum Elisäer Sitz, das prächtige Berlin."

[34] Cf. Waldron, *Lactilla*, 89–90.

metaphors for poetic creativity,[35] the parallel between the cultivation of plants (arrived at either "naturally," watered by the clouds, or "artificially," through the gardener's care) and the cultivation of minds would have been easily recognizable to contemporary readers, as would her conclusion: that her native surroundings, understood both physically and intellectually, provided little or no nourishment for her "genius" which could only flourish in the cultivated atmosphere of the king's great city. Using both nature imagery and the traditional city-country dichotomy, Karsch's poem unmasks the bourgeois concept of exclusive nature inspiration as a dreary intellectual landscape in which poetic talent withers for want of stimulus, and it is a sign of her resistance to the bourgeois ban on erudition that she employs some trappings of this education in making her central point. In likening the speaker's escape from the dreary countryside to the magnificent city to the poet's escape from drowning on the dolphin's back, she purposely employs an image gleaned not from "nature," but from a mythological source, thus once again stating the centrality of "cultivation" for her own work.

Yearsley was perhaps the most openly intertextual of all women peasant poets and simultaneously the one who most obviously flaunted her own extensive reading in her final volume of poetry, *The Rural Lyre* (1796). Like Karsch, she saw her only chance to distinguish herself through constant emphasis on her humble station, her lack of education, and in buying into the bourgeois myth that cast her as Pure Nature. In the preface to her second volume, she answered the rift with her patron Hannah More and the accusation that the poems of her first volume must have been coauthored or at least severely edited by More with a pronounced statement that her writing owed nothing to her patron,[36] but this defiance lands her — once more — squarely in the realm of Nature Inspiration. The announcement of her second volume describes it as "A Collection of Poetry in Blank Verse, on various subjects, never before published, by Ann Yearsley, the Bristol Milkwoman. This being the produce of her own uncultivated genius, without any alterations and corrections, she hopes will prove an amusing novelty to those who may prefer Nature's unclipt wing of poetic fancy."[37] Inherent in Yearsley's announcement of her volume is the same paradox that marks her sensibility poems, which, in defiance of More's claim that sensibility could only be experienced by a refined mind,

---

[35] For a discussion of the employment of nature metaphors in aesthetic writing, cf. chapter 1.

[36] Cf. Yearsley's narrative "To the Noble and Generous Subscribers," with which she prefaced her second volume (*Poems on Various Subjects*, xv-xxv, particularly xxiv).

[37] Quoted in Waldron, *Lactilla*, 132.

sing the praise of "Sensibility untaught":[38] independence from the patron can only be achieved at the price of adherence to a poetological concept, that of nature inspiration, advocated by that same patron.

In some of Yearsley's work, exclusive nature inspiration is faulted for the same deficiencies that Karsch diagnosed in her dedicatory poem to Kottwitz: the lack of stimulus and the impossibility of development. The following, taken from Yearsley's poem "On Mrs. Montagu," is perhaps one of the most concrete poetic descriptions of the process of creative inspiration ever written by a lower-class poet:

> Oft as I trod my native wilds alone,
> Strong gusts of thought would rise, but rise to die;
> The portals of the swelling soul ne'er oped
> By liberal converse, rude ideas strove
> Awhile for vent, but found it not, and died.
> Thus rust the Mind's best powers. Yon starry orbs,
> Majestic ocean, flowery vales, gay groves,
> Eye-wasting lawns, and Heaven-attempting hills,
> Which bound th' horizon, and which curb the view;
> All those, with beauteous imagery, awaked
> My ravished soul to ecstasy untaught,
> To all the transport the rapt sense can bear;
> But all expired, for want of powers to speak;
> All perished in the mind as soon as born,
> Erased more quick than cyphers on the shore,
> O'er which the cruel waves, unheedful, roll.[39]

Yearsley clearly evokes the idealized nature poet of bourgeois aesthetics — that poet whom William Duff envisioned as wandering his native groves alone, with the landscape serving as both inspiration for and subject of the creative work — while equally clearly citing her own rural origins. Unlike Karsch's description of the wilderness in which she grew up, Yearsley's native landscape appears as beautiful and inspiring, but it is the nature

---

[38] Cf. Hannah More, "Sensibility," in *Poems*, 166–87, and Yearsley, "Addressed to Sensibility," *Poems on Various Subjects*, 1–6, and "To Indifference," *Poems on Various Subjects*, 49–53. The quotation is taken from Yearsley's "Addressed to Sensibility," *Poems on Various Subjects*, 6. More's poem "Sensibility," written in 1782, predates Yearsley's *Poems on Various Subjects*, in which both of her sensibility poems appeared, by five years.

[39] Yearsley, "On Mrs. Montagu," in Lonsdale, *Eighteenth-Century Women Poets*, 395–96, the citation 396 (also in Fairer/Gerrard, 441–43). For an interpretation of the poem, cf. Waldron, *Lactilla*, 97–100, and Landry, *Muses*, 125–27; the poem is also mentioned in Tompkins, 63.

of that inspiration that is depicted as deficient. For inspiration, which the bourgeois natural-genius aesthetic would equate with the process of writing, is here limited to the moment of conceptualization and the *will* to write; the execution of the will, the power of expression, depends on "liberal converse," or "cultivation," as Karsch has stated: exchange with other writers, either directly (in conversation) or indirectly through reading. Yearsley's analysis emphasizes the transitoriness of inspiration as well as the fact that, deprived of that exchange with authors and books, that cultivation that could stir "powers to speak," the poet, even the inspired poet, will remain mute. What is *erased* here — Yearsley's choice of words suggests not only obliteration but also, indirectly, outside agency — is not only the poet's chance at posterity but her entire work, that work which wants to come into being following the initial burst of inspiration but which can find no expression without focus and direction.

Whereas most other peasant poets adhered to the bourgeois model of nature inspiration, this concept is at times problematized in the work of both Karsch and Yearsley. Although both authors clearly perceive the nature-inspired unerudite poet as the model for their own writing and recognize this as the only aesthetic context that would allow them to publish, they occasionally also critique the limitations inherent in this model. Both authors identify the lack of development, of intellectual or creative growth, as its ultimate limiting factor, thus indirectly showing up the flaws of the bourgeois aesthetic that confuses the moment of inspiration with the creation of the work. Karsch's emphasis on "cultivation," Yearsley's yearning for "converse" can be read as a rejection of the ban on formal learning that is part and parcel of the bourgeois aesthetic of nature poetry. In particular, Yearsley's concept of *assuming* ignorance to be "secure from her Critics, or Wits" and the occasional poems in which she and other poets flaunt their erudition while claiming exclusive nature inspiration point to the dilemma facing the lower-class author whose literary existence was defined by bourgeois aesthetics. That dilemma is not only defined by class difference but by the discrepancy between reception and production: whereas the marketing, the publication, the entire bourgeois reception of the peasant poet was predicated on the concept of his or her spontaneousness, lack of learning, and indebtedness to Nature in both the physical and the poetological sense, exclusive nature inspiration, from the vantage point of poetic production, proved to be a creative dead end.

## Under Love's Spell: Authors and Readers

Particularly for the work of Anna Louisa Karsch, Love, that other great inspiration of women peasant poets, is generally considered to be as central as Nature, both as a theme and as a source of inspiration. Her reception as a love poet is largely a posthumous one: Herder thought it inappropriate to confer on her the appellation Sappho because she did not publish love poems.[40] But those contemporaries who knew her unpublished love poems to Gleim both saw her as one of the greatest love poets of the age and viewed her writing as decisively influenced by the theme. No other poet, Gleim claimed, treated the subject with similar fervor and expression;[41] Karsch's "Sapphic poems,"[42] enthusiastically received by Gleim and Ebert, constituted the only portion of her work that Gleim planned to publish in entirely unedited and uncorrected form.[43] Karsch's refusal to publish these poems and the fact that Gleim accorded them an extraordinary status in Karsch's work can partly be explained by two factors: the Anacreontic game in the correspondence between Karsch and Gleim, in which both switched constantly back and forth between real and pastoral identities, particularly when love was the subject, and the disconnect between Karsch's and Gleim's interpretation of these poems, with Karsch's perception of her work as real expressions of love pitted against Gleim's desire to market them as "Sapphic" odes. In effect, what Karsch does in refusing to publish her love poems to Gleim is to draw a distinction between Anacreontic game/fiction and reality that neither her patron nor her later biographers and critics were willing to acknowledge. For in their writings, love constitutes the primary inspiration for Karsch's work precisely *because* she was supposedly incapable of distinguishing between fiction and reality. Gleim erased this distinction by refusing to acknowledge the personal nature of Karsch's verse epistles to him, indeed, many of his attempts to persuade Karsch to give her permission for their publication are predicated on his pretense that these poems had originally been written *as* fiction and conceived as such by their author: "Sappho's" love letters, in his reading, were written in jest.[44] Conversely, later scholars have

---

[40] Herder, "Gedichte von Anna Louisa Karschin," 255.
[41] Gleim to Karsch, February 18, 1783, *"Bruder in Apoll,"* II, 168.
[42] Cf. chapter 3 for a discussion of this part of Karsch's work.
[43] Cf. Gleim's and Ebert's pleas with Karsch not to correct these poems in *"Bruder in Apoll,"* II, 160, 169.
[44] Cf. Gleim's letter to Karsch, April 13, 1783, in which he answers Karsch's fear of the shame to which she would be exposed if her personal love epistles to Gleim were ever published: "Her shame! What shame? That Sappho jested" ("Und ihre Schmach? Und

often related the expressiveness of Karsch's love poetry to the assumption that they were autobiographical rather than literary, that Karsch could not distinguish between life and literature, and that this inability constituted, in fact, the principal "inspiration" for her love poems, written to Gleim in response to an Anacreontic game that she mistook for an expression of real feeling.[45]

Klencke's biography of Karsch furnishes a compelling early example for the critical assumption that Karsch was incapable of differentiating between fact and fiction: she relates an episode in which Karsch, as a young girl, is used as a go-between in an adulterous love affair between a miller's wife, in whose house she was then employed as a servant, and an officer. The girl, understandably confused by the goings-on, makes up a love story by way of possible explanation, a traditional romance featuring a forced marriage to the elderly and ugly miller, a previous love affair between the miller's beautiful wife and the dashing young officer which has been ended by the marriage, and a projected daring rescue of the wife from the miller's clutches at the hands of her lover. Klencke's story is significant in that she attributes two aspects central to the later interpretation of Karsch as a love-inspired poet to the story: first, the premise that Karsch ended up *believing her own fairy tale*, that is, that she was unable to distinguish between reality and her own fantasy, and second, that this tragic love story became Karsch's first inspiration to write. What Karsch writes in response to this self-created tragic love story is situated somewhere between elegy and sentimental tragedy: "She was so taken in by this fancy that she really ended up believing in it. Her enthusiasm inflamed, she took the part of the supposedly unhappy couple; *for the first time, she took up the pen*, and brandishing it like the knight his lance, she assailed harsh Fate in moving lamentations."[46] Klencke's rather belittling depiction of Karsch's childish romanticism aside, she presents Love not only as a central aspect and theme of Karsch's work, but — more

---

welche? Daß Sapho gescherzt hat"; *"Bruder in Apoll,"* II, 181). In another letter, Gleim cites "Thyrsis's" worries that Sappho could be seriously in love and refutes this idea in an elaborate reported conversation between his Gleim persona and Thyrsis; cf. his letter to Karsch, May 9, 1762, in *"Bruder in Apoll,"* I, 104. Karsch, however, consistently denied that she had not been in earnest; cf., for example, her verse epistle to Gleim, March 1, 1783, *"Bruder in Apoll,"* II, 169–71, particularly 171.

[45] Cf. the sources and discussion in chapter 2.

[46] Klencke, "Lebenslauf," 31–32: "Sie ward von dieser Meinung so eingenommen, daß sie es zuletzt wirklich glaubte. Ihr Enthusiasmus entflammte, sie trat auf die Seite der beiden vermeintlichen Unglücklichen, und — ergriff *ihre erste Feder* mit welcher sie wie mit einer ritterlichen Lanze, in beweglichen Klagen auf das harte Schicksal loszog." (The emphases are original.)

significantly — as the original instigation to write. As with Klencke's story of Karsch's interest in nature cited earlier, there is no confirmation of this story in any of Karsch's autobiographical writings — neither the wife's infidelity nor the piece of writing supposedly inspired by her mistress's affair are so much as mentioned.[47]

Karsch's reception as a love poet has gained currency with her posthumous critics, partly because many of her love poems only became available with the publication of her letters. Clearly, these poems are also both more accessible and appealing to the modern reader than the many dedicatory and tributary poems she wrote in honor of her patrons and subscribers, which constitute much of the work she published during her lifetime. But Karsch's work features as many poetic treatments of unrequited or unhappy love, wife beatings, rape, and divorce as it does love poems,[48] and there is little indication that she saw the topos as linked with her own poetic production. From her point of view, Gleim's "Sapphic Odes" were love letters written in verse, not intended for, and passionately defended against, publication. In her poem "An den Domherrn von Rochow, als er gesagt hatte, die Liebe müsse sie gelehret haben, so schöne Verse zu machen" (To the Canon of Rochow, When He Said That Love Must Have Taught Her to Write Such Beautiful Verse), she answers the charge as follows:

> Connoisseur of Songs of Sappho!
> Underneath your white vest, I know
> Beats a heart bless'd at Love's shrine.
> Though you may know love's affliction
> I must tell you 'tis but fiction
> To call Love a Muse of mine.
>
> My young days were oppressed with cares,
> On summer mornings I sat there,
> Sighing my poor stammered song.
> Not for a young man was my melody,
> No! for God who the crowds of men does see
> As if they were an anthill's throng.

---

[47] Cf. Karsch's description of her servitude in the mill in *"Bruder in Apoll,"* I, 345–47.

[48] Examples are her poem "Sapho an Amor" (in *Auserlesene Gedichte,* 252–54; republished in *Gedichte und Lebenszeugnisse,* 88–89); her poetic rendition of a beating she received by her husband, cited in Hausmann, 334, and her rhymed epistle to Gleim (October or November 1781), in which she pleads for his understanding of her daughter's separation from her husband and also refers to her own marital experience in defense of her daughter's decision to sue for divorce (*"Bruder in Apoll,"* II, 163–64).

> Without emotions, as I've often said,
> Without affection, I was wed,
> Became a mother, as in times of war
> A young girl would not trust love's bliss,
> On whom a soldier forced a kiss,
> Whose army reigned as conqueror.[49]

The distinction Karsch draws here is a class-based one: she begins her answer to the Canon with an allusion to his *education* — he appears as a "connoisseur" (*Kenner*), and it remains unclear whether the poem refers to his knowledge of Karsch's own poetry or to that of the historical Sappho, her namesake. She proceeds to claim that although he, the bourgeois recipient, may well be acquainted with love, love played no part in either making her a wife or a mother, and links this experience directly with her class origins and poverty in the opening line of the second stanza ("My young days were oppressed with cares"). The misery of her early life is something she insisted on because, like her lack of education and her physical plainness, it emphasized the humbleness of her origins and therefore the genuineness of her poetic existence as Nature's Child. The fact that she likens her experience with what bourgeois poets and readers consider "love" to rape in wartime makes her refutation all the more adamant, and serves to draw a distinct line between bourgeois poetic experience and her own.

Yearsley reiterated Karsch's point approximately twenty years later in her poem "To Mr. V — — , On his pronouncing the Author to be in Love, when she wrote the preceding." Although her title and message read like Karsch's, Yearsley takes a more humorous stance in her response to bourgeois expectations:

---

[49] Anna Louisa Karsch, "An den Domherrn von Rochow": Kenner von dem saphischen Gesange! / Unter deinem weissen Ueberhange / Klopft ein Herze, voller Gluth in dir! / Von der Liebe ward es unterrichtet / Dieses Herze, aber ganz erdichtet / Nennst du sie die Lehrerin von mir! // Meine Jugend ward gedrückt von Sorgen, / Seufzend sang an manchem Sommermorgen / Meine Einfalt ihr gestammelt Lied; / Nicht dem Jüngling thöneten Gesänge, / Nein, dem Gott, der auf der Menschen Menge, / Wie auf Ameishaufen niedersieht! // Ohne Regung, die ich oft beschreibe, / Ohne Zärtlichkeit ward ich zum Weibe, / Ward zur Mutter! wie im wilden Krieg, / Unverliebt ein Mädchen werden müßte, / Die ein Krieger halb gezwungen küßte, / Der die Mauer einer Stadt erstieg.

The translation of the first stanza is mine; the remainder of the poem is cited after Susan Cocalis's translation, published as "My Young Days Were Oppressed with Cares," in Cocalis's *Defiant Muse*, 25. The original appeared in Karsch's *Auserlesene Gedichte*, 110–12 (the citation 110–11) and was republished in *Gedichte und Lebenszeugnisse*, 68–69; *Herzgedanken*, 223; and as "Bekenntnis" in excerpted form in *Das Lied der Karschin*, 81. For a brief discussion of the poem, cf. Mödersheim, "Fruchtbarste Bäume," 47–48.

> On the axis of Love, wheels the Universe round,
> In rotation continued, and thrifty;
> While some tender minds at fifteen feel the wound,
> And some hold it out till they're fifty.
>
> O ye Gods, then defend me from fifty, in love,
> When that language has left the bright eye,
> Which speaks to the soul, tho' our tongues never move,
> And shall conquer, when accent must die.[50]

Yearsley's initial exposé portrays love as inescapable; her poem goes on to depict the emotion as stronger and more pervasive than all other goals and emotions, including virtue, avarice, ambition, or fame. Having thus defined Love as all-consuming and all-powerful, she topples it from its pedestal:

> And now, my good friend, your conclusion to prove,
> (Perhaps, too, I hint it in spite)
> From Precept, write Sermons; from Nature write Love;
> And then you'll be sure to do right.
>
> Yet, say, if on Love I most aptly define,
> By that, can you fathom my soul?
> No passion shall ever my spirit confine,
> Independent, I smile at controul.
>
> While a bosom like yours, soft emotions perplex,
> When bright objects strike full on the eye;
> And may Love's transitions continue to vex,
> 'Till in age ev'ry rapture must die.[51]

Yearsley's speaker thus sets out specifically to disprove her reader's conclusion that her poetry is inevitably love inspired and unmasks his assumption rather contemptuously as a formulaic poetology in which "Nature" and "Love" inspiration are linked as a matter of course and in which deliberate, contemplative writing can only result in rather prosaic (sermonizing) work. Although her speaker agrees with this dictum, the speaker's stated attitude ("spite") and the doubts she raises immediately after conceding the point ("Yet . . .") allude to the fact that this acknowledgment is not entirely unrestrained. Not unlike Karsch, she draws a clear distinction between her work and her biography in her statement that even

---

[50] Yearsley, "To Mr. V — —," *Poems on Various Subjects*, 31–33, the citation 31.
[51] Yearsley, "To Mr. V — —," *Poems on Various Subjects*, 33.

if her entire work was classified as love poetry, and correctly so, Mr. V.'s assumption that the author herself was either in love or inspired by love would be invalid. Yearsley's rejection of love as the ultimate poetic inspiration of women is not as obviously class-based as Karsch's, and neither does she cite her own biographical circumstance as an explanation for her independence from the bonds of love. Nonetheless, her final stanza makes the same comparison between reader and author that Karsch had made: it is not the author but the reader who is under love's spell, and it is this circumstance that is cited as the obvious source of the reader's desire expressed toward the poet and her writing. Both Karsch and Yearsley recognize this for what it is, a projection of bourgeois desire onto their work and a limitation of the poet's own authority over her writing.

The extraordinary level of intertextual discourse and the awareness of bourgeois concepts displayed in the work of Yearsley and Karsch in particular can be linked, in part, to the length of their careers: unlike other woman peasant writers, both had writing careers that spanned decades; whereas most other peasant women published a single volume of verse, Yearsley and Karsch published repeatedly. After their initial highly successful volumes, Yearsley went on to publish two further volumes of poetry, a drama, and a novel,[52] all with the help of patrons; Karsch, who tried unsuccessfully to persuade her patron Gleim to edit a second volume of her poems, published several smaller independent volumes.[53] Their awareness of bourgeois aesthetics and poetology and the resulting demands made on their own work must have increased substantially with extended exposure. Their writing is not dissimilar to that of other peasant poets in the sense that they both clearly perceived bourgeois Nature aesthetics as the basis not only for their publication but also for their writing, and repeatedly stated their allegiance to this model. But theirs is the only work that clearly, if only intermittently, shows up the inconsistencies and paradoxes inherent in the bourgeois Nature aesthetic, as it was applied to these writers. Thus, the work of both Karsch and Yearsley with regard to the Nature aesthetic is much more multifaceted and differentiated than later criticism of their work or accounts of their lives. In particular, Klencke's biography of Karsch indicates to what extent Karsch's occasional digressions from the Nature aesthetic were erased and how she was fashioned, posthumously, into the

---

[52] Cf. Waldron's list of Yearsley's publications in *Lactilla*, ix-xiii.

[53] *Poetische Einfälle* appeared simultaneously with Gleim's edition of her poems, *Auserlesene Gedichte*, in 1764; subsequent publications independent of his patronage included *Neue Gedichte* (1772) and a reprint of that edition in 1774 (cf. the *Zeittafel* appended to Karsch's "*Bruder in Apoll,*" II, 580–87).

quintessential nature-inspired poet who could properly exemplify bourgeois theory. A poetic existence under patronage, as both Karsch and Yearsley knew, entailed the artificial production of a persuasive image as a Nature Poet, which occasionally meant feigning ignorance, concealing formal training, learning, or reading that bourgeois critics might conceive of as detrimental to the poet's natural and spontaneous inspiration.

The three most central dichotomies discussed in the work of Karsch and Yearsley describe the polar opposites of author/reader, production/reception, and life/literature. Karsch's poem addressed to the Canon of Rochow and Yearsley's poem addressed to Mr. V. both defend their work against the reader's assumptions, but in so doing, imply the exact opposite, a poetological situation particular to poetic work produced under patronage: that state in which the determining spirit behind the poetic work is not the author's but the reader's. Their adherence to the bourgeois Nature aesthetic restates the same dilemma, for the aesthetics that exert their influence on the work are aesthetics of *reception* mapped onto the process of *production*. Because peasant poetry was produced not only in a social context (that of patronage) but also within a clearly defined aesthetic and poetological context, it can claim a somewhat exceptional status in literary history: a body of literature whose production processes were, to a considerable degree, preempted by its own reception.

One recurring theme in the work of Karsch and Yearsley that could well be seen as undermining the bourgeois reception of their work is their insistence on the distinction between life and work, expressed poetically through the refusal to admit Love, experienced in real life, as poetic inspiration for love poems. It is an aspect that constitutes perhaps the most crucial breach with the bourgeois reception of peasant poets, for this reception, as has been discussed earlier,[54] was predicated on the *identity* of life and work, on the work as an expression of the life. As countless reviews state, the poet's work is only interesting because of the peasant's life. Both the insistence on the distinction between life and Art and the insistence on poetological and thematic independence — the refusal to have one's work preempted by one's biography — clearly constitute central aspects of a bourgeois conceptualization of Art. If one reads this as an indirect attempt on the part of Karsch and Yearsley, the two most published and most prolific of all women peasant poets of the century, to participate in the bourgeois project of literary Art, it is noteworthy that these attempts were subsequently expunged, most obviously in Karsch's case, in the streamlining interpretation of the poet as incapa-

---

[54] Cf. chapter 3.

ble of distinguishing between life and Art and *therefore* adequately viewed as a Nature Poet whose inspiration is limited to the biographical rather than the literary. Peasant poets who adopted this line of reasoning, who adhered to the bourgeois Nature aesthetic, as most did, ended up caught between the direct dependence on their bourgeois patrons and an indirect dependence on bourgeois poetology: as the case of Ann Yearsley demonstrates, aesthetic independence (both from the direct indebtedness to the patron and the more general indebtedness to literary traditions) could only be declared at the cost of a new allegiance to an aesthetic model developed by bourgeois theorists and applied to lower-class authors, applied with particular emphasis to that lower-class author, the woman peasant, who was seen as best exemplifying the "Rural Muse." Thus, Nature Inspiration, in its tension between author and reader, production and reception, life and literature, constituted an acute paradox for lower-class authors, simultaneously avowing the author's aesthetic independence and restating her social subordination.

# 6: Of Patrons and Critics: Reading the Bourgeois Reader

## Reading the Reader: Of Critics and Posterity

VIRTUALLY EVERY WOMAN peasant poet's work contains several pieces in which the poet annotates, preempts, ventriloquizes, satirizes, or otherwise comments on her own projected reception in bourgeois and aristocratic circles. The critic, in particular, is accorded a major role in these poems. In nearly all works in which the professional critic appears, he assumes a spiteful and destructive personality: even in cases where reader response is depicted as positive, as it is in poetry by both Anna Louisa Karsch and Christian Milne, the critical response to their work is portrayed as inevitably devastating.[1] Hardly has the "rustic damsel issue[d] forth her lays," in the hopes of gaining admission to the lower slopes of Parnassus, when the critic appears to dash her aspirations: "'Vain are her hopes,' the snarling critic cries; / 'Rude and imperfect is her rural song.'"[2] Janet Little, in this and other poems,[3] endows her critic with two qualities designed to secure the reader's sympathies for the author rather than the critic: one is the presentation of the critic's response not as literary criticism but as class prejudice, for his objections are largely based on the author's class background, on the fact that she is a "rural" writer who cannot lay claim to the polish and sophistication of the bourgeois author. Little's poem hints at her

---

[1] Anna Louisa Karsch, "Der Criticus," cited in Becker-Cantarino's foreword to the reedition of Karsch's *Gedichte*, 1, and Christian Milne, "On Seeing the List of Subscribers to This Little Work," *Simple Poems*, 154–55. The projected reader response, however, is frequently seen as considerably more charitable than that of the critics. Karsch, for example, gratefully mentioned her popularity with the general readership in several poems: for example, her poem "An Herrn Uz" (To Mr. Uz), *Auserlesene Gedichte, 186–87 (reprinted in Gedichte und Lebenszeugnisse,* 67–68) and "An die Freyfrau von Troschke und Rosenwehrt" (To the Baroness von Troschke und Rosenwehrt), *Auserlesene Gedichte,* 103–5, republished in *O, mir entwischt nicht,* 58–59.

[2] Janet Little, "To the Public," *The Poetical Works,* 29–30, the citation 29; brief interpretation in Bold, 23.

[3] Little's implacable critic also appears in her "An Epistle to a Lady," *Poetical Works,* 125–28, the citation 125, and in "A Poem on Contentment," *Poetical Works,* 173–79, the citation 176.

awareness of the paradoxical relationship between the emerging consciousness of art as *bourgeois* Art, which is already prefigured in the critic's response, and the bourgeois Nature aesthetic which, conversely, demands rusticity and simplicity from the rural author's work. The second aspect that Little employs in disqualifying her critic's response is the fact that his judgment is preemptive rather than reactive. Rather than constituting an honest critique of published writing, it is intentionally aimed at preventing further publications, at silencing the author.

It is perhaps this anticipation of the reception of their poems that explains the predominance of poems in which the author's position is portrayed as an embattled one: "Spite and Ignorance, with sneering looks, / . . . Malicious Envy . . . And Folly" close ranks to undermine the author's resolve to continue writing;[4] "The ignorant" and "The proud" scorn her work simply because "The Author's but a Shipwright's Wife, / And was a serving Maid."[5] Occasionally, the author's humble origins and lack of formal education are seen as potential protection from, rather than provocation of, the critics' rage: Ann Candler views herself as "From snarling critics and their censure free, / They'll not bestow a single thought on me; / No strokes of satire will they lavish here, / But let me off with a contemptuous sneer."[6] Likewise, Mary Masters, in her spirited "Defence of Myrtillo," deems her savage attack on the "snarling crew" comparatively safe, for her "safety is in being mean, / A foolish thing that's plac'd below their spleen."[7] The peasant poet, in her own projected reception, will either be savaged by criticism or contemptuously ignored as beneath criticism; there is not a single work envisioning the possibility of a fair or serious reading or a positive response on the part of professional critics. The spite displayed by the critic's persona in poetry is closely related to another recurring theme: that of the author being "punished" for her writing. Writing for the lower-class author is presented as a "crime" for which she justly "suffers" the critics' rage;[8] the fact that the "crazy-pated dairy-maid"[9] insists on scribbling on is considered offensive enough to merit the contemptuous response. Correspondingly, there are also several works by such diverse

---

[4] Christian Milne, "Introductory Verses," *Simple Poems,* 33–35, the quotations 35.

[5] Christian Milne, "To a Gentleman, Desirous of Seeing My Manuscripts," *Simple Poems,* 55–56.

[6] Candler, "To the Rev. Dr. J — — n. On his being appointed one of his Majesty's Chaplains," *Poetical Attempts,* 58–60, the quotation 58–59.

[7] Masters, "Defence of Myrtillo," *Poems on Several Occasions,* 54–56, the quotation 55. The poem was reprinted in Colman/Thornton, II, 147–48.

[8] Leapor, "The Head-Ach. To Aurelia," *Poems Upon Several Occasions,* 101–3, the citation 102.

[9] Janet Little, "An Epistle to a Lady," *Poetical Works* 125–28, the quotation 128.

authors as Molly Leapor, Janet Little, Mary Masters, and Anna Louisa Karsch in which the poet either considers or vows to leave off writing to protect herself from further abuse.[10]

It is interesting to note that such a destructive and preemptive response is not always limited to the bourgeois reader but at times also projected onto "arrived" authors of the peasant class. Janet Little's satire on her idol, Robert Burns, is not only a cheerful send-up of his infamous womanizing, utilizing the allegory of Burns baking cakes for all the lasses in the county, but it also projects the plowman poet's less than charitable attitude toward the female competition:

> As Rab, who ever frugal was,
> Some oat-meal cakes was baking,
> In came a crazy scribbling lass,
> Which set his heart a-quaking.
>
> 'I fear,' says he, 'she'll verses write,
> An' to her neebors show it:
> But troth I need na care a doit,
> Though a' the country knew it.[11]

Other poets, as well, documented the near-universal distaste with which their writing was received: Molly Leapor wrote a series of poems in which she satirizes the disapproval of her poetic occupation by her critics and neighbors[12] or, alternately, dissolves in tears of atonement for her

---

[10] Most prominently, Janet Little in "To a Lady Who Sent the Author Some Papers with a Reading of Sillar's Poems," *Poetical Works*, 206–7 (brief interpretation in Hilton Brown, 19, and Ferguson, *Eighteenth-Century Women Poets*, 107); cf. also Leapor's short-lived vow to "quit the darling crime" in "Crumble-Hall," Colman/Thornton, II, 126–32, the citation 126, and Mary Masters, "To Mrs. Masters, occasion'd by her Resolution to write no more. By Mr. J. W."; "The Answer to the Foregoing Verses," and "The Resolution Broke," in *Poems on Several Occasions*, 97–99 ("To Mrs. Masters"), 99–100 ("The Answer"), and 94–96 ("The Resolution"). Karsch voiced her trepidation of the critical response in advance of every single planned publication; cf. her remarks in *"Bruder in Apoll,"* I, 250–51, 310, and II, 5, 379, and the letters cited in Beuys, 106–7, 131.

[11] Little, "On Seeing Mr. —— Baking Cakes," *Poetical Works*, 171–72, the quotation 171; brief interpretation in Ferguson, *Eighteenth-Century Women Poets*, 103–4. On Little's relationship with Robert Burns, cf. Hilton Brown.

[12] Molly Leapor, "An Epistle to Artemisia, On Fame," in Fairer/Gerrard, 292–97, excerpted in Lonsdale, *Eighteenth-Century Women Poets*, 204–6 (brief interpretation in Blunden, 68–69, and Rizzo, "Molly Leapor," 320–21); "The Epistle of Deborah Dough," in Lonsdale, *Eighteenth-Century Women Poets*, 209–10 (interpreted in Blunden, 66–67).

poetic "Mischief."[13] At times, even the instrument of writing or the medium of inspiration turn on the poet: Leapor's narrator in "The Inspired Quill" is harshly upbraided for her "unprofitable rhyme" by the quill she employs to write it.[14] Disdainful muses appear in the poetry of Molly Leapor, Mary Masters,[15] and Janet Little, motivated, in Little's case, by the same class-based prejudice that mars the critical response: "the Muses are fled far away, / They deem it disgrace with a milkmaid to stay."[16] What is hinted at here is a process of systematic discouragement through consistently devastating critique, which finally succeeds in achieving its stated objective, the undermining of the author's determination to write at all.

In poems concentrating on discouragement by critics rather than friends, neighbors, or one's own pen or muse, the author's reaction to the projected critic's response ranges from satirical amusement to abject terror. Janet Little, in "To My Aunty," imagines her work appearing in print, only to provide a field day for the sneering critics. In Little's analysis, the criticism of Tom Touchy, Will Hasty, Jack Tim'rous, and James Easy, whether devastating or indulgent, has little to do with the work and much with the background and assumed personality of both author and critic. Notably, the critique shows no respect for the integrity of the work as an independent intellectual and creative effort that bourgeois authors claim as a matter of course: one of Little's critics oversteps his authority by rewriting some poems and censoring others.[17] Molly Leapor, in "Upon Her Play Being returned to her, Stain'd with Claret," likewise upbraids her critics for their contempt for and carelessness with her work; her solution is defiant yet demoralizing: to refuse to resubmit the play and to bury it in a drawer.[18] Such carelessness and disregard is surely

---

[13] Leapor, "To Grammaticus," *Poems Upon Several Occasions* 122–25, the quotation 122 (brief discussion in Blunden, 68); cf. also her poem "The Penitent," in which she regrets not having accepted ten pounds for a volume of her poems, aspiring, with unparalleled arrogance, to sell them at a higher price (*Poems Upon Several Occasions,* 118–20). Leapor's volume, published posthumously, cleared seventy-five pounds, enabling her father to become a freeholder (cf. Lilley, 177).

[14] Leapor, "The Inspired Quill," Colman/Thornton II, 67–71; the quotation 71.

[15] Leapor, "The Proposal," *Poems Upon Several Occasions,* 173–75; Masters, "The Female Triumph," *Poems on Several Occasions,* 8–10, the citation 10.

[16] Little, "'To a Lady Who Sent the Author Some Papers with a Reading of Sillar's Poems," *Poetical Works,* 206–7, the quotation 206.

[17] Little, "To My Aunty," *Poetical Works,* 164–66. Cf. also Landry's brief interpretation of the poem in *Muses,* 237.

[18] Leapor, "Upon Her Play Being returned to her," Colman/Thornton II, 133–34; reprint in Lonsdale, *Eighteenth-Century Women Poets,* 211–12. The poem is cited but not discussed in Blunden, 70.

incompatible with the respect accorded the bourgeois author, and this indication of class bias in criticism is a recurring theme in reception poems that expressly contrast, as does Janet Little in "Given to a Lady Who Asked Me to Write a Poem,"[19] bourgeois and lower-class poetic productivity. Little's humorous exposé portrays the harsh road to literary success: on their steep and laborious ascent to Mount Parnassus, bones are broken and limbs are lost; the male bourgeois tradition is summarized in a brief genealogy including Pope, Swift, Thomson, Addison, and Young. These are "royal Anna's golden days," a blissful time in which literary activity was defined by hard work rather than spontaneous inspiration and reserved for a few male bourgeois greats. In a sarcastic quotation of the ubiquitous bourgeois complaints about the flood of lower-class writers, this literary elysium is contrasted with the more permissive modern literary climate in which "ilka dunce maun hae a pen, / To write in hamely, uncouth rhymes."[20] Particularly offensive to the critic is the emergence of women from the lower classes as authors: "But what is more surprising still, / A milkmaid must tak up her quill; / An' she will write, shame fa' the rabble! / That think to please wi' ilka bawble."[21] And although such attempts could be seen within a literary tradition, that tradition established by the growing fame of Robert Burns, whose authorship is, in Little's poem, acknowledged even by bourgeois critics, the lower-class woman is clearly deemed ineligible for such recognition:

> But then a rustic country quean
> To write — was e'er the like o't seen?
> A milk maid poem-books to print;
> Mair fit she wad her dairy tent;
> Or labour at her spinning wheel,
> An' do her wark baith swift an' weel.
> Frae that she may some profit share,
> But winna frae her rhyming ware.
> Does she, poor silly thing, pretend
> The manners of our age to mend?
> Mad as we are, we're wise enough
> Still to despise sic paultry stuff.[22]

---

[19] Little, "Given to a Lady," *Poetical Works,* 112–16, reprinted in Lonsdale, *Eighteenth-Century Women Poets,* 454–55. Interpretations are offered in Landry, *Muses,* 223–26, and briefly, in Schaff, 141–42.

[20] Little, "Given to a Lady," *Poetical Works,* 113 and 114, respectively.

[21] Little, "Given to a Lady," *Poetical Works,* 114.

[22] Little, "Given to a Lady," *Poetical Works,* 115.

In this stanza, the poem changes narrative perspective: the poetic speaker ("I") of previous stanzas who rather proudly describes Burns's success as such that even the critics cannot blame him for writing is clearly not identical with the "we" of this last stanza, a group that can easily be identified as the snarling tribe of critics that peoples other poems as well. Their verdict paraphrases not a critique of the work but a conglomerate of bourgeois class and gender prejudices directed at its author. Particularly prominent among them are the well-meaning recommendation that the poet had best return to her "real" (physical) work,[23] the bourgeois concern that the poet would be unable to make a living from her writing, and the solicitousness and condescension ("poor thing") that is an unmistakable aspect of class superiority. That it is particularly the female peasant poet who is disqualified from writing, whereas exceptions are made for male greats like Burns, is clearly expressed in the critics' shocked exclamation when faced with a "country quean's" (girl's) poetic inclinations: "was e'er the like o't seen?" In 1792, when Little's collection appeared, the like of it had been seen numerous times, with at least eighteen rural and/or laboring women authors in England and Scotland publishing poetry either in magazines or as independent volumes[24] and some women, such as Mary Collier, Molly Leapor, Ann Yearsley, and Jane West, achieving a moderate amount of fame. But this contextualization of Little's own writing is withheld from the author who is instead relegated to a barrage of venomous criticism designed to discourage further authorship:

> All this and more, a critic said;
> I heard and slunk behind the shade:
> So much I dread their cruel spite,
> My hand still trembles when I write.[25]

This final authorial response to critical attack, ironically delivered in standard English whereas the critics speak Scots throughout,[26] has led at least one reader to correlate the author's voice with English and that of

---

[23] This conclusion is reached in numerous poems ventriloquizing the critic or reader, paradigmatically in Leapor's poem "The Ten-Penny Nail," *Poems Upon Several Occasions*, 125–31, in which Mira is finally advised to leave off writing and "get thee gone to spinning, / Or wisely dearn your Father's Linen" (131). Cf. also Yearsley's sarcastic aside that she could always return to the milking pail if the muse failed her; cited in Ferguson, *Eighteenth-Century Women Poets*, 62.

[24] For a list of publishing lower-class and rural women in England, cf. the introduction.

[25] Little, "Given to a Lady," *Poetical Works*, 116.

[26] This has been pointed out by both Landry (*Muses*, 226) and Schaff (142).

the critics with the socially "inferior" Scots.[27] But the "I" that appears earlier in the poem and shows such admiration for the work of Burns is also a speaker of Scots. If we assume this "I" to be the authorial voice, no clear linguistic distinction between author and critic can be established. On the contrary, the "I" and the "we," presumably the author's and the critics' voices, although diametrically opposed in their stance, are, with the exception of the final four lines, virtually indistinguishable in terms of language use. Scots as the language of both author and critic would make sense if we assume that Little, a Scottish author, levied her attack specifically against Scottish critics who were famed for their severity and deemed considerably harsher in their judgment than critics on the English literary scene. Little's usage of a language that was (and still is) deemed inferior to English and that could therefore be disqualified as inappropriate for the lofty purposes of literary Art might also be read as an expression of the author's awareness of the perceived distance between her writing and that of the long list of male bourgeois greats listed, in standard English, at the outset of the poem. Coming from her critics, Scots as an "inferior" language, often presumed to be the speech of the ignorant,[28] could well serve to counter the critics' claim to intellectual and cultural superiority. Social concerns are clearly central to the poem and are expressed as follows: in the vacillating roles played by the lower-class speaker commenting on bourgeois criticism and bourgeois literary history, by the bourgeois critics in turn belittling the lower-class author, and in the whole being "given" by the lower class-author "to a Lady Who Asked Me to Write a Poem," in fulfillment of a charge by someone either from the aristocracy or the gentry. Little's poem thus traces the genealogy of her work from its inception to its reception: at its outset, as the title establishes, stands the fact of patronage, being asked to write by a social superior; at its end the ultimate condemnation of the

---

[27] Cf. Schaff's interpretation: "ihre eigenen Worte sind in Englisch geschrieben, die des Kritikers im sozial nieder bewerteten Scots" (142).

[28] The status of Scots as a language is still widely debated in Scotland, particularly since the establishment of the new Scottish Parliament in 1999. Scots is commonly considered a collection of dialects and a literary language; it has no presence in legal or official discourse. Even within today's Scottish Parliament, there is dispute regarding the status of Scots as a "language," even an official national language. Much of this attitude is undoubtedly due to the historical perception of Scots as supposedly socially and culturally inferior to English. In the wake of the establishment of the new Scottish Parliament, this issue has become even more controversial: critics of the anti-Scots argument point out that the disqualification of Scots as an inferior dialect (and that of Gaelic for much the same reason) would lead, paradoxically, to the preservation of English linguistic dominance at the outset of Scottish autonomy from Westminster politics. My thanks to Mark Taplin for his insights on this issue.

work and the directive to stop writing, issued, as well, by her social superiors. Little's poem, vacillating, as it does, between obedience to the patron who commissioned this poem and her fearful response to the critics' mandate to stop writing, expressed in the trembling of her hand, is perhaps one of the most expressive poems on the extent to which the predetermined reception of lower-class writing resulted in impediments to its production — to what extent a social exclusion might turn into a psychological preclusion.

Ventriloquies of the bourgeois reader of the kind that Little employs in her final stanza are quite popular in reception poems by peasant women. Elizabeth Hands and Christian Milne have repeatedly used this method. Milne, in "On a Lady, Who Spoke with Some Ill-Nature of the Advertisement of My Little Work in the 'Aberdeen Journal,'" vociferously paraphrases the lady's objections to her writing: "pert Miss Prue" states her opinion that the verse of someone "Ne'er bred at school" must necessarily be substandard.[29] Although class clearly plays a part in her condemnation, gender constitutes another central trait that should prevent further literary activity: "A wife so mean / Should nurse, and clean, / And mend her husband's jacket; / Not spend her time / In writing rhyme, / And raising such a racket!"[30] As with Little's poem, the bourgeois prohibition of lower-class literary activity is aimed, first and foremost, at the woman writer of that class.

Perhaps the most famous of such ventriloquies are contained in two poems by Elizabeth Hands: "Poem, On the Supposition of an Advertisement appearing in a Morning Paper, of the Publication of a Volume of Poems, by a Servant Maid" and her follow-up "Poem, On the Supposition of the Book having been published and read."[31] In both poems, Hands creates an elaborate scenario: a circle of ladies at tea (in the first poem) and a gender-mixed company after dinner (in the second) discuss what is clearly recognizable as Hands's own volume, ironically prefaced by these two poems. In the first poem, the ladies' idle gossip centers on the announcement of the volume, leading inevitably into a discussion of the lower-class author's license to write at all:

---

[29] Milne, "On a Lady," *Simple Poems*, 152–53, the quotation 152.

[30] Milne, "On a Lady," *Simple Poems*, 153.

[31] Hands, *The Death of Amnon*, 47–50 and 50–55, respectively, republished in Lonsdale, *Eighteenth-Century Women Poets*, 425–26 and 427–29, respectively. The second poem has been briefly analyzed in Landry, *Muses*, 188–89; both poems in Schaff, 139–41.

> A servant write verses! says Madam Du Bloom;
> Pray what is the subject? — a Mop, or a Broom?
> He, he, he, — says Miss Flounce; I suppose we shall see
> An Ode on a Dishclout — what else can it be?
> Says Miss Coquetilla, why ladies so tart?
> Perhaps Tom the Footman has fired her heart;
> And she'll tell us how charming he looks in new clothes,
> And how nimble his hand moves in brushing the shoes;
> Or how the last time that he went to May-Fair,
> He bought her some sweethearts of ginger-bread ware.
> For my part I think, says old lady Marr-joy,
> A servant might find herself other employ:
> Was she mine I'd employ her as long as 'twas light,
> And send her to bed without candle at night.
> Why so? says Miss Rhymer, displeas'd, I protest
> 'Tis pity a genius should be so deprest!
> What ideas can such low-bred creatures conceive,
> Says Mrs. Noworthy, and laught in her sleeve.
> Says old Miss Prudella, if servants can tell
> How to write to their mothers, to say they are well,
> And read of a Sunday the Duty of Man;
> Which is more I believe than one half of them can;
> I think 'tis much *properer* they should rest there,
> Than be reaching at things so much out of their sphere.[32]

Because the conversation takes place before the volume in question has even appeared, the poem's point of attack is a circumstance criticized by other lower-class women as well: that the bourgeois reception of the lower-class author's work is predetermined by her class background. The a priori contempt accorded the poetic activity of the lower-class author is partly a consequence of the perceived difference between the lofty themes accorded poetic treatment in bourgeois literature and the everyday trivialities to which the servant's perception is supposedly limited. Such trivialities, considered unpoetic by definition, disqualify the collection from serious consideration:

> O law! says young Seagram, I've seen the book, now
> I remember, there's something about a mad cow.

---

[32] Hands, "A Poem, On the Supposition," *The Death of Amnon*, 47–50; the quotation 47–48. (The emphasis is original.)

A mad cow! — ha, ha, ha, ha, return'd half the room;
What can y' expect better, says Madam Du Bloom?[33]

"Better" in this case means more appropriate to the poetic medium, the choice of a theme deemed worthy of poetic treatment on the one hand and, on the other, its treatment in a lofty style appropriate to the theme. As Madam Du Bloom's comment makes clear, lower-class writers are *principally* seen as incapable of treating such themes and thus defining themselves as authors; if they write at all, as Schaff has pointed out, then their writing must be functional and "useful," such as recipes or letters to Mother.[34] In cases in which the author usurps the right to do "better," to treat a theme generally deemed more fitting, the reader response is to map the author's background onto the poetic treatment of the theme. Thus love, perceived as one of the most central themes of the woman poet, is endowed with a class background; what is, in the bourgeois context, the ultimate theme of poetry is here read as a plebeian parody involving a romance between a footman and a serving maid. As the second poem in this sequence makes clear, poetic themes that turn out to be different from the projected ones — odes to the mop, the mad cow and the nimble footman — are censored just as severely for their inappropriateness in view of the author's class background or gender. When asked about the themes treated in the collection, Mrs. Routella informs the assembly that one of the poems — the poem alluded to here is "The Death of Amnon," the title piece and longest work in Hands's collection — has rape as its subject. Her answer provokes a sneer of the kind that, in peasant women's poetry, is the critic's most distinguishing characteristic: "A Rape! interrupted the Captain Bonair, / A delicate theme for a female I swear."[35] The limitation of themes imposed on the author is clearly related to her class background and her gender; the bourgeois bias is made obvious by the fact that the peasant author is exposed to bourgeois ridicule if she adheres to these restrictions and bourgeois censure if she does not.

In the bourgeois critique as ventriloquized by Hands and Milne, the lower-class author's lack of education, in aesthetics identified as a guarantee for her "naturalness" and spontaneity, becomes the predominant aspect

---

[33] Hands, "A Poem, On the Supposition," *The Death of Amnon*, 50–55, the quotation 54. The poem alluded to in this passage is Hands's own "Written, originally extempore, on seeing a Mad Heifer run through the Village where the Author lives," included in the same collection (115–16). The poem is discussed in chapter 4.

[34] The interpretation is Schaff's, 140, referring to the following passage in Hands's poem: "Had she wrote a receipt, to've instructed you how / To warm a cold breast of veal, like a ragou, / Or to make cowslip wine that would pass for Champaign; / It might have been useful, again and again" (*The Death of Amnon*, 49).

[35] Hands, "A Poem, On the Supposition," *The Death of Amnon*, 50–55, the quotation 51.

that disqualifies her as a writer. As Schaff has pointed out, Hands turns the tables on her audience by identifying that same aspect, lack of education, as a crucial flaw of her readership: in this group that nonetheless identifies itself as the cultural elite, only the rector recognizes the biblical origin of the story of Amnon.[36] Class superiority thus does not necessarily entail either cultural or literary preeminence over the lower-class writer, a central point in Hands's critique since it is precisely this superiority on which the bourgeois claim to cultural dominance rests. Hands's uneducated bourgeois readers nonetheless deem themselves qualified to judge a collection filled with literary and mythological allusions they are unable to understand as inadequate to the refined tastes of an erudite readership: "A stile elevated you cannot expect: / To some of her equals they may be a treasure, / And country lasses may read them with pleasure."[37] If all attempts fail to force the author to leave off writing and return to her barn, her dairy, or her spinning wheel, the next best course is obviously to limit her readership to members of her own class. Like her readers' attempts to preempt the author's creativity and intellect in the projected limitation of themes, the limitation of her audience documents the crucial difference, in the readers' perception, between Hands's work and bourgeois literary Art, whose claims to transcendence are based on artistic and intellectual freedom as well as the supposition of virtually unlimited influence.

That the poet's production cannot remain unaffected by her reception is also occasionally a theme in reception poems. In Molly Leapor's "The Proposal," Mira, Leapor's poetic persona, reports to her patron on an exchange with her Muse during which her muse presents her with an ultimatum.[38] Mira's muse objects to her plans for publication, for the reception of her poems is a foregone conclusion:

> 'So cries the peevish Maid, (and squinting)
> 'Methinks I heard you talk of Printing:
> 'Have I bestow'd a world of Pains,
> 'To spirit up your blockish Brains,
> 'To get from thence an idle Rhyme,
> 'That made me blush to call it mine?
> 'And shall I see the crippl'd Crew
> 'Discarded from their Seat and you,
> 'Turn'd out to skip from hand to hand

---

[36] Hands, "A Poem, On the Supposition," *The Death of Amnon*, 50–55, the reference 52; the interpretation by Schaff, 140.

[37] Hands, "A Poem, On the Supposition," *The Death of Amnon*, 50–55, the quotation 54–55.

[38] Leapor, "The Proposal," *Poems Upon Several Occasions*, 173–75.

'In dirty Gazettes round the Land,
'To grace the Knee of ev'ry Sot,
'And catch the Droppings of his Pot,
'While in a Rage the drowsy Swains
'Perhaps may curse you for your Pains,
'Protesting with a Critick's Spite,
'That none since *Dursey* knew to write?'[39]

What Mira's muse suggests here is a distinction that is not expressed in other reception poems, but one that may nonetheless have played a part in the universally harsh depiction of the critics' response: the distinction between unpublished Art and published drivel. Once published, she suggests, Mira's poems will be at the mercies of spiteful critics or used by the next drunkard as an undersurface for his beer mug, or worse, his chamber pot. Publication, in the muse's interpretation, is paramount to the prostitution of the work: like a whore, the work will be relegated to filthy surroundings ("dirty Gazettes") and be accessible to everyone ("skip from hand to hand"). Such a venture, the muse concludes, is beneath her dignity, but if Mira insists on publishing, she can recommend another muse who would be willing to prostitute herself in the manner described:

'But, *Mira*, if you want a Muse,
'To grace the Page of weekly News,
'The Task is much too low for me,
'Yet I've a Maid of less Degree,
'(With Spirit suiting to her State)
'Will serve you at an easy Rate:
'Whose Voice, tho' hoarse, is loud and strong,
'An Artist at a ranting Song,
'Can chaunt Lampoons without much straining,
'Or Epigrams with double Meaning,
'To join the Tavern-Harp or Viol:
'Now if you'll take her upon trial,
'To her Deservings suit your Pay,
'And then you take the safest way:
'Perhaps you'll prosper in the End,
'I'll say no more: But ask your Friend,
'Here ends the Muse — Dear Madam, say,
'Shall I reject her or obey?'[40]

---

[39] Leapor, "The Proposal," *Poems Upon Several Occasions* 173–74 (emphasis original).
[40] Leapor, "The Proposal," *Poems Upon Several Occasions,* 174–75 (emphasis original.)

Like the author herself, the muse who would agree to prostitute herself in publication is also a servant, a "maid," someone of low degree, and, as in so many other reception poems, her themes and genres are predetermined: her coarse ranting and chanting to the tune of the tavern harp distances her as far as is imaginable from the lofty aspirations of bourgeois poetry. The serious muse who inspires such poetry is once again contrasted with her sluttish pendant who is portrayed as willing to serve anyone "at an easy Rate" and whose poetic output, risqué epigrams and double entendres, are all entirely in character. Mira's timid question with which the poem closes is equally far removed from Hands's satire and Little's defiance: it asks what kinds of alternatives to obscurity on the one hand, or publication followed by scorn on the other, can be imagined for the lower-class author. Simultaneously, Leapor restates what other poets have noted: that the poet's themes and genres, the entire process of writing, can be vitally influenced by her (predetermined) reception. Publication, in Leapor's poem, is viewed as an act of giving in to this influence, a conclusion that parallels the speaker's determination in "Upon Her Play Being returned to her, Stain'd with Claret" to refuse to resubmit her play for production and instead have it disappear in the drawer.

Of all sinister outcomes projected in the reception poetry of women peasant poets, Leapor's conclusion is possibly the most disheartening, for it offers no scenario that would enable the lower-class author to publish in the bourgeois-dominated literary market and retain any semblance of creative or intellectual integrity. The alternatives she offers — the continued obscurity or prostitution and denigration of the work — are no alternatives at all for the serious writer; although publication under these circumstances may, at best, allow the author to "prosper" financially, the posthumous fame that is seen as the bourgeois poet's lasting achievement will be withheld from the peasant poet, regardless of her decision or refusal to publish. This subject, the author's posthumous reception, has been explicitly treated in poems by Anna Louisa Karsch, who repeatedly speculated that her work would be forgotten soon after her death.[41] Karsch's prediction is particularly revealing in that she links the disregard of future readers for her work to her own lack of erudition, that trait viewed by critics as most characteristic of the female and the lower-class writer. Her poem "An den berühmten Chodowiecky" (Addressed to the

---

[41] For example, in "Ueber den Unbestand des Ruhms" (On the Fickleness of Fame), *Gedichte*, 80–81, and "Ob Sappho für den Ruhm schreibt?" (In Answer to the Question Whether Sappho Writes for Fame), in *O, mir entwischt nicht*, 34–35, and *Gedichte und Lebenszeugnisse*, 74–75.

Famous Painter Chodowiecky) could be read as an elaborate expression of her admiration for his work, but the reasons she assigns for the projected canonization of his work and the disregard for hers have more to do with the artist than the art:

> He is so great — I am so small,
> I sing a song that amounts to nothing at all,
> He sings his song to endure, on and on,
> To prove to the world Apollo called him son;
> My little fame won't see posterity,
> When I have gone off to eternity
> It will soon wither and fall — but his will stand.
> For I am just a woman, he's a man,
> My verse knows only how to walk the German way,
> But his can dance to the tune of a Roman lay.[42]

Class and gender thus both play their part in denying the peasant poet's work lasting fame: the work that endures is, by definition, that of the male and erudite (classically educated) author. Few authors have diagnosed the essential paradox facing the lower-class writer and the mechanics of canonization with such clarity: the Nature and genius aesthetics that define poetic genius as antithetical to bourgeois erudition constitute the peasant woman's only chance to publish and thus furnish her entire raison d'être within her contemporary literary scene. Yet Karsch postulates that this aesthetic itself will prove a transient fad, speculating rather astutely that works capable of displaying the trappings of a bourgeois classical education are ultimately more likely to be interpreted, by an educated bourgeois readership, as works of lasting value.

Peasant poets' reception poems do more than just comment on these poets' fears of criticism; they express their awareness of the *difference*, in the bourgeois perception, between peasant poetry and bourgeois Art, between, as Karsch once put it, the "accomplished poet" and the "verse manufacturer."[43] In the critical response, this difference manifests itself

---

[42] Karsch, "An den berühmten Chodowiecky": Er ist so groß — ich bin so klein, / Ich sing' ein Lied, das nichts beweiset, / Er singt, um ewig hier zu seyn, / Und jede Welt zu überführen, / Daß Ihn Apollo Sohn genannt; / Mein Bischen Ruhm wird sich verlieren, / Wenn ich ins Geistesvaterland / Hinweggeflattert bin — und Seiner wird bestehen. / Ich bin ein Weib, Er ist ein Mann, / Mein Verschen weiß nur deutsch zu gehen, / Wenn Sein Vers nach dem Takt des Römers tanzen kann" (Gedichte, 221–23, the quotation 221). The poem was reprinted as "Als Chodowiecky sie gemalt hatte" (When Chodowiecky Painted Her) in *Das Lied der Karschin*, 82.

[43] Cf. her letter to Gleim, December 2, 1769: "The Duke signed himself a 'devoted friend,' an honor accorded only the accomplished poet, but never a manufacturer of

most prominently in three central ideas. Whereas the bourgeois author can freely choose his themes, the peasant poet's choice of themes is limited to the bucolic, the rustic, and the pastoral; by the same token, the bourgeois author's work can lay claim to a universal readership, whereas the peasant poet writes for an audience limited to her own class. Whereas bourgeois Art is defined in large measure by its *Zweckfreiheit*, its sovereignty from functionality, the critical response to the lower-class author's work preemptively ties both production and reception to a specific purpose, defining it as a work expressive *of* lower-class concerns and written *for* the lower classes. The third central idea that implicitly addresses the difference between peasant poetry and bourgeois Art, as it is ventriloquized in these poems, is the fact that bourgeois Art rapidly came to be seen as independent of its author, whereas peasant poetry was published with a clear understanding that the author's life and class background provided an indispensable background, indeed, an excuse for the publication of her work. In reception poems, the intimate connection between life and Art in the case of the peasant poet is expressed in the near-universal portrayal of the critical response being directed at the author rather than the work. Criticism is not viewed as criticism of writing but rather as an attempt to put the peasant in her place, to remove her from the literary scene. Both of these aspects of the reception poetry of women peasant writers are documented in actual reviews, of peasant women and women of other classes.

Gender, as is frequently pointed out, also plays a central role in the reception of the author's work, for the critics portrayed in these poems are considerably less willing to accept a female peasant poet than a male writer from the same class. This is particularly evident in Little's poems, in which the famous case of Robert Burns, the plowman poet, could feasibly provide a precedent for the publication of a milkmaid's verse. In a situation where class could become a unifying factor rather than a handicap, as it is portrayed in most reception poems, gender becomes the crucial aspect sanctioning the poetic activity of the male peasant and banning that of the female. What is withheld from the writing of lower-class women in the creation of this gender divide is a contextualization of their work that could lead to an interpretation of that work, read collectively, within a *tradition* of lower-class writing. Without such a tradition, aspirations to posthumous fame are futile; preempted by the critical response, there is literally no context in which the work of peasant women can be read. In contrast to

---

verse" ("Der Herzog unterschrieb: ergebener Freund, eine Ehre, die nur dem verdienstvollen Dichter, nicht aber einer Versmacherin zukommt . . ."; cited in Hausmann, 247–50, the quotation 248).

the genealogy of male bourgeois writers cited in several poems, each woman writer is treated (denigrated) individually, decontextualized from both the bourgeois literary tradition and other writers of her own class.

Most crucially, reception poems by lower-class women writers investigate the consequences of a predetermined class- and gender-based reception for future poetic production. Trepidation about the critics' spite may be a universal authorial response regardless of the author's class or gender, but there is no other body of work in which muses so consistently boycott rather than inspire, pens protest rather than write, and in which the author's determination to give up writing or publishing is voiced so frequently, if paradoxically, in published poetry. The dependence of these poems on an audience, the tremendous influence of the reception on the process of production as portrayed in women's reception poetry counters, again, an idea central to the bourgeois Nature aesthetic: the centrality of inspiration, the insignificance of publication, and the poet's complete independence not only from previous models and traditions but also from contextualization within a contemporary literary landscape.

## Castle-Building: Of Patrons and Their Empty Promises

In a body of work that was published with the support of a patron who was simultaneously its first reader and critic, the patron naturally assumes a central role. Most peasant poets repeatedly addressed their patrons in poems, most central among them Karsch's love poems to Gleim and her poems in praise of royal patrons,[44] Leapor's verse epistles to "Artemisia" (her poetic name for her patron Bridget Freemantle),[45] and Yearsley's poems addressed to "Stella" (her patron Hannah More).[46] Whereas one might presume these works to be limited to the poems of praise and gratitude traditionally expected of the social inferior, many of them take the author's relationship with her patron as occasion for reflection on the subject of patronage. Ann Yearsley's difficult relationship with her patron

---

[44] For example, "Als sie wirklich ihr Haus erhielt" (When She Was Finally Given Her House), in *Das Lied der Karschin*, 75–76, reprinted as "Versuch einer Danksagung an König Friedrich Wilhelm den Vielgeliebten Im Februar 1787" (Attempt to Sing My Thanks to King Frederick William the Much Beloved In February 1787) in *O, mir entwischt nicht*, 113–14, and *Gedichte und Lebenszeugnisse*, 128–29; and "An Ebendesselben Hochfürstl. Durchl. Den 19. October 1773" (To His Royal Highness, Written on the 19th of October 1773), *Gedichte*, 152–55.

[45] On Leapor's epistolary poetry to Artemisia, cf. Landry, *Muses*, 96–102.

[46] On Yearsley's "Stella" poems, cf. Landry, *Muses*, 150–52.

Hannah More[47] is extraordinarily well documented in her poetry. Her poem "To Stella; on a Visit to Mrs Montagu" is only one of several in her first volume, published under More's patronage, that is addressed to Hannah More. As one might expect, the poem presents More as the angel who saved the poet from destitution: "How has your bounty cheer'd my humble state, / And chang'd the colour of my gloomy fate!"[48] But the destitution from which the author was saved by Stella's intervention is not merely physical but also intellectual, a stance congruent with other poems in which Yearsley identified the deficiencies of Dame Nature as exclusive poetic inspiration.[49] In Stella's company, the poet tastes, for the first time, "the nameless sweets of wit." She now moves in circles

> Where Genius in familiar converse sits,
> Crowns real worth, and blasts pretending Wits;
> Where great ideas, fed by Fancy, glow,
> And soul-expanding notes in rapture flow;
> Where pointed thought in polish'd diction drest,
> With every grace assaults the yielding breast;
> O, powers of Genius![50]

The intellectual stimulation that Yearsley describes here is a far cry from the bourgeois notion of nature inspiration: "genius," defined in aesthetics as the result of the poet's exclusive exchange with Nature and his Muse, is here redefined as born of "converse" with others; whereas the natural-genius aesthetic presupposes the author's lack of education, Yearsley's portrayal endows the concept with distinctly cerebral qualities, as "great ideas" expressed in "polish'd diction." Essentially, Yearsley expresses her hope and expectation of being admitted, through her patron's intervention, into the community of (bourgeois) authors. The price of admission she offers to her strictly religious patron is the forswearing of her atheism, in her assertion that More and Montagu, that "Blest pair," were responsible for her conversion: "O, had not souls like your's been given, / The stupid Atheist might well doubt a Heaven, / Convinc'd, he now deserts his gloomy stand, / Owns MIND the noblest proof of a creating hand."[51] Even in this early poem, written at a time

---

[47] Cf. chapter 2.
[48] Yearsley, "To Stella," in Fairer/Gerrard, 440–41, the quotation 440.
[49] Cf. Yearsley's poem "On Mrs. Montagu" and the discussion in the previous chapter.
[50] Yearsley, "To Stella," Fairer/Gerrard, 440.
[51] Yearsley, "To Stella," Fairer/Gerrard, 441.

when Yearsley must still have had every expectation of continued support by her patron, their relationship is portrayed, inadvertently, more as a business relationship in which something is offered in exchange for this support rather than the idealized bond between angelic saviour and grateful pauper with which Yearsley frames it. In poems written after the rift with More, Yearsley emphasizes an entirely different aspect of the relationship: the vanity and arrogance with which the patron asserts her superiority over her charge[52] and the reduction of those who accept her favors to a subhuman state, "Low, groveling, and confin'd."[53] In her poem "On Being Presented with a Silver Pen," she describes the association between bourgeois patron and peasant protégée as inevitably condescending on one side and inevitably demeaning on the other:

> The cooly-wise, with self-applauding glance,
> And taunting air, cries, "Friendship's all romance:
> "It ne'er existed, but in pleasing sound;
> "Nor has it been, or ever will be found.
> "Have we not seen the World? Do we not know,
> "How far its rapid streams *exactly* flow?
> "'Tis to relieve Distress — this is the sum,
> "But let your Prudence point out what's to come.
> "Keep wretches *humble,* for when once reliev'd,
> "They oft-times prove our *Charity* deceiv'd:
> "Therefore be *cautious,* nor their *merits* trust;
> "They *may* have very few — if poor — they *must.*
> "Think not a savage virtuous — but confine,
> "His future acts by obligation's line:
> "He surely *must* be humble, grateful, true,
> "While *he's* dependent — the superior *you.*[54]

Yearsley's poem contains an astute paraphrase of the patron's design to relieve the peasant's financial distress with the proceeds of her volume,

---

[52] Cf. Yearsley's unpublished poem "To Stella," published in Ferguson, "Unpublished Poems," 31–32.

[53] Yearsley, "To those who accuse the Author of Ingratitude," *Poems on Various Subjects,* 57–60, the quotation 57 (brief interpretation in Landry, *Muses,* 157).

[54] Yearsley, "On Being Presented with a Silver Pen," *Poems on Various Subjects,* 83–91, the quotation 88. (All emphases are original.) For a brief interpretation, cf. Tompkins, 79; Waldron, "Ann Yearsley," 317; and "Muse-born Wonder," 122. On the oppressiveness of patronage in other poems by Yearsley, cf. Tompkins, 67–68, and Waldron, *Lactilla,* 97–98.

as both More and Montagu repeatedly expressed in letters.[55] Such an attitude naturally precludes an interpretation of the volume in question as a literary work: when the object of patronage is charity, the poet's literary ambitions, her hope for recognition as an equal, even "friendship," as she states at the outset of the passage, are doomed to failure. Most intriguing in Yearsley's poem is the importance she assigns to keeping the peasant in her place: there is more here than an indictment of the patron's unparalleled arrogance demonstrated in the magnanimous relief of the "wretch." Just as prevalent, throughout the poem, is the bourgeois fear of the upstart peasant, expressed in the "caution" recommended in dealing with the "savage," an animal who, unencumbered by virtue and merit, has to be kept on the tight leash of obligation, forced to feel the whip of bourgeois superiority that will ensure its perpetual submission. Yearsley's conclusion with respect to the peasant poet's poetic future is not dissimilar to that reached by Elizabeth Hands and other poets:[56] the submissive attitude exacted of the poet is diagnosed as in and of itself "confining." Authorship, as she maintained elsewhere, is predicated on a different state, that of "equality";[57] in a context where the association between patron and protégée is not one of "friendship" but one of domination and submission, authorship becomes inconceivable because it presupposes an Artistic independence that is anathema to the patronized poet's confined creativity.

It is this theme of the most principal difference between bourgeois Art and peasant poetry that is related in a poem by Anna Louisa Karsch. In "An den Apoll, daß er die Leyer zurücknehmen möchte" (To Apollo, Asking Him to Take Back His Lyre), she contrasts her poetry with that of the Sabinian poet Flacchus: his song creates an earthly paradise in which wolves and tigers forget the hunt, eat grass, and lie down with the lambs to listen to his song. She, however, cannot even influence her patron Frederick II to rescue her from poverty and the necessity to humble herself before lesser patrons. Whereas Flacchus's golden lyre enchants the world, her poetry is limited to cheap entertainment for the rabble who lives better than she does and despises her for her poverty and humble origins. Karsch concludes her poem with a plea to Apollo to send her

---

[55] For a discussion of More's and Montagu's patronage of Yearsley, cf. chapter 2.

[56] Cf., for example, Leapor's satire of the bowing and scraping recipient of patronage in "The Way of the World," in Colman/Thornton, II, 60–65. The poem was also published in *The Monthly Review* (November 1749): 20–24.

[57] Yearsley, "Address to Friendship; a Fragment," *The Rural Muse*, 74–81, the quotation 81, and "Clifton Hill," cited in "An Historical Milkwoman," 397. Both poems view "equality" as a prerequisite for friendship.

the golden strings of Flacchus and help her persuade her royal patron to elevate her above "fortune and the rabble."[58] In this, her conclusion seems incongruous with the remainder of her poem: the poem itself describes two radically different concepts of art — the Orphic irresistible and universal appeal that is recognizably a trait of High Art in contrast with the lower-class author's diminished role as an entertainer of the rabble, a role envisioned with similar clarity by Molly Leapor in "The Proposal." But Karsch's conclusion does not, unlike Yearsley's, allude to the possibility of the lower-class poet attaining the rank of author, of becoming an Artist who could, like Flacchus, conquer the world with her song. Karsch's speaker, given the poetic power to make the lion lie with the lambs, would exercise this power not over the world but merely over her patron; the poetic independence envisioned here is not absolute but relative. Whereas Yearsley, Hands, and other poets clearly saw the benefits contained in the bourgeois model of authorship, the height of this poetic speaker's professional ambition seems to be reached at the point where she is permitted to serve one master rather than many. The intellectual and creative independence of the true Artist that Yearsley cites in various poems, the possibility of universal and enduring influence that Karsch symbolizes in Flacchus's song are not imagined, or imaginable, as part of the patronized poet's existence. Whether this is presented self-consciously and critically or whether the limits of her poetic speaker's imagination describe Karsch's own,[59] her poem stands as a highly expressive example of a theory voiced frequently in peasant women's poetry: that the poet's status as a patronized poet imposes vital limitations not only on the process of publication but also on that of writing, even, as Karsch has shown, on the powers of imagination.

Molly Leapor's pastoral tale "Mopsus: Or, the Castle-Builder" is possibly the most acerbic allegory of the patronage system written in the eighteenth century.[60] Mopsus is a peasant youth who, despising his native groves, sets out for the city, initially seduced by the prediction of a gypsy who, in exchange for a handsome fee, presages his marriage to a baron's

[58] Karsch, "An den Apoll," *Gedichte,* 28–29, the citation 29: "O helfender Apoll! Geschändet / Wirst du, wenn deine Vaterhand / Mir nicht die goldnen Saiten sendet, / Die der Sabiner aufgespannt, / Wenn mich des dritten Cäsars Rechte / Nicht über Glück und Pöbel hebt. . . ." The poem was reprinted in *Gedichte und Lebenszeugnisse,* 77–78, and Muncker, 314–15. Karsch frequently voiced the same hope for the generosity of a royal patron which would spare her the necessity of accepting support from bourgeois patrons in letters, cf. the letters cited in Hausmann, 185, 374.

[59] On Karsch's self-image as a writer, cf. Pott, *Briefgespräche,* 41, and Schaffers, 113.

[60] Leapor, "Mopsus: Or, the Castle-Builder," in Colman/Thornton, II, 103–22 (interpretation in Rizzo, "Molly Leapor," 334–35, and Greene, 145–49).

daughter. Thus encouraged, he propositions the baron's daughter; he is soundly beaten by her servants and returns briefly to his humble station in his father's cottage from which dreams of greatness soon propel him to London. Once there, he spends his fortune keeping company with the nobles and is finally persuaded by a brothel keeper, in the disguise of a respectable matron, of the undying love of a fair lady of high degree and considerable wealth. Mopsus falls for the ruse, entertains the blushing bride, who turns out to be a common prostitute, and all her train, until he falls drunk under the table. When the police raid the brothel, Mopsus is arrested. In jail, he repents and is finally bailed out by his parents, who sell their oxen to free their son. The story then repeats itself: a lord, who knows a fool when he sees one, sends one of his footmen to pose as a sage. The faux sage offers Mopsus the now-familiar prediction of marriage to a rich society lady, which Mopsus believes for a third time and thus ends up marrying the lord's own cast-off and pregnant servant-class mistress. Happily, however, Mopsus soon loses his new wife to another, more generous lover and her child to disease. He returns home, where he receives the lost son's welcome and forswears all dreams of riches and greatness: "Grown grave by sorrow, by experience wise."[61]

The allegorical relevance of Mopsus's adventures to the paradigmatic peasant poet's career would be obvious even if it were not an analogy drawn by the author herself in letters in which she identified her own authorial ambitions with Mopsus's thwarted quest for greatness. Leapor's patron Bridget Freemantle described "Mopsus" as "occasioned" by her own mention of a potential subscription for Leapor's poems;[62] Leapor herself, in a letter to Freemantle, identified her own literary ambition as "castle-building."[63] But although there are clearly autobiographical connections that can be drawn to Leapor's poem, drawn quite deliberately by the author, the significance of her tale is not limited to the personal but extends to the social and the poetological. Like Karsch in her

---

[61] Leapor, "Mopsus," Colman/Thornton, II, 122.

[62] Bridget Freemantle, "To John *****, Esq.," in *The Monthly Review* (June 1751): 23–29, the citation 25.

[63] Molly Leapor in a letter to Bridget Freemantle, in which she also describes her dread of the critics after submitting her play for production in London: "I cannot hear the playhouse spoke of without trembling; and shall not dare to look into a news-paper, for fear of meeting with the name of *Cibber*. — Yet, after all, *Mira* has her gay intervals, and an excellent knack at castle-building" (emphases original). In the continuation of this letter, Leapor lists a series of grand schemes she would execute if her play succeeded and made her rich, including founding a hospital and an almshouse, enlarging the college chapel, and decking herself out splendidly with a house, an equipage, and magnificent clothes. Leapor's letter was published posthumously by Freemantle in *The Monthly Review* (June 1751): 30–31, the quotation 30.

pastoral patronage allegory "Der Sänger bey der Heerde,"[64] Leapor rather pointedly adheres to that genre in which, as a multitude of bourgeois reviews makes clear, the rural author is expected to write — namely, the pastoral tale — and thus overtly states her compliance with bourgeois myths of peasant creativity. Like Karsch, Leapor uses this genre to comment on the effect of this myth on their writing and the oppressiveness of the patronage system. In many ways, both pieces indirectly define themselves as directed writing. Both poets comment on the fact that the peasant sensation's success depends not on his own goals or accomplishments but on the largesse of others (in the case of Karsch's shepherd, the duke's generosity; in Mopsus's case, marriage to a society lady). Equally daringly, both authors voice their clear understanding of the bourgeois assumption, even the mandate, that the peasant poets' career be a fleeting one, symbolized in the premature end of the peasant's career at court or in the city. Whereas Karsch portrays this ending, in keeping with bourgeois expectations, as an idealized and voluntary return to the countryside, Leapor reinterprets this popular motif as the peasant's mistreatment and ultimate abandonment by his patrons, thus unveiling the bourgeois myth of lower-class literary creativity *as* a myth, and a parasitical one. Most important of Leapor's conclusions is her obvious suspicion, expressed in the repeated and deliberate deception of Mopsus through his patrons, that bourgeois creativity myths were not advanced in support of the literary development of the lower classes, but that, quite the reverse, the peasant poet was pressed into the service of bourgeois myths of "natural" and spontaneous poetic creativity.

It is noteworthy that both Karsch's and Leapor's tales center on a masculine hero, a significant move given that the hero of the tale clearly symbolizes, in both cases, peasant creativity in general and the author's own production in particular. Leapor does this repeatedly: for example, in "The Libyan Hunter, a Fable," in which the Libyan poet Sylvius is presented by the muses as the male symbol of poesy.[65] Such identification across gender lines is generally not atypical for the work of other women peasant poets where lower-class creativity is frequently embodied by male peasant writers, such as Stephen Duck (in Collier's case) or Robert Burns (in Little's). Karsch's shepherd and Leapor's peasant are not gender coincidences, they personify a trend: in lower class-women's poetry, class identification coexists with a gender disconnect. Conversely, no woman peasant poet has ever cast a woman peasant as the symbol of lower-class

---

[64] For an interpretation of Karsch's tale, cf. chapter 4.

[65] Leapor, "The Libyan Hunter. A Fable," in Colman/Thornton, II, 74–80, specifically, 75–76.

creativity. Perhaps this is not entirely surprising given that the two most famous lower-class poets, quite possibly the only poets from that class who reached comparative fame and success even in bourgeois circles, and most certainly the two idols on which many aspiring women peasant writers modeled themselves, were both men: Stephen Duck in England, Robert Burns in Scotland. The single text by a woman peasant that questions the elevated status of these idols, Mary Collier's poem "The Woman's Labour" (her response to Stephen Duck's poem "The Thresher's Labour") criticizes Duck's portrayal of women's *physical*, not their intellectual or creative work.[66] The battle whose outcome would define the nature of peasant poetic creativity, as portrayed in the patronage poems of lower-class women, was a class war, not a battle of the sexes: the male poet pitted against male or female patrons. In this, patronage poems differ significantly from reception poems, in which the poet's gender is often viewed as a determining factor, shown in her overtly contemptuous reception. The male lower-class writer, who is occasionally, as with Little's figure of Burns, admitted into the ranks of serious authors, is not subjected to the same degree of criticism.

Leapor's image of castle-building is one that also can be applied, in different ways, to the work of Yearsley and Karsch, for it aptly circumscribes both the peasant poet's aspirations to bourgeois fame and the acknowledgment and the hopelessness of these aspirations. Comparatively few peasant poets of the age accepted this situation, abdicating all authorial ambition and desire for recognition as an Artist in the bourgeois sense and resigning themselves, as did Elizabeth Bentley, to a second-class citizenship on Parnassus:

> O! had I POPE'S or GRAY'S harmonious lyre,
> O'er Nature's paths with THOMSON could I tread,
> Or catch one vivid ray of SHAKESPEAR'S fire,
> Or follow where seraphic MILTON led.
>
> . . . . . . . . . . . . . . . . . . . . . . .
>
> But since unerring Fate's divine decree
> Has fix'd my lot to sing in humbler strain,
> I'll sound the simplest shell, content to be
> The last and lowest of the tuneful train.[67]

[66] Cf. chapter 4 for an interpretation of Collier's poem.

[67] Elizabeth Bentley, "Lines, Addressed As a Tribute of Gratitude to the Subscribers in General. January, 1791," *Genuine Poetical Compositions,* 67–69, the quotation 68–69, all capitalizations original. The poem has been interpreted in Landry, *Muses,* 210–13.

The hopelessness of achieving acknowledgment as an author, as a creator of Art in the bourgeois sense, is the common denominator in both reception and patronage poems. In both traditions, this exclusion from authorship is linked to the peasant poet's class and her gender. Gender plays a central part in reception as well as patronage poems: in reception poems it occasionally appears as an additional feature disqualifying the woman writer of the lower classes, postulating simultaneously that male writers of the same class are accepted to a greater degree by their bourgeois readership. In patronage poems such as Karsch's "Der Sänger bey der Heerde" and Leapor's "Mopsus," the gender paradox inherent in the creation of a masculine character whose poetic career symbolizes that of the female author is deemed more acceptable than the symbolization of lower-class creativity as female. The impossibility of transcending class and gender barriers in the pursuit of authorship is thus documented in the limits of imagination, in Leapor's inability to envision creativity as female and in Karsch's inability to envision a greater purpose for her art than the gratification of her royal patron. Thus, even castle-building, the act of exercising that part of the imagination that is supposedly least beholden to reality, is curtailed, in the work of lower-class women, by the realities of class and gender. It must be considered one of the most notable achievements of these authors that they managed to portray this process quite self-consciously, that they documented a connection between the consistent undermining of the peasant author in criticism and the ultimate effect on her production. The peasant woman poet's continued literary activity relies crucially on two aspects that are depicted as most impaired in this process: her ability, or will, to write and her ability to imagine, in the sense of creative imagination and that power to imagine herself as an author on which all poetic achievement depends.

# Conclusion:
# On the Gender and Class of Art

> *Sooner or later those familiar tropes for primitives*
> *become the tropes conventionally used for women.*
> — Marianna Torgovnick, *Gone Primitive*[1]

REVIEWS OF PEASANT POETS, the forewords to their volumes, their autobiographical writings, their life stories as retold by their patrons and later scholars, and finally, their reception as reflected in their own work make one thing clear: that the bourgeoisie has, from its earliest definition of literature as Art in the wake of its own emancipation from aristocratic patronage, defined Art as an *exclusively* bourgeois enterprise. However, this state of affairs is not an accurate depiction of the literary scene in either England, Scotland, or Germany: both aristocratic and lower-class authors wrote and published in all three countries throughout the eighteenth century. But the eighteenth-century bourgeois conceptualization of Art does not describe a social reality but a claim to cultural superiority vis-à-vis art forms originating from other classes. In later literary history, this image has been extraordinarily successful: modern criticism to this day generally assumes the bourgeoisie's unparalleled dominance of artistic and intellectual life from the eighteenth century on, once a "free" literary market had replaced aristocratic patronage. In England and Scotland, but particularly in Germany, where the artistic rise of the middle class can be contrasted with its continuing political subordination, the cultural self-definition of the new bourgeoisie is assumed to have established itself in direct opposition to the aristocracy.[2] In literary history, the bourgeois political revolution that did not take place in either England, Scotland, or Germany in the eighteenth century is neatly replaced by a cultural revolution during which the middle class, politically subordinate but morally and intellectually superior, wrests control over culture from the upper classes, replacing them as the main producers and consumers of Art.[3]

---

[1] The quotation 17.
[2] Cf., for example, McCann, 3–4.
[3] Cf. Balet; Hauser, *The Social History of Art;* and Kaiser, 41–44, 52.

Throughout this book, it has been my contention that bourgeois claims to intellectual, moral, and artistic distinction in Germany, England, and Scotland were not only formulated through dissociation from the aristocracy but also, and more significantly, through dissociation from lower-class authors. In this final section, their reception is linked with that of bourgeois women authors. Such a comparison points to three important conclusions: The first and foremost is the understanding of literary Art in the eighteenth century not only as essentially bourgeois, or at least distinct from the lower orders, but also as essentially male,[4] an idea already economically expressed in Richard Steele's short list of the "chief Qualifications of a good Poet . . . : To be a very well-bred man."[5] Second, the disqualification of lower-class authors and women of any class from authorship was based on related assumptions and discourses. And finally, nineteenth- and twentieth-century criticism has, to a significant extent, adopted this definition, thereby excluding the work of women and lower-class authors, whose oeuvre is usually mined exclusively for historical or cultural interest, from *aesthetic* consideration. A reception history of bourgeois women and peasant authors, spanning three countries and three centuries, is a monumental task, one that will require decades of consistent study of canonized aesthetics as well as noncanonized art forms. In the absence of such a framework, it would be premature to present this close connection between the reception of peasant poets and that of women writers and its meaning for the establishment of bourgeois Art as anything so definite as a "conclusion." But the similarities between the reception of peasant poets and that of women writers seem to (at least) support a hypothesis that invites further study. In closing, I therefore invite readers to entertain two possibilities raised by the material presented in this book: first, that the exclusion of women's literature and nonbourgeois art forms, originally formulated aesthetically in the eighteenth century, became one of the most consequential defining characteristics of bourgeois Art; second, that the new definition of Art as essentially male and bourgeois turned out to be decisively influential in the process of canonization from the early nineteenth century onward and still dominates academic discourse today.

---

[4] John Barrell has already made this point in his *Poetry, Language, and Politics:* "The universal, the fully human position, from which properly literary texts, and properly literary criticism, can be produced, is also a masculine position" (6).

[5] Richard Steele's definition originally appeared in the *Spectator* no. 314, February 1712 and is cited in Lonsdale, "Introduction," xxiv. For a persuasive argument of the eighteenth-century definition of literary Art as essentially male, cf. Kazzazzi; also Schabert/Schaff, 9–11; Schabert, 116; Schaff, 125; and Tebben, "Vorwort," 7, and "Soziokulturelle Bedingungen," 34.

In this chapter, I focus exclusively on the bourgeois definition of Art and the degree to which that concept involved either lower-class or women's creativity, *not* on the literary history of either peasant poets or women writers. Largely due to the still predominant understanding of Art as male and middle class in scholarship and criticism, the literary history of neither lower-class authors nor women writers has so far been written to a degree that would make such generalizations permissible.[6] Similarities between their literary histories, so far as we know them, do exist to the extent that both groups conformed to bourgeois and male expectations of their writing, which are comparable in both cases. As is the case with peasant poets, poetry was the most popular genre in the literary production of bourgeois women, accounting for approximately one third of all publications. The reasons for the predominance of poetry in the work of both lower-class authors and bourgeois women can easily be related to the fact that neither group was considered eligible for primary and professional authorship, that each group was saddled with a "vocation" that lay elsewhere (physical labor for peasants, household management and childcare for bourgeois women), and that both groups of writers therefore wrote under comparable conditions. Their lack of leisure and constant interruptibility must have made novel or drama writing seem less conceivable than the production of shorter forms such as poetry.[7] Like most peasant poets, many bourgeois women writers produced only one volume of poetry.[8] But even in the absence of an authoritative literary history for either group, some important differences emerge. Landry's assumption that most peasant women poets published anonymously or under a pseudonym is based less on evidence available for lower-class writers and more on the literary history of bourgeois women, to whom that statement applies with some accuracy.[9] Of the twenty-four lower-class women writers whose works have inspired

---

[6] In particular, the history of Scottish women writers is underresearched and, in the wake of the Act of Union of 1707, difficult to separate from English women's literary history: many Scottish women writers described themselves as Englishwomen (cf. McMillan's "Introduction," xiii). Cf. also the problematization of "Scottishness" in Gifford's and McMillan's "Introduction," x-xiii.

[7] Bridget Hill has voiced the same speculation with regard to the poetic productivity of lower-class authors, cf. *Servants,* 238.

[8] Stanton, 249–51.

[9] Cf. Landry, *Muses,* 11: "Eighteenth-century laborers of both sexes, like middle- and upper-class women, doubtless enter literary history before the nineteenth century most often as Anon." Landry offers no documentation for this claim. On the anonymity of women writers, cf. Marshall, Schabert, 110–13, and Schaff, 128–31, for the English context; and Kord, *Namen,* for the German context. On class-specific differences in women's usage of anonymity and pseudonymity in Germany, cf. Kord, *Namen,* 77–92.

and influenced this study and of the fourteen authors whose works appear in it, not a single one published either anonymously or using a pseudonym. Although it is impossible to disprove the existence of any as yet undiscovered anonymous or pseudonymous publications by lower-class women, there is also no evidence in its favor, and anonymous or pseudonymous publication would be anathema to the basis on which the publication of peasant authors rested. For the application of the aesthetic principle of exclusive Nature inspiration to the peasant poet could only be justified by a convincing exhibition of the poet's class and educational background. Such a display usually not only involved revealing the poet's identity but also details of her life, in many cases an abbreviated biography, usually with an emphasis on the author's highly marketable deprivation in both the physical and intellectual sense. Another point where there are fundamental differences in the literary history of peasant poets versus bourgeois women is the point at which the poet addresses her readers or critics directly: although distinct similarities can be found in forewords by peasant poets or their patrons,[10] the peasants' defiant resistance, their satirical ventriloquies in poetry bear no relation to the "discourse of modesty" (*Bescheidenheitstopos*)[11] that feminist scholarship has recognized as one of the predominant characteristics in the forewords and prefaces of bourgeois women writers.[12] For bourgeois women writers, who in their forewords subordinated their literary activities to their "natural" feminine duty and vocation as house-

---

[10] Cf. the materials and discussion in chapter 2.

[11] One example from a character who has played a part in this study is Helmina von Chézy's view of femininity and authorship as *principally* incompatible, her wish that she could have remained "wholly feminine" ("ganz eine Frau") and her description of writing as a "family curse" passed down from her grandmother Anna Louisa Karsch to her mother Karoline von Klencke to herself. Her letter to Therese Huber, dated May 21, 1821, is cited in Heuser, "Stationen," 160. On the difference between Karsch's authorial stance and the discourse surrounding bourgeois female authorship, cf. Pott, *Briefgespräche*, 43–44.

[12] On the German context, cf. Heuser, "Poetologische Reflexionen"; on the English context, cf. Schaff, 126, and Gibson, 79–81. Although I am aware of the generic difference between these texts — poetry in the peasants' case, prefaces and forewords in the bourgeois women's — and the fact that the poetic medium would be more likely to be considered "fictional," I nonetheless consider the two analogous in the sense that both attempt to forestall or comment on the critical reception of their work and both are usually explicitly directed at the male and bourgeois critic or reader. In the case of peasant women, such poems often preface the work, thus assuming the function of the foreword. Prose forewords in the works of peasant women are more frequently authored by patrons than the poet herself; for a discussion of these forewords, many of which do echo the bourgeois discourse of modesty closely, cf. chapter 2.

wives and mothers,[13] it would have meant a severe breach of middle-class feminine propriety to put their writing before their families, as Karsch did when she claimed, in a poem written in 1758, that her four children "bothered" her when she wrote.[14] Klencke's analogous statement in her biography of Karsch that Karsch was "not born for domesticity"[15] would have been equally impossible to apply to bourgeois women: *all* women, according to bourgeois doctrine, were born for domesticity and nothing else. As feminist scholarship has since established, much of the writing of bourgeois women was explicitly directed at a readership composed of their own class and gender: this is true for many of their novels,[16] including the most famous "woman's novel" of the age, Sophie von La Roche's *Die Geschichte des Fräuleins von Sternheim* (The History of Lady Sophia Sternheim [1771]), but even more explicit in the case of conduct books for women, which are legion in both the eighteenth and the nineteenth centuries.[17] Peasant poetry, however, was not directed at a readership of its own class, but at an erudite bourgeois readership; as the poems that take the themes of bourgeois patronage, readership, or aesthetics show, their work takes a principally different authorial stance, one that cannot, unlike much work by bourgeois women writers, rely on a basic affinity between author and reader. And finally, whereas many bourgeois women writers made a profession of their writing, few lower-class women were able to do so; most of them remained as dependent on physical labor postpublication as they had

---

[13] Cf. Kord, *Blick*, 17–19, for sources and discussion, and Heuser, "Poetologische Reflexionen" for women's forewords.

[14] Karsch's poem "Ihr Freunde von den Wissenschaften," cited in Klencke's biography, 77: "Vier Kinder stöhren mich; doch das Geräusch von Kindern, / Kann nicht den Trieb in mir und nicht das Feuer mindern."

[15] Klencke, "Lebenslauf," 79: "She was not born for domesticity, and now, the more she yielded to her genius, the more onerous seemed to her the duties of housewife, mother and servant, for she was all three at once" ("Sie war für keinen häuslichen Zustand geboren, und jetzt, je mehr sie sich ihrem Genie überließ, je drückender wurden ihr die Pflichten einer Hausfrau, Mutter und Magd; denn dies war sie zugleich"). A parallel argument appears in Sulzer's foreword to Karsch's 1764 edition, in which he furnishes a precise reversal of the bourgeois women's forewords seeking to convince their readers that they would never neglect their households over their writing: Sulzer claims that before Karsch came to Berlin, it was her vocation as a *poet* that was neglected because of her household duties (xvi).

[16] Cf., for example, Breen's "Introduction" to her edition of the writings of the prose of English women Romantics, particularly xix.

[17] For some examples, see the collection by Häntzschel and the section "Conduct" in Vivien Jones; for a discussion of the German context, cf. Becker-Cantarino, *Der lange Weg*, 149–200.

been before.[18] The literary histories of bourgeois and peasant women authors obviously differ in many significant ways. Where these differences are erased, however, is in these poets' reception by their bourgeois male readership, where both were defined as part of a background against which true Art could establish its claim to cultural significance: "the status of labouring poets was never equal to that of writers from polite society. Labouring poets carried a stigma comparable to that of women writers."[19] The systematic exclusion of women and the poor from nineteenth-century anthologies[20] is only one manifestation of this principal definition of legitimate authorship as bourgeois and male.

"Male" and "bourgeois" have become rather complex terms: as feminist theorists have established, "male" describes sex as well as gender, an anatomical as well as a social reality, with essentialists and constructionists deeply divided over the question of the prediscursive existence of the anatomical category "sex."[21] "Bourgeois," as well, is an amorphous term that cannot be described exhaustively in terms of either class or social rank.[22] Whereas "rank" describes a social status composed of such diverse factors as possessions, privileges, behaviors, education, honors, duties, residence, and occupation, "class" is generally used to describe economic status.[23] Neither definition will serve here: in all three countries, the emerging bourgeoisie defined itself in opposition to the traditional social hierarchies of rank; unlike members of an economic "class," members of the bourgeoisie hailed from various economic backgrounds.[24] The most defining characteristics describing the bourgeoisie in either national context are usually not merely social

---

[18] Cf. the materials and discussion in chapter 2. Two contrastive examples that could be mentioned in this context is the lower-class author Anna Louisa Karsch, who consistently sought support from her patrons for the publication of her works, and her daughter, the bourgeois author Karoline von Klencke, who did publish independently of male patronage. Pott has viewed Karsch's inability to publish independently in connection with her gender rather than her class, echoing remarks Karsch herself made in letters (cf., e.g., *"Bruder in Apoll,"* I, 215, 273), but this interpretation fails to explain why independence from the patron, an option that had not been open to Karsch, was apparently feasible for Klencke (*Briefgespräche*, 70–71).

[19] Greene, 110. Many reviews in which the works of "unlettered" poets are principally juxtaposed with "great" literature are cited by Bold, 22. Cf. also the materials and discussion in chapter 2.

[20] As established by Lonsdale and cited in Greene, 205.

[21] Cf. especially the works of Butler and Fuss.

[22] Some of my remarks on this are condensed from the discussion in my *Sich einen Namen machen*, chapter 4.

[23] Cf. Wallech, 269.

[24] Cf. Kocka, "Bürgertum," 42, and King and Raynor for the English context.

and economic but also cultural and moral, expressed in the bourgeoisie's self-image as culturally dominant and its critical distance from the aristocracy based on its claim to moral rectitude. Kocka, Bausinger, and Kaplan have identified the emphasis on education and aesthetics, an ensemble of values and behaviors (such as order, industry, punctuality, and thrift) and, above all, a specific understanding of the role of the family in general and women in particular as defining aspects of bourgeois culture.[25] In England, and to a lesser degree in Germany, these values were largely shared between the gentry and the bourgeoisie, in stark opposition to the "corrupt" aristocracy, which served as a foil for these values.[26] Thus, a case can be made that the term "bourgeoisie," despite its clear dissociation from both the aristocracy and the lower classes, is defined more significantly through cultural and moral factors than social and economic considerations. Kocka's definition of the bourgeoisie as a culture[27] seems the only one that adequately reflects the aesthetic and ethical considerations expressed in the eighteenth-century debate, and also the one that is most helpful in clarifying the status of women within that culture.

The first and most significant paradox confronting such an investigation is the fact that women do not *have* a status in bourgeois culture. Woman's "natural" vocation as wife and mother, established by the relatively recent division of remunerative work outside of the home versus housework and cemented in pedagogical, philosophical, legal, and literary writings,[28] resulted in her economic dependence on man and thus in her

---

[25] Cf. Kocka, "Bürgertum," 43; Kaplan 9; Bausinger, 121–22.

[26] Cf. Kaiser, 39–44, and the discussion and materials cited in Kord, *Sich einen Namen machen*, 78. For class and rank issues in eighteenth-century England, see Barrell, *English Literature*, 17–50.

[27] Kocka, "Bürgertum," 43; cf. also Bausinger, 121.

[28] According to Ferguson, the ideological shift to the concept of women as exclusively housewives and mothers occurred considerably earlier in England than it did in Germany, at the outset of the eighteenth century rather than toward its end (cf. Ferguson, *First Feminists*, 16, versus Blackwell, 335). Nancy Armstrong, however, views this development as a long-term process throughout the century (4; cf. also Schabert, 105, and Jones's introduction for the English context). Some texts indicative of the shift toward women's exclusive domesticity in eighteenth-century England are cited in Stone, *Family, Sex and Marriage*, 343–60; cf. also Reynolds, 258–71, and Mahl/Koon, 9 (on the education of bourgeois girls to domesticity); Scott's famous poem "The Female Advocate" is an eloquent example for the domestic virtues now portrayed as exemplary (cf. Holladay, v-vi). For the German context, see Hausen, "Polarisierung"; Duden; Cocalis, "Vormund"; Dietrick; Dotzler; Hoffmann; Kord, *Namen*, 36–44; and Niethammer, 47, 67–72. Cf. Young, *Women*, 61, for a description of bourgeois attempts to extend the philosophy of the house as "woman's true sphere" to lower-class women in Scotland, which, although universally accepted among the bourgeoisie, met with considerably greater resistance

status as a legal unperson without civic rights. When writers such as Kant, Knigge, and Fichte asserted that a woman could "not actually be considered a person at all in civil society,"[29] they did not deny woman's essential humanity — although that, as well, was a subject of intense debate[30] — but her status as a *Bürger,* understood both as *citoyenne* and as *bourgeoise* in the sense of belonging to that new class that was rapidly staking its claim to cultural superiority.[31] Nancy Armstrong has pointed out in her discussion of the English context that the production of the new feminine ideal of exclusive domesticity is thus intimately related to the other significant cultural and social shift occurring in the eighteenth century, the rise of the middle classes.[32] According to Kant, neither lower-class men nor women are *bürgerlich* in the sense of either *citoyen* or *bourgeois;* his listing of unfortunates principally deprived of a "civic/bourgeois personality" (*"bürgerliche Persönlichkeit"*), persons "whose whole existence is, as it were, merely inherent," includes apprentices, servants, legal minors, and women of any class, age, or status.[33] As Kant's rather emphatic act of depriving lower-class men and all women of *personhood* makes clear, the essential *Unmündigkeit* he describes has transcended its economic origins; his restrictions are essential and philosophical, rather than merely social or economic. Women, thus excluded from civic personhood and the legal rights of the *citoyen,* are deemed even less eligible for the cultural accom-

---

among the lower classes. For a history of women's work in eighteenth-century Europe, cf. Simonton, 1–83.

[29] The quotation is taken from Knigge's *Über den Umgang mit Menschen,* II, 55 ("da die Frau eigentlich gar keine Person in der bürgerlichen Gesellschaft ausmacht"); cf. the discussion in Frevert's *Women,* 13; similar argumentation in Kant, "Anthropologie," 196–204, and discussion in Bovenschen, 233; and Fichte, "Grundriss des Familienrechts," 312–13. For a brief discussion of women's legal status as noncitizens into the nineteenth century, cf. Marion Gray, 241–42, and Niethammer, 55–56; on relevant contemporary texts, cf. Marion Gray, 145–72, particularly 153–54 on Kant's comments on the issue in his *Metaphysik der Sitten.*

[30] Cf. the texts cited in Sigrid Lange.

[31] Cf. Frevert, *Women,* 13.

[32] Cf. her *Desire and Domestic Fiction,* particularly 8; also Kontje, whose discussion of the French Revolution likewise assumes that the triumph of the middle class was predicated on the domestication of middle-class women (5).

[33] Kant, "Metaphysik," 131: "Der Geselle bei einem Kaufmann, oder bei einem Handwerker; der Dienstbote (nicht der im Dienste des Staats steht), der Unmündige *(naturaliter vel civiliter)*; alles Frauenzimmer, und überhaupt jedermann, der nicht nach eigenem Betrieb, sondern nach der Verfügung Anderer (außer der des Staats), genötigt ist, seine Existenz (Nahrung und Schutz) zu erhalten, entbehrt der bürgerlichen Persönlichkeit, und seine Existenz ist gleichsam nur Inhärenz." (The emphases are original.) Cf. also the discussion of this passage in Bovenschen, 235.

plishments of the *bourgeois:* this is the clear subtext of countless treatises by male bourgeois thinkers of the age who, in England as well as Germany, have excluded women from consideration as serious authors.[34] The following two aspects seem worthy of emphasis: whereas modern criticism has often endowed the bourgeoisie, precisely because of its self-definition as a culture rather than a class, with a pseudo-egalitarianism that presupposes that potentially everyone could claim membership to the middle classes,[35] indications are that, on the contrary, this self-image as culturally superior rested in no small measure on a rather pointed exclusion. Second, the exclusion of women from the bourgeoisie in the cultural sense was arguably even more central to this image than the elimination of their civic rights: if, in particular, the German bourgeoisie's self-definition as culturally superior was partly pitted against its own sense of political powerlessness, the German *Bürger's* sense of worth would necessarily rest much more strongly on his self-definition as *bourgeois* than as *citoyen.*

Because the process of women's exclusion from the new bourgeois culture has already been well documented for both the English and the German contexts, I cite only the most important eighteenth-century developments here. Pragmatically, restricting women to the home freed men from housework and childcare and enabled their cultural activities;[36] ideologically, the economic situation was validated by women's "natural" vocation to an exclusively domestic existence.[37] In literature by bourgeois men, the bourgeois housewife provided a pleasing contrast to the much-maligned aristocratic mistress;[38] as Nancy Armstrong has established for

---

[34] Cf. the sources and discussion in Kord, *Namen,* 36–44, for the German context; and Messer-Davidow and Higonnet, 160–63, for the English context.

[35] Cf., for example, Kaiser, on the establishment of the bourgeoisie's cultural preeminence: "Sofern jeder Bildungswillige in das Bildungspublikum hineinwachsen kann, gehören ihm potentiell alle an" (44). Kaiser's comment exemplifies the bourgeois myopia with respect to social realities, an aspect that was central to the aesthetic pretense in the eighteenth century and is today no less central for the continuation of such critical predilections as *Autonomieästhetik,* to cite just one example.

[36] Cf. particularly Hausen, "Polarisierung," and Tebben, "Soziokulturelle Bedingungen," 14, for the German context; Messer-Davidow for the English context; and Burness for the Scottish context.

[37] Cf. Dietrick; Cocalis, "Vormund"; Duden; Hausen, "Polarisierung"; Hoffmann; Dotzler; Marion Gray, 228–35; Simonton, 13–15; Niethammer, 67–72; and Wunder, "Gender Norms"; for the English context, cf. Ferguson, *First Feminists,* 16; Schabert, 105; and Nancy Armstrong, 4. On the "cult of domesticity" and the separate spheres in Scotland, cf. Burness, 106.

[38] Cf. the sources cited in Kord, "Protagonist/Antagonist" for the German context and Nancy Armstrong, 20, for the English context; see also McKeon, *Origins* 255–56, on the

the English context, the configuration of gender characteristics in literature and conduct books for women was central to the project of bourgeois emancipation: "it was the new domestic woman rather than her counterpart, the new economic man, who first encroached upon aristocratic culture and seized authority from it."[39] But as treatises like Friederike Helene Unger's "Etwas über das Gesinde" (A Few Remarks on Domestics [1788]) demonstrate, bourgeois femininity was defined at least as consistently in dissociation from the lower classes as in opposition to the aristocracy.[40] In both England and Germany, literary and philosophical images of femininity changed considerably during the eighteenth century, with the erudite woman of the Enlightenment being replaced by the passively sentimental heroine.[41] In both countries, the new sentimental virtue of women was personified by the same heroines, with Samuel Richardson's Clarissa and Pamela attaining the same tremendous popularity and influence in Germany that they had commanded in England.[42] The three main characteristics that defined the bourgeois man — education, work, and culture — were made taboo for bourgeois women: although the level of education permissible for women was hotly debated in the Moral Weeklies in both England and Germany,[43] women were clearly neither supposed to work (for money) nor were they supposed to produce culture (certainly not for money). Work itself was

popular theme of the "common" girl's chastity endangered by the aristocratic seducer in English literature.

[39] Nancy Armstrong, 59; cf. also 68. On women's domesticity and its relation to women's "work," cf. Simonton, 18–23. Armstrong states that conduct books for women were a new phenomenon in the eighteenth century; until then, rule books had concentrated on men of the ruling class (61–62). On the German bourgeois woman as an antithesis to the aristocratic lady, cf. Blackwell, 327–29.

[40] Unger presents her entire treatise, in which she proposes to regulate the dress and leisure activities of domestic servants, as a service to bourgeois society ("Verdienst um die bürgerliche Gesellschaft," 684). Implicitly reflected in her treatise is the contrast between the becoming reticence and modesty of the bourgeois woman with the upstart arrogance and profligate tendencies of the female domestic servant.

[41] Cf. Schabert and Holladay, iv-xi, for the English context; Bovenschen, 107–10, 158–59, 162–64, and Tebben, "Soziokulturelle Bedingungen," 17–19, for the German context. Cf. also Fulford's study on changes of gender definitions in England in the late eighteenth/early nineteenth century.

[42] Cf. Bovenschen, 158–59.

[43] The Moral Weeklies represent another major literary trend in the eighteenth century that began in England and was imported into Germany, where it became exceedingly influential (cf. Martens). Cf. Sotiropoulos for an overview of bourgeois women's education in Germany and England, chapters I, IV, V, and VI, and her "window chapters," 35–52, 152–66, 217–26.

redefined as a masculine occupation, its meaning rapidly reduced to gainful employment performed outside of the home. That home — now idealized as the haven of tranquillity to which men return after their labors and presupposed to be free of everything that now defined their labors abroad, including work, strife, and competition[44] — increasingly resembles that rural pasture of the pastoral in which fruit falls from the trees and beasts willingly offer themselves up to the slaughter. The bourgeois angel in the house, charged with running the household, was simultaneously charged to avoid the appearance of work, that is, to aestheticize her labor into a pleasing picture of domestic bliss.[45] Her unseen activities thus closely resemble those of the happy swains in pastoral literature who reap the bounty of the land without labor or strife.[46] Literary parallels aside, the taboo on women's work demonstrably represents a *bourgeois* restriction, and the same can be said to apply to the "gender characteristics" (Hausen's *Geschlechtscharaktere*)[47] that defined women as exclusive caregivers for their husbands and children and that furnished the rationale for this restriction. To the extent that women's vocation as housewife and mother, despite the attempts of bourgeois men to generalize this as "natural" and thus inherently feminine and applicable to all women, relates to the segregation of masculine work (gainful employment) and women's work (housework), this vocation describes an *exclusively* bourgeois value that was developed within the bourgeoisie, is discussed only in bourgeois literature, and is applied by bourgeois thinkers only to women of their own class.[48] The angel in the house who runs the household silently and efficiently but does not "work," the idealized mother who selflessly cares for her children, is bourgeois by definition. Neither aristocratic nor lower-class women were

---

[44] Cf., for example, Nancy Armstrong, 8.

[45] Cf. the discussion in Kord, *Namen*, 80, and Frevert, *Women*, 22–24, 67, 120; Meyer 172–73, 180–84, 190; Kaplan, 2–31; Duden, 134–35; Nipperdey, 145; and Nancy Armstrong, 76, 78–80, for the English context.

[46] Cf. chapter 4 for a more extensive discussion of this tradition.

[47] Cf. Hausen's list of "natural" female versus male characteristics ("Polarisierung," 368); a comparable listing is offered by Nancy Armstrong for the English context (18–19). Compare also Marion Gray's and Harriet Guest's more recent discussion of the separation of the public and private spheres in the eighteenth century (Gray 228–35; Guest, 5–14, 176–219, and 313–39) as well as Simonton on the effect of the separation of work and home (70–75) and of notions of gender (80–81) on women's work.

[48] Niethammer has already forcefully made this point (47, 71). Cf. also Hausen, "Polarisierung," 382–83, 393, and "Ulme," 90, 97; Stubbs, ix–50; Frevert's "Einleitung" to *Bürgerinnen und Bürger,* 13; Greven-Aschoff, 22–23, 62; Levy, 20–47, particularly 34; and Lipp, 181.

expected to spend much time with either their husbands or their children, and lower-class women's work outside of the home failed to raise a furor in either the eighteenth or subsequent centuries.[49]

Femininity fulfilled a similar role to male philosophers and aestheticists as the "natural genius" — personified in the *Volk* in the aesthetic tradition and applied to the peasant poet in the patrons' forewords — did to the bourgeois reader. Herder's elaborate daydream to "become, for a time, an ancient Caledonian" and sail, uprooted from civilization, the rough seas, past the coast that saw Fingal's deeds and heard the songs of Ossian[50] is echoed a few decades later in Friedrich Schiller's poems and aesthetic writings defining femininity. Both Herder's uncivilized *Volk* and Schiller's idea of the feminine stand for an uncomplicated unity with Nature that Man, in his monumental efforts to dominate Nature, has lost and to which he longs to return.[51] Thus, Man's return to Nature, representing both "the myth of origins and the utopia of fulfillment,"[52] can be symbolized either by class or gender difference. If men, as de Beauvoir has stated, approach women *because* women are remote from the world,[53] the same holds true for the relationship expressed in terms of class: the bourgeois approaches the peasant poet *because* he is remote from civilization. Both peasants and women appear in the works of male bourgeois thinkers as Nature Personified; in both cases, this Nature is harnessed in the service of masculine bourgeois erudite creativity:[54] the regenerative function of the *Volk* for the cultured middle classes is the same as that attributed to the Feminine for the benefit of men.[55] Because both peasants and women were also viewed as particularly corruptible through Culture, both had to be induced to internalize his or her supposed "nature":[56] thus, the flood of conduct books for women[57] served a parallel purpose to that discernible in the works of the "peasant

---

[49] Cf. Frevert, *Women*, 23, 28–30, 89.

[50] The passage in his "Auszug aus einem Briefwechsel über Ossian" is cited in chapter 1, n. 36.

[51] Bovenschen, 240–41. Bovenschen has explicitly linked the discourse of femininity in Schiller's theoretical writings with that of nature versus culture; cf. her discussion of Schiller's *Naïve und sentimentalische Dichtung*, 252. On the incompatibility of femininity and culture in theories of the naive, cf. also Geitner, 294–301.

[52] Bovenschen, 242: "Ursprungsmythos und Vollendungsutopie."

[53] From de Beauvoir's *The Second Sex*, cited in Bovenschen, 242.

[54] Cf. the discussion and examples pertaining to peasant poets' "nature" in chapter 1.

[55] Cf. Dedner, *Topos*, 134.

[56] Cf. Bovenschen, 250–51.

[57] Cf. Schabert/Schaff, "Einleitung," 13, and Nancy Armstrong, 59–63, 65–66.

enlightenment."[58] Particularly in cases where the praise of the peasant's contentment in his station and the praise of female domesticity were written by the same person,[59] the commonality of purpose in both traditions can easily be discerned in the similarity of argumentation.

It follows that the status of women authors in eighteenth-century bourgeois culture can be defined to a certain degree in relation to the reception of nonbourgeois art forms, such as peasant poetry. There are some striking similarities in the expectations directed by bourgeois men at both lower-class authors and women writers of their own class. Both peasant poets and bourgeois women were seen as particularly suited to the pastoral genre;[60] both were expected to produce primarily occasional literature.[61] As shown in previous chapters, the bourgeois goal in the treatment of peasant poets was not to encourage the development of literacy and artistry among the lower classes but to create a naive unlettered poet who would *occasionally* be poetically inspired for the entertainment of her bourgeois or aristocratic patrons: a mixture between idiot savant and court jester.[62] What links the reception of peasant poets of either gender with that of bourgeois women authors is partly that discourse, as well as the frequent attempts by male patrons of bourgeois women's writing to define their work as produced by "nature" rather than erudition or genius. Similar to peasants' literary work, bourgeois women's literature was read as the result of poetic inspiration, not literary training. In both cases, the descent from the natural genius to the mediocre occasional poet, as described in contemporary criticism, usually begins with the author's attempt to publish her second work, thus establishing herself as a professional author.[63] Perhaps the most famous example from the ranks of bourgeois women authors is Sophie von La Roche's novel *Geschichte des Fräuleins von Sternheim* (1771),[64] easily the

---

[58] Cf. the sources and discussion in chapter 1.

[59] As they were in the case of Hannah More, cf., for example her *Village Politics* and "The Practical Use of Female Knowledge."

[60] Messenger, "Pastoral Trap," 96–97.

[61] Tebben, 14; Messenger, "Pastoral Trap," 96–97.

[62] This has been Klaus's conclusion as well in his *Literature of Labour*, 21.

[63] For some examples in Germany, cf. the chapter on women's reception history in Kord, *Namen*, 135–73.

[64] I use Sophie von La Roche because she was easily the most famous German woman novelist of the century; her career was an inspiration for many subsequent bourgeois women novelists, some of whom she supported in various ways. La Roche can thus be considered the quintessential bourgeois woman writer of the century, despite the fact that she married an aristocrat (Count La Roche). Her own class origins are bourgeois.

most famous German novel of the century and the blueprint for Goethe's *Die Leiden des jungen Werther* (The Sorrows of Young Werther [1774]). Like the work of peasant poets, it was published with the help of a bourgeois male patron, La Roche's former fiancé Christoph Martin Wieland, who presented the novel in his introduction as a "spontaneous fruit of pure nature . . . that possesses special inner beauties of mind and heart, which compensate us for the absence of a plot elaborated in accordance with established rules, and indeed for the lack of everything that might pass under the heading of *authorial art*."[65] Wieland here indicates a number of prohibitions that applied to the work of peasant poets as well: like the work of peasant writers, La Roche's novel was supposedly nature-inspired and free from both masculine erudition and authorial ambition. Indeed, Wieland cites as the best indication of La Roche's "natural" talent her "felicitous" (read: coincidental) aptness of expression, "often enough in passages with which a strict grammarian would be least satisfied"[66] — those passages, in other words, that most clearly demonstrate the author's lack of formal education. As with peasant authors' work, the impetus for writing is defined as autobiographical with the statement that La Roche brought up "a paper girl" in replacement for her own two daughters who were away at boarding school;[67] some of her readers, assuming Sternheim to be an autobiographical character, voiced their disappointment when La Roche's appearance differed from the descriptions of her heroine in the novel.[68] And while the peasant poet's humbleness and gratitude expresses itself in his or her freedom from authorial ambition, restricting itself to one single publication whose purpose is defined as relieving the author's financial distress, La Roche's feminine modesty exacts the same price: Wieland claimed in the novel's foreword that it had been published without the author's knowledge or

---

[65] Wieland, "To D.F.G.R.V.," 7–8 (emphasis original). Wieland was also an enthusiastic supporter of the "nature poet" Anna Louisa Karsch, cf. his letter to Karsch cited in Chézy, "Erinnerungen," 30–32.

[66] Wieland, "To D.F.G.R.V.," 8.

[67] Cf. Lynn's introduction to the English translation (xiv-xv). The quotation is taken from La Roche's *Letters on Mannheim* of 1791 and quoted by Lynn, xiv-xv. Christa Bürger has analyzed the principal disconnection from Life as one of the principal requirements of Art in the German classical and romantic movements and linked this prerequisite with women's literary production; cf. *Leben Schreiben*.

[68] Caroline Flachsland complained about the difference in a letter to her fiancé, Herder, in 1772; cf. the citation and discussion in Bovenschen, 193. On the common identification of La Roche with her heroine, cf. Bovenschen, 190–200, and Lynn, xvii; on the broad reception of German women's writings as autobiographical, cf. Kord, *Namen*, 147–55.

consent.[69] Even the most enthusiastic reviews of La Roche's novel show few signs that the novel was ever received as *art*, or, for that matter, as a book. Goethe, one of *Sternheim's* most ardent admirers, set the tone for its reception when he said that the novel was not a book, it was a human soul.[70] The tremendous success of La Roche's novel established her, in the minds of her readers, as a literary phenomenon not dissimilar from the spectacle represented by the peasant poet; it did *not* establish her as an author. Inexplicably, in view of *Sternheim's* unprecedented success, Wieland lost interest in editing the planned second part of the novel, and La Roche's attempts to publish another novel were met with harsh criticism and emphatic disapproval — particularly from Goethe and other authors who had been *Sternheim's* most enthusiastic supporters.[71]

The case of Sophie von La Roche, the most famous and paradigmatic of all eighteenth-century women authors, is not exceptional but indicative. The argumentation in the foreword to her novel, written by her patron Christoph Martin Wieland; the recourse to "natural" inspiration; the indication that her first was intended to be the author's sole publication; and her critics' clear attempts to distinguish her writing from that of a bourgeois male author are not only highly reminiscent of the reception history of peasant poets but also paradigmatic for that of bourgeois women writers throughout the eighteenth century. The most striking parallel between the reception of lower-class writers and that of women writers is the taboo on bourgeois masculine erudition[72] and the resulting limitation

[69] Cf. Wieland, "To D.F.G.R.V.," 5. The same lack of authorial ambition has been claimed on behalf of Anna Louisa Karsch as late as 1992 by Reinhard Nickisch, who views her poetic production as "unpretentious and carefree, without any ulterior motives with respect to speedy publication" ("unprätentiös und unbekümmert, ohne den Hintergedanken an eine alsbaldige Veröffentlichung"; 77). Nickisch's obvious approval of Karsch's supposed lack of authorial ambition, particularly his use of the pejorative expression "Hintergedanke" (ulterior motive) reveals much in this context. For some parallel examples from the English context, cf. Harris, "Sappho," 240.

[70] Goethe's notice in the *Frankfurter Gelehrte Anzeigen*, February 14, 1771: "Die Herren irren sich, wenn sie glauben, sie beurteilen ein Buch — es ist eine Menschenseele." Quoted in Bovenschen, 192; cf. also the discussion of Goethe's assessment in Lynn, xvii.

[71] Cf. Becker-Cantarino, "Nachwort," 388–92, 398.

[72] Cf. paradigmatically the 1774 review of Mary Scott's *Female Advocate*, in which the reviewer excoriates the literary education for women that Scott had defended in her work as rendering the "poor girls . . . worse than ignorant; conceited without knowledge, and supercilious without taste. Hence the prejudices of men, with respect to female learning, are by no means likely to be lessened. It is dreadful for a man of real knowledge and politeness to encounter one of these literary vixens. . . . You are offended with an empty mind, bloated with vanity; while politeness obliges you to suppress your disgust, and perhaps to feign some degree of admiration. — The effects of real knowledge are gentleness and modesty, particularly in a sex where any thing approaching to assurance is intolerable. We think, therefore,

of their work to effusions of Nature, spontaneously and unconsciously produced.[73] Mellor has established for English bourgeois women writers of the late eighteenth century that a "poetess" is "distinctly different from the *male* 'poet'"; one of the manifestations of this difference is a feature that puts the bourgeois woman writer into close association with the peasant poet — namely, "the adoption of the mask of the improvisatrice."[74] The author's restriction to a single publication can be explained by recourse to the same logic, for from this perspective, the work of both peasant poets and bourgeois women can only be assessed in one of two ways, either as the sensational and commendable effusions of spontaneous Nature or as mediocre imitations of bourgeois Art.[75] But, as the former definition already implies, it can be applied only to those who are not already part of the cultural scenery; spontaneous Nature inspiration, as advertised by Wieland and countless patrons of lower-class authors, can only convincingly be claimed of a first publication. Repeated publication arouses suspicions of the natural genius's corruption through exposure to Culture, so that attempts to publish a second work are viewed as illegitimate dabbling in Art, an assumption of bourgeois and male privilege. Thus, the reception history of bourgeois women shows some of the same paradigms as that of peasant authors: initial enthusiasm for and admiration of their "natural" genius (viewed as *opposed* to bourgeois culture) followed by a far more critical assessment of their literary competence, compared with works produced *within* that culture.[76]

The central factor connecting the bourgeois reception of lower-class poets with that of bourgeois women writers is their essential difference from bourgeois culture, most notably defined through work and erudition, most frequently expressed in their identification as natural, unlettered, spontaneous, uncultured, or primitive. Torgovnick has shown that, for the

---

that the ladies can never hope, in any considerable numbers, either to rival the men in literary fame; or to render themselves such rational, entertaining, and improving companions, as to reconcile us to their *learning*" (*Monthly Review*, 389; emphasis original).

[73] Cf., for example, Gibson's depiction of the reception of Katherine Philips, 80–81, as well as Tebben's "Vorwort," 7–8. Colman's and Thornton's introduction to *Poems by Eminent Ladies,* published in 1757, assumes their authors, regardless of their class background, to be "more indebted to nature for their success, than to education" (v).

[74] Mellor, 81 (the emphasis is original).

[75] Cf. Higonnet, 161, on the English context and Kord, *Namen*, 85, on the German context.

[76] Cf. Bovenschen, 160. For several examples from the reception history of German women authors in the eighteenth and nineteenth centuries, cf. Kord, *Namen*, 135–73. For a parallel demonstration of the reception history of peasant authors of either gender, cf. Klaus, *Literature of Labour*, 19.

educated, the appeal of the primitive continues undiminished.[77] The bourgeois interest in the primitive transcends historical and geographical boundaries, but frequently, regardless of its historical or geographical provenance, relies on two aspects: the expression of a distinctly discernible power relationship between the savage and the erudite; and the denial of learning, either through autodidacticism or formal education,[78] which is defined as a bourgeois and masculine trait. Both of these aspects are expressed in numerous authorial and editorial prevarications throughout the centuries and in various national contexts. The little old peasant woman in the backwoods of Kassel who supplied the Grimm brothers with oral tales thus turned out to be a literate French-speaking Huguenot, no more than middle-aged and no less than middle class.[79] Thomas Percy's source for his border ballad "Edward," which was supposedly "taken down from the recitation of an old woman," metamorphosed into Sir David Dalrymple, later Lord Hailes, a High Court judge.[80] And when the Edinburgh novelist Kate Atkinson won the Whitbread award in 1995, she was widely represented as a miner's daughter, single mother, hotel chambermaid, and "home help" who had instinctively produced something wittily postmodern, disregarding the fact that Atkinson had done postgraduate work in English literature and would presumably be well versed in postmodern theory.[81] Torgovnick's insight that behind the Western rhetoric about the primitive is often an interest in power that is belied by the aestheticism of representation[82] applies to this context as well, with the slight amendment that in this case, the power relation is *expressed* in aesthetics. However, the power relations Torgovnick describes in her study of the Western perception of the primitive are the same as that exercised on women and lower-class authors: to elevate their works to the status of Art or to refuse this

---

[77] Cf. particularly her *Gone Primitive* and *Primitive Passions*.

[78] Schaffers has examined this process for Anna Louisa Karsch (e.g., 38).

[79] Cf. Ellis, 13–36.

[80] Quotation and discussion in Fiske, 43.

[81] Cf. the articles by Tresidder and Ellison in *The Guardian*, January 1996, outlining the response to Atkinson's award, particularly the comments quoted in Ellison's article about Atkinson's presumably unconscious postmodernism. References to Atkinson's lower-class background and menial jobs appear in both articles. These three examples (the Grimm brothers' and Percy's prevarication about their sources and Atkinson's representation on the occasion of her book award) were supplied by Howard Gaskill, to whom I am also indebted for references to book sources to confirm the cases of the Grimms and Percy. Undoubtedly, many cases in which "culture" was misrepresented as "nature" could be added to these three. I thank Howard Gaskill for permitting me to use his examples here.

[82] Torgovnick, *Gone Primitive*, 79.

status re-enacts bourgeois aesthetics and simultaneously the bourgeois power to bestow or withhold that label.[83]

Feminist scholarship on predominantly bourgeois women's literature has long since established that Art as conceptualized by male philosophers, aestheticists, and literati has a gender. The reception of peasant poets, read in the context of the eighteenth-century bourgeois aesthetic debate, indicates equally clearly that Art also has a class. Both statements run counter to the most essential pretense necessary for the establishment of (masculine bourgeois) Art: that of Art's complete freedom from nonaesthetic functionality and purpose and Art's corresponding aesthetic independence from biographical, social, or political context. Once recognized as bourgeois and male, Art loses its ability to lay claim to this essential *Zweckfreiheit*,[84] which has furnished the basic premise underlying the process of canonization and the establishment of literary criticism in the nineteenth century[85] and informed many interpretive traditions, from Old Historicism to New Criticism to *Autonomieästhetik*, in the twentieth. Art reconsidered as an expression of power relations is endowed with functionality and purpose: to perpetuate the aesthetic values and perceptions of middle-class men.[86] It does this by upholding a class- and gender-based monopoly on Culture to which only few exceptions are admitted. Beyond those exceptions, the rare canonized woman author and — so far — the only two canonized lower-class writers,[87] the literature of women and peasants is either ignored entirely or subject to evaluation by

---

[83] Torgovnick, *Gone Primitive*, 82–83; the same point has been made for the German literary context in Stüssel, 218.

[84] The term is employed, for example, in Bennholdt-Thomsen and Runge's "Vorwort," 11.

[85] On the process of literary canonization in Germany, cf. Frederiksen and Watanabe-O'Kelly.

[86] This is in marked contrast to the fiction established in eighteenth-century aesthetics and perpetuated in nineteenth-century canonization and much twentieth-century criticism: that the representation of the bourgeois in bourgeois Art can be generalized to a representation of a universal *humanitas*. Cf. paradigmatically, Kaiser's statement: "Bei der Darstellung des Bürgerlichen geht es zunächst um die Konsolidierung und Propagierung von Werten der Menschlichkeit und des Gemüts . . . das Bürgertum [neigt] dazu . . . seine Ideale und Normen nicht als schichtenspezifisch, sondern als allgemein-verbindlich zu formulieren — von hier aus gewinnen Schlagworte wie Menschlichkeit, Humanität, ihre Durchschlagskraft" (53–54). This representativeness of the bourgeois for humanity in general supposedly finds its truest expression in classical literature (Kaiser, 53). Thus, the conflation of "bourgeois" (and, unstatedly, male) values as "human" values continues to furnish an essential basis for traditional literary criticism.

[87] Robert Burns and John Clare are the only lower-class authors who still command a readership, whose works exist in modern editions, and who have elicited a somewhat consistent critical and scholarly response.

different criteria from those applied to the works of "true" (bourgeois male) Artists — for example, in the declassification of their work as autobiographical and specific rather than transcendent and universal, or in the definition of the interest in the work as historical and social rather than aesthetic. Thus, traditional twentieth-century criticism continues the work begun in eighteenth-century aesthetics and validated in nineteenth-century canonization: largely unaware of the principal contradiction between its faith in Artistic *Zweckfreiheit* and the social power it wields, largely unable or unwilling to perceive nonbourgeois and nonmasculine art forms as Art, literary criticism replicates these power relations ad infinitum.

# Appendix: Short Biographies of Women Peasant Poets

*Bentley, Elizabeth* (1767–1839; England: Norwich), poet and schoolmistress. Daughter of journeyman cordwainer/shoemaker Daniel (some sources: Christopher) Bentley and Mary Lawrence, an only child. She received no formal education and was taught to read and write by her father. She read as much as she could during her childhood. In circa 1777, her father was paralyzed by a stroke; he died of a second stroke in 1783. Bentley began to write circa 1785; her mother showed her first verses to her circle of acquaintances. Aware of the shortcomings of her education, Bentley deliberately set out to improve her writing with the help of grammar books. Early literary influences included Oliver Goldsmith, Alexander Pope, Thomas Gray, William Shakespeare, and John Milton. Her works, many of which first appeared in the *Norwich Chronicle,* include many pastorals and nature poems, an ode supporting the abolition of the slave trade and a poem on cruelty to animals. Her first volume was read by nearly 2,000 subscribers and was positively reviewed in the *Gentleman's Magazine* and in the *Monthly Review*. From the proceeds of the volume, Bentley opened a small school to support herself and her mother. She received support from the Royal Literary Fund twice, in 1799 and in 1829.

Works by Elizabeth Bentley: *Genuine Poetical Compositions* (1791); "An Ode on the Glorious Victory" (1805); *Poems* (1821); *Miscellaneous Poems* (1835). One of her poems is anthologized in Feldman, 89–90.

Works about Elizabeth Bentley (see Works Cited): Blain, Clements, and Grundy, 85; Feldman, 87–89; Jackson, 26; Landry, *Muses,* 209–16; Janet Todd, *Dictionary,* 46–47. A short autobiographical account prefaces Bentley's volume.

*Candler, Ann* (née More, 1740–1814 [some sources: 1816]; England: Suffolk/Ipswich), poet and cottager. Daughter of glover William More in Suffolk and Holder (first name unknown). Candler early showed a desire to read and received books from acquaintances. Although her father offered to pay for her to learn how to write, she declined the offer because she was aware of the family's strapped financial situation, and taught herself to write by imitating her father. Although she disliked reading poetry, she usually wrote in verse. Her parents moved to Ipswich early in her youth, where her mother died at age fifty-four (ca. 1755). Candler, at that point, assumed the care of her father, with whom she lived until she married at age twenty-two (1762). Of her nine children (five sons, four daughters), three sons died as infants. Her husband drank and frequently enlisted in the army during their married life, forcing her to bail him out repeatedly; he finally deserted her in 1794. Her poetry came to the notice of a local minister, whom she thanked in verse for his charitable support of her family; this minister showed her work around and encouraged her to continue writing. During her husband's frequent absences, she lived on donations of friends and occasional labor; on one occasion (before 1794), she followed him to London, but almost immediately returned to the Ipswich workhouse. In 1801, at the time she wrote the preface to her work, she was still living in the workhouse; support for her publication came from unnamed "ladies" (one of whom was Elizabeth Cobbold) who attempted to raise enough money to furnish a room for Candler to take her out of the workhouse. In 1802, she was settled in a cottage.

Works by Ann Candler: *Poetical Attempts* (1803). Single poems appeared in the *Ipswich Journal* (1785 onward). One of her poems is anthologized in Feldman, 182–84.

Works about Ann Candler (see Works Cited): Feldman, 180–82; "Memoirs of the Life of Ann Candler," in *Poetical Attempts;* Buck, 390; Janet Todd, *Dictionary,* 72–73.

*Cave, Jane* (c. 1754–1813; England: Bristol/Newport, Monmouthshire), poet and possibly teacher. Daughter of nonconformist parents (her father, John Cave, was an exciseman and glover). She married John (some sources: Thomas) Winscom some time before 1783. Her book *Poems, on Various Subjects* appeared in 1783 with 2,000 subscribers and was reissued in 1786, with poems added to the edition in 1789 and 1794. The 1786 edition includes "An Elegy On a Maiden Name," in which she regrets the loss of her name in marriage; the 1789 edition struck a compromise, appearing as authored "By Miss Cave, Now Mrs. W — —." Cave suffered from severe and recurring headaches, which became the subject of her poems.

Works by Jane Cave: *Poems, on Various Subjects* (1783, 2nd ed. 1786, with additions in 1789 and 1794).

Works about Jane Cave (see Works Cited): Buck, 404; Janet Todd, *Dictionary,* 76.

*Collier, Mary* (1689/90 [some sources: 1679]–after 1762; England: Heyshett/Sussex, Petersfield), poet, washerwoman, brewer, and rural laborer. Collier, having lost her mother early, received no formal education. In her autobiographical remarks prefacing her *Poems on Several Occasions,* she describes herself as a self-taught recreational reader and a self-taught writer "to assist my memory." Her employers, on hearing her quote her own poetry, encouraged her writing. Her poem *The Woman's Labour,* a response to Stephen Duck's description of women's slovenliness in *The Thresher's Labour,* was published at her own expense and went through three editions within two years, from which she reaped little profit. A well-known local poet, she was often asked for occasional poetry, including a request to write on disappointed old maids, which she refused, saying she knew no such beings (she herself never married). Similar to the work of some other women peasant poets — for example, that of Anna Louisa Karsch — much of her poetry is strongly patriotic. Among others, she wrote eulogies on the poet Stephen Duck and on the marriage of George III, and poems championing women's education. Collier, writing years before "unlettered poets" became a phenomenon, made no money from her writing and continued to work as a seasonal farm laborer, washerwoman, and brewer until her death. Collier is today credited with being the first known peasant woman to publish poetry and the first woman ever to make the female double burden the subject of poetry.

Works by Mary Collier: *A Woman's Labour* (1739; 3 eds. until 1741; new ed. 1762); *Poems of Mary Collier . . . A New Edition* (1762, also as *Poems on Several Occasions,* 1762). Some of her work has been anthologized: for example, Fairer/Gerrard, 257; Lonsdale, *Eighteenth-Century Women Poets,* 171–73, and *New Oxford Book of Eighteenth-Century Verse,* 325–26.

Works about Mary Collier (see Works Cited)*:* Blain, Clements, and Grundy, 225; Ferguson, *Eighteenth-Century Women Poets,* 7–25, *First Feminists,* 257–65, and her "Introduction" to Collier and Duck; Bridget Hill, *Women,* 34–35, 157–61, 236–37; Klaus, "Stephen Duck und Mary Collier"; Landry, "Mary Collier," *Muses,* 38–40, 56–77, and "Resignation"; Rowbotham, 24–25; Shiach, 51–53; Janet Todd, *Dictionary,* 90–91; Unwin, 73–74.

*Dippen, Maria Catharina* (c. 1737–62; Germany: Eimersleben near Halberstadt), poet and farmer. Dippen was discovered by Anna Louisa Karsch on a trip to Halberstadt, during which Karsch stopped at a village and was given Dippen's poetry by the village preacher. She was described by Karsch as a woman of great poetic talent, which manifested itself primarily in the speed and spontaneity with which she wrote. Dippen wrote in High German but spoke the local dialect of her village. After a seven-year courtship, she was persuaded by friends to marry, circa 1758, a local farmer whom Karsch described as supportive of her writing and suffering from consumption. Karsch refers to her as a "mother," so she must have had at least one child. Some of her poetry, as described by Karsch, depicts the horrors of war and its consequences for the rural population. According to Karsch, Dippen was a great inspiration for numerous fledgling women poets in her village. She died of unspecified causes at age twenty-five.

Works by Maria Catharina Dippen: Dippen did not publish her poetry; Karsch cites three of her poems in her letter to Sulzer (dated June 1762, in *"Bruder in Apoll"* I, 426–30). It is unclear to what extent Karsch may have edited or reworked these poems.

Works about Maria Catharina Dippen (see Works Cited): Karsch, letter to Sulzer (June 10, 1762, in *"Bruder in Apoll"* I, 426–30).

*Glover, Jean* (1758/59–1801; Scotland: Kilmarnock/Muirkirk), poet and nomadic singer/songwriter, allegedly prostitute and thief. Daughter of the weaver James Glover and Jean Thomson, two older siblings (one brother, James, died ca. 1824). She was locally famous for her singing. After witnessing performances by nomadic actors, Glover ran away with an actor (ca. 1790). According to Robert Burns, she "was not only a — —, but also a thief; and in one or other character has visited most of the correction-houses in the west" ("Remarks on Scottish Songs and Ballads"). He credited her with the song "O'er the Moor amang the Heather," which he sent to Johnson's *Scots Musical Museum* for inclusion, and claimed that he took the song down from her "singing as she was strolling with a slight-of-hand blackguard through the country." The song was included in numerous collections and is the only one that has survived, although she must have composed many more. Glover spent the rest of her life as a traveling performer at fairs, accompanied by Richard, the "slight-of-hand blackguard" Burns mentioned. She was famed particularly for the performance of one song, "Green Grow the Rashes." She reputedly died in Letterkenny, Ireland, in 1801.

Works by Jean Glover: "O'er the Moor amang the Heather," in *The Scots Musical Museum*, ed. James Johnson (1839); also included in McCordick, II, 76, Kerrigan, 169; and Greig (with music), 148–49.

Works about Jean Glover (see Works Cited): McCue, "Burns," 43–45; Paterson, 34–37; Stewart, 8; Janet Todd, *Dictionary*, 136–37.

*Hands, Elizabeth* (birth and death dates unknown; England: Allesley near Coventry), poet and domestic servant. Little biographical information is available. A servant in the Huddesford family of Allesley near Coventry, she married a blacksmith in Bourton (near Rugby) some time before 1785 and had a daughter in 1785. She published some pieces under the pseudonym "Daphne" in the *Coventry Mercury*. Her book, *The Death of Amnon*, which was solicited by the masters of the Rugby school, attracted 1,200 subscribers, but was condescendingly reviewed.

Works by Elizabeth Hands: *The Death of Amnon* (1789, reprinted 1996). Several of her poems have been anthologized: for example, in Feldman, 258–67, and Lonsdale, *Eighteenth-Century Women Poets*, 422–29.

Works about Elizabeth Hands (see Works Cited): Blain, Clements, and Grundy, 483; Feldman, 256–58; Franklin, "Introduction" to Hands; Jackson, 144; Landry, *Muses*, 186–208; Janet Todd, *Dictionary*, 149–50.

*Karsch, Anna Louisa* (née Dürbach, 1722–91; Germany: Tirschtiegel near Crossen/Oder, Berlin), poet and cowherd. Daughter of the innkeeper and brewer Christian (?) Dürbach who died circa 1730, she was raised from age six to ten by an uncle who taught her to read; at age ten she was returned to her mother, who had remarried. In her autobiographical letters, she cites the encounter with a herder boy as the inspiration to take up reading and eventually writing; her childhood years were spent babysitting her younger siblings, herding cows, doing household and farm chores, and reading in secret. In 1737, she married the weaver Michael (?) Hirsekorn; she had three or four children (Michael, ca. 1740–?; Johann Christian, 1748–97; no names or dates available for the third and fourth children, one of whom must have died before 1748). Hirsekorn abused her and divorced her in 1748 (?) when she was pregnant with their last child. Hers was the first divorce recorded in Silesia. She was either coerced or persuaded to marry the tailor Daniel Karsch (ca. 1720–?) in 1749 (?), and had three more children (Charlotte, ca. 1753–1759/60; another daughter, died 1759/60; Karoline Luise, 1750–1802). Her husband, an alcoholic, plunged the family into poverty; throughout most of the years of their marriage, Karsch was the wage earner of the family. She toured the surrounding villages, providing impromptu poems for weddings, funerals, and christenings; her talent for poetic improvisation eventually attracted the attention of bourgeois supporters who encouraged her to move the family to Glogau in 1755, where she might have a better environment for her poetic activity. In Glogau, her patriotic poetry in praise of Frederick II enabled her to establish contact with her first patron, the Baron von Kottwitz, who eventually offered to take her to Berlin. Karsch sold her husband off to a Prussian army recruiter (1760), put her son Johann Christian (born after her divorce from Hirsekorn and disinherited by his father) into the charge of supporters, and moved to Berlin with her daughter Karoline (later, the writer Karoline von Klencke) in January 1761. In Berlin, she was initially courted for her improvisational talents and provided the entertainment at bourgeois and aristocratic gatherings; on one of these occasions, she met her patron, the poet Johann Wilhelm Ludwig Gleim (1719–1803), editor of her first volume (1764), and the aestheticist Johann Georg Sulzer (1720–79), who wrote the biographical introduction for the volume. She corresponded with Gleim for the rest of her life. After the appearance of the highly critical reviews of her first volume, her popularity waned, and Karsch made a meager living from occasional poems and appearances in society as an impromptu poet. Although her volume had been an unprecedented commercial success, earning Karsch the record honorarium of 2,000 thalers, Karsch as a woman (and a lower-class woman) was not deemed eligible to manage her own earnings; the money was held in escrow and Karsch was meagerly supported on the interest of 100 thalers per year. Karsch's repeated and persistent attempts to gain lifelong support from the court was balanced by her own generosity toward those in need: aside from supporting her two stepbrothers, son, daughter, and eventually her grandchildren, Karsch was locally famous for her willingness to support others and write poetic appeals on their behalf. Frederick II granted her an audience in 1763; Frederick William II built her a house in 1789. Aside from short poetic collections, published in pamphlet form, no second volume of poetry appeared, although she and Gleim repeatedly mentioned the possibility of a second volume in their letters. Her last years were marred by frequent altercations with her daughter, who continued to live with her until her death in 1791. Although Karsch had been forced to subsist from the interest of her royalties, which were managed by her patrons, she died a wealthy woman, leaving her children the considerable sum of 3,600 thalers. She is commonly regarded as the first professional woman writer in Germany who was capable of supporting herself and her children exclusively by her writing.

Works by Anna Louisa Karsch: *Gesänge bey Gelegenheit der Feyerlichkeiten Berlins* (1763); *Auserlesene Gedichte* (1764, reprinted in 1966 and 1996); *Einige Oden über verschiedene hohe Gegenstände* (1764); *Poetische Einfälle, Erste Sammlung* (1764); *Kleinigkeiten* (1765); *Neue Gedichte* (1772, 2nd ed. 1774, reprinted in 1996); posthumously: *Gedichte* (ed. K. L. von Klencke, 1792, 2nd ed. 1797, reprinted in 1996); *Die Karschin* (letters, 1933); *Das Lied der Karschin* (1938); *Herzgedanken* (letters, 1981); *O mir entwischt nicht, was die Menschen fühlen* (poems and letters, 1981); *Gedichte und Lebenszeugnisse* (poems and letters, 1987); *Mein Bruder in Apoll* (letters, 2 vols., 1996).

Works about Anna Louisa Karsch (see Works Cited): Anger; Becker-Cantarino, "Belloise," "Deutsche Sappho," and "Vorwort"; Bennholdt-Thomsen and Runge; Chézy, "Meine Großmutter"; Dawson; Ives; Kastinger-Riley; Klencke; Krzywon; Menzel; Mödersheim; Molzahn; Muncker; Pott; Schaffers; Schlaffer; Stüssel, 216–25; Sulzer, "Vorrede"; Gerhard Wolf. Biographical information about Karsch can be found in numerous lexica and biobibliographical dictionaries.

*Leapor, Molly (Mary)* (1722–46; England: Brackley, Northamptonshire), poet, playwright, and domestic servant. Daughter of the gardener Philip Leapor and Ann Leapor (?–1741). Leapor attended the Free School in Brackley, where she studied with Richard Cooper. She read and wrote poetry from an early age, which was at first tolerated, later sternly discouraged. After her mother's death in 1741, Leapor was sent into service. Early literary influences include John Dryden and Alexander Pope. Although she was a well-known local poet, her chances for an aristocratic sponsorship were decreased by her unattractive appearance and her refusal to behave in a sufficiently ingratiating manner. As of 1745, Leapor was befriended and patronized by Bridget Freemantle, a country gentlewoman, who appears in her poems as "Artemisia." Freemantle bought her a writing desk, sought to have her tragedy produced, and collected subscribers for a volume of Leapor's poems; her ultimate goal was to raise enough money to free Leapor from menial labor and to enable her to spend her time in writing and study. Much of Leapor's poetry concerns the discrepancy between her class and gender and her aspirations as a serious writer, a theme that also recurs in biographical accounts: according to one source, she scorched the meat while cooking because she was so taken up with her writing; according to another, she was fired from her job as a kitchen maid for similar reasons. She died of the measles in November 1746. Her first collection, *Poems upon Several Occasions*, was published posthumously with the aid of her patron Bridget Freemantle for the benefit of her father; the second appeared in 1751 under the sponsorship of Samuel Richardson. At the time of her death, she was also working on a blank-verse tragedy, *The Unhappy Father,* and another untitled drama.

Works by Mary Leapor: *Poems upon Several Occasions* (2 vols., 1748, 1751). Much of her work was anthologized: for example, in Colman/Thornton II, 17–134; Fairer/Gerrard, 284–304; and Lonsdale, *Eighteenth-Century Women Poets,* 194–217.

Works about Mary Leapor (see Works Cited): Blain, Clements, and Grundy, 640; Colman/Thornton II, 13; Blunden; Greene; Hold, 97–102; Landry, *Muses,* 78–119; Rizzo; Janet Todd, *Dictionary,* 192–93.

*Little, Janet (Jenny)* (1759–1813; Scotland: Ecclefechan/Dumfriesshire, Ayrshire), poet, domestic servant, and dairywoman. The daughter of George Little, a hired farm laborer in Nether Bogside, Little received little formal education. She worked as a domestic servant first to the Reverend Johnstone in Glasgow, then to Frances Wallace Dunlop, patron of the poet Robert Burns (1759–96), and began to write poetry during her employment there. Both Dunlop and Burns assisted her with her subscription bill for her first volume, which appeared in 1792 and from which she cleared fifty pounds. Through Dunlop's mediation, Little began a (possibly one-sided) correspondence with Burns. In 1786, after the suicide of the Earl of Loudoun, she accompanied Dunlop's daughter to Loudoun Castle, where she supervised the dairy, a position that provided Little with financial security. There, she married John Richmond (ca. 1741–1819), a fellow laborer (December 1792), becoming the stepmother to his five children. She continued to write poems after the publication of her first volume, many of them religious, but no further publications appeared.

Little's poems, written in both English and Scots, frequently treat the dilemma occasioned by her own ambitions as a writer and the bourgeois critical response; in some of these poems, Burns appears as the icon of lower-class poetic activity.

Works by Janet Little: *The Poetical Works of Janet Little* (1792). Several of her poems are anthologized in Feldman, 426–35. An electronic version of this text is available at www.lib.ucdavis.edu/English/BWRP/Works/LittJPoeti.htm.

Works about Janet Little (see bibliography): Blain, Clements, and Grundy, 662; Bold; Hilton Brown; Feldman, 423–26; Ferguson, *Eighteenth-Century Women Poets,* 91–114; Jackson, 203–4; Landry, *Muses,* 220–37; Paterson, 78–91; Stewart, 12; Janet Todd, *Dictionary,* 199.

*Masters, Mary* (1694?–1771; some sources: 1706?–1759?; England: Norwich/Ottely near Leeds/Yorkshire), poet. The daughter of a poor Norwich schoolmaster who believed that women should be educated exclusively for housework, Masters was severely discouraged from writing as a child. The preface to her poems describes her as completely uneducated and claims that her poems had to be cleaned of grammatical errors by a friend; she makes the same claim in her dedicatory poem to the Earl of Burlington, in which she describes herself as "Unskill'd in Converse, and in Schools untaught." Her first publication consists of at least ten years' worth of philosophical, religious, and love poems. John Duncombe was one of her subscribers. She was attacked in the *London Magazine* in 1738 and published a response in the *Gentleman's Magazine* in 1739. She lived in London in the early 1750s, where she had contact with, among others, Edward Cave (with whom she is said to have lived), Elizabeth Carter, Catherine Macaulay, and Samuel Johnson. Many of her poems exhibit a religious bent (she wrote several psalms in verse), others were protofeminist: she wrote about the deplorable lack of educational opportunities for women. She is said to have lived in Derbyshire from 1755 until 1757.

Works by Mary Masters: *Poems on Several Occasions* (1733); *Familiar Letters and Poems on Several Occasions* (1755). Some of her poems were anthologized in Colman/Thornton II, 147–56.

Works about Mary Masters: Blain, Clements, and Grundy, 725; Colman/Thornton II, 120; "The Preface" to Masters, *Poems;* Janet Todd, *Dictionary,* 215–16.

*Milne, Christian* (née Ross, 1773–after 1816; Scotland: Inverness/Aberdeen), poet and domestic servant. Daughter of the housewright and cabinetmaker Thomas Ross and Mary Gordon, nine (possibly more) siblings, at least seven died young. Her parents moved to Inverness when she was a child, and her mother died soon thereafter. Her father married Mary Denton, housekeeper of George Duff. After a move to Auchentoul in Banffshire, Milne was put into school; she read at age five and read poetry at age six. Her first poetic attempts date back to that time. In her own description, she derived such joy from writing that she carried a slate around with her and wrote on it whenever she was unobserved. Her stepmother, afraid that she would neglect her housework, sternly opposed her reading and writing. She read, mostly in secret, Allan Ramsay and John Milton, among others. At age fourteen, she went to Aberdeen and into service; at this stage, she began to write in earnest. She described her own working method as memorizing her own poetry throughout the week and writing down works composed in her head during the week on Sunday evenings. She destroyed much of her writing for fear of being caught. Around 1788, her father lost his entire property to pay for a partner's debt; Milne's last surviving brother died the same year on his first sea voyage. She moved to Edinburgh with her father, whom she supported on her servant's wages. At age nineteen, she had to leave service because she fell ill with consumption; she and her father then lived off of three shillings per week provided by a charitable organization. At age twenty-two, recovered from consumption, she became a servant to Dr. Jack, the principal of

King's College in Aberdeen; her father died some time during her two years of service in that household. Dr. Jack read her writing and encouraged her to continue; from that time onward, she stopped destroying her work. She married Patrick (some sources: Peter) Milne, a journeyman ship-carpenter, at age twenty-four, and had eight children with him, four born before 1805. Through the patronage of Dr. and Mrs. Livingston, the Reverend Bishop Skinner, and Mr. Ewen, she was encouraged to publish her work, which appeared by subscription in 1805 and earned her 100 pounds, money she saved in case of widowhood. Her publication caused her severe trouble with her neighbors who accused her of idleness; as a result, she felt compelled to defend her writing, pointing out that she had written her poems while doing housework. In later years, the family was troubled by financial deprivation, and Milne herself was in poor health. In 1816, she invested money in a ship. Much of her poetry uses seafaring, shipwrecks, and quayside partings as themes.

Works by Christian Milne: *Simple Poems, on Simple Subjects* (1805). Some of her poems are anthologized in Feldman, 446–50.

Works about Christian Milne (see Works Cited): Blain, Clements, and Grundy, 743; Feldman, 443–46; Jackson, 219; "Preface" to Milne; Spence.

*Pagan, Isobel* ([some sources: Isabel] *Tibbie*) (1741–1821; Scotland: Muirkirk/Ayrshire), poet, cottager, and alehouse keeper. Pagan was reputedly lame from birth and severely deformed, an unrelenting drunkard, and blessed with "great vivacity of spirit" (Paterson). Accounts of her life are limited to the anecdotal, little reliable information about her is available. She reputedly came from a well-connected family who wanted nothing to do with her, and she lived independently as of age fourteen. She was courted by Campbell (first name unknown) and had a child with him; he deserted her on the eve of their planned marriage. For more than thirty years, she lived in a hovel (granted her for free by her landlord) that became a locally famous spot where Pagan sold illegal whiskey and entertained her customers with "a constant stream of songs, most of them of dubious taste" (Stewart). She was famed for her sarcasm and her singing voice. In 1803, she published a book of her verse, supposedly dictated because she herself could not write, in which she included the following autobiographical poem:

> I was born near four miles from Nith-head,
> Where fourteen years I got my bread,
> My learning it can soon be told,
> Ten weeks, when I was seven years old.
> With a good old religious wife,

>       Who lived a quiet and sober life:
>       Indeed, she took of me more pains
>       Than some does now of forty bairns.
>       With my attention, and her skill,
>       I read the Bible no that ill;
>       And when I grew a wee thought mair,
>       I read when I had time to spare;
>       But a' the whole tract of my time,
>       I found myself inclined to rhyme:
>       When I see merry company,
>       I sing a song with mirth and glee.
>       And sometimes I the whisky pree,
>       But 'deed it's best to let it be.
>       A' my faults I will not tell,
>       I scarcely ken them a' mysel';
>       I've come through various scenes of life,
>       Yet never was a married wife.

Aside from this autobiographical account, there is only one account of her life (Paterson), which abounds with anecdotes of Pagan's violent temper and her excessive drinking. Her volume of poems was filled "with verses on subjects connected with the sports of the moors" (Paterson) and edited for propriety by the tailor William Gemmell. She was legendary for defending herself against her defamers with impromptu couplets and maligning the clergy in verse. Her best-known songs today are the still-famous Scottish folk song "Ca the Yowes" (still taught to Scottish schoolchildren) and "The Crook and Plaid." "Ca the Yowes" was included, in edited form, in Cunningham's *Songs of Scotland* and attributed to "a gentleman by the name of Pagan"; it was also included in the *Harp of Caledonia* under her full name. Burns added a verse to this song and later wrote his own version. Her purported inability to write (cf. Blain, Clements, and Grundy; Feldman; and Paterson) is disproved by a handwritten letter in the Scottish National Library. Pagan's death at the age of eighty was a local sensation, a fact that attests to her local fame as a singer and eccentric.

Works by Isobel Pagan: *A Collection of Songs and Poems on Several Occasions* (1803, reprinted in 1805 and 1808); "Ca the Yowes," in *The Scots Musical Museum,* ed. James Johnson (1839), also included in McCordick I, 1182–83, and Kerrigan, 164; "The Crook and Plaid," in *Scottish Poetry of the Eighteenth Century,* ed. George Eyre-Todd (1896), also included in McCordick I, 1183, and Kerrigan, 165. Paterson quotes four of her poems in his biographical account of her; other poems are anthologized in Feldman, 543–55.

Works about Isobel Pagan (see Works Cited): Blain, Clements, and Grundy, 823; Feldman, 538–42; McCue, "Burns," 45–46; Paterson, 113–23; Stewart, 9.

*Yearsley, Ann Cromartie* (née Cromartie, 1752–1806; England: Clifton near Bristol), poet, playwright, novelist, and milkmaid. Yearsley received no formal education. She was taught to read and write by her mother and brother; early literary models included Shakespeare, Milton, and Edward Young. She married the laborer John Yearsley (1748–1803) in 1774; six children (Henry, 1775–79; William, 1776–99; John, 1778–1814; Charles, 1780–?; Ann Cromarty, 1782–?; Jane Jones, 1784–?). Changes in landownership made selling milk unprofitable; following an exceptionally hard winter (1783–84) which brought agriculture to a standstill, the family was reduced to starvation in 1784. They were provided with food and clothing by Richard Vaughan, who also tried to find help for them among the charitable families of Bristol. Soon thereafter, Yearsley was brought into contact with the philanthropist and writer Hannah More (1745–1833), who undertook to have a volume of her poems published to rescue her from destitution. When Yearsley rebelled against More's tight control over the earnings from the volume, More dropped her; Yearsley's second volume was published under the patronage of the Earl of Bristol. Yearsley went on to publish three more volumes of poetry, a novel, a drama, and several poems and letters in pamphlet form; in many of her works, she comments on major political events of her day (the pamphlets on Louis XVI and Marie Antoinette; also several poems in *The Rural Lyre*). A well-known local writer, she was frequently asked to write occasional poems; her work appeared regularly in various journals. Her *Poem on the Inhumanity of the Slave Trade* establishes her as a fervent opponent of slavery and an abolitionist; her *Dispute* is possibly the earliest tract advocating children's rights. In her elegies on Louis XVI, she opposed capital punishment. After circa 1791, she ran an apparently successful circulating library in the resort community Bristol Hotwells. Although biographers have frequently claimed that Yearsley died childless, destitute, and insane, at least three of her children (John, Ann, and Jane) survived her, and there is no evidence of poverty or insanity at the end of her life.

Works by Ann Yearsley: *Poems, on Several Occasions* (3 eds. in 1785, 4th ed. 1786); *Poems, on Various Subjects* (1787; reprinted in 1994); *A Poem on the Inhumanity of the Slave Trade* (1788); *Stanzas of Woe* (1790); *The Dispute: Letter to the Public from the Milkwoman* (1791); *Earl Good-*

*win: A Historical Play* (1791); *Reflections on the Death of Louis XVI* (1793); *Sequel to Reflections on the Death of Louis XVI* (1793); *An Elegy on Marie Antoinette of Austria, Ci-devant Queen of France: With a Poem on the Last Interview between the King of Poland and Loraski* (1794); *The Royal Captives: A Fragment of Secret History* (1795); *The Rural Lyre: A Volume of Poems* (1796; reprinted in 1996). Works by Ann Yearsley are included in numerous anthologies, including Feldman, 837–43; Fairer/Gerrard, 439–51; Wu, 150–70.

Works about Ann Yearsley (see Works Cited): Alvarez Saar/Schofield; Anonymous, "An Historical Milkwoman"; Blain, Clements, and Grundy, 1197; Carter, 192–232; Demers; Feldman, 831–37; Ferguson, *First Feminists*, 380–97, and "Unpublished Poems"; Jackson, 383–85; Landry, *Muses*, 120–85; Rizzo, "Patron," 259–62; Southey, 125–34, 195–98; Janet Todd, *Dictionary*, 336–37; Tompkins; Unwin, 77–81; Waldron; Zionkowski, 98–106.

# Works Cited

Abel, Wilhelm. *Geschichte der deutschen Landwirtschaft vom frühen Mittelalter bis zum 19. Jahrhundert.* Stuttgart: Eugen Ulmer, 1962.

———. *Massenarmut und Hungerkrisen im vorindustriellen Deutschland.* Göttingen: Vandenhoeck & Ruprecht, 1986.

Abrams, Lynn, and Elizabeth Harvey, eds. *Gender Relations in German History: Power, Agency and Experience from the Sixteenth to the Twentieth Century.* Durham, NC: Duke UP, 1993.

Abrams, M. H. *The Mirror and the Lamp: Romantic Theory and the Critical Tradition.* New York: W. W. Norton, 1958.

Achilles, Walter. *Die Lage der hannoverschen Landbevölkerung im späten 18. Jahrhundert.* Hildesheim: August Lax, 1982.

Alvarez Saar, Doreen, and Mary Anne Schofield, eds. *Eighteenth-Century Anglo-American Women Novelists: A Critical Reference Guide.* New York and London: G. K. Hall, 1996.

"An Historical Milkwoman." *Eclectic Magazine* (March 1856): 393–98.

Anger, Alfred. "Anna Louisa Karsch." In *Literatur Lexikon: Autoren und Werke deutscher Sprache,* vol. 6, edited by Walther Killy, 244–46. Munich: Bertelsmann, 1990.

———. "Anna Louisa Karschin." In *Deutsche Dichter: Leben und Werk deutschsprachiger Autoren,* edited by Gunter E. Grimm and Frank Rainer Max. Vol. 3: *Aufklärung und Empfindsamkeit,* 1141–44. Stuttgart: Reclam, 1988.

———. "Nachwort." In Karsch, Anna Louisa, *Auserlesene Gedichte. Faksimile-Nachdruck,* edited by Alfred Anger, 3–18. Stuttgart: Metzler, 1966.

———. "Nachwort." In Karsch, Anna Louisa, *Gedichte und Lebenszeugnisse,* edited by Alfred Anger, 184–203. Stuttgart: Reclam, 1987.

"Anna Louisa Durbach." *Gentleman's Magazine* 34 (1764): 558–59.

"Anna Louisa Karsch(in), geb. Dürbach." *Lexikon deutschsprachiger Schriftsteller. Von den Anfängen bis zum Ausgang des 19. Jahrhunderts.* Edited by K. Böttcher, H. Greiner-Mai, K. Krolop, and H. Prosche, 299–300. Leipzig: VEB Bibliographisches Institut, 1987.

"Anne Luise Karschin." *Lexikon deutscher Dichter und Prosaisten,* vol. 2. Edited by K. H. Jördens. 607–40. Hildesheim, New York: Georg Olms, 1970 [1807].

Armstrong, Isobel, and Virginia Blair, eds. *Women's Poetry in the Enlightenment: The Making of a Canon, 1730–1820.* London: Macmillan P, 1999.

Armstrong, Nancy. *Desire and Domestic Fiction: A Political History of the Novel.* New York and Oxford: Oxford UP, 1987.

Arnim, Ludwig Achim von. "*Ungedruckte Briefe der Karschin.*" In *Unbekannte Aufsätze und Gedichte. Mit einem Anhang von Clemens Brentano,* edited by Ludwig Geiger, 55–74. Berlin: Gebrüder Paetel, 1892.

Ashraf, Phyllis Mary. *Englische Arbeiterliteratur vom 18. Jahrhundert bis zum ersten Weltkrieg: Entwicklungstendenzen im Überblick.* Berlin and Weimar: Aufbau, 1980.

Ashton, T. S. *An Economic History of England: The 18th Century.* London: Methuen, 1955.

Asmus, Helmut. "Die politische Entwicklung in Magdeburg vom Ausgang des 18. Jahrhunderts bis zum ersten Weltkrieg, unter besonderer Berücksichtigung der Geschichte der Magdeburger Arbeiterbewegung." In *Bauer und Landarbeiter im Kapitalismus in der Magdeburger Börde: Zur Geschichte des dörflichen Alltags vom Ausgang des 18. Jahrhunderts bis zum Beginn des 20. Jahrhunderts,* edited by Hans-Jürgen Rach and Bernhard Weissel, 299–324. Berlin: Akademie-Verlag, 1982.

Badinter, Elisabeth. *Die Mutterliebe. Geschichte eines Gefühls vom 17. Jahrhundert bis heute.* Munich: Piper, 1991.

Balet, Leo (with E. Gerhard). *Die Verbürgerlichung der deutschen Kunst, Literatur und Musik im 18. Jahrhundert.* Strasbourg, Leipzig, and Zurich: Heitz, 1936.

Barber, Mary. *Poems on Several Occasions.* London: Printed for C. Rivington, at the Bible and Crown in St. Paul's Church-Yard, 1734.

———. *The Poetry of Mary Barber, ?1690–1757.* Edited by Bernard Tucker. Lewiston, ME: Edwin Mellen, 1992.

———. "Verses said to be written by Mrs. Mary Barber. To a Friend desiring an Account of her Health in Verse." *Gentleman's Magazine* 7 (1737): 179.

Barkhausen, Max. "Government Control and Free Enterprise in Western Germany and the Low Countries in the Eighteenth Century." In *Essays in European Economic History 1500–1800,* edited by Peter Earle, 212–73. Oxford: Clarendon P, 1974.

Barndt, Kerstin. "'Mein Dasein ward unvermerkt das allgemeine Gespräch.' Anna Louisa Karsch im Spiegel zeitgenössischer Popularphilosophie." *Anna Louisa Karsch (1722–1791): Von schlesischer Kunst und Berliner "Natur." Ergebnisse des Symposiums zum 200. Todestag der Dichterin,* edited by Anke Bennholdt-Thomsen and Anita Runge, 162–76. Göttingen: Wallstein, 1992.

Barrell, John. *English Literature in History 1730–80: An Equal, Wide Survey.* London: Hutchinson, 1983.

———. *The Idea of Landscape and the Sense of Place 1730–1840: An Approach to the Poetry of John Clare.* Cambridge: Cambridge UP, 1972.

———. *Poetry, Language and Politics.* Manchester: Manchester UP, 1988.

Barrell, John, and John Bull, eds. *The Penguin Book of English Pastoral Verse.* London: Allen Lane, 1974.

Baumann, Gerd, ed. *The Written Word: Literacy in Transition.* Oxford: Clarendon P, 1986.

Baumgart, Peter, and Ulrich Schmilewski, eds. *Kontinuität und Wandel: Schlesien zwischen Österreich und Preußen.* Sigmaringen: Jan Thorbecke, 1990.

Baur, Uwe. *Dorfgeschichte: Zur Entstehung und gesellschaftlichen Funktion einer literarischen Gattung im Vormärz.* Munich: Wilhelm Fink, 1978.

Bausinger, Hermann. "Bürgerlichkeit und Kultur." In *Bürger und Bürgerlichkeit im 19. Jahrhundert,* edited by Jürgen Kocka, 121–42. Göttingen: Vandenhoeck & Ruprecht, 1987.

Becker-Cantarino, Barbara. "'Belloisens Lebenslauf': Zu Dichtung und Autobiographie bei Anna Luisa Karsch." In *Gesellige Vernunft: Zur Kultur der literarischen Aufklärung,* edited by Ortrud Gutjahr, Wilhelm Kühlmann, and Wolf Wucherpfennig, 13–22. Würzburg: Königshausen & Neumann, 1993.

———. "Die 'deutsche Sappho' und 'des Herzogs Spießgesell': Anna Louisa Karsch und Goethe." In *Anna Louisa Karsch (1722–1791): Von schlesischer Kunst und Berliner "Natur." Ergebnisse des Symposiums zum 200. Todestag der Dichterin,* edited by Anke Bennholdt-Thomsen and Anita Runge, 110–31. Göttingen: Wallstein, 1992.

———. *Der lange Weg zur Mündigkeit: Frau und Literatur (1500–1800).* Stuttgart: Metzler, 1987.

———. "Leben als Text: Briefe als Ausdrucks- und Verständigungsmittel in der Briefkultur und Literatur des 18. Jahrhunderts." In *Frauen Literatur Geschichte: Schreibende Frauen vom Mittelalter bis zur Gegenwart,* 2nd ed., edited by Hiltrud Gnüg and Renate Möhrmann, 129–46, 684–85. Stuttgart and Weimar: Metzler, 1999.

———. "Nachwort." In Sophie von La Roche. *Geschichte des Fräuleins von Sternheim,* edited by Barbara Becker-Cantorino, 381–415. Stuttgart: Reclam, 1983.

———. "(Sozial)Geschichte der Frau in Deutschland, 1500–1800." In *Die Frau von der Reformation zur Romantik: Die Situation der Frau vor dem Hintergrund der Literatur- und Sozialgeschichte,* edited by Barbara Becker-Cantarino, 243–93. Bonn: Bouvier, 1980.

———. "Vorwort." Anna Louisa Karsch. In *Gedichte. Nach der Dichterin Tode herausgegeben von ihrer Tochter Caroline Luise von Klencke*, edited by Barbara Becker-Cantarino. Reprint, Karben: Verlag Petra Wald, 1996.

Bennholdt-Thomsen, Anke, and Anita Runge. "Vorwort." In *Anna Louisa Karsch (1722–1791): Von schlesischer Kunst und Berliner "Natur." Ergebnisse des Symposiums zum 200. Todestag der Dichterin*, edited by Anke Bennholdt-Thomsen and Anita Runge, 7–11. Göttingen: Wallstein, 1992.

———, eds. *Anna Louisa Karsch (1722–1791): Von schlesischer Kunst und Berliner "Natur." Ergebnisse des Symposiums zum 200. Todestag der Dichterin*. Göttingen: Wallstein, 1992.

Bentley, [Elizabeth]. *Genuine Poetical Compositions on Various Subjects, by E. Bentley*. Norwich: Crouse and Stevenson, 1791.

Berindei, Dan, Wolfgang Gesemann, Alfred Hoffmann, Walter Leitsch, Albrecht Timm, and Sergij Vilfan, eds. *Der Bauer Mittel- und Osteuropas im sozioökonomischen Wandel des 18. und 19. Jahrhunderts*. Cologne and Vienna: Böhlau, 1973.

Berkner, Lutz K. "Inheritance, Land Tenure and Peasant Family Structure: A German Regional Comparison." In *Family and Inheritance: Rural Society in Western Europe, 1200–1800*, edited by Jack Goody, Joan Thirsk, and E. P. Thompson, 71–95. Cambridge: Cambridge UP, 1976.

Bernstein, John Andrew. "Shaftesbury's Optimism and Eighteenth-Century Social Thought." In *Anticipations of the Enlightenment in England, France, and Germany*, edited by Alan Charles Kors and Paul J. Korshin, 86–101. Philadelphia: U of Pennsylvania P, 1987.

Beveridge, Sir William (with L. Liepmann, F. J. Nicholas, M. E. Rayner, M. Wretts-Smith, et al.). *Prices and Wages in England from the Twelfth to the Nineteenth Century*. 4 vols. London, New York, and Toronto: Longmans, Green, 1939.

Biermann, Karlheinrich. "Zwischen Bürger und 'Volk': Zum gesellschaftlichen Rollenverständnis des Schriftstellers nach der Julirevolution von 1830 (Victor Hugo)." *Zum Funktionswandel der Literatur*, edited by Peter Bürger, 127–46. Frankfurt am Main: Suhrkamp, 1983.

Blackwell, Jeannine. "Weibliche Gelehrsamkeit oder die Grenzen der Toleranz: die Fälle Karsch, Naubert und Gottsched." In *Lessing und die Toleranz: Sonderband zum Lessing Yearbook*, edited by Peter Freimark, Franklin Kopitzsch, and Helga Slessarev, 325–39. Detroit: Wayne State UP, 1986.

Blain, Virginia, Patricia Clements, and Isobel Grundy, eds. *The Feminist Companion to Literature in English: Women Writers from the Middle Ages to the Present*. London: B. T. Batsford, 1990.

Blaschke, Monika. "No Way but Out: German Women in Mecklenburg." In *Peasant Maids — City Women: From the European Countryside to Urban America*, edited by Christiane Harzig, 25–56. Ithaca, NY, and London: Cornell UP, 1997.

Blickle, Peter. "'Handarbeit,' 'gemeiner Mann' und 'Widerstand' in der vorrevolutionären Gesellschaft." In *Vom Elend der Handarbeit: Probleme historischer Unterschichtenforschung*, edited by Hans Mommsen and Winfried Schulze, 234–39. Stuttgart: Klett, 1981.

———, ed. *Landgemeinde und Stadtgemeinde in Mitteleuropa: Ein struktureller Vergleich.* Munich: R. Oldenbourg, 1991.

Blunden, Edmund. "A Northamptonshire Poetess: Glimpses of an Eighteenth-Century Prodigy." *Journal of the Northamptonshire Natural History Society and Field Club* 28 (1936): 59–74.

Bold, Valentina. "Janet Little 'The Scotch Milkmaid' and 'Peasant Poetry.'" *Scottish Literary Journal* 20, 2 (1993): 21–30.

Bovenschen, Silvia. *Die imaginierte Weiblichkeit: Exemplarische Untersuchungen zu kulturgeschichtlichen und literarischen Präsentationsformen des Weiblichen.* Frankfurt am Main: Suhrkamp, 1979.

Bowden, Peter J. "Agricultural Prices, Wages, Farm Profits, and Rents." In *The Agrarian History of England and Wales. Vol. V, 2 (1640–1750)*, edited by Joan Thirsk, 1–118. Cambridge: Cambridge UP, 1985.

Brandt, Peter, ed. (with Thomas Hofmann and Reiner Zilkenat). *Preußen: Zur Sozialgeschichte eines Staates. Eine Darstellung in Quellen.* Reinbek: Rowohlt, 1981.

Breen, Jennifer. "Introduction." *Women Romantics 1785–1832: Writing in Prose,* edited by Jennifer Breen, xix-xl. London: J. M. Dent, 1996.

———, ed. *Women Romantics 1785–1832: Writing in Prose.* London: J. M. Dent, 1996.

Brinker-Gabler, Gisela. "Anna Louisa Karsch." In *Deutsche Dichterinnen vom 16. Jahrhundert bis zur Gegenwart: Gedichte und Lebensläufe*, edited by Gisela Brinker-Gabler, 134–41. Frankfurt am Main: Fischer, 1978.

Brown, Hilton. "Burns and the Scottish Milkmaid." *Burns Chronicle*, 2nd ser. 25 (1950): 15–20.

Brown, John. *A Dissertation on the Rise, Union, and Power, the Progressions, Separations, and Corruptions, of Poetry and Music. To Which Is Prefixed, the Cure of Saul. A Sacred Ode. Written by Dr. Brown.* London: Printed for L. Davis and C. Reymers, 1763.

Brown, Mary Ellen. "Old Singing Women and the Canons of Scottish Balladry and Song." In *A History of Scottish Women's Writing*, edited by Douglas Gifford and Dorothy McMillan, 44–57. Edinburgh: Edinburgh UP, 1997.

Brümmer, Franz. *Deutsches Dichter-Lexikon. Biographische und bibliographische Mittheilungen über deutsche Dichter aller Zeiten. Unter besonderer Berücksichtigung der Gegenwart für Freunde der Literatur zusammengestellt*. 2 vols. Eichstätt and Stuttgart: Krüll, 1876.

———. *Lexikon der deutschen Dichter und Prosaisten von den ältesten Zeiten bis zum Ende des 18. Jahrhunderts*. Leipzig: Reclam, 1884.

Brunner, Otto. "Europäisches Bauerntum." In *Neue Wege der Verfassungs- und Sozialgeschichte*, 3rd ed., edited by Otto Brunner, 103–27. Göttingen: Vandenhoeck & Ruprecht, 1980.

Buck, Claire, ed. *The Bloomsbury Guide to Women's Literature*. New York: Prentice Hall, 1992.

Bürger, Christa. *Leben Schreiben: Die Klassik, die Romantik und der Ort der Frauen*. Stuttgart: Metzler, 1990.

———. "Philosophische Ästhetik und Populärästhetik: Vorläufige Überlegungen zu den Ungleichzeitigkeiten im Prozeß der Institutionalisierung der Kunstautonomie." In *Zum Funktionswandel der Literatur*, edited by Peter Bürger, 107–26. Frankfurt am Main: Suhrkamp, 1983.

Bürger, Gottfried August. "Herzensausguß über Volkspoesie." In *Sturm und Drang: Weltanschauliche und ästhetische Schriften*, vol. 2, edited by Peter Müller, 332–37. Berlin and Weimar: Aufbau Verlag, 1978.

———. "Vorrede zur ersten Ausgabe der Gedichte (April 1778)." In *Sturm und Drang: Weltanschauliche und ästhetische Schriften*, vol. 2, edited by Peter Müller, 358–66. Berlin and Weimar: Aufbau Verlag, 1978.

Bürger, Peter. "Institution Literatur und Modernisierungsprozeß." In *Zum Funktionswandel der Literatur*, edited by Peter Bürger, 9–32. Frankfurt am Main: Suhrkamp, 1983.

———. *Zur Kritik der idealistischen Ästhetik*. Frankfurt am Main: Suhrkamp, 1983.

———, ed. *Zum Funktionswandel der Literatur*. Frankfurt am Main: Suhrkamp, 1983.

Burness, Catriona. "'Kept some steps behind him': Women in Scotland 1780–1920." In *A History of Scottish Women's Writing*, edited by Douglas Gifford and Dorothy McMillan, 103–18. Edinburgh: Edinburgh UP, 1997.

Burns, Robert. "Answer to a Tiviotdale Farmer's Wife's Epistle, March 22." MS Acc. 7748, National Library of Scotland.

Burns, Robert, and Frances Dunlop. *Robert Burns and Mrs. Dunlop: Correspondence Now Published in Full for the First Time*. Edited by William Wallace. 2 vols. New York: Dodd, Mead, 1898.

Butler, Judith. "Contingent Foundations: Feminism and the Question of 'Postmodernism'." In *Feminists Theorize the Political*, edited by Judith Butler and Jean W. Scott, 3–21. New York: Routledge, 1992.

———. *Gender Trouble: Feminism and the Subversion of Identity*. New York: Routledge, 1990.

———. "Gender Trouble, Feminist Theory, and Psychoanalytic Discourse." In *Feminism/Postmodernism*, edited by Linda J. Nicholson, 324–40. New York and London: Routledge, 1990.

———. "Imitation and Gender Insubordination." In *Inside/Out: Lesbian Theories, Gay Theories*, edited by Diana Fuss, 13–31. New York: Routledge, 1991.

———. "Performative Acts and Gender Constitution: An Essay in Phenomenology and Feminist Theory." In *Performing Feminisms: Feminist Critical Theory and Theatre*, edited by Sue-Ellen Case, 270–82. Baltimore and London: Johns Hopkins UP, 1990.

Butler, Judith, and Jean W. Scott, eds. *Feminists Theorize the Political*. New York: Routledge, 1992.

"By the Reviewers, a Proclamation." *Monthly Review* 58 (1778): 162.

Calm, Marie. "Die Künste." In *Bildung und Kultur bürgerlicher Frauen 1850–1918. Eine Quellendokumentation aus Anstandsbüchern und Lebenshilfen für Mädchen und Frauen als Beitrag zur weiblichen literarischen Sozialisation*, edited by Günter Häntzschel, 353–60. Tübingen: Niemeyer, 1986.

Candler, Ann. *Poetical Attempts, By Ann Candler, A Suffolk Cottager; with a short Narrative of her Life*. Ipswich: John Raw, 1803.

Carter, Jefferson Matthew. "The Unlettered Muse: The Uneducated Poets and the Concept of Natural Genius in Eighteenth-Century England." Ph.D. diss., University of Arizona, 1972.

Cave, [Jane]. *Poems, on Various Subjects, Entertaining, Elegiac, and Religious. With a Few Select Poems, from other Authors. By Miss Cave, Now Mrs. W——*. 2d ed. Shrewsbury: T. Wood, 1789.

Chambers, Robert, coll. *The Scottish Songs*. 2 vols. Edinburgh: Ballantyne, 1829.

Charles, Lindsey, and Lorna Duffin, eds. *Women and Work in Pre-Industrial England*. London, Sydney, and Dover, NH: Croom Helm, 1985.

Chartres, John, and David Hey, eds. *English Rural Society, 1500–1800: Essays in Honour of Joan Thirsk*. Cambridge: Cambridge UP, 1990.

Chézy, Helmina von. "Erinnerungen aus meinem Leben. Von der Herausgeberin." In *Aurikeln. Eine Blumengabe von deutschen Händen, herausgegeben von Helmina von Chezy, geb. Freyin von Klencke*, 3–190. Berlin: Bei Duncker & Humblot, 1818.

———. "Meine Großmutter Anna Louisa Karschin." *Unvergessenes: Denkwuerdigkeiten aus dem Leben*, vol 1, 3–110. Leipzig: F. A. Brockhaus, 1858.

Cocalis, Susan. "Der Vormund will Vormund sein: Zur Problematik der weiblichen Unmündigkeit im 18. Jahrhundert." In *Gestaltet und Gestaltend: Frauen in der deutschen Literatur,* edited by Marianne Burkhard, 33–55. Amsterdam: Rodopi, 1980.

———, ed. and trans. *The Defiant Muse: German Feminist Poems from the Middle Ages to the Present.* New York: Feminist P, 1986.

Cole, G. D. H., and Raymond Postgate. *The British People 1746–1946.* London: Methuen, 1961.

Collier, Mary. "Some Remarks of the Author's Life Drawn by Herself." In *First Feminists: British Women Writers 1578–1799,* edited by Moira Ferguson, 264–65. Bloomington, IN.: Indiana UP, 1985.

Collier, Mary, and Stephen Duck. *The Thresher's Labour [Stephen Duck] (1736) and The Woman's Labour [Mary Collier] (1739).* Introduction by Moira Ferguson. The Augustan Reprint Society Publication no. 230. Los Angeles: UCLA William Andrews Clark Memorial Library, 1985.

[Colman, George, and Bonnell Thornton, eds.] *Poems by Eminent Ladies, to Which Is Prefixed, a Short Account of Each Writer.* 2 vols. Dublin: D. Chamberlaine, 1757.

Cooper, J. P. "Patterns of Inheritance and Settlement by Great Landowners from the Fifteenth to the Eighteenth Centuries." In *Family and Inheritance: Rural Society in Western Europe, 1200–1800,* edited by Jack Goody, Joan Thirsk, and E. P. Thompson, 192–327. Cambridge: Cambridge UP, 1976.

"Copy of a Letter from a Gentleman, Residing on Clifton-Hill, Near Bristol, to a Friend in London, Dated Nov. 30, 1784." *Gentleman's Magazine* 54 (1784): 897.

Cottle, Joseph. *Reminiscences of Samuel Taylor Coleridge and Robert Southey.* London: Houlston & Stoneman, 1847. Reprint, Highgate.: Lime Tree Bower P, 1970.

Crawford, Margaret. *The Gardener's Daughter from Stow. Featuring Rustic Lays on the Braes of the Gala Water.* Compiled and edited by David Roseburgh. Galashiels: Reiver P, 1999.

Crawford, Robert, ed. *Robert Burns and Cultural Authority.* Edinburgh: Edinburgh UP, 1997.

Cressy, David. *Literacy and the Social Order: Reading and Writing in Tudor and Stuart England.* Cambridge: Cambridge UP, 1980.

Currie, J[ames]. "Prefatory Remarks." *The Works of Robert Burns; with an Account of His Life, and a Criticism on His Writings. To Which are prefixed, Some Observations on the Character and Condition of the Scottish Peasantry,* vol. 1, edited by James Currie, 1–31. London: T. Cadell and W. Davies; Edinburgh: W. Creech, 1806.

Damm, Sigrid. *Christiane und Goethe: Eine Recherche*, 9th ed. Frankfurt am Main: Insel, 1999.

Davidoff, Leonore. *Family Fortunes: Men and Women of the English Middle Class, 1780–1850*. London: Routledge, 1992.

Davies, Mererid Puw, Beth Linklater, and Gisela Shaw, eds. *Autobiography by Women in German*. Oxford, Bern, and Berlin: Peter Lang, 2000.

Davison, Dennis, ed. *The Penguin Book of Eighteenth-Century English Verse*. Middlesex: Penguin Books, 1975.

Dawson, Ruth P. "Selbstbezähmung und weibliche Misogynie: Verserzählungen von Frauen im 18. Jahrhundert." In *Der Widerspenstigen Zähmung: Studien zur bezwungenen Weiblichkeit in der Literatur vom Mittelalter bis zur Gegenwart*, edited by Sylvia Wallinger and Monika Jonas, 133–42. Innsbruck: Institut für Germanistik der Universität Innsbruck, 1986.

Dedner, Burghard. *Topos, Ideal und Realitätspostulat: Studien zur Darstellung des Landlebens im Roman des 18. Jahrhunderts*. Tübingen: Niemeyer, 1969.

———. "Vom Schäferleben zur Agrarwirtschaft: Poesie und Ideologie des 'Landlebens' in der deutschen Literatur des 18. Jahrhunderts." *Jahrbuch der Jean-Paul-Gesellschaft* 7 (1972): 40–83.

Demers, Patricia. "'For mine's a stubborn and a savage will': 'Lactilla' (Ann Yearsley) and 'Stella' (Hannah More) Reconsidered." *Huntington Library Quarterly* (Spring 1993): 135–50.

Dietrick, Linda. "Women Writers and the Authorization of Literary Practice." In *Unwrapping Goethe's Weimar: Essays in Cultural Studies and Local Knowledge*, edited by Burkhard Henke, Susanne Kord, and Simon Richter, 213–32. Rochester, NY: Camden House, 2000.

Doody, Margaret Anne. *The Daring Muse: Augustan Poetry Reconsidered*. Cambridge: Cambridge UP, 1985.

———. "Sensuousness in the Poetry of Eighteenth-Century Women Poets." In *Women's Poetry in the Enlightenment: The Making of a Canon, 1730–1820*, edited by Isobel Armstrong and Virginia Blain, 3–32. London: Macmillan P, 1999.

———. "Swift among the Women." *The Yearbook of English Studies* 18 (1988): 68–92.

Dotzler, Bernhard J. "'Seht doch wie ihr vor Eifer schäumet . . .' Zum männlichen Diskurs über Weiblichkeit um 1800." *Jahrbuch der deutschen Schillergesellschaft* 30 (1986): 339–82.

Douglas, Sir George, ed. *Poems of the Scottish Minor Poets, from the Age of Ramsay to David Gray*. London: Walter Scott, 1891.

Duden, Barbara. "Das schöne Eigentum: Zur Herausbildung des bürgerlichen Frauenbildes an der Wende vom 18. zum 19. Jahrhundert." *Kursbuch* 47 (1977): 125–40.

Duff, William. *An Essay on Original Genius, and Its Various Modes of Exertion in Philosophy and the Fine Arts, Particularly in Poetry*. London: Edward & Charles Dilly, 1767.

Duncan, Bruce. *Lovers, Parricides, and Highwaymen: Aspects of Sturm und Drang Drama*. Rochester, NY: Camden House, 1999.

Duncombe, John. *The Feminiad: A Poem (1754)*. The Augustan Reprint Society Publication no. 207. Los Angeles: UCLA William Andrews Clark Memorial Library, 1981.

Earle, Peter, ed. *Essays in European Economic History 1500–1800*. Oxford: Clarendon P, 1974.

Eger, Elizabeth. "Fashioning a Female Canon: Eighteenth-Century Women Poets and the Politics of the Anthology." In *Women's Poetry in the Enlightenment: The Making of a Canon, 1730–1820*, edited by Isobel Armstrong and Virginia Blain, 201–15. London: Macmillan, 1999.

Ehrenpreis, Irvin. "Poverty and Poetry: Representations of the Poor in Augustan Literature." *Studies in Eighteenth-Century Culture* 1 (1971): 3–35.

Elias, A. C. "A Manuscript Book of Constantia Grierson's." *Swift Studies* 2 (1987): 33–56.

Ellis, John M. *One Fairy Story Too Many: The Brothers Grimm and Their Tales*. Chicago and London: U of Chicago P, 1983.

Ellison, Mike. "Rushdie Makes It a Losing Double." *The Guardian*, January 24, 1996, p. 3, col. 3.

Engell, James. *The Creative Imagination: Enlightenment to Romanticism*. Cambridge: Harvard UP, 1981.

Eyre-Todd, George, ed. *Scottish Poetry of the Eighteenth Century*. Glasgow: W. Hodge, 1896.

Fagan, Patrick, ed. *A Georgian Celebration: Irish Poets of the Eighteenth Century*. Dublin: Branar, 1989.

Fairer, David, and Christine Gerrard, eds. *Eighteenth-Century Poetry: An Annotated Anthology*. Oxford: Blackwell, 1999.

Fechner, Jörg-Ulrich. "Leidenschafts- und Charakterdarstellung im Drama." In *Sturm und Drang*, edited by W. Hinck, 175–91. Kronberg/Taunus: Athenäum, 1978.

Feldman, Paula R., ed. *British Women Poets of the Romantic Era: An Anthology*. Baltimore and London: Johns Hopkins UP, 1997.

Ferguson, Moira. "'The Cause of My Sex': Mary Scott and the Female Literary Tradition." *The Huntington Library Quarterly* 50, 4 (Autumn 1987): 359–77.

———. *Eighteenth-Century Women Poets: Nation, Class, and Gender.* Albany, NY: SUNY P, 1995.

———. "Feministische Polemik: Schriften englischer Frauen von der Spätrenaissance bis zur Französischen Revolution." Translated by Irina Rajewski. *Querelles: Jahrbuch für Frauenforschung* 2 (1997): 292–315.

———, ed. *First Feminists: British Women Writers 1578–1799.* Bloomington, IN: Indiana UP, 1985.

———. "Introduction." In *First Feminists: British Women Writers 1578–1799,* edited by Moira Ferguson, 1–50. Bloomington, IN: Indiana UP, 1985.

———. "The Unpublished Poems of Ann Yearsley." *Tulsa Studies in Women's Literature* 12, 1 (Spring 1993): 13–46.

Fichte, Johann Gottlieb. "Erster Anhang des Naturrechts: Grundriss des Familienrechts." *Fichtes Werke,* vol. 3, edited by Immanuel Hermann Fichte, 304–68. Berlin: Walter de Gruyter, 1971.

Fiske, Roger. *Scotland in Music: A European Enthusiasm.* Cambridge: Cambridge UP, 1983.

Foss, Michael. *The Age of Patronage: The Arts in Society 1660–1750.* London: Hamish Hamilton, 1971.

Fowler, Alastair. "Country House Poems: The Politics of a Genre." *The Seventeenth Century* 1, 1 (January 1986): 1–14.

Franklin, Caroline. "Introduction." In Elizabeth Hands. *The Death of Amnon: A Poem.* [Bound with: Ann Yearsley, *The Rural Lyre: A Volume of Poems,* edited by Caroline Franklin.] Coventry: N. Rollason, 1789. Reprint, London: Routledge, 1996.

———. "Introduction." In Ann Yearsley. *The Rural Lyre: A Volume of Poems.* [Bound with: Elizabeth Hands, *The Death of Amnon: A Poem,* edited by Caroline Franklin.] Coventry: N. Rollason, 1789. Reprint, London: Routledge, 1996.

Franz, Günther. *Geschichte des deutschen Bauernstandes vom frühen Mittelalter bis zum 19. Jahrhundert.* Stuttgart: Eugen Ulmer, 1976.

Frederiksen, Elke. "The Challenge of 'Missing Contents' for Canon Formation in German Studies." In *Gender and Germanness: Cultural Productions of Nation,* edited by Patricia Herminghouse and Magda Mueller, 101–12. Providence, RI, and Oxford: Berghahn, 1997.

Freemantle, Bridget. "To John *****, Esq." *Monthly Review* 5 (June 1751): 23–29.

Frels, Wilhelm. *Deutsche Dichterhandschriften von 1400 bis 1900: Gesamtkatalog der eigenhändigen Handschriften deutscher Dichter in den Bibliotheken und Archiven Deutschlands, Österreichs, der Schweiz und der CSR*. 1934. Reprint, Stuttgart: Hiersemann, 1970.

French, Lorely. *German Women As Letter Writers: 1750–1850*. Madison, WI, and London: Associated University P, 1996.

Frevert, Ute. "Bürgerliche Meisterdenker und das Geschlechterverhältnis: Konzepte, Erfahrungen, Visionen an der Wende vom 18. zum 19. Jahrhundert." In *Bürgerinnen und Bürger: Geschlechterverhältnisse im 19. Jahrhundert*, edited by Ute Frevert, 17–48. Göttingen: Vandenhoeck & Ruprecht, 1988.

———. "Einleitung." In *Bürgerinnen und Bürger: Geschlechterverhältnisse im 19. Jahrhundert*, edited by Ute Frevert, 11–16. Göttingen: Vandenhoeck & Ruprecht, 1988.

———. *Frauen-Geschichte: Zwischen bürgerlicher Verbesserung und neuer Weiblichkeit*. Frankfurt am Main: Suhrkamp, 1986.

———. *Women in German History: From Bourgeois Emancipation to Sexual Liberation*. Translated by Stuart McKinnon-Evans with Terry Bond and Barbara Norden. Oxford and New York: Berg, 1988.

———, ed. *Bürgerinnen und Bürger: Geschlechterverhältnisse im 19. Jahrhundert*. Göttingen: Vandenhoeck & Ruprecht, 1988.

Friedrichs, Elisabeth. *Die deutschsprachigen Schriftstellerinnen des 18. und 19. Jahrhunderts. Ein Lexikon*. Stuttgart: Metzler, 1981.

Frühsorge, Gotthard, and Rainer Gruenter, eds. *Gesinde im 18. Jahrhundert*. Hamburg: Meiner, 1995.

Frühwald, Wolfgang, and Alberto Martino, eds. *Zwischen Aufklärung und Restauration: Sozialer Wandel in der deutschen Literatur (1700–1848)*. Tübingen: Niemeyer, 1989.

Fulford, Tim. *Romanticism and Masculinity: Gender, Politics and Poetics in the Writings of Burke, Coleridge, Cobbett, Wordsworth, De Quincey and Hazlitt*. New York: St. Martin's P, 1999.

Fuss, Diana. *Essentially Speaking: Feminism, Nature and Difference*. New York and London: Routledge, 1989.

Gärtner, Johannes. *Das Journal Etranger und seine Bedeutung für die Verbreitung deutscher Literatur in Frankreich*. Mainz, 1905. Reprint, Geneva: Slatkins Reprints, 1971.

Garland, H. B. *Storm and Stress (Sturm und Drang)*. London, Sydney, Toronto, and Wellington: George G. Harrap, 1952.

Garve, Christian. *Über den Charakter der Bauern und ihr Verhältniss gegen die Gutsherrn und gegen die Regierung*. Breslau: Wilhelm Gottlieb Korn, 1786.

Gaskill, Howard. "'Blast, rief Cuchullin . . .!' J. M. R. Lenz and Ossian." In *From Gaelic to Romantic: Ossianic Translations*, edited by Fiona Stafford and Howard Gaskill, 107–18. Amsterdam: Rodopi, 1998.

———. "The 'Joy of Grief': Moritz and Ossian." *Colloquia Germanica* 28, 2 (1995): 101–25.

———. "'Ossian hat in meinem Herzen den Humor verdrängt': Goethe and Ossian Reconsidered." In *Goethe and the English-Speaking World*, edited by Nicholas Boyle and John Guthrie, 47–59. Rochester, NY: Camden House, 2002.

Gay, Pamela Diane. "Rousseau and the Lyric Natural: The Self As Representation." Ph.D. diss., Louisiana State University, Baton Rouge, 1998.

Gee, James Paul. "Orality and Literacy: From the Savage Mind to Ways with Words." *Tesol Quarterly* 20, 4 (1986): 719–46.

Geitner, Ursula. *Die Sprache der Verstellung: Studien zum rhetorischen und anthropologischen Wissen im 17. und 18. Jahrhundert.* Tübingen: Niemeyer, 1992.

Gerard, Alexander. *An Essay on Genius.* London: Printed for W. Strahan and T. Cadell in the Strand and W. Creech at Edinburgh, 1774.

Gerth, Klaus. "Die Poetik des Sturm und Drang." In *Sturm und Drang: Ein literaturwissenschaftliches Studienbuch,* edited by Walter Hinck, 55–80. Kronberg/Taunus: Athenäum, 1978.

Gibson, A. J. S., and T. C. Smout. *Prices, Food and Wages in Scotland 1550–1780.* Cambridge: Cambridge UP, 1995.

Gibson, Rebecca Gould. "'My Want of Skill': Apologias of British Women Poets, 1660–1800." In *Eighteenth-Century Women and the Arts,* edited by Frederick M. Keener and Susan E. Lorsch, 79–86. Westport, CT: Greenwood, 1988.

Gifford, Douglas, and Dorothy McMillan. "Introduction." *A History of Scottish Women's Writing,* edited by Douglas Gifford and Dorothy McMillan, ix-xxiii. Edinburgh: Edinburgh UP, 1997.

———, eds. *A History of Scottish Women's Writing.* Edinburgh: Edinburgh UP, 1997.

Gilboy, Elizabeth W. *Wages in Eighteenth Century England.* Cambridge, MA: Harvard UP, 1934.

Gisborne, Thomas. *An Enquiry into the Duties Of Men in the Higher and Middle Classes of Society in Great Britain: Resulting from Their Respective Stations, Professions, and Employments.* 2 vols. London: J. Davis, for B. and J. White, 1795.

Goebel, Gerhard. "'Literatur' und Aufklärung." In *Zum Funktionswandel der Literatur*, edited by Peter Bürger, 79–97. Frankfurt am Main: Suhrkamp, 1983.

Goedeke, Karl. *Grundrisz zur Geschichte der deutschen Dichtung aus den Quellen*, 2nd ed., vol. 5. Dresden: L. Ehlermann, 1893.

Götze, Walter. *Die Begründung der Volksbildung in der Aufklärungsbewegung*. Berlin and Leipzig: J. Beltz, 1932.

Goetzinger, Germaine. "Männerphantasie und Frauenwirklichkeit: Kindermörderinnen in der Literatur des Sturm und Drang." In *Frauen — Literatur — Politik*, edited by Annegret Pelz, Marianne Schuller, Inge Stephan, Sigrid Weigel, and Kerstin Wilhelms, 263–86. Hamburg: Argument, 1988.

Goodridge, John. *Rural Life in Eighteenth-Century English Poetry*. Cambridge: Cambridge UP, 1995.

Goody, Jack. "Inheritance, Property, and Women: Some Comparative Considerations." In *Family and Inheritance: Rural Society in Western Europe, 1200–1800*, edited by Jack Goody, Joan Thirsk, and E. P. Thompson, 10–36. Cambridge: Cambridge UP, 1976.

Goody, Jack, Joan Thirsk, and E. P. Thompson, eds. *Family and Inheritance: Rural Society in Western Europe, 1200–1800*. Cambridge: Cambridge UP, 1976.

Gray, Marion W. *Productive Men, Reproductive Women: The Agrarian Household and the Emergence of Separate Spheres during the German Enlightenment*. New York and Oxford: Berghahn, 2000.

Gray, Richard T. "Lavater's Physiognomical 'Surface Hermeneutics' and the Ideological (Con-)Text of Bourgeois Modernism." *The Lessing Yearbook* 23 (1992): 127–48.

Greene, Richard. *Mary Leapor: A Study in Eighteenth-Century Women's Poetry*. Oxford: Clarendon P, 1993.

Greig, John, ed. *Scots Minstrelsie: A National Monument of Scottish Song*. 6 vols. Edinburgh: T. C. & E. C. Jack, Grange Publishing Works, 1893.

Greven-Aschoff, Barbara. *Die bürgerliche Frauenbewegung in Deutschland 1894–1933*. Göttingen: Vandenhoeck & Ruprecht, 1981.

Groß, Heinrich. *Deutschlands Dichterinen und Schriftstellerinen. Eine literarische Skizze*, 2nd ed. Vienna: Gerold, 1882.

Guest, Harriet. *Small Change: Women, Learning, Patriotism, 1750–1810*. Chicago and London: Chicago UP, 2000.

Häntzschel, Günter, ed. *Bildung und Kultur bürgerlicher Frauen 1850–1918. Eine Quellendokumentation aus Anstandsbüchern und Lebenshilfen für Mädchen und Frauen als Beitrag zur weiblichen literarischen Sozialisation*. Tübingen: Niemeyer, 1986.

Hahn, Barbara. "Brief und Werk: Zur Konstitution von Autorschaft um 1800." In *Autorschaft: Genus und Genie in der Zeit um 1800,* edited by Ina Schabert and Barbara Schaff, 145–56. Berlin: Erich Schmidt, 1994.

Hammer, Stephanie. "Creation and Constipation: Don Carlos and Schiller's Blocked Passage to Weimar." In *Unwrapping Goethe's Weimar: Essays in Cultural Studies and Local Knowledge,* edited by Burkhard Henke, Susanne Kord, and Simon Richter, 273–94. Rochester, NY: Camden House, 2000.

Hands, Elizabeth. *The Death of Amnon: A Poem* [Bound with: Ann Yearsley, *The Rural Lyre: A Volume of Poems*]. Edited by Caroline Franklin. Coventry: N. Rollason, 1789. Reprint, London: Routledge, 1996.

Harris, Jocelyn. "Introduction." In John Duncombe, *The Feminiad: A Poem (1754).* The Augustan Reprint Society Publication no. 207]. Los Angeles: UCLA William Andrews Clark Memorial Library, 1981.

———. "Sappho, Souls, and the Salic Law of Wit." In *Anticipations of the Enlightenment in England, France, and Germany,* edited by Alan Charles Kors and Paul J. Korshin, 232–58. Philadelphia: U of Pennsylvania P, 1987.

Harrison, Susannah. *Songs in the Night. Written by Susannah Harrison. A Young Woman under Heavy Afflictions,* edited by John Conder. London: T. Vallance & Alexander Hogg, 1780.

Harzig, Christiane, Deirdre Mageean, Margareta Matovic, Maria Anna Knothe, and Monika Blaschke. *Peasant Maids — City Women: From the European Countryside to Urban America.* Ithaca, NY, and London: Cornell UP, 1997.

Hausen, Karin. "Die Polarisierung der 'Geschlechtscharaktere' — Eine Spiegelung der Dissoziation von Erwerbs- und Familienleben." In *Sozialgeschichte der Familie in der Neuzeit Europas,* edited by Werner Conze, 363–93. Stuttgart: Ernst Klett, 1976.

———. "'. . . eine Ulme für das schwankende Efeu.' Ehepaare im Bildungsbürgertum: Ideale und Wirklichkeiten im späten 18. und 19. Jahrhundert." In *Bürgerinnen und Bürger: Geschlechterverhältnisse im 19. Jahrhundert,* edited by Ute Frevert, 85–117. Göttingen: Vandenhoeck & Ruprecht, 1988.

———, ed. *Frauen suchen ihre Geschichte: Historische Studien zum 19. und 20. Jahrhundert.* Munich: C. H. Beck, 1983.

Hauser, Arnold. *The Social History of Art.* 2 vols. London: Routledge & Kegan Paul, 1951.

———. *Sozialgeschichte der Kunst und Literatur.* 2 vols. Munich: C. H. Beck, 1953.

Hausmann, Elisabeth. *Die Karschin: Friedrichs des Großen Volksdichterin. Ein Leben in Briefen.* Frankfurt am Main: Societäts-Verlag, 1933.

Hecht, J. Jean. *The Domestic Servant Class in Eighteenth-Century England.* London: Routledge & Kegan Paul, 1956.

Heinse, J. J. "Sappho." *Iris* 3, 2 (May 1775): 114–50.

Henke, Burkhard, Susanne Kord, and Simon Richter, eds. *Unwrapping Goethe's Weimar: Essays in Cultural Studies and Local Knowledge*. Rochester, NY: Camden House, 2000.

Henning, Friedrich Wilhelm. "Bestimmungsfaktoren der bäuerlichen Einkommen im 18. Jahrhundert." *Jahrbuch für Wirtschaftsgeschichte* 1 (1970): 165–83.

———. *Dienste und Abgaben der Bauern im 18. Jahrhundert*. Stuttgart: G. Fischer, 1969.

Herder, Johann Gottfried. "Abhandlung über den Ursprung der Sprache." In *Sturm und Drang: Weltanschauliche und ästhetische Schriften*, vol. 1, edited by Peter Müller, 127–221. Berlin and Weimar: Aufbau Verlag, 1978.

———. "Aus dem Deutschen Museum. Von Ähnlichkeit der mittlern englischen und deutschen Dichtkunst, nebst verschiednem, das daraus folget." In *Sämtliche Werke*, vol. 9, edited by Bernhard Suphan, 522–35. Berlin, 1893. Reprint, Hildesheim and New York: Georg Olms, 1967.

———. "Auszug aus einem Briefwechsel über Ossian und die Lieder alter Völker." In *Sturm und Drang: Weltanschauliche und ästhetische Schriften*, vol. 1, edited by Peter Müller, 233–73. Berlin and Weimar: Aufbau Verlag, 1978.

———. "Batteux, Einschränkung der schönen Künste auf einen einzigen Grundsatz. Übersetzt und mit Abhandlungen begleitet von Joh. Adolf Schlegeln. Dritte, von neuem verbesserte und vermehrte Ausgabe. Leipzig 1770. 2 Bände" [review]. In *Sturm und Drang: Weltanschauliche und ästhetische Schriften*, vol. 1, edited by Peter Müller, 222–32. Berlin and Weimar: Aufbau Verlag, 1978.

———. "Gedichte von Anna Louisa Karschin." In Anna Louisa Karsch. *O, mir entwischt nicht, was die Menschen fühlen: Anna Louisa Karschin. Gedichte und Briefe, Stimmen von Zeitgenossen*, edited by Gerhard Wolf, 250–60. Berlin: Buchverlag Der Morgen, 1981.

———. "Grundsätze, die da zeigen, wie das Genie und der Charakter eines Menschen von dem Grade der Stärke . . . abhängt." In *Sturm und Drang: Weltanschauliche und ästhetische Schriften*, vol. 1, edited by Peter Müller, 423–31. Berlin and Weimar: Aufbau Verlag, 1978.

———. "Sappho und Karschin." In "Von der Griechischen Litteratur in Deutschland." *Ueber die neuere Deutsche Litteratur: Eine Beilage zu den Briefen, die neueste Litteratur betreffend. 1766. 1767. Sämtliche Werke*, vol. 1, edited by Bernhard Suphan, 350–54. Berlin, 1877. Reprint, Hildesheim and New York: Georg Olms, 1967.

———. "Übers Erkennen und Empfinden in der menschlichen Seele." In *Sturm und Drang: Weltanschauliche und ästhetische Schriften*, vol. 1, edited by Peter Müller, 399–431. Berlin and Weimar: Aufbau Verlag, 1978.

———. "Von Ähnlichkeit der mittlern englischen und deutschen Dichtkunst, nebst verschiednem, das daraus folget." In *Sturm und Drang: Weltanschauliche und ästhetische Schriften*, vol. 1, edited by Peter Müller, 486–97. Berlin and Weimar: Aufbau Verlag, 1978.

Heuser, Magdalene. "'Ich wollte dieß und das von meinem Buche sagen, und gerieth in ein Vernünfteln': Poetologische Reflexionen in den Romanvorreden." In *Untersuchungen zum Roman von Frauen um 1800*, edited by Helga Gallas and Magdalene Heuser, 52–65. Tübingen: Niemeyer, 1990.

———. "Stationen einer Karsch-Nachfolge in der Literatur von Frauen des 18. Jahrhunderts: Caroline von Klencke, Helmina von Chézy und Therese Huber." In *Anna Louisa Karsch (1722–1791): Von schlesischer Kunst und Berliner "Natur." Ergebnisse des Symposiums zum 200. Todestag der Dichterin*, edited by Anke Bennholdt-Thomsen and Anita Runge, 149–61. Göttingen: Wallstein, 1992.

Heydemann, Evelyne. "Institution und Autonomie: Zur Diskussion des Aufsatzes von G. Goebel: 'Literatur' und Aufklärung." In *Zum Funktionswandel der Literatur*, edited by Peter Bürger, 98–106. Frankfurt am Main: Suhrkamp, 1983.

Hibbard, G. R. "The Country House Poem of the Seventeenth Century." *Journal of the Warburg and Courtauld Institute* 19 (1956): 159–74.

Higgonet, Margaret. "Verräterischer Diebstahl: Authentizität, Autorität und männliche Angst in der englischen Romantik." In *Autorschaft: Genus und Genie in der Zeit um 1800*, edited by Ina Schabert and Barbara Schaff, 157–74. Berlin: Erich Schmidt, 1994.

Hill, Bridget. *Eighteenth-Century Women: An Anthology*. London: George Allen & Unwin, 1984.

———. *Servants: English Domestics in the Eighteenth Century*. Oxford: Clarendon P, 1996.

———. *Women, Work, and Sexual Politics in Eighteenth-Century England*. Oxford and New York: Basil Blackwell, 1989.

Hill, Christopher. *Reformation to Industrial Revolution: A Social and Economic History of Britain, 1530–1780*. London: Weidenfeld & Nicolson, 1967.

Hill, David. "Bürger und 'das schwankende Wort Volk.'" In *The Challenge of German Culture: Essays Presented to Wilfried van der Will*, edited by Michael Butler and Robert Evans, 25–36. Houndmills: Palgrave, 2000.

Hinck, Walter. "Einleitung." *Sturm und Drang: Ein literaturwissenschaftliches Studienbuch*, edited by Walter Hinck, vii-xii. Kronberg/Taunus: Athenäum, 1978.

———, ed. *Sturm und Drang: Ein literaturwissenschaftliches Studienbuch*. Kronberg/Ts.: Athenäum, 1978.

Hindenburg, Carl Friedrich, Georg Heinrich Borz, Christian Theophil Seydlitz, and Georg Eck. *Elegi in Mortem Annae Ludovicae Karschiae. Creationi XVI. Magistrorum Philos. et L. L. A. A Rectore Magnifico Carolo Friderico Hindenburgio Physices Professore Publico Ordinario Academiae Scientiarum Moguntinae Aliarumque Socio, Procancellario Splendidissimo Georgio Henrico Borzio Mathematum Professore Publico Ordinario Collegii B. M. V. Seniore Societatis Scientiar Iablonovianae Praeside, Decano Spectabili Christiano Theophilo Seydlitio Methaphysices Professore Publico Ordinario Acad. Decemviro Maioris Collegii Principum Collegiato Alumnorum Electoralium Ephoro, Dicati ab Io. Georgio Eccio Poetices Professore*. Leipzig: Klaubarth, 1792.

Hobsbawm, E. J. *Industry and Empire: An Economic History of Britain since 1750.* London: Weidenfeld & Nicolson, 1968.

Hoffmann, Volker. "Elisa und Robert oder das Weib und der Mann, wie sie sein sollten: Anmerkungen zur Geschlechtercharakteristik der Goethezeit." In *Klassik und Moderne: Die Weimarer Klassik als historisches Ereignis und Herausforderung im kulturgeschichtlichen Prozeß*, edited by Karl Richter and Jörg Schönert, 80–97. Stuttgart: Metzler, 1983.

Hold, Trevor, ed. *A Northamptonshire Garland: An Anthology of Northamptonshire Poets with Biographical Notes*. Northampton: Northamptonshire Libraries, 1989.

Holdenried, Michaela. "Autobiographik von Frauen — eine eigene Geschichte? Anmerkungen zum Forschungsstand." In *Autobiography by Women in German,* edited by Mererid Puw Davies, Beth Linklater, and Gisela Shaw, 17–33. Oxford, Bern, and Berlin: Peter Lang, 2000.

Holladay, Gae. "Introduction." Mary Scott. *The Female Advocate; a Poem. Occasioned by Reading Mr. Duncombe's Feminead (1774).* The Augustan Reprint Society Publication no. 224. Los Angeles: UCLA William Andrews Clark Memorial Library, 1984.

Hopkins, Mary Alden. *Hannah More and Her Circle*. New York and Toronto: Longmans, Green, 1947.

Humboldt, Wilhelm von. "Plan einer vergleichenden Anthropologie." In *Werke*, vol. 1, edited by Andreas Flitner, 337–75. Stuttgart: J. G. Cotta, 1960.

———. "Über den Geschlechtsunterschied und dessen Einfluß auf die organische Natur." *Werke*, vol. 1, edited by Andreas Flitner, 268–95. Stuttgart: J. G. Cotta, 1960.

———. "Über männliche und weibliche Form." *Werke*, vol. 1, edited by Andreas Flitner, 296–336. Stuttgart: J. G. Cotta, 1960.

Huyssen, Andreas. *Drama des Sturm und Drang: Kommentar zu einer Epoche.* Munich: Winkler, 1980.

Isdell-Carpenter, Andrew. "On a Manuscript of Poems Catalogued As by Mary Barber in the Library of TCD." *Hermathena: A Dublin University Review* 109 (Autumn 1969): 54–64.

Ives, Margaret. "Anna-Louisa Karsch and Her Relationship with Gleim." In *Women Writers of the Age of Goethe*, vol. 2, edited by Margaret C. Ives, 4–15. Lancaster: Department of Modern Languages, 1989.

———. "Anna Luise Karsch (1722–1791): A Brave Woman Goes to War." In *Sappho in the Shadows: Essays on the Work of German Women Poets of the Age of Goethe (1749–1832), with Translations of Their Poetry into English*, edited by Anthony J. Harper and Margaret C. Ives, 15–52. Bern: Peter Lang, 2000.

Jackson, J. R. de J. *Romantic Poetry by Women: A Bibliography, 1770–1835*. Oxford: Clarendon P, 1993.

Jacobeit, Wolfgang, and Heinz Nowak. "Zur Lebensweise und Kultur der werktätigen Dorfbevölkerung in der Zeit der Herausbildung des Kapitalismus in der Landwirtschaft vom Ende des 18. Jahrhunderts bis in die dreißiger/vierziger Jahre des 19. Jahrhunderts." In *Bauer und Landarbeiter im Kapitalismus in der Magdeburger Börde: Zur Geschichte des dörflichen Alltags vom Ausgang des 18. Jahrhunderts bis zum Beginn des 20. Jahrhunderts*, edited by Hans-Jürgen Rach and Bernhard Weissel, 1–41. Berlin: Akademie-Verlag, 1982.

Jacobi, Johann Georg. *Saemtliche Werke*. 3 vols. Halberstadt: Johann Heinrich Gros, 1770–74.

Jameson, Fredric. "From *The Political Unconscious: Narrative as a Socially Symbolic Act*." In *Theory of the Novel: A Historical Approach*, edited by Michael McKeon, 400–13. Baltimore and London: Johns Hopkins UP, 2000.

Joeres, Ruth-Ellen B., and Mary Jo Maynes, eds. *German Women in the Eighteenth and Nineteenth Centuries: A Social and Literary History*. Bloomington, IN: Indiana UP, 1986.

Johnson, James. *The Scots Musical Museum 1787–1803*. Edited by D. A. Low. 2 vols. Portland, OR: Amadeus P, 1991.

Johnston, Thomas. *The History of the Working Classes in Scotland*. East Ardsley, Wakefield, and Yorkshire: EP Publishing, 1974.

Jones, Vivien. "Introduction." *Women in the Eighteenth Century: Constructions of Femininity*, edited by Vivien Jones, 1–13. London and New York: Routledge, 1990.

———, ed. *Women in the Eighteenth Century: Constructions of Femininity*. London, New York: Routledge, 1990.

Kagel, Martin. *Strafgericht und Kriegstheater: Studien zur Ästhetik von Jakob Michael Reinhold Lenz*. St. Ingbert: Röhrig, 1997.

Kaiser, Gerhard. *Aufklärung, Empfindsamkeit, Sturm und Drang*, 3rd ed. Munich: Francke, 1979.

Kant, Immanuel. "Anthropologie in pragmatischer Hinsicht." In *Immanuel Kants Werke*, vol. 8, edited by Hermann Cohen, 1–228. Berlin: Bruno Cassirer, 1922.

———. "Metaphysik der Sitten." In *Metaphysische Anfangsgründe der Rechtslehre*, edited by Bernd Ludwig, 37–200. Hamburg: Felix Meiner, 1986.

Kaplan, Marion A. *The Making of the Jewish Middle Class: Women, Family and Identity in Imperial Germany*. New York and Oxford: Oxford UP, 1991.

Karsch, Anna Louisa. *Auserlesene Gedichte. Faksimile-Nachdruck*. Edited by Alfred Anger. Stuttgart: Metzler, 1966.

———. *Auserlesene Gedichte*. Edited by Barbara Becker-Cantarino. 1764. Reprint, Karben: Verlag Petra Wald, 1996.

———. *Gedichte. Nach der Dichterin Tode herausgegeben von ihrer Tochter Caroline Luise von Klencke*. Edited by Barbara Becker-Cantarino. 1792. Reprint, Karben: Verlag Petra Wald, 1996.

———. *Gedichte und Lebenszeugnisse*. Edited by Alfred Anger. Stuttgart: Reclam, 1987.

———. *Herzgedanken. Das Leben der "deutschen Sappho" von ihr selbst erzählt*. Edited by Barbara Beuys. Frankfurt: Societäts-Verlag, 1981.

———. *Die Karschin. Friedrichs des Großen Volksdichterin. Ein Leben in Briefen*. Edited by Elisabeth Hausmann. Frankfurt am Main: Societäts-Verlag, 1933.

———. "Lebensbericht von Anna Louisa Karsch in vier Briefen an Sulzer." In *"Mein Bruder in Apoll": Briefwechsel zwischen Anna Louisa Karsch und Johann Wilhelm Ludwig Gleim*, vol. 1, edited by Regina Nörtemann, 342–63. Göttingen: Wallstein, 1996.

———. *Das Lied der Karschin. Die Gedichte der Anna Luise Karschin mit einem Bericht ihres Lebens*. Edited by Herybert Menzel. Hamburg: Hanseatische Verlagsanstalt, 1938.

———. *"Mein Bruder in Apoll": Briefwechsel zwischen Anna Louisa Karsch und Johann Wilhelm Ludwig Gleim*. 2 vols. Edited by Regina Nörtemann (Vol. 1) and Ute Pott (Vol. 2). Göttingen: Wallstein, 1996.

———. "Meine Jugend war gedrückt von Sorgen." In *The Defiant Muse: German Feminist Poems from the Middle Ages to the Present*, edited by Susan Cocalis, 24–25. New York: Feminist P, 1986.

———. *Neue Gedichte*. Edited by Barbara Becker-Cantarino. 1772. Reprint, Karben: Verlag Petra Wald, 1996.

———. *O, mir entwischt nicht, was die Menschen fühlen: Anna Louisa Karschin. Gedichte und Briefe, Stimmen von Zeitgenossen*. Edited by Gerhard Wolf. Berlin: Buchverlag Der Morgen, 1981.

Kastinger-Riley, Helene M. "Anna Louisa Karsch." *Dictionary of Literary Biography* 97 (1990): 139–44.

———. "Wölfin unter Schäfern: Die sozialkritische Lyrik der Anna Louisa Karsch." In *Die weibliche Muse: Sechs Essays über künstlerisch schaffende Frauen der Goethezeit*, 1–25. Columbia, SC: Camden House, 1986.

Kaufhold, Karl Heinrich. "Friderizianische Agrar-, Siedlungs- und Bauernpolitik." In *Kontinuität und Wandel: Schlesien zwischen Österreich und Preußen*, edited by Peter Baumgart and Ulrich Schmilewski, 167–201. Sigmaringen: Jan Thorbecke, 1990.

Kaufman, Ulrich, ed. *Lenz in Weimar: Jakob Michael Reinhold Lenz 1776 am Weimarer Hof. Zeugnisse — Beiträge — Chronik*. Munich: Kirchheim, 1999.

Kazzazzi, Kerstin. "Eine Hand mit Armbändern: Zur sprachgeschichtlichen Asymmetrie des Autorenbegriffs." In *Autorschaft: Genus und Genie in der Zeit um 1800*, edited by Ina Schabert and Barbara Schaff, 21–39. Berlin: Erich Schmidt, 1994.

Keener, Frederick M., and Susan E. Lorsch, eds. *Eighteenth-Century Women and the Arts*. Westport, CT: Greenwood, 1988.

Kent, D. A. "Ubiquitous but Invisible: Female Domestic Servants in Mid-Eighteenth Century London." *History Workshop Journal* 28 (1989): 111–28.

Kerrigan, Catherine, ed., and Meg Bateman, trans. *An Anthology of Scottish Women Poets*. Edinburgh: Edinburgh UP, 1991.

Ketelsen, Uwe K. "Science and Literature in the Early German Enlightenment." In *Anticipations of the Enlightenment in England, France, and Germany*, edited by Alan Charles Kors and Paul J. Korshin, 165–84. Philadelphia: U of Pennsylvania P, 1987.

Kiesel, Helmuth, and Paul Münch. *Gesellschaft und Literatur im 18. Jahrhundert: Voraussetzungen und Entstehung des literarischen Markts in Deutschland*. Munich: Beck, 1977.

King, Roger. *The Middle Class*, 2nd ed. London: Longman, 1981.

Kistler, Mark O. *Drama of the Storm and Stress*. New York: Twayne, 1969.

Klaus, H. Gustav. *The Literature of Labour: Two Hundred Years of Working-Class Writing*. Brighton and Sussex: Harvester P, 1985.

———. "Stephen Duck und Mary Collier: Plebejische Kontro-Verse über Frauenarbeit vor 250 Jahren." *Gulliver: Deutsch-Englische Jahrbücher* 10 (1981): 115–23.

Klencke, Caroline Luise von. "Vorberichtender Lebenslauf der Dichterin Anna Louise Karschin, geb. Dürbach." In Anna Louisa Karsch, *Gedichte. Nach der Dichterin Tode herausgegeben von ihrer Tochter Caroline Luise von Klencke*, edited by Barbara Becker-Cantarino, 1–128. Berlin, 1792. Reprint, Karben: Verlag Petra Wald, 1996.

———. "Vorrede." In Anna Louisa Karsch, *Gedichte. Nach der Dichterin Tode herausgegeben von ihrer Tochter Caroline Luise von Klencke*, edited by Barbara Becker-Cantarino, vii-x. Berlin, 1792. Reprint, Karben: Verlag Petra Wald, 1996.

Knigge, Adolph Freiherr von. *Über den Umgang mit Menschen*. 3 vols. in 1. Hanover: Christian Ritscher, 1796. Reprint of the 5th ed., Nendeln / Liechtenstein: KTO, 1978.

Kocka, Jürgen. "Bürgertum und Bürgerlichkeit als Probleme der deutschen Geschichte vom späten 18. zum frühen 20. Jahrhundert." In *Bürger und Bürgerlichkeit im 19. Jahrhundert*, edited by Jürgen Kocka, 21–63. Göttingen: Vandenhoeck & Ruprecht, 1987.

———. "The European Pattern and the German Case." In *Bourgeois Society in Nineteenth-Century Europe*, edited by Jürgen Kocka and Allen Mitchell, 3–39. Oxford: Berg, 1993.

———, ed. *Bürger und Bürgerlichkeit im 19. Jahrhundert*. Göttingen: Vandenhoeck & Ruprecht, 1987.

Kocka, Jürgen, Karl Ditt, Josef Mooser, Heinz Reif, and Reinhard Schüren, eds. *Familie und soziale Plazierung: Studien zum Verhältnis von Familie, sozialer Mobilität und Heiratsverhalten an westfälischen Beispielen im späten 18. und 19. Jahrhundert*. Opladen: Westdeutscher Verlag, 1980.

Koepke, Wulf. "Das Wort 'Volk' im Sprachgebrauch Johann Gottfried Herders." *The Lessing Yearbook* 19 (1987): 209–21.

Kontje, Todd. *Women, the Novel, and the German Nation 1771–1871*. Cambridge: Cambridge UP, 1998.

Kord, Susanne. *Ein Blick hinter die Kulissen: Deutschsprachige Dramatikerinnen im 18. und 19. Jahrhundert*. Stuttgart: Metzler, 1992.

———. "Discursive Dissociations: Women Writers As Observers of the Sturm und Drang." In *A Companion to the Sturm und Drang*, edited by David Hill. Rochester, NY: Camden House, 2002. 241–73.

———. "Frauennatur und Kinderspiel: Über die geschlechtsspezifische Sozialisation in Kinderdramen weiblicher Autoren 1820–1865." *Jahrbuch des Freien Deutschen Hochstifts* (Winter 1994): 221–53.

———. "Protagonist/Antagonist." In *The Feminist Encyclopedia of German Literature*, edited by Friederike Eigler and Susanne Kord, 420–22. Westport, CT, and London: Greenwood P, 1997.

———. *Sich einen Namen machen: Anonymität und weibliche Autorschaft 1700–1900*. Stuttgart: Metzler, 1996.

———. "Women as Children, Women as Childkillers: Poetic Images of Infanticide in Eighteenth-Century Germany." *Eighteenth-Century Studies* 26, 3 (Spring 1993): 449–66.

Kors, Alan Charles, and Paul J. Korshin, eds. *Anticipations of the Enlightenment in England, France, and Germany.* Philadelphia: U of Pennsylvania P, 1987.

Korshin, Paul J. "Types of Eighteenth-Century Literary Patronage." *Eighteenth-Century Studies* 7, 2 (1974): 453–73.

Kosch, Wilhelm. *Deutsches Literatur-Lexikon. Biographisches und bibliographisches Handbuch,* 2nd ed. 4 vols. Bern: Francke, 1949–58.

Krauss, Werner. "Zur Periodisierung Aufklärung, Sturm und Drang, Weimarer Klassik (1961)." In *Sturm und Drang,* edited by Manfred Wacker, 67–95. Darmstadt: Wissenschaftliche Buchgesellschaft, 1985.

Krüger, Hermann Anders. *Deutsches Literatur-Lexikon. Biographisches und bibliographisches Handbuch mit Motivübersichten und Quellennachweisen.* Munich: Beck, 1914.

Krzywon, Ernst Josef. "'Ich bin Empfindung und Gesang'. Schlesiens deutsche Sappho Anna Louisa Karsch (1722–1791)." In *Kontinuität und Wandel: Schlesien zwischen Österreich und Preußen,* edited by Peter Baumgart and Ulrich Schmilewski, 335–48. Sigmaringen: Jan Thorbecke, 1990.

———. "Tradition und Wandel: Die Karschin in Schlesien (1722–1761)." In *Anna Louisa Karsch (1722–1791): Von schlesischer Kunst und Berliner "Natur." Ergebnisse des Symposiums zum 200. Todestag der Dichterin,* edited by Anke Bennholdt-Thomsen and Anita Runge, 12–56. Göttingen: Wallstein, 1992.

Kussmaul, Ann. *Servants in Husbandry in Early Modern England.* Cambridge: Cambridge UP, 1981.

La Roche, Sophie von. *Die Geschichte des Fräuleins von Sternheim.* Edited by Barbara Becker-Cantarino. Stuttgart: Reclam, 1983.

———. *The History of Lady Sophia Sternheim.* Edited by James Lynn. Translated by Joseph Collyer. London: Pickering & Chatto, 1991.

Landry, Donna. "Mary Collier (1690– after 1762)." In *Dictionary of Literary Biography: Eighteenth-Century British Poets, First Series,* edited by John Sitter, 3–6. Detroit, New York, and London: Gale Research, 1990.

———. *The Muses of Resistance: Laboring-Class Women's Poetry in Britain, 1739–1796.* Cambridge: Cambridge UP, 1990.

———. "The Resignation of Mary Collier: Some Problems in Feminist Literary History." In *The New Eighteenth Century: Theory, Politics, English Literature,* edited by Felicity Nussbaum and Laura Brown, 99–120, 287–93. New York and London: Methuen, 1987.

Lange, Sigrid. *Spiegelgeschichten: Geschlechter und Poetiken in der Frauenliteratur um 1800.* Frankfurt am Main: Ulrike Helmer, 1995.

———, ed. *Ob die Weiber Menschen sind: Geschlechterdebatten um 1800.* Leipzig: Reclam, 1992.

Lavater, Johann Caspar. *Physiognomische Fragmente, zur Beförderung der Menschenkenntniß und Menschenliebe*, vol. 3. Leipzig and Winterthur: Weidmanns Erben & Reich and H. Steiner, 1777.

Law, Alexander. "Scottish Schoolbooks of the Eighteenth and Nineteenth Centuries." In *Studies in Scottish Literature*, edited by Ross Roy. Columbia, SC: University of South Carolina English Department, 1983.

Leapor, [Mary]. *Poems upon Several Occasions. By Mrs. Leapor of Brackley in Northamptonshire*. London: J. Roberts in Warwick-Lane, 1748.

———. "The Rural Maid's Reflexions, Written by a Gardener's Daughter. Inscribed to a Lady." *The London Magazine, or, Gentleman's Monthly Intelligencer* 16 (1747): 45.

Leidner, Alan C. *The Impatient Muse: Germany and the Sturm und Drang*. Chapel Hill, NC, and London: U of North Carolina P, 1994.

Levy, Anita. *Other Women: The Writing of Class, Race, and Gender, 1832–1898*. Princeton: Princeton UP, 1991.

*Lexikon deutscher Dichter und Prosaisten*, s.v. "Anne Luise Karschin."

*Lexikon deutschsprachiger Schriftsteller. Von den Anfängen bis zum Ausgang des 19. Jahrhunderts*, s.v. "Anna Louisa Karsch(in), geb. Dürbach."

Lilley, Kate. "Homosocial Women: Martha Sansom, Constantia Grierson, Mary Leapor and Georgic Verse Epistle." In *Women's Poetry in the Enlightenment: The Making of a Canon, 1730–1820*, edited by Isobel Armstrong and Virginia Blain, 167–83. London: Macmillan, 1999.

Lipp, Carola, ed. *Schimpfende Weiber und patriotische Jungfrauen: Frauen im Vormärz und in der Revolution 1848/49*. Moos and Baden-Baden: Elster, 1986.

Little, Janet. *The Poetical Works of Janet Little, the Scotch Milkmaid*. Air: John & Peter Wilson, 1792.

Lonsdale, Roger, ed. *Eighteenth Century Women Poets. An Oxford Anthology*. Oxford and New York: Oxford UP, 1990.

———. "Introduction." *The New Oxford Book of Eighteenth Century Verse*, edited by Roger Lonsdale, xxxiii–xli. Oxford and New York: Oxford UP, 1984.

———, ed. *The New Oxford Book of Eighteenth Century Verse*. Oxford and New York: Oxford UP, 1984.

Low, Donald A. "Burns as a West Country Poet." In *The Paisley Poets: A Critical Appraisal of their Work and Reputation. Proceedings of a Seminar Held in Paisley College on 10th September 1988*, edited by Stuart James and Gordon McCrae, 4–24. Paisley: U of Paisley Library, 1993.

Lowth, Robert. *Lectures on the Sacred Poetry of the Hebrews*, 4th ed. Translated from the Latin of the Late Right Rev. Robert Lowth, D. D. F. R. S. by G. Gregory, F. A. S. London: Printed for Thomas Tegg, Cheapside, 1834.

Lützeler, Paul Michael. *Klio oder Kalliope? Literatur und Geschichte: Sondierung, Analyse, Interpretation.* Berlin: Erich Schmidt, 1997.

Lugowski, Clemens. "Der junge Herder und das Volkslied. Eine Interpretation (1938)." In *Sturm und Drang,* edited by Manfred Wacker, 215–33. Darmstadt: Wissenschaftliche Buchgesellschaft, 1985.

Luserke, Matthias. *Die Bändigung der wilden Seele: Literatur und Leidenschaft in der Aufklärung.* Stuttgart and Weimar: Metzler, 1995.

———. *Sturm und Drang: Autoren — Texte — Themen.* Stuttgart: Reclam, 1997.

Lyle, E. B., ed. *Andrew Crawford's Collection of Ballads and Songs.* 2 vols. Edinburgh: Scottish Text Society, 1996.

Lynn, James. "Introduction." Sophie von La Roche. *The History of Lady Sophia Sternheim.* Translated by Joseph Collyer, vii-xxxi. London: Pickering & Chatto, 1991.

Mabee, Barbara. "Die Kindesmörderin in den Fesseln der bürgerlichen Moral: Wagners Evchen und Goethes Gretchen." In *Feminist Studies and German Culture,* edited by Marianne Burkhard and Edith Waldstein, 29–45. Lanham, MD: U P of America, 1986.

Macintosh, John. *The Poets of Ayrshire from the Fourteenth Century till the Present Day.* Dumfries: T. Hunter, 1910.

Macpherson, James. *The Poems of Ossian and Related Works.* Edited by Howard Gaskill. Edinburgh: Edinburgh UP, 1996.

Madland, Helga. "Gender and the German Literary Canon: Marianne Ehrmann's Infanticide Fiction." *Monatshefte* 84, 4 (1992): 405–16.

———. "Infanticide as Fiction: Goethe's *Urfaust* and Schiller's 'Kindsmörderin' as Models." *The German Quarterly* 62, 1 (Winter 1989): 27–38.

Mahl, Mary R., and Helene Koon, eds. *The Female Spectator: English Women Writers Before 1800.* Bloomington, IN and London: Indiana UP, 1977.

Marshall, Alice Kahler. *Pen Names of Women Writers from 1600 to the Present. A Compendium of the Literary Identities of 2650 Women Novelists, Playwrights, Poets, Diarists, Journalists and Miscellaneous Writers.* Camp Hill, PA: From the Alice Marshall Collection, 1985.

Martens, Wolfgang. *Die Botschaft der Tugend: Die Aufklärung im Spiegel der deutschen Moralischen Wochenschriften.* Stuttgart: Metzler, 1971.

———. "Leserezepte fürs Frauenzimmer: Die Frauenzimmerbibliotheken der deutschen Moralischen Wochenschriften." *Archiv für Geschichte des Buchwesens* 15 (1975): 1143–1200.

Martini, Fritz. *Literarische Form und Geschichte: Aufsätze zu Gattungstheorie und Gattungsentwicklung vom Sturm und Drang bis zum Erzählen heute.* Stuttgart: Metzler, 1984.

———. "Von der Aufklärung zum Sturm und Drang." In *Annalen der deutschen Literatur*, 2nd ed., edited by Heinz Otto Burger, 405–63. Stuttgart: Metzler, 1971.

Masters, Mary. *Poems on Several Occasions*. London: T. Browne, 1733.

———. "A Thought at First Waking; from Mrs. Master's Poems, Now in the Press." *Gentleman's Magazine* 22 (1752): 528.

Mattenklott, Gert. *Melancholie in der Dramatik des Sturm und Drang*. Königstein/Taunus: Athenäum, 1985.

Mayhew, Alan. *Rural Settlement and Farming in Germany*. New York: Barnes & Noble, 1973.

McCann, Andrew. *Cultural Politics in the 1790s: Literature, Radicalism and the Public Sphere*. New York: St. Martin's, 1999.

McClung, William A. *The Country House Poem in English Renaissance Poetry*. Berkeley, Los Angeles, and London: U of California P, 1977.

McCordick, David, ed. *Scottish Literature: An Anthology*. 2 vols. Bern, New York, and Frankfurt: Peter Lang, 1996.

McCue, Kirsteen. "Burns, Women, and Song." In *Robert Burns and Cultural Authority*, edited by Robert Crawford, 40–57. Edinburgh: Edinburgh UP, 1997.

———. "Women and Song 1750–1850." In *A History of Scottish Women's Writing*, edited by Douglas Gifford and Dorothy McMillan, 58–70. Edinburgh: Edinburgh UP, 1997.

McInnes, Edward. *"Ein ungeheures Theater": The Drama of the Sturm und Drang*. Frankfurt, Bern, and New York: Peter Lang, 1987.

McKeon, Michael. "Generic Transformation and Social Change: Rethinking the Rise of the Novel." In *Theory of the Novel: A Historical Approach*, edited by Michael McKeon, 382–99. Baltimore and London: Johns Hopkins UP, 2000.

———. *The Origins of the English Novel 1600–1740*. Baltimore and London: Johns Hopkins UP, 1987.

———. *Politics and Poetry in Restoration England: The Case of Dryden's Annus Mirabilis*. Cambridge, MA: Harvard UP, 1975.

———, ed. *Theory of the Novel: A Historical Approach*. Baltimore and London: Johns Hopkins UP, 2000.

McMillan, Dorothy. "Introduction." *The Scotswoman at Home and Abroad: Non-Fictional Writing 1700–1900*, edited by Dorothy McMillan, xi-xiv. Glasgow: Association for Scottish Literary Studies, 1999.

———, ed. *The Scotswoman at Home and Abroad: Non-Fictional Writing 1700–1900*. Glasgow: Association for Scottish Literary Studies, 1999.

Meier, Ulrich. "Soziologische Bemerkungen zur Institution Kunst." In *Zum Funktionswandel der Literatur,* edited by Peter Bürger, 33–58. Frankfurt am Main: Suhrkamp, 1983.

Mellor, Anne K. "The Female Poet and the Poetess: Two Traditions of British Women's Poetry, 1780–1830." In *Women's Poetry in the Enlightenment: The Making of a Canon, 1730–1820,* edited by Isobel Armstrong and Virginia Blain, 81–98. London: Macmillan, 1999.

Mendelssohn, Moses. *Rezensionsartikel in Briefe, die neueste Litteratur betreffend (1759–1765).* Edited by Eva J. Engel. *Gesammelte Schriften* 5,1. Stuttgart and Bad Cannstadt: Friedrich Frommann, 1991.

Menzel, Herybert. "Wie ich zur Karschin fand." In *Das Lied der Karschin. Die Gedichte der Anna Luise Karschin mit einem Bericht ihres Lebens,* edited by Herybert Menzel, 9–52. Hamburg: Hanseatische Verlagsanstalt, 1938.

Messenger, Ann. "'Daughter of Shenstone'?: Being a Brief Life of Mary Whateley Darwall." *Bulletin of Research in the Humanities* 87 (1986): 462–81.

———. *Woman and Poet in the Eighteenth Century: The Life of Mary Whateley Darwall (1738–1825).* New York: AMS P, 1999.

———. "Women Poets and the Pastoral Trap: The Case of Mary Whateley." In *Eighteenth-Century Women and the Arts,* edited by Frederick M. Keener and Susan E. Lorsch, 93–105. Westport, CT: Greenwood, 1988.

Messer-Davidow, Ellen. "'For Softness She': Gender Ideology and Aesthetics in Eighteenth-Century England." In *Eighteenth-Century Women and the Arts,* edited by Frederick M. Keener and Susan E. Lorsch, 45–55. Westport, CT: Greenwood, 1988.

Meyer, Sibylle. "Die mühsame Arbeit des demonstrativen Müßiggangs: Über die häuslichen Pflichten der Beamtenfrauen im Kaiserreich." In *Frauen suchen ihre Geschichte: Historische Studien zum 19. und 20. Jahrhundert,* edited by Karin Hausen, 172–94. Munich: Beck, 1983.

Michalkiewicz, Stanislaw. "Das Bauernproblem in Schlesien in der Publizistik und in den Quellen an der Wende vom 18. zum 19. Jahrhundert." In *Der Bauer Mittel- und Osteuropas im sozioökonomischen Wandel des 18. und 19. Jahrhunderts,* edited by Dan Berindei, Wolfgang Gesemann, Alfred Hoffmann, Walter Leitsch, Albrecht Timm, and Sergij Vilfan, 293–306. Cologne and Vienna: Böhlau, 1973.

Milne, Christian. *Simple Poems on Simple Subjects. By Christian Milne, Wife of a Journeyman Ship-Carpenter, in Footdee, Aberdeen.* Aberdeen: J. Chalmers, 1805.

Mödersheim, Sabine. "'Auch die fruchtbarsten Bäume wollen beschnitten sein': Georg Friedrich Meyers Konzept der Einbildungskraft und Dichtungskraft und die Kritik an Anna Louisa Karsch." In *Dichtungstheorien der deutschen Frühaufklärung*, edited by Theodor Verweyen with Hans-Joachim Kertscher, 37–54. Tübingen: Niemeyer, 1995.

———. "Igel oder Amor? Zum Briefwechsel zwischen Anna Louisa Karsch und Johann Wilhelm Ludwig Gleim." In *G. A. Bürger und J. W. L. Gleim*, edited by Hans-Joachim Kertscher, 29–39. Tübingen: Niemeyer, 1996.

"Molly Leapor." *Gentleman's Magazine* 54 (1784): 806–7.

Molzahn, Ilse. "'Die Karschin,' eine 'Schlesische Nachtigall.'" *Schlesien* 10 (1965): 76–80.

Mommsen, Hans, and Winfried Schulze, eds. *Vom Elend der Handarbeit: Probleme historischer Unterschichtsforschung*. Stuttgart: Klett, 1981.

Montrose, Louis A. "Professing the Renaissance: The Poetics and Politics of Culture." In *The New Historicism*, edited by H. Aram Veeser, 15–36. New York and London: Routledge, 1989.

Mooser, Josef. *Ländliche Klassengesellschaft 1770–1848: Bauern und Unterschichten, Landwirtschaft und Gewerbe im östlichen Westfalen*. Göttingen: Vandenhoeck & Ruprecht, 1984.

More, Hannah. "Letters to Elizabeth Robinson Montagu." In *The Female Spectator: English Women Writers before 1800*, edited by Mary R. Mahl and Helene Koon, 277–86. Bloomington, IN and London: Indiana UP, 1977.

———. *Poems*. Introduction by Caroline Franklin. London: Cadell and Davies, 1816. Reprint, London: Routledge/Thoemmes P, 1996.

———. "The Practical Use of Female Knowledge, with a Sketch of the Female Character and a Comparative View of the Sexes." In *The Female Spectator: English Women Writers before 1800*, edited by Mary R. Mahl and Helene Koon, 287–96. Bloomington, IN and London: Indiana UP, 1977.

———. "A Prefatory Letter to Mrs. Montagu." Ann Yearsley. *Poems, on Various Subjects, by Ann Yearsley, a Milkwoman of Clifton, Near Bristol, Being Her Second Work*. London: G. G. J. and J. Robinson, Pater-Noster Row. 1787. Reprint, with an introduction by Jonathan Wordsworth, Oxford and New York: Woodstock Books, 1994.

———. *Strictures on the Modern System of Female Education. In Two Volumes*. Introduction by Gina Luria. New York and London: Garland, 1974.

"More Than Just a Gardener's Daughter!" *Border Telegraph* (May 4, 1999).

Moritz, Karl Philipp. *Journeys of a German in England in 1782*. Translated and edited by Reginald Nettel. London: Jonathan Cape, 1965.

———. *Reisen eines Deutschen in England im Jahr 1782*. Edited by Otto zur Linde. Berlin, 1903. Reprint, Nendeln/Liechtenstein: Kraus, 1968.

Müller, Peter. "Einleitung." *Sturm und Drang: Weltanschauliche und ästhetische Schriften*, vol. 1, edited by Peter Müller, xi-cxxiv. Berlin and Weimar: Aufbau Verlag, 1978.

———, ed. *Sturm und Drang: Weltanschauliche und ästhetische Schriften*. 2 vols. Berlin and Weimar: Aufbau Verlag, 1978.

Muncker, Franz. "Anna Luisa Karschin." In *Anakreontiker und preußischpatriotische Lyriker. Zwei Teile in einem Bande*, edited by Franz Muncker, 285–334. Stuttgart: Union Deutsche Verlagsgesellschaft, 1894. Reprint, Tübingen: Niemeyer, 1974.

Neuburg, Victor E. *Popular Education in Eighteenth Century England*. London: Woburn P, 1971.

Nickisch, Reinhard M. G. "'Daß sind . . . sehr unbeträchtliche Papiere.' Über die Epistel-Dichtung und die lyrischen Brief-Einlagen der Anna Louisa Karsch." In *Anna Louisa Karsch (1722–1791): Von schlesischer Kunst und Berliner "Natur." Ergebnisse des Symposiums zum 200. Todestag der Dichterin*, edited by Anke Bennholdt-Thomsen and Anita Runge, 66–80. Göttingen: Wallstein, 1992.

Niethammer, Ortrun. *Autobiographien von Frauen im 18. Jahrhundert*. Tübingen and Basel: Francke, 2000.

Nipperdey, Thomas. "Kommentar: 'Bürgerlich' als Kultur." In *Bürger und Bürgerlichkeit im 19. Jahrhundert*, edited by Jürgen Kocka, 143–48. Göttingen: Vandenhoeck & Ruprecht, 1987.

Nörtemann, Regina. "Nachwort." *"Mein Bruder in Apoll": Briefwechsel zwischen Anna Louisa Karsch und Johann Wilhelm Ludwig Gleim*, vol. 1, edited by Regina Nörtemann, 523–58. Göttingen: Wallstein, 1996.

———. "Verehrung, Freundschaft, Liebe: Zur Erotik im Briefwechsel zwischen Anna-Louisa Karsch und Johann Wilhelm Ludwig Gleim." In *Anna Louisa Karsch (1722–1791): Von schlesischer Kunst und Berliner "Natur." Ergebnisse des Symposiums zum 200. Todestag der Dichterin*, edited by Anke Bennholdt-Thomsen and Anita Runge, 81–93. Göttingen: Wallstein, 1992.

Nörtemann, Regina, and Ute Pott, eds. *"Mein Bruder in Apoll": Briefwechsel zwischen Anna Louisa Karsch und Johann Wilhelm Ludwig Gleim*. 2 vols. Göttingen: Wallstein, 1996.

"Of Genius." In *The Occasional Paper*, vol. 3 no. 10. London: Printed for E. Matthews, J. Roberts, J. Harrison, and A. Dodd, 1719.

Osborn, James M. "Spence, Natural Genius and Pope." *Philological Quarterly* 14, 1 (1966): 123–44.

Pagan, Isabel [sic]. *A Collection of Songs and Poems on Several Occasions*. Glasgow: Niven, Napier, & Khull, 1808.

———. "Letter to Samuel Tylor, Marchmante, Muirkirk (July 5, 1821)." MS 5406, f. 21, National Library of Scotland.

Palm, H. "Karschin: Anna Luise K." In *Allgemeine Deutsche Biographie,* vol. 15, edited by Königliche Akademie der Wissenschaften, 421–22. Leipzig: Duncker & Humblot, 1882.

Pascal, Roy. "Die Sturm-und-Drang-Bewegung (1952)." In *Sturm und Drang,* edited by Manfred Wacker, 25–66. Darmstadt: Wissenschaftliche Buchgesellschaft, 1985.

Paterson, James. *The Contemporaries of Burns, and the More Recent Poets of Ayrshire, with Selections Drawn from Their Writings.* Edinburgh: Hugh Paton, Carver, & Gilder, 1840. Reprint, New York: AMS, 1976.

Patton, Julia. *The English Village: A Literary Study, 1750–1850.* New York: Macmillan, 1919.

Pinchbeck, Ivy. *Women Workers and the Industrial Revolution 1750–1850.* London: Virago, 1981.

Pockels, Carl Friedrich. *Versuch einer Charakteristik des weiblichen Geschlechts. Ein Sittengemählde des Menschen, des Zeitalters und des geselligen Lebens.* 5 vols. Hanover: Christian Ritscher, 1797–1802.

Polewhele, Richard. *The Unsex'd Females; a Poem, Addressed to the Author of the Pursuits of Literature. By the Rev. Richard Polewhele.* New York: W. M. Cobbett, 1800.

Porter, Roy. *English Society in the Eighteenth Century.* London: Penguin Books, 1982.

Pott, Ute. "Berlin — Halberstadt — Berlin: Anna-Louisa Karsch und Caroline Luise von Klencke als Autorinnen im Briefwechsel mit Johann Wilhelm Ludwig Gleim." In *Anna Louisa Karsch (1722–1791): Von schlesischer Kunst und Berliner "Natur." Ergebnisse des Symposiums zum 200. Todestag der Dichterin,* edited by Anke Bennholdt-Thomsen and Anita Runge, 94–109. Göttingen: Wallstein, 1992.

———. *Briefgespräche: Über den Briefwechsel zwischen Anna Louisa Karsch und Johann Wilhelm Ludwig Gleim.* Göttingen: Wallstein, 1998.

———. "Die Freundschaft und die Musen. Gleim in seinen Briefen an die Dichterin Anna Louisa Karsch und ihre Tochter Caroline Luise von Klencke." In *G. A. Bürger und J. W. L. Gleim,* edited by Hans-Joachim Kertscher, 40–57. Tübingen: Niemeyer, 1996.

Pott, Ute, and Regina Nörtemann, eds. *"Mein Bruder in Apoll": Briefwechsel zwischen Anna Louisa Karsch und Johann Wilhelm Ludwig Gleim.* 2 vols. Göttingen: Wallstein, 1996.

Prandi, Julie. "Anna Louisa Karsch (1722–91)." Poetry translated by Julie Prandi and Walter Arndt. In *Bitter Healing: German Women Writers 1700–1830. An Anthology,* edited by Jeannine Blackwell and Susanne Zantop, 125–45. Lincoln, Nebr., and London: U of Nebraska P, 1990.

"Prayer to the Deity, A." *Gentleman's Magazine* 22 (1752): 529.

Rach, Hans-Jürgen, and Bernhard Weissel, eds. *Bauer und Landarbeiter im Kapitalismus in der Magdeburger Börde: Zur Geschichte des dörflichen Alltags vom Ausgang des 18. Jahrhunderts bis zum Beginn des 20. Jahrhunderts.* Berlin: Akademie-Verlag, 1982.

Radcliffe, David Hall. "Ancient Poetry and British Pastoral." In *From Gaelic to Romantic: Ossianic Translations,* edited by Fiona Stafford and Howard Gaskill, 27–40. Amsterdam and Atlanta, GA: Editions Rodopi, 1998.

Ramm, Elke. *Autobiographische Schriften deutschsprachiger Autorinnen um 1800.* Hildesheim: Olms, 1998.

Rassmann, Friedrich, comp. *Deutscher Dichternekrolog, oder gedrängte Übersicht der verstorbenen deutschen Dichter, Romanschriftsteller, Erzähler und Übersetzer nebst genauer Angabe ihrer Schriften.* Nordhausen: Happach, 1818.

———. *Literarisches Handwörterbuch der verstorbenen deutschen Dichter und zur schönen Literatur gehörenden Schriftsteller in 8 Zeitabschnitten, von 1137–1824.* Leipzig: Lauffer, 1826.

Raynor, John. *The Middle Class.* Harlow: Longmans, 1969.

Review of Ann Yearsley, *Earl Goodwin, an Historical Play. Monthly Review* (November 1791): 347–48.

Review of Ann Yearsley, *Poems on Several Occasions. Monthly Review* (September 1785): 216–21.

Review of Ann Yearsley, *Poems, on Various Subjects. Monthly Review* (December 1787): 485–89.

Review of Ann Yearsley, *The Rural Lyre, a Volume of Poems. Critical Review* 19 ns (1797): 462–63.

Review of Anna Louisa Karsch, *Auserlesene Gedichte. Journal Encyclopédique* 16 (1763): 76–86.

Review of Elizabeth Hands, *The Death of Ammon* [sic]. *Gentleman's Magazine* 60 (1790): 540.

Review of Elizabeth Hands, *The Death of Amnon. Analytical Review* 6 (1790): 96.

Review of Elizabeth Hands, *The Death of Amnon. Monthly Review* 3 ns (1790): 345–46.

Review of Mary Leapor, *Poems on Several Occasions,* vol. 1. *Monthly Review* 2 (1749): 14–25 [includes three poems appended to the review].

Review of Mary Leapor, *Poems on Several Occasions,* vol. 2. *Monthly Review* 5 (1751) 23–32 [includes some letters by Mary Leapor and Bridget Freemantle appended to the review].

Review of Mary Scott, *The Female Advocate. Critical Review* (1774): 218–20.

Review of Mary Scott, *The Female Advocate. Gentleman's Magazine* 44 (1774): 375–77.

Review of Mary Scott, *The Female Advocate. Monthly Review* 51 (1774): 387–90.

Review of Mary Scott, *Messiah: A Poem. Analytical Review* 2 (1788): 460.

Reynolds, Myra. *The Learned Lady in England 1650–1760.* Gloucester: Peter Smith, 1964.

Richardson, W. "Letter to Mr. William Craig, Gallowgate, Glasgow (June 3, 1765)." MS 9931, f. 81, National Library of Scotland.

Rizzo, Betty. "Christopher Smart, The 'C. S.' Poems, and Molly Leapor's Epitaph." *The Library: A Quarterly Journal of Bibliography* 5 (1983): 22–31.

———. "Molly Leapor: An Anxiety for Influence." *The Age of Johnson: A Scholarly Annual* 4 (1991): 313–43.

———. "The Patron as Poet Maker: The Politics of Benefaction." *Studies in Eighteenth-Century Culture* 20 (1990): 241–66.

Robbins, Bruce. *The Servant's Hand: English Fiction from Below.* New York: Columbia UP, 1986.

Roberts, William, ed. *Memoirs of the Life and Correspondence of Mrs. Hannah More,* 2nd ed. 4 vols. London: R. B. Seeley & W. Burnside, 1834.

Robisheaux, Thomas. "The Peasantries of Western Germany, 1300–1750." In *The Peasantries of Europe from the Fourteenth to the Eighteenth Centuries,* edited by Tom Scott, 111–44. London and New York: Longman, 1998.

———. *Rural Society and the Search for Order in Early Modern Germany.* Cambridge: Cambridge UP, 1989.

Roebling, Irmgard. "Sturm und Drang — weiblich: Eine Untersuchung zu Sophie Albrechts Schauspiel 'Theresgen'." *Der Deutschunterricht* 48 (1996): 63–77.

Rowbotham, Sheila. *Hidden from History: Rediscovering Women in History from the 17th Century to the Present.* New York: Pantheon, 1974.

Rowe, N. "Some Account of the Life, etc., of Mr. *William Shakespear.*" *The Works of Mr.* William Shakespear; *in Six Volumes. Adorn'd with Cuts. Revis'd and Corrected, with an Account of the Life and Writings of the Author.* Vol. 1, edited by Nicholas Rowe, i-xl. London: Printed for Jacob Tonson, 1709.

Runge, Edith Amelie. *Primitivism and Related Ideas in Sturm und Drang Literature.* New York: Russell & Russell, 1972.

Sabean, David. "Aspects of Kinship Behaviour and Property in Rural Western Europe before 1800." In *Family and Inheritance: Rural Society in Western Europe, 1200–1800*, edited by Jack Goody, Joan Thirsk, and E. P. Thompson, 96–111. Cambridge: Cambridge UP, 1976.

Sales, Roger. "The Maid and the Minister's Wife: Literary Philanthropy in Regency York." In *Women's Poetry in the Enlightenment: The Making of a Canon, 1730–1820*, edited by Isobel Armstrong and Virginia Blain, 127–41. London: Macmillan, 1999.

Sauder, Gerhard. "Reise eines Deutschen in England im Jahr 1782: Karl Philipp Moritz." In *"Der curieuse Passagier": Deutsche Englandreisende des achtzehnten Jahrhunderts als Vermittler kultureller und technologischer Anregungen*, 93–108. Heidelberg: Carl Winter, 1983.

Schabert, Ina. "Amazonen der Feder und verschleierte Ladies: Schreibende Frauen im England der Aufklärung und der nachaufklärerischen Zeit." In *Autorschaft: Genus und Genie in der Zeit um 1800*, edited by Ina Schabert and Barbara Schaff, 105–23. Berlin: Erich Schmidt, 1994.

Schabert, Ina, and Barbara Schaff, eds. *Autorschaft: Genus und Genie in der Zeit um 1800*. Berlin: Erich Schmidt, 1994.

———. "Einleitung." *Autorschaft: Genus und Genie in der Zeit um 1800*, edited by Ina Schabert and Barbara Schaff, 9–19. Berlin: Erich Schmidt, 1994.

Schaff, Barbara. "'Earth, air, and sky, and ocean has its bubbles, and verse is one of them — this most of all': Poetische Freiräume britischer Dichterinnen der Romantik." In *Autorschaft: Genus und Genie in der Zeit um 1800*, edited by Ina Schabert and Barbara Schaff, 125–44. Berlin: Erich Schmidt, 1994.

Schaffers, Uta. *Auf überlebtes Elend blick ich nieder: Anna Louisa Karsch in Selbst- und Fremdzeugnissen*. Göttingen: Wallstein, 1997.

Schiller, Friedrich. "On the Necessary Limitations in the Use of Beauty of Form." In *The Works of Frederick Schiller*, vol. 6. Translated by A. J. W. Morrison, 223–47. 6 vols. London: Henry G. Bohn (vols. 1–3) and George Bell & Sons (vols. 4–6). 1847–75.

———. "Über die notwendigen Grenzen beim Gebrauch schöner Formen." In *Sämtliche Werke. Vol. 5: Erzählungen/Theoretische Schriften*, 4th ed., edited by Gerhard Fricke and Herbert G. Göpfert, 670–93. Munich: Carl Hanser, 1967.

Schilling, Renate. *Schwedisch-Pommern um 1700: Studien zur Agrarstruktur eines Territoriums extremer Gutsherrschaft, untersucht auf der Grundlage des schwedischen Matrikelwerkes 1692–1698*. Weimar: Hermann Böhlaus Nachfolger, 1989.

Schindel, Carl Wilhelm Otto August von. *Die deutschen Schriftstellerinnen des neunzehnten Jahrhunderts*. 3 vols. in 1. Leipzig, 1823–25. Reprint of the 2nd ed., Hildesheim, Zurich, and New York: Georg Olms, 2000.

Schissler, Hanna. *Preußische Agrargesellschaft im Wandel: Wirtschaftliche, gesellschaftliche und politische Transformationsprozesse von 1763 bis 1847.* Göttingen: Vandenhoeck & Ruprecht, 1978.

Schlaffer, Hannelore. "Naturpoesie im Zeitalter der Aufklärung: Anna Luisa Karsch (1722–1791). Ein Portrait." In *Deutsche Literatur von Frauen,* vol. 1, edited by Gisela Brinker-Gabler, 313–24, 499–500, 539–40. Munich: Beck, 1988.

Schlumbohm, Jürgen, ed. *Kinderstuben: Wie Kinder zu Bauern, Bürgern, Aristokraten wurden.* Munich: dtv, 1983.

Schmidt, Jochen. *Die Geschichte des Genie-Gedankens in der deutschen Literatur, Philosophie und Politik 1750–1945.* 2 vols. Darmstadt: Wissenschaftliche Buchgesellschaft, 1985.

Schmidt-Dengler, Wendelin. *Genius: Zur Wirkungsgeschichte antiker Mythologeme in der Goethezeit.* Munich: C. H. Beck, 1978.

Schneider, Ferdinand Josef. *Die deutsche Dichtung der Geniezeit.* Stuttgart: Metzler, 1952.

Scholz, Hannelore. "'Doch mein Herz, . . . dieses ist ganz Gefühl, ganz Freundschaft, so wie es den Dichtern geziemt.' Die Karschin im Kontext der Volkspoesiedebatte in Deutschland." In *Anna Louisa Karsch (1722–1791): Von schlesischer Kunst und Berliner "Natur." Ergebnisse des Symposiums zum 200. Todestag der Dichterin,* edited by Anke Bennholdt-Thomsen and Anita Runge, 132–48. Göttingen: Wallstein, 1992.

Schröder, Rainer. *Das Gesinde war immer frech und unverschämt: Gesinde und Gesinderecht vornehmlich im 18. Jahrhundert.* Frankfurt am Main: Keip, 1992.

Scott, Mary. *The Female Advocate; a Poem. Occasioned by Reading Mr. Duncombe's Feminead (1774).* Introduction by Gae Holladay. The Augustan Reprint Society Publication no. 224. Los Angeles: UCLA William Andrews Clark Memorial Library, 1984.

Scott, Tom, ed. *The Peasantries of Europe from the Fourteenth to the Eighteenth Centuries.* London and New York: Longman, 1998.

———. *The Penguin Book of Scottish Verse.* Harmondsworth and Middlesex: Penguin Books, 1981.

Seward, Anna. *Letters of Anna Seward, Written between the Years 1784 and 1807.* 6 vols. Edinburgh: George Ramsay, 1811.

Shanks, Henry. *The Peasant Poets of Scotland and, Musings under the Beeches.* Bathgate: L. Gilbertson, 1881.

Shapin, Steven. *A Social History of Truth: Civility and Science in Seventeenth-Century England.* Chicago and London: U of Chicago P, 1994.

Sharp, [Elizabeth A.], ed. *Women's Voices: An Anthology of the Most Characteristic Poems by English, Scottish, and Irish Women.* London: Walter Scott, 1887.

Shiach, Morag. *Discourse on Popular Culture: Class, Gender and History in the Analysis of Popular Culture.* Oxford: Polity Press, 1989.

Simonton, Deborah. *A History of European Women's Work, 1700 to the Present.* London and New York: Routledge, 1998.

Sotiropoulos, Carol Strauss. "Frictions, Fictions, and Forms: Woman's Coming of Age in Eighteenth-Century Educational Discourses." Ph.D. diss., University of Connecticut, Storrs, 2001.

Southey, Robert. *The Lives and Works of the Uneducated Poets.* Edited by J. S. Childers. London: Humphrey Milford, 1925.

Spence, [Elizabeth]. "Letters from the Northern Highlands." In *Sketches of Obscure Poets, with Specimens of Their Writings,* 178–90. London: Cochrane & McCrone, 1833.

Spufford, Margaret. "Peasant Inheritance Customs and Land Distribution in Cambridgeshire from the Sixteenth to the Eighteenth Centuries." In *Family and Inheritance: Rural Society in Western Europe, 1200–1800,* edited by Jack Goody, Joan Thirsk, and E. P. Thompson, 156–76. Cambridge: Cambridge UP, 1976.

———. *Small Books and Pleasant Histories: Popular Fiction and Its Readership in Seventeenth-Century England.* Athens, Ga.: U of Georgia P, 1981.

Stadelmann, Rudolph. *Friedrich Wilhelm I. in seiner Thätigkeit für die Landescultur Preussens.* Leipzig: S. Hirzel, 1878.

Stanton, Judith Phillipps. "Statistical Profile of Women Writing in English from 1660 to 1800." In *Eighteenth-Century Women and the Arts,* edited by Frederick M. Keener and Susan E. Lorsch, 247–54. Westport, CT: Greenwood P, 1988.

Stellmacher, Wolfgang. "Grundfragen der Shakespeare-Rezeption in der Frühphase des Sturm und Drang." In *Sturm und Drang,* edited by Manfred Wacker, 112–43. Darmstadt: Wissenschaftliche Buchgesellschaft, 1985.

Stenhouse, William. *Illustrations of the Lyric Poetry and Music of Scotland.* Edinburgh and London: William Blackwood, 1853.

Stephan, Inge. "Geniekult und Männerbund: Zur Ausgrenzung des 'Weiblichen' in der Sturm und Drang-Bewegung." In *Jakob Michael Reinhold Lenz,* edited by Martin Kagel, 46–54. Munich: text + kritik, 2000.

Stewart, Karen A. *Scottish Women Writers to 1987. A Select Guide and Bibliography.* Glasgow: The Mitchell Library, 1987.

Stone, Lawrence. *The Family, Sex and Marriage in England 1500–1800.* New York, Hagerstown, MD, San Francisco, and London: Harper & Row, 1977.

———. "Literacy and Education in England 1640–1900." *Past and Present* 42 (1969): 69–139.

Strodtmann, Adolf, ed. *Briefe von und an Gottfried August Bürger. Ein Beitrag zur Literaturgeschichte seiner Zeit. Aus dem Nachlasse Bürger's und anderen, meist handschriftlichen Quellen.* 4 vols. Berlin: Gebrüder Paetel, 1874.

Stubbs, Patricia. *Women and Fiction: Feminism and the Novel, 1880–1920.* Sussex and New York: Barnes & Noble, 1979.

Stüssel, Kerstin. *Poetische Ausbildung und dichterisches Handeln: Poetik und autobiographisches Schreiben im 18. und beginnenden 19. Jahrhundert.* Tübingen: Niemeyer, 1993.

Sulzer, Johann Georg. "Entwickelung des Begriffs vom Genie." In *Vermischte philosophische Schriften. 2 Theile in 1 Band,* 307–22. Leipzig: Weidmanns Erben and Reich, 1773. Reprint, Hildesheim, and New York: Georg Olms, 1974.

———. "General Theory of the Fine Arts (1771–74): Selected Articles, trans. and ed. Thomas Christensen." In *Aesthetics and the Art of Musical Composition in the German Enlightenment: Selected Writings of Johann Georg Sulzer and Heinrich Christoph Koch,* edited by Nancy Kovaleff Baker and Thomas Christensen, 3–108. Cambridge: Cambridge UP, 1995.

———. *Vermischte philosophische Schriften. 2 Theile in 1 Band.* Leipzig: Weidmanns Erben and Reich, 1773. Reprint, Hildesheim, and New York: Georg Olms, 1974.

———. "Von der Kraft (Energie) in den Werken der schönen Künste." In *Vermischte philosophische Schriften. 2 Theile in 1 Band,* 122–45. Leipzig: Weidmanns Erben and Reich, 1773. Reprint, Hildesheim, New York: Georg Olms, 1974.

———. "Vorrede." Anna Louisa Karsch. *Auserlesene Gedichte. Faksimile-Nachdruck,* edited by Alfred Anger, vii-xxvi. Stuttgart: Metzler, 1966.

Tebben, Karin, ed. *Beruf Schriftstellerin: Schreibende Frauen im 18. und 19. Jahrhundert.* Göttingen: Vandenhoeck & Ruprecht, 1998.

———. "Soziokulturelle Bedingungen weiblicher Schriftkultur im 18. und 19. Jahrhundert: Zur Einleitung." In *Beruf Schriftstellerin: Schreibende Frauen im 18. und 19. Jahrhundert,* edited by Karin Tebben, 10–46. Göttingen: Vandenhoeck & Ruprecht, 1998.

———. "Vorwort." In *Beruf Schriftstellerin: Schreibende Frauen im 18. und 19. Jahrhundert,* edited by Karin Tebben, 7–9. Göttingen: Vandenhoeck & Ruprecht, 1998.

Thirsk, Joan. *England's Agricultural Regions and Agrarian History, 1500–1750.* Houndmills, Basingstoke, Hampshire and London: Macmillan Education, 1987.

———. *English Peasant Farming: The Agrarian History of Lincolnshire from Tudor to Recent Times.* London and New York: Methuen, 1981.

———, ed. *The Agrarian History of England and Wales. Vol. V (1640–1750)*. Cambridge: Cambridge UP, 1984–85.

———, ed. *The Rural Economy of England: Collected Essays*. London: Hambledon, 1984.

Thomas, Keith. "The Meaning of Literacy in Early Modern England." In *The Written Word: Literacy in Transition*, edited by Gerd Baumann, 97–131. Oxford: Clarendon P, 1986.

Thompson, E. P. "The Grid of Inheritance: A Comment." In *Family and Inheritance: Rural Society in Western Europe, 1200–1800*, edited by Jack Goody, Joan Thirsk, and E. P. Thompson, 328–60. Cambridge: Cambridge UP, 1976.

Thüme, Hans. *Beiträge zur Geschichte des Geniebegriffs in England*. Halle: Karras, Kröber, and Nietschmann, 1927.

Todd, Barbara. "Freebench and Free Enterprise: Widows and Their Property in Two Berkshire Villages." In *English Rural Society, 1500–1800: Essays in Honour of Joan Thirsk*, edited by John Chartres and David Hey, 175–200. Cambridge: Cambridge UP, 1990.

Todd, Janet. *Sensibility: An Introduction*. London and New York: Methuen, 1986.

———, ed. *A Dictionary of British and American Women Writers 1660–1800*. Totowa, NJ: Rowman & Allanheld, 1985.

Tompkins, Joyce Marjorie Sanxter. "The Bristol Milkwoman." In *The Polite Marriage*, 58–102. Freeport, NY: Books for Libraries P, 1969.

Torgovnick, Marianna. *Gone Primitive: Savage Intellects, Modern Lives*. Chicago and London: U of Chicago P, 1990.

———. *Primitive Passions: Men, Women, and the Quest for Ecstasy*. New York: Random House, 1997.

Touaillon, Christine. *Der deutsche Frauenroman des 18. Jahrhunderts*. Vienna: Braumüller, 1919. Reprint, Bern and Frankfurt: Lang, 1979.

Tresidder, Megan. "Big Sister of the Anti-Family." *The Guardian* (January 27, 1996): p. 25, col. 1.

[Unger, Friederike Helene.] "Etwas über das weibliche Gesinde. Von einer Hausfrau." *Berlinische Monatsschrift* 1 (1788): 676–84.

Unwin, Rayner. *The Rural Muse: Studies in the Peasant Poetry of England*. London: George Allen & Unwin, 1954.

Uphaus, Robert W. and Gretchen M. Foster, eds. *The Other Eighteenth Century: English Women of Letters 1660–1800*. East Lansing, MI: Colleagues P, 1991.

Vaughan, Larry. *The Historical Constellation of the Sturm und Drang*. New York, Berne, and Frankfurt am Main: Peter Lang, 1985.

Veeser, H. Aram, ed. *The New Historicism*. New York and London: Routledge, 1989.

Verweyen, Theodor, ed. (with Hans-Joachim Kertscher). *Dichtungstheorien der deutschen Frühaufklärung*. Tübingen: Niemeyer, 1995.

Vilfan, Sergij. "Die Agrarsozialpolitik von Maria Theresia bis Kudlich." In *Der Bauer Mittel- und Osteuropas im soziöökonomischen Wandel des 18. und 19. Jahrhunderts*, edited by Dan Berindei, Wolfgang Gesemann, Alfred Hoffmann, Walter Leitsch, Albrecht Timm, and Sergij Vilfan, 1–52. Cologne and Vienna: Böhlau, 1973.

Vollhardt, Friedrich. "Die Grundregel des Geschmacks." In *Dichtungstheorien der deutschen Frühaufklärung*, edited by Theodor Verweyen with Hans-Joachim Kertscher, 26–36. Tübingen: Niemeyer, 1995.

Voss, Jürgen. "Der Gemeine Mann und die Volksaufklärung im späten 18. Jahrhundert." In *Vom Elend der Handarbeit: Probleme historischer Unterschichtenforschung*, edited by Hans Mommsen and Winfried Schulze, 208–33. Stuttgart: Klett, 1981.

Wacker, Manfred. "Einleitung." *Sturm und Drang*, edited by Manfred Wacker, 1–15. Darmstadt: Wissenschaftliche Buchgesellschaft, 1985.

———, ed. *Sturm und Drang*. Darmstadt: Wissenschaftliche Buchgesellschaft, 1985.

Waldron, Mary. "Ann Yearsley and the Clifton Records." *Age of Johnson* 3 (1990): 301–29.

———. "'By No Means Milk and Water Matters': The Contribution to English Poetry of Ann Yearsley, Milkwoman of Clifton, 1753–1806." *Studies on Voltaire and the Eighteenth Century* 304 (1992): 801–4.

———. *Lactilla, the Milkwoman of Clifton: The Life and Writings of Ann Yearsley, 1753–1806*. Athens, Ga., and London: U of Georgia P, 1996.

———. "'This Muse-Born Wonder': The Occluded Voice of Ann Yearsley, Milkwoman and Poet of Clifton." In *Women's Poetry in the Enlightenment: The Making of a Canon, 1730–1820*, edited by Isobel Armstrong and Virginia Blain, 113–26. London: Macmillan, 1999.

Wallech, Stephen. "'Class versus Rank': The Transformation of Eighteenth-Century English Social Terms and Theories of Production." In *Race, Gender, and Rank: Early Modern Ideas of Humanity*, edited by Maryanne Cline Horowitz, 269–91. Rochester, NY: U of Rochester P, 1992.

Walpole, Horace. *Yale Edition of the Correspondence of Horace Walpole*. 48 vols. Edited by W. S. Lewis. London and New Haven, CT: Yale UP, 1937–83.

Wappler, Gerlinde. "Editionspraxis im 18. Jahrhundert: Die verlegerischen Bemühungen im Gleim-Kreis im Zusammenhang mit Anna Louisa Karsch." In *Anna Louisa Karsch (1722–1791): Von schlesischer Kunst und Berliner "Natur." Ergebnisse des Symposiums zum 200. Todestag der Dichterin,* edited by Anke Bennholdt-Thomsen and Anita Runge, 57–65. Göttingen: Wallstein, 1992.

———. *Gleims Leben und seine Beziehungen zu berühmten Zeitgenossen in Daten.* Halberstadt: Druckerei "Freundschaft," 1988.

Watanabe-O'Kelly, Helen. "What Difference Does Feminism Make to the Study of German Literature?" In *Gendering German Studies: New Perspectives on German Literature and Culture,* edited by Margaret Littler, 2–11. Oxford: Blackwell, 1997.

Watt, Helga Schutte. "Sophie La Roche as a German Patriot." In *Gender and Germanness: Cultural Productions of Nation,* edited by Patricia Herminghouse and Magda Mueller, 36–50. Providence, RI, and Oxford: Berghahn, 1997.

Watt, Ian. "From *The Rise of the Novel: Studies in Defoe, Richardson, and Fielding.*" In *Theory of the Novel: A Historical Approach,* edited by Michael McKeon, 363–81, 441–66. Baltimore and London: Johns Hopkins UP, 2000.

———. *The Rise of the Novel: Studies in Defoe, Richardson, and Fielding.* Berkeley: U of California P, 1957.

Wehinger, Brunhilde. "'Die Frucht ist fleckig und der Spiegel trübe': Lyrikerinnen im 19. Jahrhundert." In *Frauen Literatur Geschichte: Schreibende Frauen vom Mittelalter bis zur Gegenwart,* 2nd ed., edited by Hiltrud Gnüg and Renate Möhrmann, 299–312. Stuttgart and Weimar: Metzler, 1999.

Wehler, Hans-Ulrich. *Deutsche Gesellschaftsgeschichte: Vom Feudalismus des Alten Reiches bis zur defensiven Modernisierung der Reformära: 1700–1815,* vol. 1. Munich: C. H. Beck, 1987.

Weinstein, Cindy. *The Literature of Labor and the Labors of Literature: Allegory in Nineteenth-Century American Fiction.* Cambridge: Cambridge UP, 1995.

[West, Jane]. *A Gossip's Story, and A Legendary Tale.* By the Author of *Advantages of Education.* In two volumes, 3rd ed. London: T. N. Longman, 1798.

———. *Letters Addressed to a Young Man, on His First Entrance into Life, and Adapted to the Peculiar Circumstances of the Present Times.* By Mrs. West, Author of *"A Tale of the Times," "A Gossip's Story,"* etc. etc. In Three Volumes. London: Printed by A. Strahan, Printers-Street, for T. N. Longman and O. Rees, Paternoster-Row, 1801.

———. *Letters to a Young Lady, in Which the Duties and Character of Women Are Considered, Chiefly with a Reference to Prevailing Opinions.* By Mrs. West, Author of *Letters to a Young Man,* etc. 3 vols. London: Longman, Hurst, Rees, and Orme, Paternoster-Row, 1806.

[———]. *The Loyalists, an Historical Novel. By the Author of "Letter to a Young Man," "A Tale of the Times," etc,* 2nd ed., 3 vols. London: Longman, Hurst, Rees, Orme, and Brown, 1812.

———. *Miscellaneous Poems, and A Tragedy. By Mrs. West.* York: W. Blanchard, 1791.

[———]. *The Refusal. By the Author of the "Tale of the Times," "Infidel Father," etc.* 3 vols. London: Printed for Longman, Hurst, Rees, and Orme, Paternoster Row, 1810.

[———]. *Ringrove, or, Old Fashioned Notions. By the Author of "Letters to a Young Man," A Tale of the Times," etc. etc.* 2 vols. London: Longman, Rees, Orme, Brown, and Green, 1827.

[———]. *A Tale of the Times. By the Author of a Gossip's Story.* 3 vols. London: T. N. Longman and O. Rees, 1799.

Whateley Darwall, Mary. *Original Poems on Several Occasions. By Miss Whateley.* London: Printed for R. & J. Dodsley, 1764.

Whitney, Lois. *Primitivism and the Idea of Progress in English Popular Literature of the Eighteenth Century.* New York: Octagon Books, 1973.

Wieland, Christoph Martin. "To D.F.G.R.V." Sophie von La Roche. In *The History of Lady Sophia Sternheim*, edited by James Lynn, translated by Joseph Collyer, 5–9. London: Pickering & Chatto, 1991.

Wierling, Dorothee. "'Ich hab meine Arbeit gemacht — was wollte sie mehr?' Dienstmädchen im städtischen Haushalt der Jahrhundertwende." In *Frauen suchen ihre Geschichte: Historische Studien zum 19. und 20. Jahrhundert,* edited by Karin Hausen, 144–71. Munich: C. H. Beck, 1983.

Wilcox, Lance E. "Gibbon versus Law: Enlightenment and Pietist Standards for Women." In *Eighteenth-Century Women and the Arts,* edited by Frederick M. Keener and Susan E. Lorsch, 11–17. Westport, CT: Greenwood, 1988.

Willey, Basil. *The Eighteenth Century Background: Studies on the Idea of Nature in the Thought of the Period.* London: Chatto & Windus, 1946.

Williams, Raymond. *The Country and the City.* New York: Oxford UP, 1973.

———. *Marxism and Literature.* Oxford and New York: Oxford UP, 1977.

Wilson, James Grant, ed. *The Poets and Poetry of Scotland: From the Earliest to the Present Time.* 4 vols. London: Blackie & Son, 1877.

Wilson, W. Daniel. "Illuminatenideologie: Revolution, Anarchie oder aufgeklärter Absolutismus? Mit vorläufigen Ergebnissen aus der 'Schwedenkiste.'" In *Der Illuminatenorden (1776–1785/87): Ein politischer Geheimbund der Aufklärungszeit,* edited by Helmut Reinalter, 281–304. Bern: Peter Lang, 1998.

———. "The Young Goethe's Political Fantasies." In *Sturm und Drang,* edited by David D. Hill, 187–215. Rochester, NY: Camden House, 2002.

Winter, Hans-Gerd. *J. M. R. Lenz*. Stuttgart: Metzler, 1987.

Wiseman, Jane. *Antiochus the Great: Or, the Fatal Relapse. A Tragedy. As It Is Now Acted at the New-Theatre in Lincolns-Inn-Fields. By His Majesty's Servants. Written by Mrs. Jane Wiseman.* London: William Turner & Richard Bassett, 1702.

Wittmann, Reinhard. "Der lesende Landmann: Zur Rezeption aufklärerischer Bemühungen durch die bäuerliche Bevölkerung im 18. Jahrhundert." In *Der Bauer Mittel- und Osteuropas im sozioökonomischen Wandel des 18. und 19. Jahrhunderts*, edited by Dan Berindei, Wolfgang Gesemann, Alfred Hoffmann, Walter Leitsch, Albrecht Timm, and Sergij Vilfan, 142–96. Cologne and Vienna: Böhlau, 1973.

Wolf, Gerhard. "Die Gaben der Musen sind mancherlei: Anna Louisa Karschin — die preußische Sappho." Anna Louisa Karsch. *O, mir entwischt nicht, was die Menschen fühlen: Anna Louisa Karschin. Gedichte und Briefe, Stimmen von Zeitgenossen*, edited by Gerhard Wolf, 267–307. Berlin: Buchverlag Der Morgen, 1981.

Wolf, Herman. "Die Genielehre des jungen Herder (1925)." In *Sturm und Drang*, edited by Manfred Wacker, 184–214. Darmstadt: Wissenschaftliche Buchgesellschaft, 1985.

———. *Versuch einer Geschichte des Geniebegriffs in der deutschen Ästhetik des 18. Jahrhunderts*. 2 vols. Heidelberg: C. Winter, 1923.

Wolf-Graaf, Anke. *Frauen Arbeit: Eine Bildchronik*. Weinheim and Basel: Beltz, 1983.

Wright, David, ed. and intro. *The Penguin Book of Everyday Verse*. Middlesex: Penguin Books, 1983.

Wu, Duncan, ed. *Romantic Women Poets: An Anthology*. Malden, MA: Blackwell, 1997.

Wunberg, Gotthart. "Mnemosyne. Literatur unter den Bedingungen der Moderne: Ihre technik- und sozialgeschichtliche Begründung." In *Mnemosyne: Formen und Funktionen der kulturellen Erinnerung*, edited by Aleida Assmann and Dietrich Herth, 83–100. Frankfurt am Main: Fischer, 1991.

Wunder, Heide. *Die bäuerliche Gemeinde in Deutschland*. Göttingen: Vandenhoeck & Ruprecht, 1986.

———. "Gender Norms and their Enforcement in Early Modern Germany." In *Gender Relations in German History: Power, Agency and Experience from the Sixteenth to the Twentieth Century*, edited by Lynn Abrams and Elizabeth Harvey, 39–56. Durham, NC: Duke UP, 1993.

———. "Die ländliche Gemeinde als Strukturprinzip der mittelalterlich-frühneuzeitlichen Geschichte Mitteleuropas." In *Landgemeinde und Stadtgemeinde in Mitteleuropa: Ein struktureller Vergleich*, suppl. 13, edited by Peter Blickle, 385–402. Munich: R. Oldenbourg, 1991.

Yearsley, Ann. *Poems, on Several Occasions. By Ann Yearsley, a Milkwoman of Bristol*. London: T. Cadell, 1785.

———. *Poems, on Various Subjects, by Ann Yearsley, a Milkwoman of Clifton, Near Bristol; Being Her Second Work*. London: Printed for the Author and Sold by G. G. J. and J. Robinson, Pater-Noster Row. 1787. Reprint, with an introduction by Jonathan Wordsworth, Oxford and New York: Woodstock Books, 1994.

———. *The Rural Lyre; A Volume of Poems* [Bound with: Elizabeth Hands, *The Death of Amnon: A Poem*]. Introduction by Caroline Franklin. London: G. G. and J. Robinson, 1796. Reprint, London: Routledge, 1996.

———. "To the Noble and Generous Subscribers." In *Poems, on Various Subjects, by Ann Yearsley, a Milkwoman of Clifton, Near Bristol; Being Her Second Work*. London: Printed for the Author and Sold by G. G. J. and J. Robinson, Pater-Noster Row. 1787. Reprint, with an introduction by Jonathan Wordsworth, Oxford and New York: Woodstock Books, 1994.

Young, James D. *The Rousing of the Scottish Working Class*. London: Croom Helm, 1979.

———. *Women and Popular Struggles: A History of British Working-Class Women, 1560–1984*. Edinburgh: Mainstream Publishing, 1985.

Zantop, Susanne. "The Beautiful, the Ugly, and the German: Race, Gender, and Nationality in Eighteenth-Century Anthropological Discourse." In *Gender and Germanness: Cultural Productions of Nation*, edited by Patricia Herminghouse and Magda Mueller, 21–35. Providence, RI, and Oxford: Berghahn, 1997.

Zeman, Herbert. *Die deutsche anakreontische Dichtung. Ein Versuch zur Erfassung ihrer ästhetischen und literarhistorischen Erscheinungsformen im 18. Jahrhundert*. Stuttgart: Metzler, 1972.

Zilsel, Edgar. *Die Entstehung des Geniebegriffes: Ein Beitrag zur Ideengeschichte der Antike und des Frühkapitalismus*. Tübingen: J. C. B. Mohr, 1926.

Zionkowski, Linda. "Strategies of Containment: Stephen Duck, Ann Yearsley, and the Problem of Polite Culture." *Eighteenth-Century Life* 13 (November 1989): 91–108.

# Index

Adams, Jean, 68
agriculture, 177–81
Alighieri, Dante, 91
*Analytical Review, The,* 67, 303, 304
anonymity, of women writers, 242–43
Arnim, Achim von, 10–11, 91–92, 102, 274
art, as a bourgeois concept, 1, 2, 7–8, 10–11, 13, 19, 21, 27–28, 49–53, 65–66, 69, 87, 89–91, 98, 100–103, 105, 174–75, 199, 213–14, 216–17, 219–20, 224, 226, 228, 230–31, 234, 240–58, 274, 275, 276; definitions of, 12–14, 92–93, 176–77; and masculinity, 2, 13, 100, 158, 220–21, 225, 230–31, 239–58
Ashraf, Phyllis Mary, 5, 46, 47, 67, 68–69, 158, 274
Atkinson, Kate, 256
autobiographical writing, as an aspect in natural genius aesthetics, 33, 105; by peasant women, 11–12, 108–17, 120, 123–28, 158, 195
*Autonomieästhetik.* See autonomy, artistic
autonomy, artistic, 89–91, 101–2, 234, 257–58. See also art; genius, natural; imitation; originality

Barber, Mary, 3, 4, 274, 291; reprints of, 6

*Bauernaufklärung,* 42–43, 191, 251–52, 310
Becker-Cantarino, Barbara, 40, 70, 92, 108, 109, 216, 244, 254, 265, 275–76, 292, 293, 294, 295
Bennholdt-Thomsen, Anke, and Anita Runge, 4, 5, 70, 92, 257, 265, 274, 275, 276, 289, 295, 301, 302, 306, 311
Bentley, Elizabeth, 3, 53, 57, 58, 259, 276; and authorship, 62, 238; biographical descriptions of, 56–58; and pastorals, 164–65; and patronage, 62, 64, 66
Bentley, Elizabeth, works by: "Lines, Addressed as a Tribute," 238; "On a Summer Morning, 1786," 165
*Bescheidenheitstopos,* 243–44, 253–54, 285
Beuys, Barbara, 6, 9, 72, 74, 120, 145, 201, 218, 292
biography, and Art, 10–11, 77, 90, 100–103, 105–8, 214; as literature, 105–8, 128–59; and patronage, 64–66, 78, 214, 243
*Bildungsbürgertum.* See Bürger
Bloomfield, Robert, 45, 51
Brown, John, 29, 277
*Bürger, Bürgertum* (bourgeois/bourgeoisie, as a concept), 14, 16, 23, 25–26, 133, 245–51, 294, 301; in opposition to the aristocracy, 19, 22–23
Bürger, Christa, 11, 253, 278
Bürger, Gottfried August, 5, 24, 46, 278, 308; aesthetic treatises

by, 24, 25, 26, 29, 30–32, 34, 145–46
Bürger, Peter, 14, 276, 278, 286, 289, 299
Burns, Robert, 3, 5, 10, 55, 58, 61, 139, 152, 238, 262, 266, 269, 277, 278, 280, 296, 298, 302; as character in Little's poetry, 218, 220–22, 230, 237–38, 266; and criticism, 9, 257; and patronage, 68

Candler, Ann, 3, 53, 174, 259–60, 279; biographical descriptions of, 56–58, 113–14, 173; and criticism, 217; as natural genius, 58, 197; and patronage, 55
Candler, Ann, works by: "Reflections on my Own Situation," 173; "To the Rev. Dr. J——n," 197, 217
Carter, Jefferson Matthew, 3, 5, 9, 24, 25, 27, 45, 46, 93, 96, 98, 99, 108, 155, 197, 271, 279
Cave, Jane, 3, 66, 169, 196, 260, 279; and authorship, 61; and pastorals, 164
Cave, Jane, works by: "The Author's Plea," 196
Chézy, Helmina von, 123, 253, 279–80, 289; and authorship, 243; biography of Karsch, 70, 92, 111, 124, 128, 131–33, 134, 140, 142, 145, 154, 158, 197, 243, 265
Chodowiecki, Daniel Nikolaus, 142, 143, 145, 228–29
Clare, John, 9, 51, 257, 275
class, 245–46
Collier, Mary, 3, 45, 51, 56, 221, 237, 238, 260–61, 280, 293, 295; and authorship, 61; biographical descriptions of, 56–57, 184; and criticism, 66; and gender roles, 184–85; as natural genius, 60–61; and patronage, 54, 68
Collier, Mary, works by: "The Woman's Labour," 176–77, 181–86, 191, 238
Colman, George, and Bonnell Thornton, 4, 66, 112, 148, 161, 164, 167, 168, 169, 198, 217, 218, 219, 234, 235, 236, 237, 255, 266, 267
country house poem, 168–71, 298

Dalrymple, Sir David, 256
Dante Alighieri. See Alighieri, Dante
Darwall, Mary Whateley. See Whateley Darwall, Mary
Dippen, Maria Catharina, 5, 157, 261–62; as natural genius, 115–17; physical descriptions of, 139
discourse of modesty. See Bescheidenheitstopos
Dodsley, Robert, 51
domestic servants, 181, 186, 249, 289, 293, 306, 312; in works by peasant women, 185–87
domesticity, women's, 248–49
Duck, Stephen, 3, 5, 46–47, 61, 63, 64, 69, 94, 102, 237–38, 261, 293, 314; biographical descriptions of, 52–53, 62–63; as natural genius, 46, 60, 103; and patronage, 45, 50–53, 54, 63, 68, 70
Duck, Stephen, works by: "The Thresher's Labour," 176, 177, 181–84, 193, 238, 261, 280
Duff, William, 26, 28, 32, 33, 68, 161–62, 167, 192, 200, 206, 282
Duncombe, John, 14, 59, 267, 282, 287, 290

Dunlop, Frances Wallace, 55, 58, 61, 139, 266, 278

Ebert, Johann Arnold, 208
education. *See* erudition; literacy
enclosure, 178–79
erudition (and art), 7–8, 11, 15, 25, 27–28, 32, 33, 35, 37, 38, 85–87, 89, 98, 100, 106, 109–11, 114, 116, 127–28, 184, 254–56; as a theme in peasant women's works, 195–207, 211, 216–17, 220, 225–26, 228–29, 232
exploitation, as a theme in peasant women's works, 176–92

Ferguson, Moira, 2, 3, 5, 42, 61, 66, 68, 93, 97, 181, 184, 196, 198, 202, 218, 221, 233, 246, 248, 261, 266, 271, 280, 283
Fichte, Johann Gottlieb, 247
Flachsland, Caroline, 253
folklore, 25, 29–30, 68
Frederick II, King of Prussia, 15, 49, 70, 76, 77, 264; as addressee of or character in Karsch's poems, 71–72, 187, 190, 197, 198, 231, 234, 263
Frederick William II, King of Prussia, 70, 264; as addressee in Karsch's poems, 231
Freemantle, Bridget, 55, 57–59, 62, 63, 64–65, 76, 231, 236, 265, 283, 304
Friedrich II. *See* Frederick II
Friedrich Wilhelm II. *See* Frederick William II

Gee, James Paul, 42, 285
genius, natural, 2, 11, 16, 19–29, 31–36, 38, 39, 121, 161, 229, 255, 279, 301; critique of, 38, 87–91, 97–98, 99–104 112, 175, 232, 314; exemplified by peasant authors, 28–38, 45–46, 50–51, 54, 56–65, 67–68, 70, 76–80, 85–86, 91, 92, 93, 94, 96–99, 101–4, 110–11, 114–16, 128, 131, 141, 175, 193, 213–14, 243; and masculinity, 28, 36–38, 128, 131, 158, 237, 251, 255; and patronage, 44–47, 67–69, 72, 96–97, 117, 255; and physical ugliness, 140, 142–43, 146–53, 157; as a theme in the works of peasant women, 108–17, 125–28, 165–67, 194–207, 232, 237. *See also* nature; originality
*Gentleman's Magazine, The*, 54, 59, 63, 66, 99, 125, 140, 150, 259, 267, 274, 280, 298, 300, 303, 304
georgic poetry, 172, 176–77, 188–89, 190, 296
Gerard, Alexander, 26, 29, 32, 33, 34, 68, 105, 285
Gerstenberg, Heinrich Wilhelm von, 26, 91
Gleim, Johann Wilhelm Ludwig, 5, 43, 62, 87, 89, 92, 94, 95, 123, 144, 161, 175, 208, 210, 213, 231, 264, 291, 311; correspondence with Karsch, 6, 70, 72–75, 77, 78–86, 96, 109, 110, 118–21, 141, 142, 143, 145, 157, 173, 194, 196, 201, 208–9, 229, 292, 300, 301, 302; on patronage, 72–75; as "Thyrsis," 81–82, 84, 110, 119–20, 194, 209
Gleim, Johann Wilhelm Ludwig, works by: *Lieder für das Volk* (Songs for the People), 43
Glover, Jean, 3, 53, 262; biographical descriptions of, 153; physical descriptions of, 152–53

Goethe, Johann Wolfgang von, 10, 22, 23, 25, 29, 124, 253, 254, 275, 281, 312; as a Sturm und Drang author, 8, 24, 285, 297
Gottsched, Johann Christoph, 188
Greene, Richard, 2, 5, 13, 59, 63, 163, 169, 235, 245, 266, 286
Grierson, Constantia, 4, 282, 296
Grimm, Jakob, 256
Grimm, Wilhelm, 256

Haller, Albrecht von, 23, 24; aesthetic treatises by, 46
Haller, Albrecht von, works by: "Die Alpen" (The Alps), 135
Hamann, Johann Georg, 23, 24, 32; aesthetic treatises by, 26
Hands, Elizabeth, 3, 53, 234, 262–63, 283, 287, 314; and criticism, 223–26, 228, 234; and pastorals, 164, 168, 172–73; reviews of, 54, 67, 303
Hands, Elizabeth, works by: "Critical Fragments," 198
"Perplexity," 168
"Poem, on the Supposition," 223–26
"Written, originally extempore," 172–73, 225
Harrison, Susannah, 3, 53, 287
Hausmann, Elisabeth, 6, 22, 72, 76, 78, 81, 92, 103, 119, 120, 130, 210, 230, 235, 287, 292
Heinse, J. J., 88, 121–23, 142, 288
Hempel, Ernst Wilhelm, 130, 131, 142, 144
Herder, Johann Gottfried, 23, 122–23, 208, 253, 288, 294, 297, 313; aesthetic treatises by, 15, 24, 25, 26, 28–32, 33–34, 36, 145–46, 251; reviews of Karsch, 88, 122–23, 208; as

Sturm und Drang author, 6, 8, 15
Hiller, Gottlieb, 5
Hippel, Theodor Gottlieb von, 23
Hirsekorn, Michael (?), 129–30, 131, 132, 263
Holt, Jane, 3
Homer, 25, 29
Huber, Therese, 243
Humboldt, Wilhelm von, 132, 290

idleness, poetic, 51, 60, 63, 75, 95–96, 101, 160–61, 171, 175, 268
imitation, in art, 7, 15, 19, 20, 25, 32, 46, 58, 63, 78, 106, 110, 164, 193; as a factor in reviews of peasant authors, 99, 103, 255
inspiration, poetic, in aesthetics, 161–62, 200, 203–4, 206, 252; in works by peasant women, 194–215, 227–28, 231

Jacobi, Johann Georg, 81, 83–84, 119, 291
Jones, John, 104

Kant, Immanuel, 22, 132, 247, 292
Karl August, Duke of Weimar, 8, 22, 23
Karsch, Anna Louisa, 4, 5, 11, 15, 38, 54, 175, 186, 238, 261–62, 263–65, 273, 274, 275, 276, 277, 279, 287, 289, 290, 291, 292, 293, 294, 295, 296, 299, 300, 301, 302, 303, 305, 306, 308, 311, 313; and authorship, 62, 128, 235, 254; autobiographical writing by, 114–15, 117, 123–28, 132, 136, 157, 158, 244; biographical descriptions of, 66, 77–78, 107–11,

123–33, 129–35, 138, 154, 158, 199–200, 209–10, 243; correspondence with Gleim, 6, 70, 72–75, 78–86, 96, 109, 110, 118–21, 130, 141, 142, 143, 145, 157, 173, 194, 196, 208–9, 229; correspondence with Sulzer, 46, 77–78, 109–10, 113, 115–17, 123–25, 128, 136, 139, 143, 157, 200, 262, 292; and criticism, 9, 11, 35, 38–39, 69, 87–93, 96, 102, 111–12, 121, 210, 216, 218, 228–29, 256; and gender roles, 123–33, 158, 244; *illustrations*, 135, 136, 137, 142, 143, 144; as "Lalage," 81–82, 119, 164; on love as poetic inspiration, 194, 208, 210–11, 212–13; as natural genius, 33, 46, 69, 76–80, 84–89, 90, 91–93, 96, 103, 110–12, 113–15, 125, 141, 157, 161, 166, 175, 196–202, 211, 213–14, 253, 256; on nature as poetic inspiration, 195–96, 198–99, 203–5, 207, 213; and pastorals, 161, 164–67, 171; and patronage, 18, 53, 69–93, 94–95, 113, 118–21, 123, 157, 165–67, 171, 213, 231, 234–35, 237, 239, 245; physical descriptions of, 109, 135–37, 140–46, 147, 152, 157; and physiognomy, 143, 145–46, 149, 157; reception of, 10, 87–88, 91–93, 103, 111–12, 121–23, 210, 214–15; reprints of, 6; reviews of, 38–39, 87–91, 99, 100, 112, 288, 303; as "Sappho," 81–82, 118–23, 142, 208, 210–11

Karsch, Anna Louisa, works by: "An den Apoll" (To Apollo), 234–35

"An den berühmten Chodowiecki" (Addressed to the Famous Painter Chodowiecki), 228–29
"An den Domherrn von Rochow" (To the Canon of Rochow), 210–11, 213–14
"An den Freyherrn von Kottwitz" (To Baron von Kottwitz), 198–99
"An die Chartenspieler" (Addressed to Players at Cards), 125–28
"An die Freyfrau von Troschke" (To the Baroness von Troschke), 216
"An einen jungen Freund" (To a Young Friend), 110
"An Herrn Uz" (To Mr. Uz), 216
"Ann meine Mutter" (To My Mother), 201–2
"Bei Friedrich dem Großen" (On an Audience with Frederick the Great), 198
"Belloisens Lebenslauf" (Belloise's Life Story), 109
"Der Criticus" (The Critic), 216
"Drei Musen hüpfen auf" (Three Muses Jump Up), 196
"Der Frühling" (Spring), 196
"Ihr Freunde von den Wissenschaften" (You Friends of Learning), 197
"Lied an gefangene Lerchen" (Addressed to Larks in Captivity), 196
"Meine Zufriedenheit" (My Contentment), 173–74
"Ob Sappho für den Ruhm schreibt?" (In Answer to the Question Whether Sappho Writes for Fame), 228

Karsch, Anna Louisa, works by: (continued)
"Ode an Freund Bachmann" (Ode to My Friend Bachmann), 203
"Der Sänger bey der Heerde" (The Singing Shepherd Tending His Flock), 165–67, 171, 237, 239
"Sapho an Amor" (Sappho to Amor), 210
"Schlesisches Bauerngespräch" (Silesian Peasant Talk), 177, 187–91, 193
"Ueber den Unbestand des Ruhms" (On the Fickleness of Fame), 228
"Der unnachahmliche Pindar" (Inimitable Pindarus), 196
"Zueignungs-Gesang an den Baron von Kottwitz" (Dedicatory Poem to Baron von Kottwitz), 113, 166, 203–5, 206
untitled poem on poverty, 173
Karsch, Daniel, 130, 131, 263
Kehrer, Karl Christian, 142, 144
Klaus, H. Gustav, 3, 5, 10, 16–17, 39, 45, 50, 61, 181, 183, 252, 255, 261, 293
Klencke, Caroline Luise von, 264, 289, 302; biography of Karsch, 70, 78, 92, 103, 111–12, 124, 128–31, 132–35, 138, 140–42, 146, 147, 149, 152, 153, 154, 158, 199–200, 209–10, 213–14, 243, 244, 265, 293–94; edition of Karsch's poems, 72, 264, 276, 292; and patronage, 245
Klinger, Friedrich Maximilian, 23
Klopstock, Friedrich Gottlob, 23
Knigge, Adolf Franz Friedrich Freiherr von, 132, 247, 294

Kocka, Jürgen, 16, 245, 246, 275, 294, 301
Kottwitz, Rudolf Gotthard Baron von, 70, 134, 263–64; as addressee of Karsch's poetry, 113, 166, 198–99, 203–4, 206
Kotzebue, August von, 23

La Roche, Sophie von, 244, 252–54, 275, 295, 297, 311, 312
labor, as antithesis to writing, 51, 60, 63, 64, 75, 95–96, 113–14, 116, 160–61, 174–75, 268; and gender, 249–50; in pastoral literature, 176, 181, 192, 250; as a theme in lower-class women's writing, 112–13, 115–16, 160–61, 171, 176–93
laborers, women, 181, 307; in works by peasant women, 182–91
Lake, John, 47
Landry, Donna, 2, 3, 5, 57, 58, 61, 63, 64, 68, 93, 102, 103–4, 118, 150, 164, 165, 167–69, 171–72, 181, 183–85, 197–98, 202, 206, 219, 220, 221, 223, 231, 233, 238, 242, 259, 261, 263, 266, 271, 295
Lavater, Johann Caspar, 25, 286; aesthetic treatises by, 25, 26
Lavater, Johann Caspar, works by: *Physiognomische Fragmente*, 143–46, 147, 149, 296
Leapor, Molly (Mary), 3, 5, 6, 10, 11, 13, 53, 56, 62, 63, 116, 117, 175, 217–19, 221, 265–66, 286, 296, 300; biographical descriptions of, 56–58, 154; correspondence with Freemantle, 64, 231; and criticism, 218–19, 221, 226–28; as natural genius, 58–59, 63, 76, 157, 198; and pastorals, 164, 167, 193; and patronage, 55,

63–65, 157, 231, 234, 239; physical descriptions of, 140, 148–50, 157; and physiognomy, 146–47, 157; reviews of, 66, 303–4
Leapor, Molly, works by:
"Crumble Hall," 168–71
"Epistle of Deborah Dough," 218
"Epistle to a Lady," 112–13, 114, 157, 160
"An Epistle to Artemisia," 218
"The Inspired Quill," 218–19
"The Libyan Hunter," 237
"Mira's Picture," 148–50
"The Mistaken Lover," 167
"The Month of August," 164
"Mopsus, or, the Castle-Builder," 235–39
"On Mr. Pope's Universal Prayer," 198
"The Penitent," 219
"The Proposal," 219, 226–28, 235
"The Rural Maid's Reflexions," 175
"Strephon to Celia," 168
"The Ten-Penny Nail," 221
"To Grammaticus," 219; "The Head-Ach," 217
"Upon Her Play Being Returned to Her," 219, 228
"The Visit," 146–47
"The Way of the World," 234
Lessing, Gotthold Ephraim, 22, 23, 43, 93
Lenz, Jakob Michael Reinhold, 8, 22–23, 125, 285, 291, 293, 313; aesthetic treatises by, 25, 28
Lévi-Strauss, Claude, 42
Lips, Johann Heinrich, 143, 144, 145–46
literacy, of the lower classes: in England, 2, 39–42, 309; in Germany, 3, 40–41; in Scotland, 2, 39–42, 179
Little, Janet, 3, 5, 53, 266, 277, 310; and authorship, 61, 230, 237–38; biographical descriptions of, 58, 107; and criticism, 10, 216–23, 228; as natural genius, 58; and pastorals, 164, 168, 173; and patronage, 55; physical descriptions of, 139
Little, Janet, works by:
"An Epistle to a Lady," 216–17
"Given to a Lady," 220–23
"On Seeing Mr. — Baking Cakes," 218, 230
"Poem on Contentment," 173–74, 216
"To a Lady," 219
"To My Aunty," 219
"To the Public," 216–17
Lowth, Robert, 26, 28–29, 32, 34, 296
Lucas, John, 46
Ludwig, Sophie, 4, 17

Macpherson, James, 6, 15, 24, 26, 29, 36, 46, 93, 96, 124–25, 251, 285, 288, 297, 303
Masters, Mary, 3, 6, 56, 266–67, 298; and authorship, 61–62; biographical descriptions of, 56–57, 66; and criticism, 217–19; as a natural genius, 61–62, 196–97; and pastorals, 168
Masters, Mary, works by:
"Defence of Myrtillo," 217
"The Female Triumph," 219
"The Morning Frolick," 168
"To a Gentleman," 196–97
"To the Right Honourable Earl of Burlington," 196
Matthisson, Friedrich von, 23
Meier, Georg Friedrich, 25, 26, 34

Mendelssohn, Moses, 177; aesthetic treatises by, 32, 100–101; reviews of Karsch, 38, 88–91, 92, 98, 99, 100, 111, 112, 125, 154, 299
Messenger, Ann, 3, 5, 162, 163, 252, 299
Milne, Christian, 3, 6, 53, 54, 116, 173, 174, 191, 267–68, 299; and authorship, 56; biographical descriptions of, 56–57, 114; and criticism, 216–17, 223, 225; as natural genius, 57–61, 63, 114, 196, 225; and patronage, 54–55
Milne, Christian, works by:
  "Introductory Verses," 114, 196, 217
  "On a Lady," 223
  "On Seeing the List of Subscribers," 216
  "To a Gentleman, Desirous," 217
  "To a Gentleman, Who Sent Me a Present," 196
  "The Wounded Soldier," 173
  "Written at Fourteen," 177, 185–87, 191
Milton, John, 28, 36, 46, 59, 68, 93, 97, 153, 198, 238, 259, 267, 270
Montagu, Elizabeth, 95, 234; as addressee of Yearsley's poems, 206–7, 232; correspondence with More, 94–96, 97, 99, 138, 300
*Monthly Review, The,* 51–52, 55, 58, 59, 62, 63, 64, 65, 66, 67, 98, 99, 100, 101, 162–63, 167, 234, 236, 255, 260, 279, 283, 303, 304
Montrose, Louis, 106–7, 300
More, Hannah, 41, 42, 45–46, 93–94, 138, 154–56, 205, 231–32, 252, 270, 281, 290, 300, 304; correspondence with Montagu, 94–96, 97, 98, 99, 138, 300; correspondence with Walpole, 51, 94; on natural genius, 97–98
More, Hannah, works by:
  "The Ploughman's Ditty," 43
  "The Practical Use of Female Knowledge," 97–98, 252, 300
  "Sensibility," 25–26, 206
  *Village Politics,* 42, 191, 252
Moritz, Karl Philipp, 124, 285, 300, 305
Murray, Jean, 3
muse. *See* inspiration

nature (as aesthetic concept), 6–7, 15, 19–20, 24–28, 32–35, 46–47, 59, 68, 106, 108–17, 128, 141, 145, 148, 150, 161–62, 165–67, 193, 199, 215–17, 225, 229, 232, 251–52, 255; critique of, 7–8, 9; metaphoric use of in aesthetics, 33–35, 37, 204–5; in works by peasant women, 194–207, 228, 237. *See also* genius, natural; originality
Nörtemann, Regina, 6, 70, 72, 78, 80, 81, 119–20, 125, 142, 292, 301, 302

Oeser, Adam Friedrich, 145
Opitz, Martin, 188
oral literature, 68–69
originality (as a prerequisite for natural genius), 7, 21, 23–24, 25–26, 33–35, 110, 164, 193, 196–97, 201. *See also* genius, natural; nature
Ossian. *See* Macpherson, James

Pagan, Isobel (Tibbie), 3, 268–70, 301; and authorship, 62;

biographical descriptions of, 110, 140, 147, 153, 268–70; and criticism, 9, 66; as natural genius, 60, 110; physical descriptions of, 139–40, 149–50
pastoral literature, 35, 44–45, 108, 109, 161–76, 192–93, 204, 250; depictions of labor in, 164; as a genre particularly suitable for lower-class authors, 45, 46, 109, 160–64, 192, 230, 252; as a genre particularly suitable for women, 162–63, 252, 299; by individual authors: Bentley, 164–65, 259; Hands, 164, 168, 172–73; Karsch, 113, 117, 127, 164–67, 188–91, 236–37; Leapor, 148, 164, 167–68, 169–71, 193, 235–39; Little, 173–75; Masters, 168
Paterson, James, 3, 5, 9, 55, 60, 62, 139, 140, 150, 152, 153, 262, 266, 268, 269, 270, 302
patronage, aristocratic, 1, 7, 14, 19, 21–23, 44, 47, 48–49, 72–75, 101, 235, 295
patronage, bourgeois, 44, 47, 48–104, 153–56, 192–93, 197, 214, 255, 295, 304; in the works of lower-class authors, 165–67, 170–71, 222–23, 231–39
pay, rural laborers'. *See* wages
peasants, as literary characters, 43–44, 117, 157, 163, 168, 176–77, 187–91, 193
peasant enlightenment. *See Bauernaufklärung*
Percy, Thomas, 256
physiognomy, 142–43, 145–47, 149, 286, 296
Pockels, Carl Friedrich, 132, 302
poor laws, 180
Pope, Alexander, 43–44, 50–51, 63, 94, 169, 259, 265, 301; as a character in lower-class women's writing, 198, 220, 238
Pott, Ute, 4, 5, 6, 9, 70, 71, 72, 103, 108, 125, 235, 243, 245, 265, 292, 301, 302
poverty, 180; as a theme in lower-class women's writing, 113–14, 157, 172–74
pseudonyms. *See* anonymity

Ramler, Karl Wilhelm, 80, 83, 87, 93, 111, 196; correspondence with Karsch, 74; and patronage, 73–74
Ramsay, Allan, 267
reception:
of lower-class women writers, 2, 9–11, 13, 14, 87–88, 118, 214, 240–58; as represented in their works, 216–31
of lower-class writers, 51–52, 102–3, 105, 240–58
of middle-class women writers, 2, 98, 118, 194, 230, 240–58
Richardson, W., 192
Richter, Jean Paul, 23
Rizzo, Betty, 3, 10, 48, 50, 51, 63, 93, 140, 153–54, 218, 235, 266, 271, 304
Runge, Anita. *See* Bennholdt-Thomsen, Anke

Santen, Laurens van, 86
Sappho, 118, 121–22, 153, 211; as an appellation for Karsch, 81–82, 118–23, 208, 210–11; as an appellation for women writers, 118, 158
Schaffers, Uta, 4, 5, 10, 70, 72, 76, 77, 92, 93, 109, 111, 124, 128, 130, 141, 142, 235, 256, 265, 305

Schelling, Friedrich Wilhelm von, 23
Schiller, Friedrich, 15, 22, 23, 287, 297; aesthetic writings by, 36–37, 251, 305
Schlegel, August Wilhelm, 23
Schlegel, Friedrich, 23
Schmidt, Georg Friedrich, 142, 143
Schubart, Christian Friedrich Daniel, 122–23
Scott, Mary, 3, 18, 246, 283, 290, 306; reviews of, 254, 304
Scott, Mary, works by: "The Female Advocate," 246, 254
Shaftesbury, Anthony Ashley Cooper, Earl of, 24, 25, 26, 276
Shakespeare, William, 28, 32, 36, 46, 47, 59, 91, 93, 97, 99, 153, 198, 238, 259, 270, 304, 307
Shanks, Henry, 5, 10, 306
shepherds, as literary characters, 44, 117, 157–58, 163, 168, 176, 188, 192–93
Southey, Robert, 5, 13, 50, 51, 52–53, 63, 68, 93, 102, 103, 104, 107, 139, 154, 156, 271, 280, 307
Spence, Elizabeth, 3, 46, 51, 57, 60, 101, 155, 268, 307
spontaneity (of poetic production). *See* genius, natural; nature; originality
Städele (poet), 5, 46
Stubinitzki (sculptor), 145
Stüssel, Kerstin, 5, 11, 24, 25, 27, 28, 32, 33, 77, 106, 123–25, 257, 265, 308
Sturm und Drang (Storm and Stress movement), 2, 6–7, 8, 20, 282, 284, 286, 289, 292, 295, 296, 297, 298, 301, 302, 307, 309, 310; aesthetic ideas in, 24–25, 285; concepts of nature in, 24, 304; critique of, 8; drama, 23, 290, 298; influence on English Romanticism, 21; reception of Sturm und Drang authors, 8, 22; and women writers, 36–37, 294, 304, 307
Sulzer, Johann Georg, aesthetic treatises by, 11, 24, 26, 32, 33, 34, 35, 38, 68, 76–78, 93, 308; correspondence with Karsch, 5, 46, 77–78, 109–10, 113, 115–17, 123–25, 128, 136, 139, 143, 157, 200, 262, 292; as Karsch's patron, 46, 76–80, 83, 85, 90, 94, 103, 244, 264, 265

Taylor, Ellen, 4
Thomsen, Johann Heinrich, 5, 46
Thornton, Bonnell. *See* Colman, George
Torgovnick, Marianna, 240, 255–57, 309

Unger, Friederike Helene, 249, 309
Unwin, Rayner, 5, 154, 261, 271, 309
Uz, Johann Peter, 81, 85, 119, 143, 175; as addressee of Karsch's poems, 216

Vergilius Maro, Publius, 46, 93, 161
Virgil. *See* Vergilius Maro, Publius
Voß, Johann Heinrich, 23
*Volk* (as a concept), 14, 19–20, 23, 24, 25–26, 28–31, 251
Vulpius, Christian August, 22–23

wages: rural laborers', 179–80; women laborers', 179–81, 183–84, 285
Waldron, Mary, 2, 3, 5, 10, 13, 27, 93, 96, 97, 103, 138, 139,

154, 155, 162, 198, 202, 204, 205, 206, 213, 233, 271, 310
Walpole, Horace, 75, 94, 95, 96, 154, 310; correspondence with More, 51, 94
West, Jane, 3, 18, 221, 311–12
Whateley Darwall, Mary, 3, 5, 18, 299, 312; and pastorals, 162
Wieland, Christoph Martin, 23, 253–54, 255, 312
Williams, Raymond, 12–14, 24, 35, 44, 45, 47, 163–64, 169, 176–78, 312
witches, as characters representing lower-class women writers, 108, 139–40, 142–43, 145, 147–50, 152, 153, 158
Woodhouse, James, 94

Yearsley, Ann Cromartie, 3, 5, 11, 18, 109, 117, 238, 270–71, 281, 283, 287, 300, 310, 314; and authorship, 96; biographical descriptions of, 93, 107, 138–39, 154–56; and criticism, 9, 13; *illustrations,* 149, 151; literary career of, 213, 221; on love as poetic inspiration, 211–13; as natural genius, 93, 96–97, 103, 108, 150, 196–97, 204; on nature inspiration, 194, 197–98, 202–3, 205–7, 213–14, 232; and pastorals, 168; and patronage, 45–46, 51, 53, 54, 69, 70, 93–100, 231–35, 238; physical descriptions of, 146, 150; and physiognomy, 146; reception of, 10, 97, 99–100, 215; reprints of, 6, 9; reviews of, 98–101, 303
Yearsley, Ann Cromartie, works by: "Addressed to Friendship," 234
"Addressed to Ignorance," 202–3, 207
"Addressed to Sensibility," 206

"Brutus, A Fragment," 198
"Clifton Hill," 234
"The Dispute," 270
"On Being Presented With a Silver Pen," 233–34
"On Mrs. Montagu," 206–7, 232
"Poem on the Inhumanity of the Slave Trade," 270
*Poems, on Various Subjects,* 205, 211–13
*The Rural Lyre,* 205
"To Indifference," 206
"To Mr. \*\*\*, on Genius Unimproved," 198
"To Mr. V—," 211–14
"To Stella," 232
"To the King," 196
"To Those Who Accuse," 233
"Written on a Visit," 197
Young, Edward, 6, 46, 93, 197, 270; aesthetic treatises by, 25, 26, 33, 36, 88, 197; in Hands's writing, 198; influence on German aesthetics, 21; in Karsch's writing, 77, 110; in Little's writing, 220

*Zweckfreiheit. See* autonomy, artistic